Praise for *Continuous Delivery*

"If you need to deploy software more frequently, this book is for you. Applying it will help you reduce risk, eliminate tedious work, and increase confidence. I'll be using the principles and practices here on all my current projects."

—*Kent Beck, Three Rivers Institute*

"Whether or not your software development team already understands that continuous integration is every bit as necessary as source code control, this is required reading. This book is unique in tying the whole development and delivery process together, providing a philosophy and principles, not just techniques and tools. The authors make topics from test automation to automated deployment accessible to a wide audience. Everyone on a development team, including programmers, testers, system administrators, DBAs, and managers, needs to read this book."

—*Lisa Crispin, co-author of* Agile Testing

"For many organizations Continuous Delivery isn't just a deployment methodology, it's critical to doing business. This book shows you how to make Continuous Delivery an effective reality in your environment."

—*James Turnbull, author of* Pulling Strings with Puppet

"A clear, precise, well-written book that gives readers an idea of what to expect for the release process. The authors give a step-by-step account of expectations and hurdles for software deployment. This book is a necessity for any software engineer's library."

—*Leyna Cotran, Institute for Software Research, University of California, Irvine*

"Humble and Farley illustrates what makes fast-growing web applications successful. Continuous deployment and delivery has gone from controversial to commonplace and this book covers it excellently. It's truly the intersection of development and operations on many levels, and these guys nailed it."

—*John Allspaw, VP Technical Operations, Etsy.com and author of* The Art of Capacity Planning *and* Web Operations

"If you are in the business of building and delivering a software-based service, you would be well served to internalize the concepts that are so clearly explained in Continuous Delivery. But going beyond just the concepts, Humble and Farley provide an excellent playbook for rapidly and reliably delivering change."

—*Damon Edwards, President of DTO Solutions and co-editor of dev2ops.org*

"I believe that anyone who deals with software releases would be able to pick up this book, go to any chapter and quickly get valuable information; or read the book from cover to cover and be able to streamline their build and deploy process in a way that makes sense for their organization. In my opinion, this is an essential handbook for building, deploying, testing, and releasing software."

—*Sarah Edrie, Director of Quality Engineering, Harvard Business School*

"Continuous Delivery is the logical next step after Continuous Integration for any modern software team. This book takes the admittedly ambitous goal of constantly delivering valuable software to customers, and makes it achievable through a set of clear, effective principles and practices."

—*Rob Sanheim, Principal at Relevance, Inc.*

Continuous Delivery

Continuous Delivery

Jez Humble and David Farley

✦ Addison-Wesley

Upper Saddle River, NJ • Boston • Indianapolis • San Francisco
New York • Toronto • Montreal • London • Munich • Paris • Madrid
Cape Town • Sydney • Tokyo • Singapore • Mexico City

Many of the designations used by manufacturers and sellers to distinguish their products are claimed as trademarks. Where those designations appear in this book, and the publisher was aware of a trademark claim, the designations have been printed with initial capital letters or in all capitals.

The authors and publisher have taken care in the preparation of this book, but make no expressed or implied warranty of any kind and assume no responsibility for errors or omissions. No liability is assumed for incidental or consequential damages in connection with or arising out of the use of the information or programs contained herein.

The publisher offers excellent discounts on this book when ordered in quantity for bulk purchases or special sales, which may include electronic versions and/or custom covers and content particular to your business, training goals, marketing focus, and branding interests. For more information, please contact:

U.S. Corporate and Government Sales
(800) 382–3419
corpsales@pearsontechgroup.com

For sales outside the United States please contact:

International Sales
international@pearson.com

Visit us on the Web: informit.com/aw

Library of Congress Cataloging-in-Publication Data:

Humble, Jez.
  Continuous delivery : reliable software releases through build, test, and deployment automation / Jez Humble, David Farley.
      p. cm.
  Includes bibliographical references and index.
  ISBN 978-0-321-60191-9 (hardback : alk. paper) 1. Computer software--Development.
2. Computer software--Reliability. 3. Computer software--Testing. I. Farley, David, 1959-
II. Title.
  QA76.76.D47H843 2010
  005.1--dc22
                            2010022186

ISBN-13: 978–0–321–60191–9
ISBN-10: 0–321–60191–2
Text printed in the United States on recycled paper at RR Donnelley in Crawfordsville, Indiana.
First printing August 2010

This book is dedicated to my dad, who has always given me his unconditional love and support.

—Jez

This book is dedicated to my dad, who always showed me the right direction.

—Dave

Contents

Foreword by Martin Fowler

In the late 90s, I paid a visit to Kent Beck, then working in Switzerland for an insurance company. He showed me around his project, and one of the interesting aspects of his highly disciplined team was the fact that they deployed their software into production every night. This regular deployment gave them many advantages: Written software wasn't waiting uselessly until it was deployed, they could respond quickly to problems and opportunities, and the rapid turnaround led to a much deeper relationship between them, their business customer, and their final customers.

In the last decade I've worked at ThoughtWorks, and a common theme of our projects has been reducing the cycle time between an idea and usable software. I see plenty of project stories, and almost all involve a determined shortening of that cycle. While we don't usually do daily deliveries into production, it's now common to see teams doing bi-weekly releases.

Dave and Jez have been part of that sea change, actively involved in projects that have built a culture of frequent, reliable deliveries. They and our colleagues have taken organizations that struggled to deploy software once a year into the world of Continuous Delivery, where releasing becomes routine.

The foundation for the approach, at least for the development team, is Continuous Integration (CI). CI keeps the entire development team in sync, removing the delays due to integration issues. A couple of years ago, Paul Duvall wrote a book on CI in this series. But CI is just the first step. Software that's been successfully integrated into a mainline code stream still isn't software that's out in production doing its job. Dave and Jez's book pick up the story from CI to deal with that "last mile," describing how to build the deployment pipeline that turns integrated code into production software.

This kind of delivery thinking has long been a forgotten corner of software development, falling into a hole between developers and operations teams. So it's no surprise that the techniques in this book rest upon bringing these teams together—a harbinger of the nascent but growing DevOps movement. This process also involves testers, as testing is a key element of ensuring error-free releases.

Threading through all this is a high degree of automation, so things can be done quickly and without error.

Getting all this working takes effort, but benefits are profound. Long, high-intensity releases become a thing of the past. Customers of software see ideas rapidly turn into working code that they can use every day. Perhaps most importantly, we remove one of the biggest sources of baleful stress in software development. Nobody likes those tense weekends trying to get a system upgrade released before Monday dawns.

It seems to me that a book that can show you how to deliver your software frequently and without the usual stresses is a no-brainer to read. For your team's sake, I hope you agree.

Preface

Introduction

Yesterday your boss asked you to demonstrate the great new features of your system to a customer, but you can't show them anything. All your developers are halfway through developing new features and none of them can run the application right now. You have code, it compiles, and all the unit tests pass on your continuous integration server, but it takes a couple of days to release the new version into the publicly accessible UAT environment. Isn't it unreasonable to expect the demo at such short notice?

You have a critical bug in production. It is losing money for your business every day. You know what the fix is: A one-liner in a library that is used in all three layers of your three-tier system, and a corresponding change to one database table. But the last time you released a new version of your software to production it took a weekend of working until 3 A.M., and the person who did the deployment quit in disgust shortly afterward. You know the next release is going to overrun the weekend, which means the application will be down for a period during the business week. If only the business understood our problems.

These problems, although all too common, are not an inevitable outcome of the software development process: They are an indication that something is wrong. Software release should be a fast, repeatable process. These days, many companies are putting out multiple releases in a *day*. This is possible even with large projects with complex codebases. In this book, we will show you how this is done.

Mary and Tom Poppendieck asked, "How long would it take your organization to deploy a change that involves just one single line of code? Do you do this on a repeatable, reliable basis?"[1] The time from deciding that you need to make a change to having it in production is known as the *cycle time*, and it is a vital metric for any project.

---

1. *Implementing Lean Software Development*, p. 59.

In many organizations, cycle time is measured in weeks or months, and the release process is certainly not repeatable or reliable. It is manual and often requires a team of people to deploy the software even into a testing or staging environment, let alone into production. However, we have come across equally complex projects which started out like this but where, after extensive reengineering, teams were able to achieve a cycle time of hours or even minutes for a critical fix. This was possible because a fully automated, repeatable, reliable process was created for taking changes through the various stages of the build, deploy, test, and release process. Automation is the key. It allows all of the common tasks involved in the creation and deployment of software to be performed by developers, testers, and operations personnel, at the push of a button.

This book describes how to revolutionize software delivery by making the path from idea to realized business value—the cycle time—shorter and safer.

Software delivers no revenue until it is in the hands of its users. This is obvious, but in most organizations the release of software into production is a manually intensive, error-prone, and risky process. While a cycle time measured in months is common, many companies do much worse than this: Release cycles of more than a year are not unknown. For large companies every week of delay between having an idea and releasing the code that implements it can represent millions of dollars in opportunity costs—and yet these are often the ones with the longest cycle times.

Despite all this, the mechanisms and processes that allow for low-risk delivery of software have not become part of the fabric in most of today's software development projects.

Our aim is to make the delivery of software from the hands of developers into production a reliable, predictable, visible, and largely automated process with well-understood, quantifiable risks. Using the approach that we describe in this book, it is possible to go from having an idea to delivering working code that implements it into production in a matter of minutes or hours, while at the same time improving the quality of the software thus delivered.

The vast majority of the cost associated with delivering successful software is incurred after the first release. This is the cost of support, maintenance, adding new features, and fixing defects. This is especially true of software delivered via iterative processes, where the first release contains the minimum amount of functionality providing value to the customer. Hence the title of this book, *Continuous Delivery*, which is taken from the first principle of the Agile Manifesto: "Our highest priority is to satisfy the customer through early and continuous delivery of valuable software" [bibNp0]. This reflects the reality: For successful software, the first release is just the beginning of the delivery process.

All the techniques we describe in this book reduce the time and risks associated with delivering new versions of your software to users. They do this by increasing feedback and improving collaboration between the development, testing, and operations personnel responsible for delivery. These techniques ensure that when you need to modify applications, either to fix bugs or deliver new features, the time between making modifications and having the results deployed and in use is as low as possible, problems are found early when they are easy to fix, and associated risks are well understood.

Who Is This Book for, and What Does It Cover?

One of the major aims of this book is to improve collaboration between the people responsible for delivering software. In particular, we have in mind developers, testers, systems and database administrators, and managers.

We cover topics from traditional configuration management, source code control, release planning, auditing, compliance, and integration to the automation of your building, testing, and deployment processes. We also describe techniques such as automated acceptance testing, dependency management, database migration, and the creation and management of testing and production environments.

Many people involved in creating software consider these activities secondary to writing code. However, in our experience they take up a great deal of time and effort, and are critical to successful software delivery. When the risks surrounding these activities are not managed adequately, they can end up costing a lot of money, often more than the cost of building the software in the first place. This book provides the information that you need to understand these risks and, more importantly, describes strategies to mitigate them.

This is an ambitious aim, and of course we can't cover all these topics in detail in one book. Indeed we run the risk of alienating each of our target audiences: developers, by failing to treat topics such as architecture, behavior-driven development, and refactoring in depth; testers, by not spending sufficient time on exploratory testing and test management strategies; operations personnel, by not paying due attention to capacity planning, database migration, and production monitoring.

However, books exist that address each of these topics in detail. What we think is lacking in the literature is a book that discusses how all the moving parts fit together: configuration management, automated testing, continuous integration and deployment, data management, environment management, and release management. One of the things that the lean software development movement teaches is that it is important to optimize the whole. In order to do this, a holistic approach is necessary that ties together every part of the delivery process and everybody involved in it. Only when you have control over the progression of every change from introduction to release can you begin to optimize and improve the quality and speed of software delivery.

Our aim is to present a holistic approach, as well as the principles involved in this approach. We will provide you with the information that you will need to decide how to apply these practices in your own projects. We do not believe that there is a "one size fits all" approach to any aspect of software development, let alone a subject area as large as the configuration management and operational control of an enterprise system. However, the fundamentals that we describe in this book are widely applicable to all sorts of different software projects—big, small, highly technical or short sprints to early value.

As you begin to put these principles into practice, you will discover the areas where more detail is required for your particular situation. There is a bibliography at the end of this book, as well as pointers to other resources online where you can find more information on each of the topics that we cover.

This book consists of three parts. The first part presents the principles behind continuous delivery and the practices necessary to support it. Part two describes the central paradigm of the book—a pattern we call the deployment pipeline. The third part goes into more detail on the ecosystem that supports the deployment pipeline—techniques to enable incremental development; advanced version control patterns; infrastructure, environment and data management; and governance.

Many of these techniques may appear to apply only to large-scale applications. While it is true that much of our experience is with large applications, we believe that even the smallest projects can benefit from a thorough grounding in these techniques, for the simple reason that projects grow. The decisions that you make when starting a small project will have an inevitable impact on its evolution, and by starting off in the right way, you will save yourself (or those who come after you) a great deal of pain further down the line.

Your authors share a background in lean and iterative software development philosophies. By this we mean that we aim to deliver valuable, working software to users rapidly and iteratively, working continuously to remove waste from the delivery process. Many of the principles and techniques that we describe were first developed in the context of large agile projects. However, the techniques that we present in this book are of general applicability. Much of our focus is on improving collaboration through better visibility and faster feedback. This will have a positive impact on every project, whether or not it uses iterative software development processes.

We have tried to ensure that chapters and even sections can be read in isolation. At the very least, we hope that anything you need to know, as well as references to further information, are clearly sign-posted and accessible so that you can use this book as a reference.

We should mention that we don't aim for academic rigor in our treatment of the subjects covered. There are plenty of more theoretical books on the market, many of which provide interesting reading and insights. In particular, we will not spend much time on standards, concentrating instead on battle-tested skills and techniques every person working on a software project will find useful, and explaining them clearly and simply so that they can be used every day in the real world. Where appropriate, we will provide some war stories illustrating these techniques to help place them in context.

Conspectus

We recognize that not everyone will want to read this book from end to end. We have written it so that once you have covered the introduction, you can attack it in several different ways. This has involved a certain amount of repetition, but hopefully not at a level that becomes tedious if you do decide to read it cover-to-cover.

This book consists of three parts. The first part, Chapters 1 to 4, takes you through the basic principles of regular, repeatable, low-risk releases and the practices that support them. Part two, Chapters 5 through 10, describe the deployment pipeline. From Chapter 11 we dive into the ecosystem that supports continuous delivery.

We recommend that everybody read Chapter 1. We believe that people who are new to the process of releasing software, even experienced developers, will find plenty of material challenging their view of what it means to do professional software development. The rest of the book can be dipped into either at your leisure—or when in a panic.

Part I—Foundations

Part I describes the prerequisites for understanding the deployment pipeline. Each chapter builds upon the last.

Chapter 1, "The Problem of Delivering Software," starts by describing some common antipatterns that we see in many software development teams, and moves on to describe our goal and how to realize it. We conclude by setting out the principles of software delivery upon which the rest of the book is based.

Chapter 2, "Configuration Management," sets out how to manage everything required to build, deploy, test, and release your application, from source code and build scripts to your environment and application configuration.

Chapter 3, "Continuous Integration," covers the practice of building and running automated tests against every change you make to your application so you can ensure that your software is always in a working state.

Chapter 4, "Implementing a Testing Strategy," introduces the various kinds of manual and automated testing that form an integral part of every project, and discusses how to decide which strategy is appropriate for your project.

Part II—The Deployment Pipeline

The second part of the book covers the deployment pipeline in detail, including how to implement the various stages in the pipeline.

Chapter 5, "Anatomy of the Deployment Pipeline," discusses the pattern that forms the core of this book—an automated process for taking every change from check-in to release. We also discuss how to implement pipelines at both the team and organizational levels.

Chapter 6, "Build and Deployment Scripting," discusses scripting technologies that can be used for creating automated build and deployment processes, and the best practices for using them.

Chapter 7, "The Commit Stage," covers the first stage of the pipeline, a set of automated processes that should be triggered the moment any change is introduced into your application. We also discuss how to create a fast, effective commit test suite.

Chapter 8, "Automated Acceptance Testing," presents automated acceptance testing, from analysis to implementation. We discuss why acceptance tests are essential to continuous delivery, and how to create a cost-effective acceptance test suite that will protect your application's valuable functionality.

Chapter 9, "Testing Nonfunctional Requirements," discusses nonfunctional requirements, with an emphasis on capacity testing. We describe how to create capacity tests, and how to set up a capacity testing environment.

Chapter 10, "Deploying and Releasing Applications," covers what happens after automated testing: push-button promotion of release candidates to manual testing environments, UAT, staging, and finally release, taking in essential topics such as continuous deployment, roll backs, and zero-downtime releases.

Part III — The Delivery Ecosystem

The final part of the book discusses crosscutting practices and techniques that support the deployment pipeline.

Chapter 11, "Managing Infrastructure and Environments," covers the automated creation, management, and monitoring of environments, including the use of virtualization and cloud computing.

Chapter 12, "Managing Data," shows how to create and migrate testing and production data through the lifecycle of your application.

Chapter 13, "Managing Components and Dependencies," starts with a discussion of how to keep your application in a releasable state at all times without branching. We then describe how to organize your application as a collection of components, and how to manage building and testing them.

Chapter 14, "Advanced Version Control," gives an overview of the most popular tools, and goes into detail on the various patterns for using version control.

Chapter 15, "Managing Continuous Delivery," sets out approaches to risk management and compliance, and provides a maturity model for configuration and release management. Along the way, we discuss the value of continuous delivery to the business, and the lifecycle of iterative projects that deliver incrementally.

Web Links in This Book

Rather than putting in complete links to external websites, we have shortened them and put in the key in this format: [bibNp0]. You can go to the link in one of two ways. Either use bit.ly, in which case the url for the example key would be http://bit.ly/bibNp0. Alternatively, you can use a url shortening service we've installed at http://continuousdelivery.com/go/ which uses the same keys—so the url for the example key is http://continuousdelivery.com/go/bibNp0. The idea is that if for some reason bit.ly goes under, the links are preserved. If the web pages change address, we'll try to keep the shortening service at http://continuousdelivery.com/go/ up-to-date, so try that if the links don't work at bit.ly.

About the Cover

All books in Martin Fowler's Signature Series have a bridge on the cover. We'd originally planned to use a photo of the Iron Bridge, but it had already been chosen for another book in the series. So instead, we chose another British bridge: the Forth Railway Bridge, captured here in a stunning photo by Stewart Hardy.

The Forth Railway Bridge was the first bridge in the UK constructed using steel, manufactured using the new Siemens-Martin open-hearth process, and delivered from two steel works in Scotland and one in Wales. The steel was delivered in the form of manufactured tubular trusses—the first time a bridge in the UK used mass-produced parts. Unlike earlier bridges, the designers, Sir John Fowler, Sir Benjamin Baker, and Allan Stewart, made calculations for incidence of erection stresses, provisions for reducing future maintenance costs, and calculations for wind pressures and the effect of temperature stresses on the structure—much like the functional and nonfunctional requirements we make in software. They also supervised the construction of the bridge to ensure these requirements were met.

The bridge's construction involved more than 4,600 workers, of whom tragically around one hundred died and hundreds more were crippled. However, the end result is one of the marvels of the industrial revolution: At the time of completion in 1890 it was the longest bridge in the world, and at the start of the 21st century it remains the world's second longest cantilever bridge. Like a long-lived software project, the bridge needs constant maintenance. This was planned for as part of the design, with ancillary works for the bridge including not only a maintenance workshop and yard but a railway "colony" of some fifty houses at Dalmeny Station. The remaining working life of the bridge is estimated at over 100 years.

Colophon

This book was written directly in DocBook. Dave edited the text in TextMate, and Jez used Aquamacs Emacs. The diagrams were created with OmniGraffle. Dave and Jez were usually not in the same part of the world, and collaborated by having everything checked in to Subversion. We also employed continuous integration, using a CruiseControl.rb server that ran dblatex to produce a PDF of the book every time one of us committed a change.

A month before the book went to print, Dmitry Kirsanov and Alina Kirsanova started the production work, collaborating with the authors through their Subversion repository, email, and a shared Google Docs table for coordination. Dmitry worked on copyediting of the DocBook source in XEmacs, and Alina did everything else: typesetting the pages using a custom XSLT stylesheet and an XSL-FO formatter, compiling and editing the Index from the author's indexing tags in the source, and final proofreading of the book.

Acknowledgments

Many people have contributed to this book. In particular, we'd like to thank our reviewers: David Clack, Leyna Cotran, Lisa Crispin, Sarah Edrie, Damon Edwards, Martin Fowler, James Kovacs, Bob Maksimchuk, Elliotte Rusty Harold, Rob Sanheim, and Chris Smith. We'd also like to extend special thanks to our editorial and production team at Addison-Wesley: Chris Guzikowski, Raina Chrobak, Susan Zahn, Kristy Hart, and Andy Beaster. Dmitry Kirsanov and Alina Kirsanova did a fantastic job of copyediting and proofreading the book, and typesetting it using their fully automated system.

Many of our colleagues have been instrumental in developing the ideas in this book, including (in no particular order) Chris Read, Sam Newman, Dan North, Dan Worthington-Bodart, Manish Kumar, Kraig Parkinson, Julian Simpson, Paul Julius, Marco Jansen, Jeffrey Fredrick, Ajey Gore, Chris Turner, Paul Hammant, Hu Kai, Qiao Yandong, Qiao Liang, Derek Yang, Julias Shaw, Deepthi, Mark Chang, Dante Briones, Li Guanglei, Erik Doernenburg, Kraig Parkinson, Ram Narayanan, Mark Rickmeier, Chris Stevenson, Jay Flowers, Jason Sankey, Daniel Ostermeier, Rolf Russell, Jon Tirsen, Timothy Reaves, Ben Wyeth, Tim Harding, Tim Brown, Pavan Kadambi Sudarshan, Stephen Foreshew, Yogi Kulkarni, David Rice, Chad Wathington, Jonny LeRoy, and Chris Briesemeister.

Jez would like to thank his wife, Rani, for being the most loving partner he could wish for, and for cheering him up when he was grumpy during the writing of this book. He also thanks his daughter, Amrita, for her babbling, cuddles, and big gummy smiles. He is also profoundly grateful to his colleagues at ThoughtWorks for making it such an inspiring place to work, and to Cyndi Mitchell and Martin Fowler for their support of this book. Finally, a big shout out to Jeffrey Fredrick and Paul Julius for creating CITCON, and to the people he met there for many great conversations.

Dave would like to thank his wife Kate, and children Tom and Ben, for their unfailing support at every point, in this project and in many others. He would also like to make a special mention of ThoughtWorks, who, although no longer his employer, provided an environment of enlightenment and encouragement for the people that worked there, thus fostering a creative approach to finding solutions, many of which populate the pages of this book. In addition, he would like to thank his current employer, LMAX, with a special mention for Martin Thompson, for their support, trust, and willing adoption of the techniques described in this book in an intensely challenging technical environment of world-class high-performance computing.

About the Authors

Jez Humble has been fascinated by computers and electronics since getting his first ZX Spectrum at age 11, and spent several years hacking on Acorn machines in 6502 and ARM assembler and BASIC until he was old enough to get a proper job. He got into IT in 2000, just in time for the dot-com bust. Since then he has worked as a developer, system administrator, trainer, consultant, manager, and speaker. He has worked with a variety of platforms and technologies, consulting for nonprofits, telecoms, financial services, and online retail companies. Since 2004 he has worked for ThoughtWorks and ThoughtWorks Studios in Beijing, Bangalore, London, and San Francisco. He holds a BA in Physics and Philosophy from Oxford University and an MMus in Ethnomusicology from the School of Oriental and African Studies, University of London. He is presently living in San Francisco with his wife and daughter.

Dave Farley has been having fun with computers for nearly 30 years. Over that period he has worked on most types of software—from firmware, through tinkering with operating systems and device drivers, to writing games and commercial applications of all shapes and sizes. He started working in large-scale distributed systems about twenty years ago, doing research into the development of loose-coupled, message-based systems—a forerunner of SOA. He has a wide range of experience leading the development of complex software in teams, both large and small, in the UK and USA. Dave was an early adopter of agile development techniques, employing iterative development, continuous integration, and significant levels of automated testing on commercial projects from the early 1990s. He honed his approach to agile development during his four-and-a-half-year stint at ThoughtWorks where he was a technical principal working on some of their biggest and most challenging projects. Dave is currently working for the London Multi-Asset Exchange (LMAX), an organization that is building one of the highest-performance financial exchanges in the world, where they rely upon all of the major techniques described in this book.

Part I

Foundations

Chapter 1

The Problem of Delivering Software

Introduction

The most important problem that we face as software professionals is this: If somebody thinks of a good idea, how do we deliver it to users as quickly as possible? This book shows how to solve this problem.

We focus on the build, deploy, test, and release process, about which relatively little has been written. This is not because we think that software development approaches are not important; rather, that without a focus on the other aspects of the software lifecycle—aspects that are all too commonly treated as peripheral to the overall problem—it is impossible to achieve reliable, rapid, low-risk software releases that get the fruits of our labors into the hands of our users in an efficient manner.

There are many software development methodologies, but they focus primarily on requirement management and its impact on the development effort. There are many excellent books that cover in detail different approaches to software design, development, and testing; but these, too, cover only a fragment of the *value stream* that delivers value to the people and organizations that sponsor our efforts.

What happens once requirements are identified, solutions designed, developed, and tested? How are these activities joined together and coordinated to make the process as efficient and reliable as we can make it? How do we enable developers, testers, build and operations personnel to work together effectively?

This book describes an effective pattern for getting software from development to release. We describe techniques and best practices that help to implement this pattern and show how this approach interfaces with other aspects of software delivery.

The pattern that is central to this book is the *deployment pipeline*. A deployment pipeline is, in essence, an automated implementation of your application's build, deploy, test, and release process. Every organization will have differences in the implementation of their deployment pipelines, depending on their value

3

stream for releasing software, but the principles that govern them do not vary. An example of a deployment pipeline is given in Figure 1.1.

Figure 1.1 *The deployment pipeline*

The way the deployment pipeline works, in a paragraph, is as follows. Every change that is made to an application's configuration, source code, environment, or data, triggers the creation of a new instance of the pipeline. One of the first steps in the pipeline is to create binaries and installers. The rest of the pipeline runs a series of tests on the binaries to prove that they can be released. Each test that the release candidate passes gives us more confidence that this particular combination of binary code, configuration information, environment, and data will work. If the release candidate passes all the tests, it can be released.

The deployment pipeline has its foundations in the process of *continuous integration* and is in essence the principle of continuous integration taken to its logical conclusion.

The aim of the deployment pipeline is threefold. First, it makes every part of the process of building, deploying, testing, and releasing software visible to everybody involved, aiding collaboration. Second, it improves feedback so that problems are identified, and so resolved, as early in the process as possible. Finally, it enables teams to deploy and release any version of their software to any environment at will through a fully automated process.

Some Common Release Antipatterns

The day of a software release tends to be a tense one. Why should this be the case? For most projects, it is the degree of risk associated with the process that makes release a scary time.

In many software projects, release is a manually intensive process. The environments that host the software are often crafted individually, usually by an operations or IS team. Third-party software that the application relies on is installed. The software artifacts of the application itself are copied to the production host environments. Configuration information is copied or created through the admin consoles of web servers, applications servers, or other third-party components of the system. Reference data is copied, and finally the application is started, piece by piece if it is a distributed or service-oriented application.

The reason for the nervousness should be clear: There is quite a lot to go wrong in this process. If any step is not perfectly executed, the application won't run properly. At this point it may not be at all clear where the error is, or which step went wrong.

The rest of this book discusses how to avoid these risks—how to reduce the stress on release days, and how to ensure that each release is predictably reliable.

Before that, let's be clear about the kinds of process failures that we are trying to avoid. Here are a few common antipatterns that prevent a reliable release process, but nevertheless are so common as to be the norm in our industry.

Antipattern: Deploying Software Manually

Most modern applications of any size are complex to deploy, involving many moving parts. Many organizations release software manually. By this we mean that the steps required to deploy such an application are treated as separate and atomic, each performed by an individual or team. Judgments must be made within these steps, leaving them prone to human error. Even if this is not the case, differences in the ordering and timing of these steps can lead to different outcomes. These differences are rarely good.

The signs of this antipattern are:

- The production of extensive, detailed documentation that describes the steps to be taken and the ways in which the steps may go wrong

- Reliance on manual testing to confirm that the application is running correctly

- Frequent calls to the development team to explain why a deployment is going wrong on a release day

- Frequent corrections to the release process during the course of a release

- Environments in a cluster that differ in their configuration, for example application servers with different connection pool settings, filesystems with different layouts, etc.

- Releases that take more than a few minutes to perform

- Releases that are unpredictable in their outcome, that often have to be rolled back or run into unforeseen problems

- Sitting bleary-eyed in front of a monitor at 2 A.M. the day after the release day, trying to figure out how to make it work

Instead . . .

Over time, deployments should tend towards being fully automated. There should be two tasks for a human being to perform to deploy software into a development, test, or production environment: to pick the version and environment and to press the "deploy" button. Releasing packaged software should involve a single automated process that creates the installer.

We discuss automation a lot in the course of this book, and we know that some people aren't totally sold on the idea. Let us explain why we see automated deployment as an indispensable goal.

- When deployments aren't fully automated, errors will occur every time they are performed. The only question is whether or not the errors are significant. Even with excellent deployment tests, bugs can be hard to track down.

- When the deployment process is not automated, it is not repeatable or reliable, leading to time wasted on debugging deployment errors.

- A manual deployment process has to be documented. Maintaining the documentation is a complex and time-consuming task involving collaboration between several people, so the documentation is generally incomplete or out-of-date at any given time. A set of automated deployment scripts serves as documentation, and it will always be up-to-date and complete, or the deployment will not work.

- Automated deployments encourage collaboration, because everything is explicit in a script. Documentation has to make assumptions about the level of knowledge of the reader and in reality is usually written as an aide-memoire for the person performing the deployment, making it opaque to others.

- A corollary of the above: Manual deployments depend on the deployment expert. If he or she is on vacation or quits work, you are in trouble.

- Performing manual deployments is boring and repetitive and yet needs significant degree of expertise. Asking experts to do boring and repetitive, and yet technically demanding tasks is the most certain way of ensuring human error that we can think of, short of sleep deprivation, or inebriation. Automating deployments frees your expensive, highly skilled, overworked staff to work on higher-value activities.

- The only way to test a manual deployment process is to do it. This is often time-consuming and expensive. An automated deployment process is cheap and easy to test.

- We have heard it said that a manual process is more auditable than an automated one. We are completely baffled by this statement. With a manual process, there is no guarantee that the documentation has been followed. Only an automated process is fully auditable. What is more auditable than a working deployment script?

The automated deployment process must be used by everybody, and it should be the only way in which the software is ever deployed. This discipline ensures that the deployment script will work when it is needed. One of the principles that we describe in this book is to use the same script to deploy to every environment. If you use the same script to deploy to every environment, then the deployment-to-production path will have been tested hundreds or even thousands of times before it is needed on release day. If any problems occur upon release, you can be certain they are problems with environment-specific configuration, not your scripts.

We are certain that, occasionally, manually intensive releases work smoothly. We may well have been unlucky in having mostly seen the bad ones. However, if this is not recognized as a potentially error-prone step in the process of software production, why is it attended by such ceremony? Why all the process and documentation? Why are the teams of people brought in during weekends? Why have people waiting on standby in case things go less than well?

Antipattern: Deploying to a Production-like Environment Only after Development Is Complete

In this pattern, the first time the software is deployed to a production-like environment (for example, staging) is once most of the development work is done—at least, "done" as defined by the development team.

The pattern looks a bit like this.

- If testers have been involved in the process up to this point, they have tested the system on development machines.

- Releasing into staging is the first time that operations people interact with the new release. In some organizations, separate operations teams are used to deploy the software into staging and production. In this case, the first time an operations person sees the software is the day it is released into production.

- Either a production-like environment is expensive enough that access to it is strictly controlled, or it is not in place on time, or nobody bothered to create one.

- The development team assembles the correct installers, configuration files, database migrations, and deployment documentation to pass to the people who perform the actual deployment—all of it untested in an environment that looks like production or staging.

- There is little, if any, collaboration between the development team and the people who actually perform deployments to create this collateral.

When the deployment to staging occurs, a team is assembled to perform it. Sometimes this team has all the necessary skills, but often in very large organizations the responsibilities for deployment are divided between several groups. DBAs, middleware teams, web teams, and others all take a hand in deploying the latest version of the application. Since the various steps have never been tested in staging, they often have errors. The documentation misses important steps. The documentation and scripts make assumptions about the version or configuration of the target environment that are wrong, causing the deployment to fail. The deployment team has to guess at the intentions of the development team.

Often the poor collaboration that causes so many problems in deployment to staging is shored up with ad-hoc telephone calls, emails, and quick fixes. A very disciplined team will incorporate all of this communication into the deployment plan—but it is rare for this process to be effective. As pressure increases, the defined process for collaboration between the development and deployment teams is subverted, in order to get the deployment done within the time allocated to the deployment team.

In the process of performing the deployment, it is not uncommon to find that incorrect assumptions about the production environment have been baked into the design of the system. For example, one application we had a hand in deploying used the filesystem to cache data. This worked fine on a developer workstation, but less well in a clustered environment. Solving problems like this one can take a long time, and the application cannot be said to have been deployed until they are resolved.

Once the application is deployed into staging, it is common for new bugs to be found. Unfortunately, there is often no time to fix them all because the deadline is fast approaching and, at this stage of the project, deferring the release date is unacceptable. So the most critical bugs are hurriedly patched up, and a list of known defects is stored by the project manager for safekeeping, to be deprioritized when work begins on the next release.

Sometimes it can be even worse than this. Here are a few things that can exacerbate the problems associated with a release.

- When working on a new application, the first deployment to staging is likely to be the most troublesome.

- The longer the release cycle, the longer the development team has to make incorrect assumptions before the deployment occurs, and the longer it will take to fix them.

- In large organizations where the delivery process is divided between different groups such as development, DBA, operations, testing, etc., the cost of coordination between these silos can be enormous, sometimes stalling the release process in ticketing hell. In this scenario, developers, testers, and operations personnel are constantly raising tickets (or sending emails) to each other to perform any given deployment—and worse, to resolve problems that arise during deployment.

- The bigger the difference between development and production environments, the less realistic are the assumptions that have to be made during development. This can be difficult to quantify, but it's a good bet that if you're developing on a Windows machine and deploying to a Solaris cluster, you are in for some surprises.

- If your application is installed by users or contains components that are, you may not have much control over their environments, especially outside of a corporate setting. In this case, a great deal of extra testing will be required.

Instead . . .

The remedy is to integrate the testing, deployment, and release activities into the development process. Make them a normal and ongoing part of development so that by the time you are ready to release your system into production there is little to no risk, because you have rehearsed it on many different occasions in a progressively more production-like sequence of test environments. Make sure everybody involved in the software delivery process, from the build and release team to testers to developers, work together from the start of the project.

We are test addicts, and the extensive use of continuous integration and continuous deployment, as a means of testing both our software and our deployment process, is a cornerstone of the approach that we describe.

Antipattern: Manual Configuration Management of Production Environments

Many organizations manage the configuration of their production environments through a team of operations people. If a change is needed, such as a change to database connection setting or an increase in the number of threads in a thread pool on an application server, then it is carried out manually on the production servers. If a record is kept of such a change, it is probably an entry in a change management database.

Signs of this antipattern are:

- Having deployed successfully many times to staging, the deployment into production fails.

- Different members of a cluster behave differently—for example, one node sustaining less load or taking longer to process requests than another.

- The operations team take a long time to prepare an environment for a release.

- You cannot step back to an earlier configuration of your system, which may include operating system, application server, web server, RDBMS, or other infrastructural settings.

- Servers in clusters have, unintentionally, different versions of operating systems, third-party infrastructure, libraries, or patch levels.

- Configuration of the system is carried out by modifying the configuration directly on production systems.

Instead . . .

All aspects of each of your testing, staging, and production environments, specifically the configuration of any third-party elements of your system, should be applied from version control through an automated process.

One of the key practices that we describe in this book is configuration management, part of which means being able to repeatably re-create every piece of infrastructure used by your application. That means operating systems, patch levels, OS configuration, your application stack, its configuration, infrastructure configuration, and so forth should all be managed. You should be able to re-create your production environment exactly, preferably in an automated fashion. Virtualization can help you get started with this.

You should know exactly what is in production. That means that every change made to production should be recorded and auditable. Often, deployments fail because somebody patched the production environment last time they deployed, but the change was not recorded. Indeed it should not be possible to make manual changes to testing, staging, and production environments. The only way to make changes to these environments should be through an automated process.

Applications often depend on other applications. It should be possible to see at a glance exactly what the currently released version of every piece of software is.

While releases can be exhilarating, they can also be exhausting and depressing. Almost every release involves last-minute changes, such as fixing the database login details or updating the URL for an external service. There should be a way of introducing such changes so that they are both recorded and tested. Again, automation is essential. Changes should be made in version control and then propagated to production through an automated process.

It should be possible to use the same automated process to roll back to a previous version of production if the deployment goes wrong.

Can We Do Better?

You bet, and the goal of this book is to describe how. The principles, practices, and techniques we describe are aimed at making releases boring, even in complex "enterprise" environments. Software release can—and should—be a low-risk, frequent, cheap, rapid, and predictable process. These practices have been developed over the last few years, and we have seen them make a huge difference in many projects. All of the practices in this book have been tested in large enterprise projects with distributed teams as well as in small development groups. We know that they work, and we know that they scale to large projects.

The Power of Automated Deployment

One of our clients used to have a large team of people dedicated to each release. The team worked together for seven days, including the entire weekend, to get the application into production. Their success rate was poor, with many releases introducing errors or requiring high levels of intervention on the day of release as well as, often, patches and fixes on subsequent days to correct errors introduced with the release or caused by human errors in configuring the new software.

We helped them to implement a sophisticated automated build, deploy, test, and release system and to introduce the development practices and techniques necessary to support it. The last release we saw took seven seconds to deploy the application into production. No one noticed anything had happened, except of course that the new behaviors that the release implemented suddenly became available. Had the successful deployment of the system behind this major website failed for any reason, we could have backed out the change in the same amount of time.

Our goal is to describe the use of deployment pipelines, combined with high levels of automation of both testing and deployment and comprehensive configuration management to deliver push-button software releases. That is, push-button software releases to any deployment target—development, test, or production.

Along the way we will describe the pattern itself and the techniques that you will need to adopt to make it work. We will provide advice on different approaches to solving some of the problems that you will face. We have found that the advantages of such an approach vastly outweigh the costs of achieving it.

None of this is outside the reach of any project team. It does not require rigid process, significant documentation, or lots of people. By the end of this chapter, we hope that you will understand the principles behind this approach.

How Do We Achieve Our Goal?

As we said, our goal as software professionals is to deliver useful, working software to users as quickly as possible.

Speed is essential because there is an opportunity cost associated with not delivering software. You can only start to get a return on your investment once your software is released. So, one of our two overriding goals in this book is to find ways to reduce *cycle time*, the time it takes from deciding to make a change, whether a bugfix or a feature, to having it available to users.

Delivering fast is also important because it allows you to verify whether your features and bugfixes really are useful. The decision maker behind the creation of an application, who we'll call the customer, makes hypotheses about which features and bugfixes will be useful to users. However, until they are in the hands of users who vote by choosing to use the software, they remain hypotheses. It is therefore vital to minimize cycle time so that an effective feedback loop can be established.

An important part of usefulness is quality. Our software should be fit for its purpose. Quality does not equal perfection—as Voltaire said, "The perfect is the enemy of the good,"—but our goal should always be to deliver software of sufficient quality to bring value to its users. So while it is important to deliver our software as quickly as possible, it is essential to maintain an appropriate level of quality.

So, to slightly refine our goal, we want to find ways to deliver high-quality, valuable software in an efficient, fast, and reliable manner.

We, and our fellow practitioners, have discovered that in order to achieve these goals—low cycle time and high quality—we need to make frequent, automated releases of our software. Why is this?

- **Automated.** If the build, deploy, test, and release process is not automated, it is not repeatable. Every time it is done, it will be different, because of changes in the software, the configuration of the system, the environments, and the release process. Since the steps are manual, they are error-prone, and there is no way to review exactly what was done. This means there is no way to gain control over the release process, and hence to ensure high quality. Releasing software is too often an art; it should be an engineering discipline.

- **Frequent.** If releases are frequent, the delta between releases will be small. This significantly reduces the risk associated with releasing and makes it much easier to roll back. Frequent releases also lead to faster feedback—indeed, they require it. Much of this book concentrates on getting feedback on changes to your application and its associated configuration (including its environment, deployment process, and data) as quickly as possible.

Feedback is essential to frequent, automated releases. There are three criteria for feedback to be useful.

- Any change, of whatever kind, needs to trigger the feedback process.

- The feedback must be delivered as soon as possible.

- The delivery team must receive feedback and then act on it.

Let's examine these three criteria in detail and consider how we can achieve them.

Every Change Should Trigger the Feedback Process

A working software application can be usefully decomposed into four components: executable code, configuration, host environment, and data. If any of them changes, it can lead to a change in the behavior of the application. Therefore we need to keep all four of these components under control and ensure that a change in any one of them is verified.

Executable code changes when a change is made to the source code. Every time a change is made to the source code, the resulting binary must be built and tested. In order to gain control over this process, building and testing the binary should be automated. The practice of building and testing your application on every check-in is known as continuous integration; we describe it in detail in Chapter 3.

This executable code should be the same executable code that is deployed into every environment, whether it is a testing environment or a production environment. If your system uses a compiled language, you should ensure that the binary output of your build process—the executable code—is reused everywhere it is needed and never rebuilt.

Anything that changes between environments should be captured as configuration information. Any change to an application's configuration, in whichever environment, should be tested. If the software is to be installed by the users, the possible configuration options should be tested across a representative range of example systems. Configuration management is discussed in Chapter 2.

If the environments the application is to be deployed into change, the whole system should be tested with the changes to the environment. This includes changes in the operating system configuration, the software stack that supports the application, the network configuration, and any infrastructure and external systems. Chapter 11 deals with managing infrastructure and environments, including automation of the creation and maintenance of testing and production environments.

Finally, if the structure of the data changes, this change must also be tested. We discuss data management in Chapter 12.

What is the feedback process? It involves testing every change in a fully automated fashion, as far as possible. The tests will vary depending on the system, but they will usually include at least the following checks.

- The process of creating the executable code must work. This verifies that the syntax of your source code is valid.

- The software's unit tests must pass. This checks that your application's code behaves as expected.

- The software should fulfill certain quality criteria such as test coverage and other technology-specific metrics.

- The software's functional acceptance tests must pass. This checks that your application conforms to its business acceptance criteria—that it delivers the business value that was intended.

- The software's nonfunctional tests must pass. This checks that the application performs sufficiently well in terms of capacity, availability, security, and so on to meet its users' needs.

- The software must go through exploratory testing and a demonstration to the customer and a selection of users. This is typically done from a manual testing environment. In this part of the process, the product owner might decide that there are missing features, or we might find bugs that require fixing and automated tests that need creating to prevent regressions.

The environments these tests run in must be as similar as possible to production, to verify that any changes to our environments have not affected the application's ability to work.

The Feedback Must Be Received as Soon as Possible

The key to fast feedback is automation. With fully automated processes, your only constraint is the amount of hardware that you are able to throw at the problem. If you have manual processes, you are dependent on people to get the job done. People take longer, they introduce errors, and they are not auditable. Moreover, performing manual build, test, and deployment processes is boring and repetitive—far from the best use of people. People are expensive and valuable, and they should be focused on producing software that delights its users and then delivering those delights as fast as possible—not on boring, error-prone tasks like regression testing, virtual server provisioning, and deployment, which are best done by machines.

However, implementing a deployment pipeline is resource-intensive, especially once you have a comprehensive automated test suite. One of its key objectives is to optimize for human resource usage: We want to free people to do the interesting work and leave repetition to machines.

We can characterize the tests in the commit stage of the pipeline (Figure 1.1) as follows.

- They run fast.

- They are as comprehensive as possible—that is to say, they cover more than 75% or so of the codebase, so that when they pass, we have a good level of confidence that the application works.

- If any of them fails, it means our application has a critical fault and should not be released under any circumstances. That means that a test to check the color of a UI element should not be included in this set of tests.

- They are as environment-neutral as possible—that is, the environment does not have to be an exact replica of production, which means it can be simpler and cheaper.

On the other hand, the tests in the later stages have the following general characteristics.

- They run more slowly and therefore are candidates for parallelization.

- Some of them may fail, and we may still choose to release the application under some circumstances (perhaps there is a critical fix in the release candidate that causes the performance to drop below a predefined threshold—but we might make the decision to release anyway).

- They should run on an environment that is as similar as possible to production, so in addition to the direct focus of the test they also test the deployment process and any changes to the production environment.

This organization of the testing process means that we have a high level of confidence in the software after the first set of tests, which run fastest on the cheapest hardware. If these tests fail, the release candidate does not progress to later stages. This ensures optimal use of resources. There is much more on pipelining in Chapter 5, "Anatomy of the Deployment Pipeline," and the later Chapters 7, 8, and 9 which describe the commit testing stage, automated acceptance testing, and testing nonfunctional requirements.

One of the fundamentals of our approach is the need for fast feedback. Ensuring fast feedback on changes requires us to pay attention to the process of developing software—in particular, to how we use version control and how we organize our code. Developers should commit changes to their version control system frequently, and split code into separate components as a way of managing large or distributed teams. Branching should, in most circumstances, be avoided. We discuss incremental delivery and the use of components in Chapter 13, "Managing Components and Dependencies," and branching and merging in Chapter 14, "Advanced Version Control."

The Delivery Team Must Receive Feedback and Then Act on It

It is essential that everybody involved in the process of delivering software is involved in the feedback process. That includes developers, testers, operations staff, database administrators, infrastructure specialists, and managers. If people in these roles do not work together on a day-to-day basis (although we recommend that teams should be cross-functional), it is essential that they meet frequently and work to improve the process of delivering software. A process based on continuous improvement is essential to the rapid delivery of quality software. Iterative processes help establish a regular heartbeat for this kind of activity—at least once per iteration a retrospective meeting is held where everybody discusses how to improve the delivery process for the next iteration.

Being able to react to feedback also means broadcasting information. Using big, visible dashboards (which need not be electronic) and other notification mechanisms is central to ensuring that feedback is, indeed, fed-back and makes the final step into someone's head. Dashboards should be ubiquitous, and certainly at least one should be present in each team room.

Finally, feedback is no good unless it is acted upon. This requires discipline and planning. When something needs doing, it is the responsibility of the whole team to stop what they are doing and decide on a course of action. Only once this is done should the team carry on with their work.

Does This Process Scale?

One common objection we hear is that the process we describe is idealistic. It may work in small teams, these detractors say, but it can't possibly work in my huge, distributed project!

We have worked on many large projects over the years in several different industries. We have also been lucky enough to work alongside colleagues with a vast range of experiences. All the techniques and principles that we describe in this book have been proven in real projects in all kinds of organizations, both large and small, in all kinds of situations. Experiencing the same problems over and over again in such projects is what drove us to write this book.

Readers will notice that much of this book is inspired by the philosophy and ideas of the lean movement. The goals of lean manufacturing are to ensure the rapid delivery of high-quality products, focusing on the removal of waste and the reduction of cost. Lean manufacturing has resulted in huge cost and resource savings, much higher-quality products, and faster time-to-market in several industries. This philosophy is starting to become mainstream in the field of software development too, and it informs much of what we discuss in this book. Lean is certainly not limited in its application to small systems. It was created and applied to huge organizations, and even whole economies.

Both the theory and the practice are as relevant to large teams as they are to small, and our experience has been that they work. However, we don't ask you to believe what we say. Try it yourself and find out. Keep what works, discard what doesn't, and write about your experiences so that other people can benefit.

What Are the Benefits?

The principal benefit of the approach that we describe in the preceding section is that it creates a release process that is repeatable, reliable, and predictable, which in turn generates large reductions in cycle time, and hence gets features and bugfixes to users fast. The cost savings alone are worth not just the cover price of this book, but also the investment in time that the establishment and maintenance of such a release system entails.

Beyond that there are many other benefits, some of which we would have predicted beforehand, while others were more like pleasant surprises when we observed them.

Empowering Teams

One of the key principles of the deployment pipeline is that it is a pull system—it allows testers, operations or support personnel to self-service the version of the application they want into the environment of their choice. In our experience, a major contributor to cycle time is people involved in the delivery process waiting to get a "good build" of the application. Often getting a good build requires endless emails being sent, tickets being raised, or other inefficient forms of communication. When the teams involved in delivery are distributed, this becomes a major source of inefficiency. With a deployment pipeline implementation, this problem is completely removed—everybody should have the ability to see which builds are available to be deployed into the environments they care about and be able to perform a deployment at the push of a button.

What we often see as a result of this is several different versions in play in various environments, as different members of the team go about their work. The ability to easily deploy any version of the software into any environment has many advantages.

- Testers can select older versions of an application to verify changes in behavior in newer versions.

- Support staff can deploy a released version of the application into an environment to reproduce a defect.

- Operations staff can select a known good build to deploy to production as part of a disaster recovery exercise.

- Releases can be performed at the push of a button.

The flexibility that our deployment tools offer to them changes the way that they work—for the better. Overall, team members are more in control of their work, and so the quality of their work improves, which makes the quality of the application improve. They collaborate more effectively, are less reactive, and can work more efficiently because they don't spend so much time waiting for good builds to be pushed to them.

Reducing Errors

Errors can creep into software from all sorts of places. The people who commission the software in the first place can ask for the wrong thing. The analysts who capture the requirements can misunderstand, the developers can write buggy code. The errors we are talking about here, though, are specifically those introduced into production by poor *configuration management*. We will describe what we mean by configuration management in more detail in Chapter 2. For now, think of the things that have to be just right to make a typical application work—the right version of the code, sure, but also the correct version of the database schema, the correct configuration for load-balancers, the correct URL to that web service that you use to look up prices, and so forth. When we talk about configuration management, we mean the processes and mechanisms that allow you to identify and control that complete set of information, every last bit and byte.

What a Difference a Byte Makes

A few years ago, Dave was working on a large-scale point of sale system for a well-known retailer. This was in the early days of our thinking about automating the deployment process, so while some aspects of it were quite well automated others were not. A very nasty bug cropped up in production. We were suddenly getting an explosion of error traces in our logs under some unknown, hard to determine combination of circumstances. We couldn't reproduce the problem in any of our test environments. We tried all sorts of things: load testing in our performance environment, trying to simulate what looked like our production pathological case—but we just couldn't reproduce the problem. Finally, after a lot more investigation than described here, we decided to audit everything we could think of that could possibly be different between the two systems. We eventually found that a single binary library that our application depended upon, belonging to the application server software we were using, was different in the production environment and test environments. We changed the version of the binary in production, and the problem vanished.

The point of this story is not that we weren't diligent, or weren't cautious enough, or even that we were really smart because we thought to audit the system. The real point is that software can be immensely fragile. This was a fairly big system with tens of thousands of classes, thousands of libraries, and many integration points with external systems. Yet a serious error was introduced into production by a few bytes of difference between versions of a third-party binary file.

Of the many gigabytes of information that collectively comprise a modern software system, no human being—or team of human beings—is going to be able to spot a change on the scale of the example described in the preceding sidebar without machine assistance. Instead of waiting until the problem occurs, why not employ the machine assistance to prevent it happening in the first place?

By actively managing everything that can change in version control—such as configuration files, scripts to create databases and their schemas, build scripts, test harnesses, even development environments and operating system configurations—we allow computers to do what they are good at: ensure that every last bit and byte is in the place that we expect it to be, at least up until the point when our code starts running.

The Cost of Manual Configuration Management

Another project we worked on had a large number of dedicated test environments. Each ran a popular EJB application server. This application was developed as an agile project and had good automated test coverage. The local build was well managed, so it was comparatively easy for a developer to get the code running quickly locally so that they could develop it. However, this was before we had started being more careful about the automation of our application's deployment. Each test environment was configured manually, using the console-based tools of the application server vendor. Even though a copy of the configuration files that the developers used to configure their local installations was kept under version control, the configuration of each test environment was not. Each was different from its siblings. They had properties in different orders, some were missing, some were set to different values, some had different names, some had properties that didn't occur on any of the others. No two test environments were the same, and they were all different from the production environments. It was incredibly hard to determine which properties were essential, which were redundant, which should be common between environments, and which should be unique. As a result, that project employed a team of five people responsible for managing the configuration of these different environments.

In our experience, this dependence on manual configuration management is common. In many organizations that we have worked with, this is true of both their production systems and their test environments. Sometimes it may not matter that server A has its connection pool limited to 100 while server B has its pool set to 120. At other times it matters a lot.

Which configuration differences matter and which do not is not something that you want to discover by accident during your busiest trading period. This kind of configuration information defines the environment in which code runs and frequently, in effect, specifies new paths through the code. Changes to such configuration information need to be considered, and the environment in which the code runs needs to be as well defined and controlled as the behavior of the code itself. If we have access to the configuration of your database, application server, or web server, we guarantee that we can make your application fail faster than if you give us access to a compiler and your source code.

When such configuration parameters are manually defined and managed, they suffer from the human propensity for making mistakes in repetitive tasks. A simple typo in just the wrong place can stop an application in its tracks. Worse than that, programming languages have syntax checks and perhaps unit tests to verify that there are no typos. There are rarely checks of any kind applied to configuration information, particularly if that configuration information is typed directly into some console.

The simple act of adding your configuration information to your version control system is an enormous step forward. At its simplest, the version control system will alert you to the fact that you have changed the configuration inadvertently. This eliminates at least one very common source of errors.

Once all of your configuration information is stored in a version control system, the next obvious step is to eliminate the middleman and get the computer to apply the configuration rather than to type it back in. Some technologies are more amenable to this than others, but you, and often the infrastructure vendors, will be surprised how far you can take this if you think carefully about the configuration of even the most intractable third-party systems. We will discuss the details of this later in Chapter 4, and at length in Chapter 11.

Lowering Stress

Of the obvious benefits, the most pleasant is the reduction in stress in all parties that are associated with a release. Most people who have ever come anywhere near a software project that is approaching its release date will be aware that these are indeed stressful events. That in itself can be a source of problems in our experience. We have seen sensible, conservative, quality-conscious project managers asking their developers, "Can't you just modify the code?" or otherwise sane database administrators entering data into tables in databases for applications that they don't know. On both occasions, and many others like them, the change was in direct response to the pressure to "just get something working."

Don't get us wrong, we have been there too. We are not even suggesting that this is always the wrong response: If you have just released some code into production that is causing your organization to bleed money, almost anything that stops the bleed may be justified.

Our point here is different. Both examples of quick hacks to get the newly deployed production system running weren't being driven by such immediate commercial imperatives, but rather by the more subtle pressure to release on the day that was planned. The problem here is that releases into production are big events. As long as this is true they will be surrounded with a lot of ceremony and nervousness.

For a moment, imagine that your upcoming release could be performed with the push of a button. Imagine that it could be performed within a few minutes, or even a few seconds, and that if the worst came to the worst, you could back out the release in the same few minutes or seconds. Imagine that you released frequently, so the delta between what is currently in production and the new release is small. If that were true, then the risk of release would be greatly diminished, and the unpleasant feeling that you are betting your career on its success significantly reduced.

For a small set of projects, this ideal may not be practically achievable. However, in most projects it certainly is, albeit with some degree of effort. The key to reducing stress is to have the kind of automated deployment process that we have described, to perform it frequently, and to have a good story when it comes to your ability to back changes out should the worst happen. The first time you do automation, it will be painful—but it will become easier, and the benefits to the project and to yourself are almost incalculably large.

Deployment Flexibility

It should be a simple task to start your application in a new environment—ideally just a matter of commissioning the machines or virtual images and creating some configuration information that describes the environment's unique properties. Then you should be able to use your automated deployment process to prepare the new environment for deployment and deploy the chosen version of your application to it.

Running Enterprise Software on a Laptop

We were working on a project recently that had its business case invalidated by an unexpected change in government legislation. The project was intended to create the core enterprise system for a new business. The business was to be distributed across international boundaries, and the software was designed to run on a large heterogeneous collection of expensive computers. Naturally everyone was somewhat deflated by the news that the project's raison d'étre had just vanished out of the window.

There was one small high point for us though. The organization for whom we were developing the software did a downsizing analysis. "What is the minimum hardware footprint of the new system, how could we limit our capital costs?" they asked. "Well, it runs on this laptop," we answered. They were surprised, since this was a sophisticated multiuser system. "How do you know it works?" they asked after thinking it through. "Well, we can run all of the acceptance tests like this . . . ," and we showed them. "What load would it have to take?" we asked them. They told us the load, we made a single-line change to the scaling parameters for our performance tests and ran them. We showed that the laptop was too slow, but not by all that much. A single decently configured server would meet their needs, and when it was made available it would be a matter of a few minutes to get the application up and running on it.

This kind of deployment flexibility isn't only a function of the kind of automated deployment techniques that we describe in this book; the application was pretty well designed too. However, our ability to place the software wherever it was needed, on demand, gave us and our clients great confidence in our ability to manage any release at any point. As releases become less fraught, it is easier to consider things like the agile ideal of a release at the end of each iteration. Even if that isn't appropriate for a particular project, it means that we get our weekends back.

Practice Makes Perfect

In projects we work on, we try to achieve a dedicated development environment for each developer or pair of developers. However, even in projects that don't take it that far, any team that uses continuous integration or iterative, incremental development techniques will need to deploy the application frequently.

The best strategy to adopt is to use the same deployment approach whatever the deployment target. There should not be a special QA deployment strategy, or a special acceptance test, or production deployment strategy. In this way every time the application is deployed, we are confirming that our deployment mechanism is working correctly. In essence, the final deployment into production is being rehearsed every single time the software is deployed to any target.

There is one special case where some variation is permissible: the development environment. It makes sense that the developers will need to build binaries rather than take pre-prepared binaries built elsewhere, so this constraint can be relaxed for those deployments. Even on developer workstations, though, we try as much as possible to deploy and manage things in the same way.

The Release Candidate

What is a *release candidate*? A change to your code may or may not be releasable. If you were to look at a change and ask, "Should we release this change?" then the answer could only be a guess. It is the build, deployment, and test process that we apply to that change that validates whether the change can be released. This process gives us increasing confidence that the change is safe to release. We take that small change—whether it is new functionality, a bugfix, or a retuning of the system to achieve some change in performance—and verify whether or not we can release the system with that change with a high level of confidence. In order to reduce the risk further, we want to perform this validation in the shortest possible time.

While any change may lead to an artifact that can be released to users, they don't start off that way. Every change must be evaluated for its fitness. If the resulting product is found to be free of defects, and it meets the acceptance criteria set out by the customer, then it can be released.

Most approaches to releasing software identify release candidates at the end of the process. This makes some sense when there is work associated with the tracking. At the time of writing, the Wikipedia entry describing development stages shows "release candidate" as a distinct step in the process (Figure 1.2). We see things a little differently.

Figure 1.2   *Traditional view of release candidates*

Traditional approaches to software development delay the nomination of a release candidate until several lengthy and expensive steps have been taken to ensure that the software is of sufficient quality and functionally complete. However, in an environment where build and deployment automation is aggressively pursued along with comprehensive automated testing, there is no need to spend time and money on lengthy and manually intensive testing at the end of the project. At this stage the quality of the application is usually significantly higher, so manual testing is only an affirmation of the functional completeness.

Indeed, delaying testing until after the development process is, in our experience, a sure-fire way to *decrease* the quality of your application. Defects are best discovered and fixed at the point where they are introduced. When they are discovered later, they are always more expensive to fix. The developers have forgotten what they were doing at the time when they introduced the defect, and the functionality may have changed in the meantime. Leaving testing until the end normally means that there is no time to actually fix the bugs, or that only a small proportion of them can be fixed. So we want to find and fix them at the earliest possible opportunity, preferably *before* they are checked in to the code.

Every Check-in Leads to a Potential Release

Every change that a developer makes to a codebase is intended to add value in some manner. Every change committed to version control is supposed to enhance the system that we are working on. How do we know if that is true? The only way in which we can tell is through exercising the software to see if it achieves the value that we had expected. Most projects defer this part of the process until later in the life of the feature under development. This means that as far as anybody knows, the system is broken until it is found to be working when it is tested or used. If it is found to be broken at this point, it usually takes a significant amount of work to get the system running as it should. This phase is usually described as integration and is often the most unpredictable and unmanageable part of the development process. Since it is so painful, teams defer it, integrating infrequently, which only makes it worse.

In software, when something is painful, the way to reduce the pain is to do it more frequently, not less. So instead of integrating infrequently, we should integrate frequently; in fact, we should integrate as a result of every single change to the system. This practice of continuous integration takes the idea of integrating frequently to its logical extreme. In doing so, it creates a paradigm shift in the software development process. Continuous integration detects any change that breaks the system or does not fulfill the customer's acceptance criteria at the time it is introduced into the system. Teams then fix the problem as soon as it occurs (this is the first rule of continuous integration). When this practice is followed, then the software is *always* in a working state. If your tests are sufficiently comprehensive and you are running tests on a sufficiently production-like environment, then the software is in fact always in a *releasable* state.

Every change is, in effect, a release candidate. Every time a change is committed to version control, the expectation is that it will pass all of its tests, produce working code, and can be released into production. This is the starting assumption. The job of a continuous integration system is to disprove this assumption, to show that a particular release candidate is not fit to make it into production.

Principles of Software Delivery

The ideas behind this book were informed by a large number of projects that the authors have worked on over a period of many years. As we commenced the activity of synthesizing our thoughts and capturing them in these pages, we noticed that the same principles came up over and over again. We've enumerated them here. Some of what we say is subject to interpretation or caveats; the principles below are not. These are the things that we can't imagine doing without if we want our delivery process to be effective.

Create a Repeatable, Reliable Process for Releasing Software

This principle is really a statement of our aim in writing this book: Releasing software should be easy. It should be easy because you have tested every single part of the release process hundreds of times before. It should be as simple as pressing a button. The repeatability and reliability derive from two principles: automate almost everything, and keep everything you need to build, deploy, test, and release your application in version control.

Deploying software ultimately involves three things:

- Provisioning and managing the environment in which your application will run (hardware configuration, software, infrastructure, and external services).

- Installing the correct version of your application into it.

- Configuring your application, including any data or state it requires.

The deployment of your application can be implemented using a fully automated process from version control. Application configuration can also be a fully automated process, with the necessary scripts and state kept in version control or databases. Clearly, hardware cannot be kept in version control; but, particularly with the advent of cheap virtualization technology and tools like Puppet, the provisioning process can also be fully automated.

The rest of this book essentially describes strategies for realizing this principle.

Automate Almost Everything

There are some things it is impossible to automate. Exploratory testing relies on experienced testers. Demonstrations of working software to representatives of your user community cannot be performed by computers. Approvals for compliance purposes by definition require human intervention. However, the list of things that cannot be automated is much smaller than many people think. In general, your build process should be automated up to the point where it needs specific human direction or decision making. This is also true of your deployment process and, in fact, your entire software release process. Acceptance tests can be automated. Database upgrades and downgrades can be automated too. Even network and firewall configuration can be automated. You should automate as much as you possibly can.

Your authors can honestly say that they haven't found a build or deployment process that couldn't be automated with sufficient work and ingenuity.

Most development teams don't automate their release process because it seems such a daunting task. It's easier just to do things manually. Perhaps that is true the first time they perform a step in the process, but it is certainly not true by the time they perform that step for the tenth time, and is probably not true by the time they have done it three or four times.

Automation is a prerequisite for the deployment pipeline, because it is only through automation that we can guarantee that people will get what they need at the push of a button. However, you don't need to automate everything at once. You should start by looking at that part of your build, deploy, test, and release process that is currently the bottleneck. You can, and should, automate gradually over time.

Keep Everything in Version Control

Everything you need to build, deploy, test, and release your application should be kept in some form of versioned storage. This includes requirement documents, test scripts, automated test cases, network configuration scripts, deployment scripts, database creation, upgrade, downgrade, and initialization scripts, application stack configuration scripts, libraries, toolchains, technical documentation, and so on. All of this stuff should be version-controlled, and the relevant version should be identifiable for any given build. That is, these *change sets* should have a single identifier, such as a build number or a version control change set number, that references every piece.

It should be possible for a new team member to sit down at a new workstation, check out the project's revision control repository, and run a single command to build and deploy the application to any accessible environment, including the local development workstation.

It should also be possible to see which build of your various applications is deployed into each of your environments, and which versions in version control these builds came from.

If It Hurts, Do It More Frequently, and Bring the Pain Forward

This is the most general principle on our list, and could perhaps best be described as a heuristic. But it is perhaps the most useful heuristic we know of in the context of delivering software, and it informs everything we say. Integration is often a very painful process. If this is true on your project, integrate every time somebody checks in, and do it from the start of the project. If testing is a painful process that occurs just before release, don't do it at the end. Instead, do it continually from the beginning of the project.

If releasing software is painful, aim to release it every time somebody checks in a change that passes all the automated tests. If you can't release it to real users upon every change, release it to a production-like environment upon every check-in. If creating application documentation is painful, do it as you develop new features instead of leaving it to the end. Make documentation for a feature part of the definition of done, and automate the process as far as possible.

Depending on your current level of expertise, it could take a serious amount of effort to reach this goal, and of course you still have to deliver software in the meantime. Aim for intermediate goals, such as an internal release every few weeks or, if you're already doing that, every week. Gradually work to approach the ideal—even small steps will deliver great benefits.

Extreme programming is essentially the result of applying this heuristic to the software development process. Much of the advice in this book comes from our experience of applying the same principle to the process of releasing software.

Build Quality In

This principle and the last one we mention in this section—continuous improvement—are shamelessly stolen from the lean movement. "Build quality in" was the motto of W. Edwards Deming who was, among his other distinctions, one of the pioneers of the lean movement. The earlier you catch defects, the cheaper they are to fix. Defects are fixed most cheaply if they are never checked in to version control in the first place.

The techniques that we describe in this book, such as continuous integration, comprehensive automated testing, and automated deployment, are designed to catch defects as early in the delivery process as possible (an application of the principle "Bring the pain forward"). The next step is to fix them. A fire alarm is useless if everybody ignores it. Delivery teams must be disciplined about fixing defects as soon as they are found.

There are two other corollaries of "Build quality in." Firstly, testing is not a phase, and certainly not one to begin after the development phase. If testing is left to the end, it will be too late. There will be no time to fix the defects. Secondly, testing is also not the domain, purely or even principally, of testers. Everybody on the delivery team is responsible for the quality of the application all the time.

Done Means Released

How often have you heard a developer say a story or feature is "done"? Perhaps you have heard a project manager asking that developer if it is "done done"? What does "done" mean? Really, a feature is only done when it is delivering value to users. This is part of the motivation behind the practice of continuous deployment (see Chapter 10, "Deploying and Releasing Applications").

For some agile delivery teams, "done" means released into production. This is the ideal situation for a software development project. However, it is not always practical to use this as a measure of done. The initial release of a software system can take a while before it is in a state where real external users are getting benefit from it. So we will dial back to the next best option and say that a functionality is "done" once it has been successfully showcased, that is, demonstrated to, and tried by, representatives of the user community, from a production-like environment.

There is no "80% done." Things are either done, or they are not. It is possible to estimate the work remaining before something is done—but those will only ever be estimates. Using an estimate to determine the total amount of remaining work leads to recriminations and finger-pointing when those quoting the percentage turn out, as they invariably do, to be wrong.

This principle has an interesting corollary: It is not in the power of one person to get something done. It requires a number of people on a delivery team to work together to get anything done. That's why it's so important for everybody—testers, build and operations personnel, support teams, developers—to work together from the beginning. It's also why the whole delivery team is responsible for delivering—a principle so important that it gets a section of its own . . .

Everybody Is Responsible for the Delivery Process

Ideally, everybody within an organization is aligned with its goals, and people work together to help each to meet them. Ultimately the team succeeds or fails as a team, not as individuals. However, in too many projects the reality is that developers throw their work over the wall to testers. Then testers throw work over the wall to the operations team at release time. When something goes wrong, people spend as much time blaming one another as they do fixing the defects that inevitably arise from such a siloed approach.

If you are working in a small organization or in a relatively independent department, you may have complete control over the resources that you need to release software. If so, fantastic. If not, realizing this principle may require hard work over a long period of time to break down the barriers between the silos that isolate people in different roles.

Start by getting everybody involved in the delivery process together from the start of a new project, and ensure that they have an opportunity to communicate on a frequent regular basis. Once the barriers are down, this communication should occur continuously, but you may need to move towards that goal incrementally. Initiate a system where everyone can see, at a glance, the status of the application, its health, its various builds, which tests they have passed, and the state of the environments they can be deployed to. This system should also make it possible for people to perform the actions that they need to do their job, such as deployment to environments under their control.

This is one of the central principles of the DevOps movement. The DevOps movement is focused on the same goal we set out in this book: encouraging greater collaboration between everyone involved in software delivery in order to release valuable software faster and more reliably [aNgvoV].

Continuous Improvement

It is worth emphasizing that the first release of an application is just the first stage in its life. All applications evolve, and more releases will follow. It is important that your delivery process also evolves with it.

The whole team should regularly gather together and hold a retrospective on the delivery process. This means that the team should reflect on what has gone well and what has gone badly, and discuss ideas on how to improve things. Somebody should be nominated to own each idea and ensure that it is acted upon. Then, the next time that the team gathers, they should report back on what happened. This is known as the *Deming cycle*: plan, do, study, act.

It is essential that everybody in the organization is involved in this process. Allowing feedback to happen only within silos and not across them is a recipe for disaster: It leads to local optimization at the expense of general optimization—and, ultimately, finger-pointing.

Summary

Traditionally, the point of software release has been a time fraught with stress. At the same time, when compared to the disciplines associated with creation and management of code, it is treated as an unverified, manual process that relies on ad-hoc configuration management techniques for crucial aspects of the configuration of the system. In our view, the stress associated with software releases and their manual, error-prone nature are related factors.

By adopting the techniques of automated build, test, and deployment, we gain many benefits. We gain the ability to verify changes, to make the process reproducible across a range of environments, and to largely eliminate the opportunity for errors to creep into production. We gain the ability to deploy changes, and so bring business benefits more quickly, because the release process itself is no longer a hurdle. Implementing an automated system encourages us to implement other good practices, such as behavior-driven development and comprehensive configuration management.

We also gain the ability to spend more weekends with our families and friends and to live our lives with less stress, while at the same time being more productive. What is not to like about that? Life is too short to spend our weekends in server rooms deploying applications.

The automation of the development, test, and release processes has a profound impact on the speed, quality, and cost of releasing software. One of the authors works on a complex distributed system. Release into production for this system, including data migration in large-scale databases, takes between 5 and 20 minutes depending on the scale of the data migration associated with a particular release. Moving the data takes a long time. A closely related, and comparable, system of which we are aware takes 30 days for the same part of the process.

The rest of this book will be more concrete in the advice that we offer and the recommendations that we make, but we wanted this chapter to give you an ideal, but nevertheless realistic, view of the scope of this book—from twenty thousand feet. The projects that we have referred to here are all real projects, and while we may have disguised them a little to protect the guilty, we have tried very hard not to exaggerate any technical detail or the value of any technique.

Chapter 2

Configuration Management

Introduction

Configuration management is a term that is widely used, often as a synonym for version control. It is worth setting the context for this chapter with our own informal definition:

> Configuration management refers to the process by which all artifacts relevant to your project, and the relationships between them, are stored, retrieved, uniquely identified, and modified.

Your configuration management strategy will determine how you manage all of the changes that happen within your project. It thus records the evolution of your systems and applications. It will also govern how your team collaborates—a vital but sometimes overlooked consequence of any configuration management strategy.

Although version control systems are the most obvious tool in configuration management, the decision to use one (and every team should use one, no matter how small) is just the first step in developing a configuration management strategy.

Ultimately, if you have a good configuration management strategy, you should be able to answer "yes" to all of the following questions:

- Can I exactly reproduce any of my environments, including the version of the operating system, its patch level, the network configuration, the software stack, the applications deployed into it, and their configuration?

- Can I easily make an incremental change to any of these individual items and deploy the change to any, and all, of my environments?

- Can I easily see each change that occurred to a particular environment and trace it back to see exactly what the change was, who made it, and when they made it?

- Can I satisfy all of the compliance regulations that I am subject to?

- Is it easy for every member of the team to get the information they need, and to make the changes they need to make? Or does the strategy get in the way of efficient delivery, leading to increased cycle time and reduced feedback?

The last point is important, as we all too often encounter configuration management strategies which address the first four points but put all kinds of barriers in the way of collaboration between teams. This is unnecessary—with sufficient care, this last constraint does not need to be antithetical to the others. We don't tell you how to answer all of these questions in this chapter, although we do address them all through the course of this book. In this chapter, we divide the problem into three:

1. Getting the prerequisites in place to manage your application's build, deploy, test, and release process. We tackle this in two parts: getting everything into version control and managing dependencies.

2. Managing an application's configuration.

3. Configuration management of whole environments—the software, hardware, and infrastructure that an application depends upon; the principles behind environment management, from operating systems to application servers, databases, and other commercial off-the-shelf (COTS) software.

Using Version Control

Version control systems, also known as source control, source code management systems, or revision control systems, are a mechanism for keeping multiple versions of your files, so that when you modify a file you can still access the previous revisions. They are also a mechanism through which people involved in software delivery collaborate.

The first popular version control system was a proprietary UNIX tool called SCCS (Source Code Control System) which dates back to the 1970s. This was superseded by RCS, the Revision Control System, and later CVS, Concurrent Versions System. All three of these systems are still in use today, although with an increasingly small market share. Nowadays there is a wealth of better version control systems, both open source and proprietary, designed for a variety of different environments. In particular, we believe that there are few circumstances in which the open source tools—Subversion, Mercurial, or Git—would not satisfy most teams' requirements. We will spend much more time exploring version control systems and patterns for using them, including branching and merging, in Chapter 14, "Advanced Version Control."

In essence, the aim of a version control system is twofold: First, it retains, and provides access to, every version of every file that has ever been stored in it. Such systems also provide a way for metadata—that is, information that describes the data stored—to be attached to single files or collections of files. Second, it allows teams that may be distributed across space and time to collaborate.

Why would you want to do this? There are a few reasons, but ultimately it's about being able to answer these questions:

- What constitutes a particular version of your software? How can you reproduce a particular state of the software's binaries and configuration that existed in the production environment?

- What was done when, by whom, and for what reason? Not only is this useful to know when things go wrong, but it also tells the story of your application.

These are the fundamentals of version control. Most projects use version control. If yours doesn't yet, read the next few sections, then put this book aside and add it immediately. The following few sections are our advice on how to make the most effective use of version control.

Keep Absolutely Everything in Version Control

One reason that we use the term version control in preference to source control is that version control isn't just for source code. Every single artifact related to the creation of your software should be under version control. Developers should use it for source code, of course, but also for tests, database scripts, build and deployment scripts, documentation, libraries and configuration files for your application, your compiler and collection of tools, and so on—so that a new member of your team can start working from scratch.

It is also important to store all the information required to re-create the testing and production environments that your application runs on. This should include configuration information for your application's software stack and the operating systems that comprise the environment, DNS zone files, firewall configuration, and so forth. At the bare minimum, you need *everything* required to re-create your application's binaries and the environments in which they run.

The objective is to have everything that can possibly change at any point in the life of the project stored in a controlled manner. This allows you to recover an exact snapshot of the state of the entire system, from development environment to production environment, at any point in the project's history. It is even helpful to keep the configuration files for the development team's development environments in version control since it makes it easy for everyone on the team to use the same settings. Analysts should store requirements documents. Testers should keep their test scripts and procedures in version control. Project managers should save their release plans, progress charts, and risk logs here. In short, every member of the team should store any document or file related to the project in version control.

Check Everything In

Many years ago one of the authors worked on a project that was being developed by three different teams operating from three different locations. The subsystems that each team was working on communicated with one another using a proprietary message protocol via IBM MQSeries. This was before we started using continuous integration as a guard against issues with configuration management.

We had been rigorous in our use of version control for our source code. We had learned that lesson even earlier in our careers. However, our version control had stopped at the source code.

When the time came, close to the first release of the project, to integrate the three separate subsystems, we discovered that one of the teams was using a different version of the functional specification describing the message protocol. In fact, the document that they had implemented was six months out-of-date. Naturally, there was a lot of late-night work as we tried to fix the problems this caused and keep the project on schedule.

Had we simply checked the document into our version control system, we would not have had the problem, or the late nights! Had we used continuous integration, the project would have finished significantly earlier.

We really can't emphasize enough how important good configuration management is. It enables everything else in this book. If you don't have absolutely every source artifact of your project in version control, you won't enjoy any of the benefits that we discuss in this book. All of the practices that we discuss to reduce your software's cycle time and increase its quality, from continuous integration and automated testing to push-button deployments, depend on having everything related to your project in a version control repository.

In addition to storing source code and configuration information, many projects also store binary images of their application servers, compilers, virtual machines, and other parts of their toolchain in version control. This is fantastically useful, speeding up the creation of new environments and, even more importantly, ensuring that base configurations are completely defined, and so known to be good. Simply checking everything you need out of the version control repository assures a stable platform for development, test, or even production environments. You can then store whole environments, including base operating systems with configuration baselines applied, as virtual images for an even higher level of assurance and deployment simplicity.

This strategy offers the ultimate in control and assured behavior. There is no way for a system under such rigorous configuration management to have errors added at a later stage in the process. This level of configuration management ensures that, provided you keep the repository intact, you will always be able to retrieve a working version of the software. This safeguards you even when the compilers, programming languages, or other tools associated with the project have fallen into the bit-bucket of obscurity.

One thing that we don't recommend that you keep in version control is the binary output of your application's compilation. This is for a few reasons. First, they are big, and unlike compilers, they proliferate rapidly (we create new binaries for every check-in that compiles and passes the automated commit tests). Second, if you have an automated build system, you should be able to re-create them easily from source by rerunning the build script. Please note: We don't recommend recompilation as a normal part of your build process. However, the combination of your build system and source code is all that should be required to re-create an instance of your application in an emergency. Finally, storing the binary output of the build breaks the idea of being able to identify a single version of your repository for each application version because there may be two commits for the same version, one for source code and another for the binaries. This may seem obscure, but it becomes extremely important when creating deployment pipelines—one of the central topics of this book.

Version Control: The Freedom to Delete

A corollary of having every version of every file in version control is that it allows you to be aggressive about deleting things that you don't think you need. With version control, you can answer the question "Should we delete this file?" with a "Yes!" without risk; if you make the wrong decision, it is simple to fix by retrieving the file from an earlier configuration set.

This freedom to delete is in itself a significant step forward in the maintainability of a large configuration set. Consistency and organization are key to keeping a large team working efficiently. The ability to weed out old ideas and implementations frees the team to try new things and to improve the code.

Check In Regularly to Trunk

There is a tension at the heart of working with version control. On one hand, to gain access to many of its benefits, such as the ability to step back to a recent, known-good version of your artifacts, it is important to check in frequently.

On the other hand, once you check your changes into version control, they become public, instantly available to everybody else on the team. Further, if you are using continuous integration, as we recommend, your changes are not only visible to the other developers on the team; you have just given birth to a build that could potentially end up in acceptance testing or even production.

Since checking in is a form of publication, it is important to be sure that your work, whatever it may be, is ready for the level of publicity that a check-in implies. This applies to developers in particular who, given the nature of their work, need to be cautious about the effects of their check-ins. If a developer is in the middle of working on a complex part of the system, they won't want to commit their code until it is finished; they want to feel confident that their code is in a good state and won't adversely affect other functions of the system.

In some teams, this can lead to days or even weeks between check-ins, which is problematic. The benefits of version control are enhanced when you commit regularly. In particular, it is impossible to safely refactor an application unless everybody commits frequently to mainline—the merges become too complex. If you commit frequently, your changes are available for other people to see and interact with, you get a clear indication that your changes haven't broken the application, and merges are always small and manageable.

A solution that some people use to resolve this dilemma is to create a separate branch within the version control system for new functionality. At some point, when the changes are deemed satisfactory, they will be merged into the main development branch. This is a bit like a two-stage check-in; in fact, some version control systems work naturally in this way.

However, we are opposed to this practice (with three exceptions, discussed in Chapter 14). This is a controversial viewpoint, especially to users of tools like ClearCase. There are a few problems with this approach.

- It is antithetical to continuous integration, since the creation of a branch defers the integration of new functionality, and integration problems are only found when the branch is merged.

- If several developers create branches, the problem increases exponentially, and the merge process can become absurdly complex.

- Although there are some great tools for automated merging, these don't solve semantic conflicts, such as somebody renaming a method in one branch while somebody else adds a new call to that method in another branch.

- It becomes very hard to refactor the codebase, since branches tend to touch many files which makes merging even more difficult.

We will discuss the complexities of branching and merging in more detail in Chapter 14, "Advanced Version Control."

A much better answer is to develop new features incrementally and to commit them to the trunk in version control on a regular and frequent basis. This keeps the software working and integrated at all times. It means that your software is always tested because your automated tests are run on trunk by the continuous integration (CI) server every time you check in. It reduces the possibility of large merge conflicts caused by refactoring, ensures that integration problems are caught immediately when they are cheap to fix, and results in higher-quality software. We discuss techniques to avoid branching in more detail in Chapter 13, "Managing Components and Dependencies."

To ensure you aren't going to break the application when you check in, two practices are useful. One is to run your commit test suite before the check-in.

This is a quick-running (less than ten minutes) but relatively comprehensive set of tests which validate that you haven't introduced any obvious regressions. Many continuous integration servers have a feature called pretested commit which allows you to run these tests on a production-like environment before you check in.

The second is to introduce changes incrementally. We recommend that you aim to commit changes to the version control system at the conclusion of each separate incremental change or refactoring. If you use this technique correctly, you should be checking in at the very minimum once a day, and more usually several times a day. This may sound unrealistic if you are not used to doing it, but we assure you, it leads to a far more efficient software delivery process.

Use Meaningful Commit Messages

Every version control system has the facility to add a description to your commit. It is easy to omit these messages, and many people get into the bad habit of doing so. The most important reason to write descriptive commit messages is so that, when the build breaks, you know who broke the build and why. But this is not the only reason. Your authors have been caught out by not using sufficiently descriptive commit messages on several occasions, most often when trying to debug a complex problem under a tight deadline. The usual scenario runs like this:

1. You find a bug that is down to a rather obscure line of code.

2. You use your version control system to find out who put in that line of code and when.

3. That person is off on holiday or has gone home for the night, and left a commit message that said "fixed obscure bug."

4. You change the obscure line of code to fix the bug.

5. Something else breaks.

6. You spend hours trying to get the application working again.

In these situations, a commit message explaining what the person was doing when they committed that change can save you hours of debugging. The more this happens, the more you will wish you had used good commit messages. There is no prize for writing the shortest commit message. A couple of medium-to-long sentences with an overview of what you were doing will often save you many times the effort later on.

One style we like is a multiparagraph commit message in which the first paragraph is a summary and the following paragraphs add more detail. The first paragraph is what gets shown on line-per-commit displays—think of it as a newspaper headline, giving the reader enough information to figure out if she is interested in reading on.

You should also include a link to the identifier in your project management tool for the feature or bug you're working on. On many teams we've worked on, the system administrators locked down their version control systems so that commits that do not include this information fail.

Managing Dependencies

The most common external dependencies within your application are the third-party libraries it uses and the relationships between components or modules under development by other teams within your organization. Libraries are typically deployed in the form of binary files, are never changed by your application's development team, and are updated very infrequently. Components and modules are typically under active development by other teams and change quite frequently.

We spend a great deal of time discussing dependencies in Chapter 13, "Managing Components and Dependencies." Here, however, we will touch on some of the key issues of dependency management as it impacts configuration management.

Managing External Libraries

External libraries usually come in binary form, unless you're using an interpreted language. Even with interpreted languages, external libraries are normally installed globally on your system by a package management system such as Ruby Gems or Perl modules.

There is some debate as to whether or not to version-control libraries. For example, Maven, a build tool for Java, allows you to specify the JARs your application depends on and downloads them from repositories on the Internet (or a local cache, if you have one).

This is not always desirable; a new team member may be forced to "download the Internet" (or at least decently sized chunks of it) in order to get started on a project. However, it makes the version control check-out much smaller.

We recommend that you keep copies of your external libraries somewhere locally (in the case of Maven, you should create a repository for your organization containing approved versions of libraries to use). This is essential if you have to follow compliance regulations, and it also makes getting started on a project faster. It also means you always have the ability to reproduce your build. Furthermore, we emphasize that your build system should always specify the exact version of the external libraries that you use. If you don't do this, you can't reproduce your build. Failure to be absolutely specific also leads to an occasional long debugging session tracking down strange errors due to people or build systems using different versions of libraries.

Whether you keep external libraries in version control or not involves some trade-offs. It makes it much easier to correlate versions of your software with the versions of the libraries that were used to build them. However, it makes version control repositories bigger and check-outs longer.

Managing Components

It's good practice to split all but the smallest applications into components. Doing so limits the scope of changes to your application, reducing regression bugs. It also encourages reuse and enables a much more efficient development process on large projects.

Typically, you would start off with a monolithic build creating binaries or an installer for your entire application in one step, usually running unit tests at the same time. Depending on the technology stack you use, a monolithic build is usually the most efficient way to build small and medium-size applications.

However, if your system grows or you have components that several projects depend on, you may consider splitting out your components' builds into separate pipelines. If you do so, it's important to have binary dependencies between your pipelines rather than source dependencies. Recompiling dependencies is not only less efficient; it also means you're creating an artifact that is potentially different from the one that you already tested. Using binary dependencies can make it hard to track back a breakage to the source code change that caused it, but a good CI server will help you with this problem.

While modern CI servers do a pretty good job of managing dependencies, they often do so at the cost of making it harder to reproduce the entire end-to-end build process for your application on a developer workstation. Ideally, if I have a few components checked out on my machine it should be relatively straight-forward to make changes in some of them and run a single command that rebuilds the necessary bits in the right order, creates the appropriate binaries, and runs relevant tests. This is, unfortunately, beyond the capability of most build systems, at least without much clever hackery by build engineers, although tools such as Ivy and Maven and scripting technologies such as Gradle and Buildr do make life easier than it used to be.

There is much more on managing components and dependencies in Chapter 13.

Managing Software Configuration

Configuration is one of the three key parts that comprise an application, along with its binaries and its data. Configuration information can be used to change the behavior of software at build time, deploy time, and run time. Delivery teams need to consider carefully what configuration options should be available, how to manage them throughout the application's life, and how to ensure that configuration is managed consistently across components, applications, and technologies. We believe that you should treat the configuration of your system in the same way you treat your code: Make it subject to proper management and testing.

Configuration and Flexibility

If asked, everyone wants flexible software. Why would you not? But flexibility usually comes at a cost.

Clearly there is a continuum: At one end, there is single-purpose software that does one job well but has little or no ability to have its behavior modified. At the other end of the spectrum is a programming language that you can use to write a game, an application server, or a stock control system—that is flexibility! Most applications, though, are at neither extreme. Instead, they are designed for a specific purpose, but within the bounds of that purpose they will usually have some ways in which their behavior can be modified.

The desire to achieve flexibility may lead to the common antipattern of "ultimate configurability" which is, all too frequently, stated as a requirement for software projects. It is at best unhelpful, and at worst, this one requirement can kill a project.

Any time, you change the behavior of an application you are programming. The language in which you are programming the changes may be more or less constrained, but it is programming nevertheless. The more configurability you intend to offer users, by definition, the fewer constraints you can afford to place on the configuration of the system, and so the more sophisticated the programming environment needs to become.

In our experience, it is an enduring myth that configuration information is somehow less risky to change than source code. Our bet is that, given access to both, we can stop your system at least as easily by changing the configuration as by changing the source code. If we change the source code, there are a variety of ways in which we are protected from ourselves; the compiler will rule out nonsense, and automated tests should catch most other errors. On the other hand, most configuration information is free-form and untested. In most systems there is nothing to prevent us from changing a URI from "http://www.asciimation.co.nz/" to "this is not a valid URI." Most systems won't catch a change like this until run time—at which point, instead of enjoying the ASCII version of Star Wars, your users are presented with a nasty exception report because the URI class can't parse "this is not a valid URI."

There are many significant pitfalls on the road to highly configurable software, but perhaps the worst are the following.

- It frequently leads to analysis paralysis, in which the problem seems so big and so intractable that the team spends all of their time thinking about how to solve it and none of their time actually solving anything.

- The system becomes so complex to configure that many of the benefits of its flexibility are lost, to the extent where the effort involved in its configuration is comparable to the cost of custom development.

The Danger of Ultimate Configurability

We were once approached by a client who had spent three years working with a vendor of a packaged application in their particular vertical market. This application was designed to be very flexible and configured to meet the needs of its customers, albeit by specialists in its configuration.

Our client was concerned that the system was still not close to being ready for use in production. Our organization implemented a custom-built equivalent in Java from scratch in eight months.

Configurable software is not always the cheaper solution it appears to be. It's almost always better to focus on delivering the high-value functionality with little configuration and then add configuration options later when necessary.

Don't misunderstand us: Configuration is not inherently evil. But it needs to be managed carefully and consistently. Modern computer languages have evolved all sorts of characteristics and techniques to help them reduce errors. In most cases, these protections do not exist for configuration information, and more often than not there are not even any tests in place to verify that your software has been configured correctly in testing and production environments. Deployment smoke tests, as described in the "Smoke-Test Your Deployments" section on page 117, are one way to mitigate this problem and should always be used.

Types of Configuration

Configuration information can be injected into your application at several points in your build, deploy, test, and release process, and it's usual for it to be included at more than one point.

- Your build scripts can pull configuration in and incorporate it into your binaries at **build time**.

- Your packaging software can inject configuration at **packaging time**, such as when creating assemblies, ears, or gems.

- Your deployment scripts or installers can fetch the necessary information or ask the user for it and pass it to your application at **deployment time** as part of the installation process.

- Your application itself can fetch configuration at **startup time or run time**.

Generally, we consider it bad practice to inject configuration information at build or packaging time. This follows from the principle that you should be able to deploy the same binaries to every environment so you can ensure that the thing that you release is the same thing that you tested. The corollary of this is that anything that changes between deployments needs to be captured as configuration, and not baked in when the application is compiled or packaged.

> **Packaging Configuration Information**
>
> One serious problem with the J2EE specification is that the configuration has to be packaged in the war or ear along with the rest of the application. Unless you use another configuration mechanism instead of that provided by the specification, this means that you have to create a different war or ear file for every environment that you deploy to if there are any configuration differences. If you are stuck with this, you need to find another way to configure your application at deployment time or run time. We provide some suggestions below.

It is usually important to be able to configure your application at deployment time so that you can tell it where the services it depends upon (such as database, messaging servers, or external systems) belong. For example, if the runtime configuration of your application is stored in a database, you may want to pass the database's connection parameters to the application at deployment time so it can retrieve it when it starts up.

If you control your production environment, you can usually arrange for your deployment scripts to fetch this configuration and supply it to your application. In the case of packaged software, the default configuration is normally part of the package, but there needs to be some way to override it at deployment time for testing purposes.

Finally, you may need to configure your application at startup time or at run time. Startup-time configuration can be supplied either in the form of environment variables or as arguments to the command used to start the system. Alternatively, you can use the same mechanisms that you use for runtime configuration: registry settings, a database, configuration files, or an external configuration service (accessed via SOAP or a REST-style interface, for example).

Whatever mechanism you choose, we strongly recommend that, as far as practically possible, you should try and supply all configuration information for all the applications and environments in your organization through the same mechanism. This isn't always possible, but when it is, it means that there is a single source of configuration to change, manage, version-control, and override (if necessary). In organizations where this practice isn't followed, we have seen people regularly spend hours tracking down the source of some particular setting in one of their environments.

Managing Application Configuration

There are three questions to consider when managing your application's configuration:

1. How do you represent your configuration information?

2. How do your deployment scripts access it?

3. How does it vary between environments, applications, and versions of applications?

Configuration information is often modeled as a set of name-value strings.[1] Sometimes it is useful to use types in your configuration system and to organize it hierarchically. Windows properties files that contain name-value strings organized by headings, YAML files popular in the Ruby world, and Java properties files are relatively simple formats that provide enough flexibility in most cases. Probably the useful limit of complexity is to store configuration as an XML file.

There are a few obvious choices for where to store your application configuration: a database, a version control system, or a directory or registry. Version control is probably the easiest—you can just check in your configuration file, and you get the history of your configuration over time for free. It is worth keeping a list of the available configuration options for your application in the same repository as its source code.

Note that the place where you store configuration is not the same as the mechanism by which your application accesses it. Your application can access its configuration via a file on its local filesystem, or through more exotic mechanisms such as a web or directory service, or via a database; more on this in the next section.

It is often important to keep the actual configuration information specific to each of your application's testing and production environments in a repository separate from your source code. This information generally changes at a different rate to other version-controlled artifacts. However, if you take this route, you will have to be careful to track which versions of configuration information match with which versions of the application. This separation is particularly relevant for security-related configuration elements, such as passwords and digital certificates, to which access should be restricted.

---

1. Technically, configuration information can be thought of as a set of tuples.

Don't Check Passwords into Source Control or Hard-Code Them in Your Application

Operations staff will remove your eyes with a spoon if they catch you doing this. Don't give them the pleasure. If you must store your password somewhere other than the inside of your head, you could try putting them in your home directory in an encrypted form.

One egregious variation of this technique is to have the password for one layer of your application stored somewhere in the code or filesystem in the layer that accesses it. Passwords should always be entered by the user performing the deployment. There are several acceptable ways to handle authentication for a multilayer system. You could use certificates, a directory service, or a single sign-on system.

Databases, directories, and registries are convenient places to store configuration since they can be accessed remotely. However, make sure to keep the history of changes to configuration for the purposes of audit and rollback. Either have a system that automatically takes care of this, or treat version control as your system of reference for configuration and have a script that loads the appropriate version into your database or directory on demand.

Accessing Configuration

The most efficient way to manage configuration is to have a central service through which every application can get the configuration it needs. This is as true for packaged software as it is for internal corporate applications and software as a service hosted on the Internet. The main difference between these scenarios is in when you inject the configuration information—at packaging time for packaged software, or at deploy time or run time otherwise.

Probably the easiest way for an application to access its configuration is via the filesystem. This has the advantage of being cross-platform and supported in every language—although it may not be suitable for sand-boxed runtimes such as applets. There is also the problem of keeping configuration on filesystems in sync if, for example, you need to run your application on a cluster.

Another alternative is to fetch configuration from a centralized repository such as a RDBMS, LDAP, or a web service. An open source tool called ESCAPE [apvrEr] makes it easy to manage and access configuration information via a RESTful interface. Applications can perform an HTTP GET which includes the application and environment name in the URI to fetch their configuration. This mechanism makes most sense when configuring your application at deployment time or run time. You pass the environment name to your deployment scripts (via a property, command-line switch, or environment variable), and then your scripts fetch the appropriate configuration from the configuration service and make it available to the application, perhaps as a file on the filesystem.

Whatever the nature of the configuration information store, we recommend that you insulate the detail of the technology from your application with a simple façade class providing a

```
getThisProperty()
getThatProperty()
```

style of interface, so you can fake it in tests and change the storage mechanism when you need to.

Modeling Configuration

Each configuration setting can be modeled as a tuple, so the configuration for an application consists of a set of tuples. However, the set of the tuples available and their values typically depend on three things:

- The application

- The version of the application

- The environment it runs in (for example, development, UAT, performance, staging, or production)

So, for example, version 1.0 of your reporting application will have a set of tuples different from version 2.2, or from version 1.0 of your portfolio management application. The values of those tuples will, in turn, vary depending on the environment they are deployed into. For example, the database server used by the application in UAT will typically be different from that used in production and may even vary between developer machines. The same applies to packaged software or external integration points—an update service used by your application will be different when running integration tests from when it is accessed from a customer's desktop.

Whatever you use to represent and serve configuration information—XML files in source control or a RESTful web service—should be able to handle these various dimensions. Here are some use cases to consider when modeling configuration information.

- Adding a new environment (a new developer workstation perhaps, or a capacity testing environment). In this case you'd need to be able to specify a new set of values for applications deployed into this new environment.

- Creating a new version of the application. Often, this will introduce new configuration settings and get rid of some old ones. You should ensure that when you deploy this new version to production, it can get its new settings, but if you have to roll back to an older version it will use the old ones.

- Promoting a new version of your application from one environment to another. You should ensure that any new settings are available in the new environment, but that the appropriate values are set for this new environment.

- Relocating a database server. You should be able to update, very simply, every configuration setting that references this database to make it point to the new one.

- Managing environments using virtualization. You should be able to use your virtualization management tool to create a new instance of a particular environment that has all the VMs configured correctly. You may want to include this information as part of the configuration settings for the particular version of the application deployed into that environment.

One approach to managing configuration across environments is to make the expected production configuration the default and to override this default in other environments as appropriate (ensure you have firewalls in place so that production systems don't get hit by mistake). This means that any environment-specific tailoring is reduced to only those configuration properties that must be changed for the software to work in that particular environment. This simplifies the picture of what needs to be configured where. However, it also depends on whether or not your application's production configuration is privileged—some organizations expect the production configuration to be kept in a separate repository from that of other environments.

Testing System Configuration

In the same way that your application and build scripts need testing, so do your configuration settings. There are two parts to testing configuration.

The first stage is to ensure that references to external services in your configuration settings are good. You should, as part of your deployment script, ensure that the messaging bus you are configured to use is actually up and running at the address configured, and that the mock order fulfillment service your application expects to use in the functional testing environment is working. At the very least, you could ping all external services. Your deployment or installation script should fail if anything your application depends on is not available—this acts as a great smoke test for your configuration settings.

The second stage is to actually run some smoke tests once your application is installed to make sure it is operating as expected. This should involve just a few tests exercising functionality that depends on the configuration settings being correct. Ideally, these tests should stop the application and fail the installation or deployment process if the results are not as expected.

Managing Configuration across Applications

The problem of managing configuration is particularly complex in medium and large organizations where many applications have to be managed together. Usually in such organizations, legacy applications exist with esoteric configuration options that are poorly understood. One of the most important tasks is to keep a catalogue of all the configuration options that each of your applications has, where they are stored, what their lifecycle is, and how they can be changed.

If possible, such information should be generated automatically from each application's code as part of the build process. But where this is not possible, it should be collected in a wiki or other document management system.

When managing applications that are not entirely user-installed, it is important to know what the current configuration of each running application is. The goal is to be able to see each application's configuration through your operation team's production monitoring system, which should also display which version of each application is deployed in each environment. Tools such as Nagios, OpenNMS, and HP OpenView all provide services to record such information. Alternatively, if you manage your building and deployment process in an automated fashion, your configuration information should always be applied through this process, and hence be stored in version control or a tool like Escape.

It is especially important to have access to this information on a real-time basis when your applications depend on each other and deployments must be orchestrated. Countless hours have been lost by one application having a few configuration options set wrongly and thereby bringing down an entire set of services. Such problems are extremely hard to diagnose.

Configuration management of every application should be planned as part of project inception. Consider how other applications in your ecosystem manage their configuration and use the same method, if possible. Too often, decisions on how to manage configuration are done on an ad-hoc basis, and as a result every application packages its configuration in a different place and uses a different mechanism for accessing it. This makes it unnecessarily hard to determine the configuration of your environments.

Principles of Managing Application Configuration

Treat your application's configuration the same way you treat your code. Manage it properly, and test it. Here is a list of principles to consider when creating an application configuration system:

- Consider where in your application's lifecycle it makes sense to inject a particular piece of configuration—at the point of assembly where you are packaging your release candidate, at deployment or installation time, at startup time, or at run time. Speak to the operations and support team to work out what their needs are.

- Keep the available configuration options for your application in the same repository as its source code, but keep the values somewhere else. Configuration settings have a lifecycle completely different from that of code, while passwords and other sensitive information should not be checked in to version control at all.

- Configuration should always be performed by automated processes using values taken from your configuration repository, so that you can always identify the configuration of every application in every environment.

- Your configuration system should be able to provide different values to your application (including its packaging, installation, and deployment scripts) based on the application, its version, and the environment it is being deployed into. It should be easy for anyone to see what configuration options are available for a particular version of an application across all environments it will be deployed into.

- Use clear naming conventions for your configuration options. Avoid obscure or cryptic names. Try to imagine someone reading the configuration file without a manual—it should be possible to understand what the configuration properties are.

- Ensure that your configuration information is modular and encapsulated so that changes in one place don't have knock-on effects for other, apparently unrelated, pieces of configuration.

- Use the DRY (don't repeat yourself) principle. Define the elements of your configuration so that each concept has only one representation in the set of configuration information.

- Be minimalist: Keep the configuration information as simple and as focused as possible. Avoid creating configuration options except where there is a requirement or where it makes sense to do so.

- Avoid overengineering the configuration system. Keep it as simple as you can.

- Ensure that you have tests for your configuration that are run at deployment or installation time. Check that the services your application depends upon are available, and use smoke tests to assert that any functionality depending on your configuration settings works as it should.

Managing Your Environments

No application is an island. Every application depends on hardware, software, infrastructure, and external systems in order to work. We refer to this, throughout this book, as your application's environment. We deal, at some length, with the topic of environment management in Chapter 11, "Managing Infrastructure and Environments," but the topic deserves some discussion in the context of configuration management, so we will introduce it here.

The principle to bear in mind when managing the environment that your application runs in is that the configuration of that environment is as important as the configuration of the application. If, for example, your application depends on a messaging bus, the bus needs to be configured correctly or the application will not work. Your operating system's configuration is also important. For example, you may have an application that relies on a large number of file descriptors being available. If the operating system defaults to a lower limit for the number of file descriptors, your application won't work.

The worst approach to managing configuration information is to deal with it on an ad-hoc basis. This means installing the requisite pieces of software by hand and editing the relevant configuration files. This is the most common strategy that we encounter. Although seemingly simple, this strategy has several common problems that arise in all but the most trivial of systems. The most obvious pitfall is that if, for any reason, the new configuration doesn't work, it's difficult to return to a known good state with any certainty since there is no record of the previous configuration. The problem can be summed up as follows:

- The collection of configuration information is very large.

- One small change can break the whole application or severely degrade its performance.

- Once it is broken, finding the problem and fixing it takes an indeterminate amount of time and requires senior personnel.

- It is extremely difficult to precisely reproduce manually configured environments for testing purposes.

- It is difficult to maintain such environments without the configuration, and hence behavior, of different nodes drifting apart.

In *The Visible Ops Handbook* the authors refer to manually configured environments as "works of art." In order to reduce the cost and risk of managing environments, it is essential to turn our environments into mass-produced objects whose creation is repeatable and takes a predictable amount of time. We have been involved in too many projects where poor configuration management has meant significant expense—paying for teams of people to work on this aspect of the system alone. It also acts as a continual drag on the productivity of the development process, making deployments to test environments, development environments, and into production much more complex and costly than they need to be.

The key to managing environments is to make their creation a fully automated process. It should always be cheaper to create a new environment than to repair an old one. Being able to reproduce your environments is essential for several reasons.

- It removes the problem of having random pieces of infrastructure around whose configuration is only understood by somebody who has left the organization and cannot be reached. When such things stop working, you can usually assume a significant downtime. This is a large and unnecessary risk.

- Fixing one of your environments can take many hours. It is always better to be able to rebuild it in a predictable amount of time so as to get back to a known good state.

- It is essential to be able to create copies of production environments for testing purposes. In terms of software configuration, testing environments should be exact replicas of the production ones, so configuration problems can be found early.

The kinds of environment configuration information you should be concerned about are:

- The various operating systems in your environment, including their versions, patch levels, and configuration settings

- The additional software packages that need to be installed on each environment to support your application, including their versions and configuration

- The networking topology required for your application to work

- Any external services that your application depends upon, including their versions and configuration

- Any data or other state that is present in them (for example, production databases)

There are two principles that, as we have found, form the basis of an effective configuration management strategy: Keep binary files independent from configuration information, and keep all configuration information in one place. Applying these fundamentals to every part of your system will pave the way to the point where creating new environments, upgrading parts of your system, and rolling out new configurations without making your system unavailable becomes a simple, automated process.

All of these things need to be considered. Although it's obviously unreasonable to check your operating system into version control, it's certainly not unreasonable to version-control its configuration. A combination of remote installation systems and environment management tools such as Puppet and CfEngine make centralized management and configuration of operating systems straightforward. This topic is covered in detail in Chapter 11, "Managing Infrastructure and Environments."

For most applications, it is even more important to apply this principle to the third-party software stack that they depend on. Good software has installers that can be run from the command line without any user intervention. It has configuration that can be managed in version control and does not require manual intervention. If your third-party software dependencies don't meet these criteria, you should find alternatives—these criteria for third-party software selection are of such importance that they should be at the core of every software evaluation exercise. When evaluating third-party products and services, start by asking the following questions:

- Can we deploy it?

- Can we version its configuration effectively?

- How will it fit into our automated deployment strategy?

If the answer to any of these questions is in any way negative, there are various possible responses—we discuss them at greater length in Chapter 11.

An environment that is in a properly deployed state is known as a *baseline* in configuration management terminology. Your automated environment provisioning system should be able to establish, or reestablish, any given baseline that has existed in the recent history of your project. Any time you change any aspect of the host environment of your applications, you should store the change, creating a new version of the baseline and associating that version of the application with the new version of the baseline. This ensures that the next time that you deploy the application or create a new environment, it will include the change.

Essentially, you should treat your environment the same way you treat your code—changing it incrementally and checking the changes into version control. Every change should be tested to ensure that it doesn't break any of the applications that run in the new version of the environment.

Applying Configuration Management to Infrastructure

We worked on two projects recently that highlighted the differences between an effective use of configuration management and a less than effective approach.

In the first project, we decided to replace the messaging infrastructure on which the project was based. We had very effective configuration management, and good modular design in place. Before we replaced the infrastructure, we attempted an upgrade to the latest version that the vendor assured us would address most of our concerns.

Our client, and the vendor, clearly thought that this upgrade was a big deal. They had been planning it for several months and worrying about the disruptive impact to the development team. In the event, two members of our team worked to prepare a new baseline in the manner described in this section. We tested it locally, including running our full acceptance test pack on the trial version. Our tests highlighted a number of problems.

We fixed the most glaring problems, but did not get all of our acceptance tests passing. However, we had reached a point at which we were confident that the fixes should be straightforward, and our worst case was that we would have to revert to our previous baseline image, all safely stored in version control. With the agreement of the rest of the development team, we committed our changes so that the whole team could work together on fixing the bugs that the version change of the messaging infrastructure introduced. This entire process took a single day, including running all of the automated tests to verify our work. We watched carefully for more bugs in manual testing during the subsequent iteration, but there were none. Our automated test coverage was proven to be sufficiently good.

In the second project, we were asked to do some repair work on an ailing legacy system which had been in production for several years and was slow and error-prone. It had no automated testing when we arrived and only the most basic configuration management at the source-code level. One of our tasks was to update the version of the application server, since the version on which the system was running was no longer supported by its vendor. For an application in this state, without a supporting continuous integration system and without any automated testing, the process went reasonably smoothly. However, it took a small team of six people two months to get the changes done, tested, and deployed into production.

As ever with software projects, it is impossible to make direct comparisons. The technologies in question were quite different, as were the codebases. However, both involved upgrading a piece of core middleware infrastructure. One took a team of six two months, and the other took two people half a day.

Tools to Manage Environments

Puppet and CfEngine are two examples of tools that make it possible to manage operating system configuration in an automated fashion. Using these tools, you can declaratively define things such as which users should have access to your boxes and what software should be installed. These definitions can be stored in your version control system. Agents running on your systems regularly pull the latest configuration and update the operating system and the software installed on it. With systems like these, there is no reason to log into a box to make fixes: All changes can be initiated through the version control system, so you have a complete record of every change—when it was made and by whom.

Virtualization can also improve the efficiency of the environment management process. Instead of creating a new environment from scratch using an automated process, you can simply take a copy of each box in your environment and store it as a baseline. Then it is trivial to create new environments—it can be done by clicking a button. Virtualization has other benefits, such as the ability to consolidate hardware and to standardize your hardware platform even if your applications require heterogeneous environments.

We discuss these tools in more detail in Chapter 11, "Managing Infrastructure and Environments."

Managing the Change Process

Finally, it is essential to be able to manage the process of making changes to your environments. A production environment should be completely locked down. It should not be possible for *anybody* to make a change to it without going through your organization's change management process. The reason for this is simple: Even a tiny change could break it. A change must be tested before it goes into production, and for that it should be scripted and checked into version control. Then, once the change has been approved, it can be rolled out to the production environments in an automated fashion.

In this sense, a change to your environment is just like a change to your software. It has to go through your build, deploy, test, and release process in exactly the same way as a change to the application's code.

In this respect, testing environments should be treated the same as production environments. The approval process will usually be simpler—it should be in the hands of the people managing the testing environment—but in all other respects their configuration management is the same. This is essential because it means that you are testing the process that you use to manage your production environments during the more frequent deployments into test environments. It bears repeating that your test environments should closely resemble your production environments in terms of software configuration—that way there should be no surprises when you deploy to production. This does not imply that test environments must be clones of expensive production environments; rather, that they should be managed, deployed to, and configured by the same mechanisms.

Summary

Configuration management is the foundation of everything else in this book. It is impossible to do continuous integration, release management, and deployment pipelining without it. It also makes a huge positive impact on collaboration within delivery teams. As we hope we have made clear, it is not just a question of choosing and implementing a tool, although that is important; it is also, crucially, a question of putting good practices into place.

If your configuration management process is sound, you should be able to answer "yes" to the following questions:

- Could you completely re-create your production system, excluding production data, from scratch from the version-controlled assets that you store?

- Could you regress to an earlier, known good state of your application?

- Can you be sure that each deployed environment in production, in staging, and in test is set up in precisely the same way?

If not, then your organization is at risk. In particular, we recommend having a strategy for storing baselines and controlling changes to:

- Your applications' source code, build scripts, tests, documentation, requirements, database scripts, libraries, and configuration files

- Your development, testing, and operations toolchains

- All environments used in development, testing, and production

- The entire application stack associated with your applications—both binaries and configuration

- The configuration associated with every application in every environment it runs in, across the entire application lifecycle (building, deployment, testing, operation)

Chapter 3

Continuous Integration

Introduction

An extremely strange, but common, feature of many software projects is that for long periods of time during the development process the application is not in a working state. In fact, most software developed by large teams spends a significant proportion of its development time in an unusable state. The reason for this is easy to understand: Nobody is interested in trying to run the whole application until it is finished. Developers check in changes and might even run automated unit tests, but nobody is trying to actually start the application and use it in a production-like environment.

This is doubly true in projects that use long-lived branches or defer acceptance testing until the end. Many such projects schedule lengthy integration phases at the end of development to allow the development team time to get the branches merged and the application working so it can be acceptance-tested. Even worse, some projects find that when they get to this phase, their software is not fit for purpose. These integration periods can take an extremely long time, and worst of all, nobody has any way to predict how long.

On the other hand, we have seen projects that spend at most a few minutes in a state where their application is not working with the latest changes. The difference is the use of continuous integration. Continuous integration requires that every time somebody commits any change, the entire application is built and a comprehensive set of automated tests is run against it. Crucially, if the build or test process fails, the development team stops whatever they are doing and fixes the problem immediately. The goal of continuous integration is that the software is in a working state all the time.

Continuous integration was first written about in Kent Beck's book *Extreme Programming Explained* (first published in 1999). As with other Extreme Programming practices, the idea behind continuous integration was that, if regular integration of your codebase is good, why not do it all the time? In the context of integration, "all the time" means every single time somebody commits any

55

change to the version control system. As one of our colleagues, Mike Roberts, says, "Continuously is more often than you think" [aEu8Nu].

Continuous integration represents a paradigm shift. Without continuous integration, your software is broken until somebody proves it works, usually during a testing or integration stage. With continuous integration, your software is proven to work (assuming a sufficiently comprehensive set of automated tests) with every new change—and you know the moment it breaks and can fix it immediately. The teams that use continuous integration effectively are able to deliver software much faster, and with fewer bugs, than teams that do not. Bugs are caught much earlier in the delivery process when they are cheaper to fix, providing significant cost and time savings. Hence we consider it an essential practice for professional teams, perhaps as important as using version control.

The rest of this chapter describes how to implement continuous integration. We'll explain how to solve common problems that occur as your project becomes more complex, listing effective practices that support continuous integration and its effects on the design and development process. We'll also discuss more advanced topics, including how to do CI with distributed teams.

Continuous integration is dealt with at length in a companion volume to this one: Paul Duvall's book *Continuous Integration* (Addison-Wesley, 2006). If you want more detail than we provide in this chapter, that is the place to go.

This chapter is mainly aimed at developers. However, it also contains some information that we think will be useful for project managers who want to know more about the *practice* of continuous integration.

Implementing Continuous Integration

The practice of continuous integration relies on certain prerequisites being in place. We'll cover these, then look at the tools available. Perhaps most importantly, continuous integration depends on teams following a few essential practices, so we'll spend some time discussing these.

What You Need Before You Start

There are three things that you need before you can start with continuous integration.

1. Version Control

Everything in your project must be checked in to a single version control repository: code, tests, database scripts, build and deployment scripts, and anything else needed to create, install, run, and test your application. This may sound obvious, but surprisingly, there are still projects that don't use any form of version control. Some people don't consider their project big enough to warrant the use of version control. We don't believe that there is a project small enough to do without it. When we write code on our own, for our own needs on our own computers, we still use version control. There exist several simple, powerful, lightweight, and free version control systems.

We describe the choice and use of revision control systems in more detail in the "Using Version Control" section on page 32 and in Chapter 14, "Advanced Version Control."

2. An Automated Build

You must be able to start your build from the command line. You can start off with a command-line program that tells your IDE to build your software and then runs your tests, or it can be a complex collection of multistage build scripts that call one another. Whatever the mechanism, it must be possible for either a person or a computer to run your build, test, and deployment process in an automated fashion via the command line.

IDEs and continuous integration tools have become pretty sophisticated these days, and you can usually build your software and run tests without going anywhere near the command line. However, we think that you should still have build scripts that can be run via the command line without your IDE. This might seem controversial, but there are several reasons for this:

- You need to be able to run your build process in an automated way from your continuous integration environment so that it can be audited when things go wrong.

- Your build scripts should be treated like your codebase. They should be tested and constantly refactored so that they are tidy and easy to understand. It's impossible to do this with an IDE-generated build process. This gets more and more important the more complex the project becomes.

- It makes understanding, maintaining, and debugging the build easier, and allows for better collaboration with operations people.

3. Agreement of the Team

Continuous integration is a practice, not a tool. It requires a degree of commitment and discipline from your development team. You need everyone to check in small incremental changes frequently to mainline and agree that the highest priority task on the project is to fix any change that breaks the application. If people don't adopt the discipline necessary for it to work, your attempts at continuous integration will not lead to the improvement in quality that you hope for.

A Basic Continuous Integration System

You don't need a continuous integration software in order to do continuous integration—as we say, it is a practice, not a tool. James Shore describes the simplest way to get started with continuous integration in an article called "Continuous Integration on a Dollar a Day" [bAJpjp] using only an unused development machine, a rubber chicken, and a bell. It's worth reading this article because it demonstrates wonderfully the essentials of CI without any tool except version control.

In reality, though, CI tools these days are extremely simple to install and get running. There are several open source options, such as Hudson and the venerable CruiseControl family (CruiseControl, CruiseControl.NET, and CruiseControl.rb). Hudson and CruiseControl.rb in particular are extremely straightforward to get up and running. CruiseControl.rb is very lightweight and can be easily extended by anyone with some knowledge of Ruby. Hudson has a large pool of plugins allowing it to integrate with pretty much every tool in the build and deployment ecosystem.

At the time of writing, two commercial CI servers had free editions designed for small teams: Go from ThoughtWorks Studios and TeamCity from JetBrains. Other popular commercial CI servers include Atlassian's Bamboo and Zutubi's Pulse. High-end release management and build acceleration systems which can also be used for plain and simple CI include UrbanCode's AntHillPro, ElectricCloud's ElectricCommander, and IBM's BuildForge. There are plenty more systems out there; for a complete list, go to the CI feature matrix [bHOgH4].

Once you have your CI tool of choice installed, given the preconditions described above, it should be possible to get started in just a few minutes by telling your tool where to find your source control repository, what script to run in order to compile, if necessary, and run the automated commit tests for your application, and how to tell you if the last set of changes broke the software.

The first time you run your build on a CI tool, you are likely to discover that the box you're running your CI tool on is missing a stack of software and settings. This is a unique learning opportunity—make a note of everything that you did to get things working, and put it on your project's wiki. You should take the time to check any software or settings that your system depends on into version control and automate the process of provisioning a new box.

The next step is for everybody to start using the CI server. Here is a simple process to follow.

Once you're ready to check in your latest change:

1. Check to see if the build is already running. If so, wait for it to finish. If it fails, you'll need to work with the rest of the team to make it green before you check in.

2. Once it has finished and the tests have passed, update the code in your development environment from this version in the version control repository to get any updates.

3. Run the build script and tests on your development machine to make sure that everything still works correctly on your computer, or alternatively use your CI tool's personal build feature.

4. If your local build passes, check your code into version control.

5. Wait for your CI tool to run the build with your changes.

6. If it fails, stop what you're doing and fix the problem immediately on your development machine—go to step 3.

7. If the build passes, rejoice and move on to your next task.

If everybody on the team follows these simple steps every time they commit any change, you will know that your software works on any box with the same configuration as the CI box at all times.

Prerequisites for Continuous Integration

Continuous integration won't fix your build process on its own. In fact, it can be very painful if you start doing it midproject. For CI to be effective, the following practices will need to be in place before you start.

Check In Regularly

The most important practice for *continuous integration* to work properly is frequent check-ins to trunk or mainline. You should be checking in your code at least a couple of times a day.

Checking in regularly brings lots of other benefits. It makes your changes smaller and thus less likely to break the build. It means you have a recent known-good version of the software to revert to when you make a mistake or go down the wrong path. It helps you to be more disciplined about your refactoring and stick to small changes that preserve behavior. It helps to ensure that changes altering a lot of files are less likely to conflict with other people's work. It allows developers to be more explorative, trying out ideas and discarding them by reverting back to the last committed version. It forces you to take regular breaks and stretch your muscles to help avoid carpal tunnel syndrome or RSI. It also means that if something catastrophic happens (such as deleting something by mistake) you haven't lost too much work.

We mention checking into trunk on purpose. Many projects use branches in version control to manage large teams. But it is impossible to truly do continuous integration while using branches because, by definition, if you are working on a branch, your code is not being integrated with that of other developers. Teams who use long-lived branches face exactly the same integration problems as we described at the beginning of this chapter. We can't recommend using branches except in very limited circumstances. There is a much more detailed discussion of these issues in Chapter 14, "Advanced Version Control."

Create a Comprehensive Automated Test Suite

If you don't have a comprehensive suite of automated tests, a passing build only means that the application could be compiled and assembled. While for some teams this is a big step, it's essential to have some level of automated testing to provide confidence that your application is actually working. There are many kinds of automated tests, and we discuss them in more detail in the next chapter. However, there are three kinds of tests we are interested in running from our continuous integration build: unit tests, component tests, and acceptance tests.

Unit tests are written to test the behavior of small pieces of your application in isolation (say, a method, or a function, or the interactions between a small group of them). They can usually be run without starting the whole application. They do not hit the database (if your application has one), the filesystem, or the network. They don't require your application to be running in a production-like environment. Unit tests should run very fast—your whole suite, even for a large application, should be able to run in under ten minutes.

Component tests test the behavior of several components of your application. Like unit tests, they don't always require starting the whole application. However, they may hit the database, the filesystem, or other systems (which may be stubbed out). Component tests typically take longer to run.

Acceptance tests test that the application meets the acceptance criteria decided by the business, including both the functionality provided by the application and its characteristics such as capacity, availability, security, and so on. Acceptance tests are best written in such a way that they run against the whole application in a production-like environment. Acceptance tests can take a long time to run—it's not unheard of for an acceptance test suite to take more than a day to run sequentially.

These three sets of tests, combined, should provide an extremely high level of confidence that any introduced change has not broken existing functionality.

Keep the Build and Test Process Short

If it takes too long to build the code and run the unit tests, you will run into the following problems:

- People will stop doing a full build and running the tests before they check in. You will start to get more failing builds.

- The continuous integration process will take so long that multiple commits will have taken place by the time you can run the build again, so you won't know which check-in broke the build.

- People will check in less often because they have to sit around for ages waiting for the software to build and the tests to run.

Ideally, the compile and test process that you run prior to check-in and on your CI server should take no more than a few minutes. We think that ten minutes is about the limit, five minutes is better, and about ninety seconds is ideal. Ten minutes will seem like a long time to people used to working on small projects. It will seem like a very short time to old-timers who have experienced hour-long compiles. It's around the amount of time you can devote to making a cup of tea, a quick chat, checking your email, or stretching your muscles.

This requirement may seem to contradict the previous one—having a comprehensive set of automated tests. But there are a number of techniques that you can use to reduce the build time. The first thing to consider is making your tests run faster. XUnit-type tools, such as JUnit and NUnit, provide a breakdown of how long each test took in their output. Find out which tests are performing slowly, and see if there's a way to optimize them or get the same coverage and confidence in your code with less processing. This is a practice that you should perform regularly.

However, at some point you will need to split your test process into multiple stages, as described in detail in Chapter 5, "Anatomy of the Deployment Pipeline." How do you split them up? Your first action should be creating two stages. One should compile the software, run your suite of unit tests that test individual classes making up your application, and create a deployable binary. This stage is called the commit stage. We go into a great deal of detail about this stage of your build in Chapter 7.

The second stage should take the binaries from the first stage and run the acceptance tests, as well as integration tests, and performance tests if you have them. Modern CI servers make it easy to create staged builds in this way, run multiple tasks concurrently, and aggregate the results up so you can see the state of your build at a glance.

The commit stage should be run before checking in, and should run on the CI server for every check-in. The stage that runs the acceptance tests should be run once the check-in test suite passes, but can take a longer time. If you find that the second build takes longer than half an hour or so, you should consider running this test suite in parallel on a larger multiprocessor box, or perhaps establish a build grid. Modern CI systems make this simple. It is often useful to incorporate a simple smoke test suite into your commit stage. This smoke test should perform a few simple acceptance and integration tests to make sure that the most commonly used functionality isn't broken—and report back quickly if it is.

It is often desirable to group your acceptance tests into functional areas. This allows you to run collections of tests that focus on particular aspects of the behavior of your system after making a change in that area. Many unit testing frameworks allow you to categorize your tests in this way.

You may get to a stage where your project needs to be split up into several modules, each of which is functionally independent. This requires some careful thought in terms of how you organize these subprojects both in revision control and on your CI server. We'll deal with this in more detail in Chapter 13, "Managing Components and Dependencies."

Managing Your Development Workspace

It is important for developers' productivity and sanity that their development environment is carefully managed. Developers should always work from a known-good starting point when they begin a fresh piece of work. They should be able to run the build, execute the automated tests, and deploy the application in an environment under their control. In general, this should be on their own local machine. Only in exceptional circumstances should you use shared environments for development. Running the application in a local development environment should use the same automated processes that are used in the continuous integration and testing environments and ultimately in production.

The first prerequisite to achieve this is careful configuration management, not just of source code, but also of test data, database scripts, build scripts, and deployment scripts. All of these must be stored in version control, and the most recent known-good version of these should be the starting point when coding begins. In this context, "known-good" means that the revision you are working from has passed all automated tests on your continuous integration server.

The second step is configuration management of third-party dependencies, libraries, and components. It is vital that you have the correct versions of all libraries or components, which means the same versions that are know to work with the version of the source code you are working from. There are open source tools to help manage third-party dependencies, Maven and Ivy being the most common. However, when working with these tools you need to be careful to make sure they are configured correctly so you don't always get the latest available version of some dependency in your local working copy.

For most projects, the third-party libraries they depend on don't change very frequently, so the simplest solution of all is to commit these libraries into your version control system along with your source code. There is more information on all this in Chapter 13, "Managing Components and Dependencies."

The final step is to make sure that the automated tests, including smoke tests, can be run on developer machines. On a large system this might involve configuring middleware systems and running in-memory or single-user versions of databases. This can involve a certain degree of effort, but enabling developers to run a smoke test against a working system on a developer machine prior to each check-in can make a huge difference to the quality of your application. In fact, one sign of a good application architecture is that it allows the application to be run without much trouble on a development machine.

Using Continuous Integration Software

There are many products on the market that can provide the infrastructure for your automated build and test process. The most basic functionality of continuous integration software is to poll your version control system to see if any commits have occurred and, if so, check out the latest version of the software, run your build script to compile the software, run the tests, and then notify you of the results.

Basic Operation

At heart, continuous integration server software has two components. The first is a long-running process which can execute a simple workflow at regular intervals. The second provides a view of the results of the processes that have been run, notifies you of the success or failure of your build and test runs, and provides access to test reports, installers, and so on.

The usual CI workflow polls your revision control system at regular intervals. If it detects any change, it will check out a copy of your project to a directory on the server, or to a directory on a build agent. It will then execute the commands you specify. Typically, these commands build your application and run the relevant automated tests.

Most CI servers include a web server that shows you a list of builds that have run (Figure 3.1) and allows you to look at the reports that define the success or failure of each build. This sequence of build instructions should culminate in the production and storage of the resulting artifacts such as binaries or installation packages, so that testers and clients can easily download the latest good version of the software. Most CI servers are configurable using a web interface or through simple scripts.

Bells and Whistles

You can use your CI package's workflow capabilities to do lots of other things beyond the basic functionality. For example, you can get the status of the most recent build sent to an external device. We've seen people use red and green lava lamps to show the status of the last build, or a CI system that sent the status to a Nabaztag wireless electronic rabbit. One developer we know, with some skill in electronics, created an extravagant tower of flashing lights and sirens which would explode into action to indicate the progress of various builds on a complex project. Another trick is to use text-to-speech to read out the name of the person who broke the build. Some continuous integration servers can display the status of the build, along with the avatars of the people who checked in—and this can be displayed on a big screen.

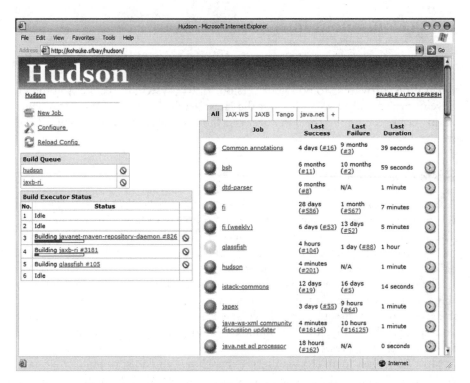

Figure 3.1   *Screenshot of Hudson, by Kohsuke Kawaguchi*

Projects use gadgets like these for the simple reason: They're a great way to allow everyone to see the status of the build at a glance. Visibility is one of the most important benefits of using a CI server. Most CI server software ships with a widget that you can install on your development machine to show you the status of the build in the corner of your desktop. Tools like this are especially useful for teams that are distributed, or at least not working in the same room together.

The only drawback of such visibility is that if your development team is working in close quarters with their customers, as should be the case in most agile projects, build failures—a natural part of the process—may become regarded as a sign of problems with the quality of the application. The fact is that the reverse is true: Every time a build fails, it indicates that a problem has been found that may otherwise have made it into production. However, this can sometimes be hard to explain. Having been through this several times, including having some difficult conversations with clients when the build was broken for a longer period than any of us liked, we can only recommend that you keep the high-visibility build monitor and work hard at explaining its very real benefits. Of course, the best answer of all is to work hard to keep the build green.

You can also get your build process to perform analysis of your source code. Teams commonly determine test coverage, code duplication, adherence to coding standards, cyclomatic complexity, and other indications of health, and have the results displayed on the summary page for each build. You can also run programs to produce graphs of the object model or database schema. This is all about visibility.

Today's advanced CI servers can distribute work across a build grid, manage the builds and dependencies of collections of collaborating components, report directly into your project management tracking system, and do lots of other useful things.

Predecessors to Continuous Integration

Back before continuous integration was introduced, many development teams used a nightly build. It was a common practice at Microsoft for many years. Anyone who broke the build was required to stay and monitor subsequent builds until the next person caused a break.

Many projects still have nightly builds. The idea is that a batch process will compile and integrate the codebase every night when everybody goes home. This is a step in the right direction, but it isn't very helpful when the team arrives the next morning only to find that the code didn't compile. The next day they make new changes—but are unable to verify if the system integrates until the next night. So the build stays red for days and days—until, you guessed it, integration time rolls around again. In addition, this strategy is less than useful when you have a geographically dispersed team working on a common codebase from different time zones.

The next evolutionary step was to add automated testing. The first time we tried this was many years ago. The testing in question was the most basic smoke test that simply asserted that the application would run following compilation. This was a big step in our build process at the time, and we were very pleased with ourselves. These days, we'd expect a little more in even the most basic of automated builds. Unit testing has come a long way, and even a simple unit test suite will provide a significantly improved level of confidence in the resulting build.

The next level of sophistication which was used in some projects (though we confess we haven't seen it recently) was a process of "rolling builds" where, instead of a scheduled batch process to build the software overnight, the build is run continuously. Each time a build finishes, the latest version is collected from version control and the process starts all over again. Dave used this to good effect in the early 1990s; it was much better than overnight builds. The problem with this approach is that there is no direct link between a particular check-in and the build. So, while there was a useful feedback loop for the developer, it provided insufficient traceability back to whatever broke the build to really scale to larger teams.

Essential Practices

So far, much of what we have described has been related to the automation of building and deployment. However, that automation exists within an environment of human processes. Continuous integration is a practice, not a tool, and it depends upon discipline to make it effective. Keeping a continuous integration system operating, particularly when you are dealing with large and complex CI systems, requires a significant degree of discipline from the development team as a whole.

The objective of our CI system is to ensure that our software is working, in essence, all of the time. In order to ensure that this is the case, here are the practices that we enforce on our teams. Later we will discuss practices that are optional but desirable, but those listed here are mandatory for continuous integration to work.

Don't Check In on a Broken Build

The cardinal sin of continuous integration is checking in on a broken build. If the build breaks, the developers responsible are waiting to fix it. They identify the cause of the breakage as soon as possible and fix it. If we adopt this strategy, we will always be in the best position to work out what caused the breakage and fix it immediately. If one of our colleagues has made a check-in and broken the build as a result, then to have the best chance of fixing it, they will need a clear run at the problem. They don't want us checking in further changes, triggering new builds, and compounding the failure with more problems.

When this rule is broken, it inevitably takes much longer for the build to be fixed. People get used to seeing the build broken, and very quickly you get into a situation where the build stays broken all of the time. This continues until somebody on the team decides that enough is enough, a Herculean effort ensues to get the build green, and the process starts all over again. Just after this work is finished it's a great time to get everybody together to remind them that following this principle will ensure a green build, and thus working software, all of the time.

Always Run All Commit Tests Locally before Committing, or Get Your CI Server to Do It for You

As we have already established, a commit triggers the creation of a release candidate. It is a kind of publication. Most people will check their work before publishing it in any form, and a check-in is no different.

We want check-ins to be lightweight enough so we can be happy to check in regularly every twenty minutes or so, but also formal enough so that we will briefly pause to think about it before committing. Running the commit tests locally is a sanity check before committing to the action. It is also a way to ensure that what we believe to work actually does.

As developers come to a pause and are ready to commit, they should refresh their local copy of the project by updating from the version control system. They should then initiate a local build and run the commit tests. Only when this is successful is the developer ready to commit the changes to the version control system.

If you haven't encountered this approach before, you may be wondering why we run the commit tests locally before checking in, if the first thing that will happen on check-in is that the code will be compiled and the commit tests rerun. There are two reasons for this approach:

1. Other people may have checked in before your last update from version control, and the combination of your new changes and theirs might cause tests to fail. If you check out and run the commit tests locally, you will identify this problem without breaking the build.

2. A common source of errors on check-in is to forget to add some new artifact to the repository. If you follow this procedure, and your local build passes, and then your CI management system fails the *commit stage*, you know that it is either because someone checked in in the meantime, or because you forgot to add the new class or configuration file that you have just been working on into the version control system.

Following this practice ensures the build stays green.

Many modern CI servers offer a feature variously known as pretested commit, personal build, or preflight build. Using this facility, instead of checking in yourself, your CI server will take your local changes and run a build with them on the CI grid. If the build passes, the CI server will check your changes in for you. If the build fails, it will let you know what went wrong. This is a great way to follow this practice without having to wait until the commit tests pass to start working on the next feature or bugfix.

At the time of writing, the CI servers Pulse, TeamCity, and ElectricCommander all offer this feature. This practice is best combined with a distributed version control system which lets you store commits locally without pushing them to the central server. In this way, it is very easy to shelve your changes by creating a patch and revert back to the version of the code you sent to the CI server if your personal build fails.

Wait for Commit Tests to Pass before Moving On

The CI system is a shared resource for the team. When a team is using CI effectively, following our advice and checking in frequently, any breakage of the build is a minor stumbling block for the team and project as a whole.

However, build breakages are a normal and expected part of the process. Our aim is to find errors and eliminate them as quickly as possible, without expecting perfection and zero errors.

At the point of check-in, the developers who made it are responsible for monitoring the build's progress. Until their check-in has compiled and passed its *commit tests*, the developers should not start any new task. They shouldn't go out for lunch or start a meeting. They should be paying sufficient attention to the build to know its outcome within a few seconds of the *commit stage* completing.

If the commit succeeds, the developers are then, and only then, free to move on to their next task. If it fails, they are at hand to start determining the nature of the problem and fixing it—with another check-in or a revert to the previous version in version control, that is, backing out their changes until they understand how to make them work.

Never Go Home on a Broken Build

It is 5:30 P.M. on Friday, all your colleagues are walking out of the door, and you have just committed your changes. The build has broken. You have three options. You can resign yourself to the fact that you will be leaving late, and try to fix it. You can revert your changes and return to your check-in attempt next week. Or you can leave now and leave the build broken.

If you leave the build broken, when you return on Monday your memory of the changes you made will no longer be fresh, and it will take you significantly longer to understand the problem and fix it. If you aren't the first person back fixing the build on Monday morning, your name will be mud with the rest of the team when they arrive to find the build broken and their ability to work compromised. If you are taken ill over the weekend, and don't make it in to work the next day, expect either several phone calls asking for details of how you messed up the build and how to fix it, or having your revision unceremoniously dumped by one of your colleagues. Still, your name will be mud.

The effect of a broken build generally, and specifically a build left broken at the end of a day's work, is magnified if you are working in a distributed development team with groups in different time zones. In these circumstances, going home on a broken build is perhaps one of the most effective ways of alienating your remote colleagues.

Just to be absolutely clear, *we are not recommending that you stay late to fix the build after working hours.* Rather, we recommend that you check in regularly and early enough to give yourself time to deal with problems should they occur. Alternatively, save your check-in for the next day; many experienced developers make a point of not checking in less than an hour before the end of work, and instead leave that to do first thing the next morning. If all else fails, simply revert your change from source control and leave it in your local working copy. Some version control systems, including all the distributed ones, make this easier by allowing you to accumulate check-ins within your local repository without pushing them to other users.

Build Discipline on Distributed Projects

Your authors once worked on what we believe to have been, at the time, the largest agile project in the world. This was a geographically distributed project working on a shared codebase. The team as a whole was, at various points in the life of the project, working simultaneously in San Francisco and Chicago in the USA, in London, UK, and in Bangalore, India. During any given 24-hour period there were only about 3 hours when someone, somewhere in the world, was not working on the code. For the rest of the time, there was a constant stream of changes committed to the version control system and a constant stream of new builds being triggered.

If the team in India broke the build and went home, the London team could have their day's work dramatically affected. Similarly, if the London team went home on a broken build, their colleagues in the USA would be swearing under their breath for the next eight hours.

Rigorous build discipline was essential, to the extent that we had a dedicated build master who not only maintained the build but also sometimes policed it, ensuring that whoever broke the build was working to fix it. If not, the build engineer would revert their check-in.

Always Be Prepared to Revert to the Previous Revision

As we described earlier, while we try hard to be diligent, we all make mistakes, so we expect that everyone will break the build from time to time. On larger projects, it is often a daily occurrence, though pretested commits will greatly alleviate this. In these circumstances, the fixes are normally simple things that we will recognize immediately and fix by committing a small one-line change. However, sometimes we get it more wrong than that, and either can't find where the problem lies, or just after the check-in fails we realize that we missed something important about the nature of the change that we have just made.

Whatever our reaction to a failed *commit stage*, it is important that we get everything working again quickly. If we can't fix the problem quickly, for whatever reason, we should revert to the previous change-set held in revision control and remedy the problem in our local environment. After all, one of the reasons that we want a revision control system in the first place is to allow us precisely this freedom to revert.

Airplane pilots are taught that every time they land, they should assume that something will go wrong, so they should be ready to abort the landing attempt and "go around" to make another try. Use the same mindset when checking in. Assume that you may break something that will take more than a few minutes, and know what to do to revert the changes and get back to the known-good revision in version control. You know that the previous revision was good because you *don't check in on a broken build*.

Time-Box Fixing before Reverting

Establish a team rule: When the build breaks on check-in, try to fix it for ten minutes. If, after ten minutes, you aren't finished with the solution, revert to the previous version from your version control system. Sometimes, if we are feeling particularly lenient, we will allow you a little leeway. If you are in the middle of your local build preparing for the check-in, for example, we will let you finish that to see if it works. If it works, you can check in and hopefully your fix will be good; if it fails either locally or following check-in, revert to the last known-good state.

Experienced developers will often enforce this rule in any case, happily reverting other people's builds that are broken for ten minutes or more.

Don't Comment Out Failing Tests

Once you begin to enforce the previous rule, the result is often that developers comment out failing tests in order to get their changes checked in. This impulse is understandable, but wrong. When tests that have been passing for a while begin to fail, it can be hard to work out why. Has a regression problem really been found? Perhaps one of the assumptions of the test is no longer valid, or the application really has changed the functionality being tested for a valid reason. Working out which of these conditions is applicable can involve talking to a whole bunch of people and take time, but it is essential to put in the work to find out what is going on and either fix the code (if a regression has been found), modify the test (if one of the assumptions has changed), or delete it (if the functionality under test no longer exists).

Commenting out tests that fail should always be a last resort, very rarely and reluctantly used, unless you are disciplined enough to fix it right away. It is OK to very occasionally comment out a test pending either some serious development work that needs to be scheduled or some extended discussions with the customer. However, this can push you down a slippery slope. We've seen code where half the tests were commented out. It's advisable to track the number of commented tests and display it on a big, visible chart or screen. You could even fail the build if the number of commented tests exceeds some threshold, maybe 2% of the total.

Take Responsibility for All Breakages That Result from Your Changes

If you commit a change and all the tests you wrote pass, but others break, the build is still broken. Usually this means that you have introduced a regression bug into the application. It is your responsibility—because you made the change—to fix all tests that are not passing as a result of your changes. In the context of CI this seems obvious, but actually it is not common practice in many projects.

This practice has several implications. It means that you need to have access to any code that you can break through your changes, so you can fix it if it breaks. It means that you can't afford to have developers own a subset of the code that only they can work on. To do CI effectively, everybody needs access to the whole codebase. If for some reasons you are forced into a situation where access to code cannot be shared with the whole team, you can manage around it through good collaboration with the people who have the necessary access. However, this is very much a second-best, and you should work hard to get such restrictions removed.

Test-Driven Development

Having a comprehensive test suite is essential to continuous integration. While we deal at length with strategies for automated testing in the next chapter, it is worth highlighting that the fast feedback, which is the core outcome of continuous integration, is only possible with excellent unit test coverage (excellent acceptance test coverage is also essential, but these tests take longer to run). In our experience, the only way to get excellent unit test coverage is through test-driven development. While we have tried to avoid being dogmatic about agile development practices in this book, we think test-driven development is essential to enable the practice of continuous delivery.

For those not familiar with test-driven development, the idea is that when developing a new piece of functionality or fixing a bug, developers first create a test that is an executable specification of the expected behavior of the code to be written. Not only do these tests drive the application's design, they then serve both as regression tests and as documentation of the code and the application's expected behavior.

A discussion of test-driven development is beyond the scope of this book. It is, however, worth noting that as with all such practices it is important to be both disciplined and pragmatic about test-driven development. We have two book recommendations for further reading on this topic: Steve Freeman and Nat Pryce's *Growing Object-Oriented Software, Guided by Tests*, and Gerard Meszaros' *xUnit Test Patterns: Refactoring Test Code*.

Suggested Practices

The following practices aren't required, but we have found them useful, and you should at least consider using them for your project.

Extreme Programming (XP) Development Practices

Continuous integration is one of the twelve core XP practices described in Kent Beck's book, and as such it complements and is complemented by the other XP practices. Continuous integration can make a huge difference to any team even if they are not using any of the other practices, but it is even more effective in conjunction with the other practices. In particular, in addition to test-driven development and shared code ownership, which we described in the previous section, you should also consider refactoring as a cornerstone of effective software development.

Refactoring means making a series of small, incremental changes that improve your code without changing your application's behavior. CI and test-driven development enable refactoring by assuring you that your changes don't alter the existing behavior of the application. Thus your team becomes free to make changes which might touch large areas of the code without worrying that they can break the application. This practice also enables frequent check-ins—developers check in after each small, incremental change.

Failing a Build for Architectural Breaches

Sometimes there are aspects of the architecture of a system that are too easy for developers to forget. One technique that we have used is to place some commit-time tests that prove that breaches of these rules are not taking place.

This technique is really only a tactical one and difficult to describe other than by example.

Enforcing Remote Calls at Build Time

The best example we can recall was from a project that was implemented as a collection of distributed services. This was a genuinely distributed system in the sense that it had significant business logic executed in client systems, and real business logic executed at the server too—this was because of real business requirements, not just poor programming.

Our development team deployed all of the code for both the client system and server system in their development environments. It was too easy for a developer to make a local call from the client to the server or from the server to the client, without realizing that if they really want that behavior they have to make a remote call.

We had organized our code into packages representing a facet of the layering strategy to help us with deployment. We used this information and some open source software that would evaluate code dependencies, and used grep to search the output from the dependency tool to see if there were any dependencies between packages that broke our rules.

This prevented unnecessary breakages at functional test time and helped reinforce the architecture of our system—reminding the developers of the importance of the process boundary between the two systems.

This technique can seem a little heavyweight and is not a replacement for a clear understanding of the architecture of the system under development within the development team. However, it can be very useful when there are important architectural issues to defend—things that could otherwise be difficult to catch early.

Failing the Build for Slow Tests

As we have said before, CI works best with small, frequent commits. If the commit tests take a long time to run, it can have a seriously detrimental effect on the productivity of the team because of the time spent waiting for the build and test process to complete. This will, in turn, discourage frequent check-ins, so the team will start to store up their check-ins, making each one more complex—with more likelihood of merge conflicts and more chance of introducing errors, and so failing the tests. All this slows everything down even further.

To keep the development team focused on the importance of keeping the tests fast, you can fail the commit tests if you find an individual test that takes longer than some specified time. Last time we used this approach we failed the build for any test that took more than two seconds to run.

We tend to like practices where a small change can have a wider effect. This is just such a practice. If a developer writes a commit test that takes too long to run, the build will fail when they get ready to commit their change. This encourages them to think carefully about strategies to make their tests run quickly. If the tests run quickly, developers will check in more frequently. If the developers check in more frequently, there is less chance of merge problems, and any problem that does arise is likely to be small and quick to solve, so developers are more productive.

There is a caveat though: This practice can be a bit of a two-edged sword. You need to be wary of creating flaky intermittent tests that fail if your CI environment is, for some reason, under unusual load. We have found that the most effective way to use this approach is as a strategy to get a large team focused on a specific problem, not as something we would employ in every build. If your build becomes slow, you can use this approach to keep the team focused, for a while, on speeding things up.

Please note: We are talking about test performance, not performance testing here. Capacity testing is covered in Chapter 9, "Testing Nonfunctional Requirements."

Failing the Build for Warnings and Code Style Breaches

Compiler warnings are usually warning you for good reasons. A strategy that we have adopted with some success, though it is often referred to as the "code Nazi" by our development teams, is to fail the build on warnings. This can be a bit draconian in some circumstances, but as a way to enforce good practice it is effective.

You can strengthen this technique as much as you wish by adding checks for specific or general coding lapses. We have used one of the many open source code-quality tools with some success:

- Simian is a tool that identifies duplication in most popular languages (including plain text).

- JDepend for Java, and its commercial .NET cousin NDepend, generate a wealth of useful (and some less useful) design quality metrics.

- CheckStyle can test for bad coding practices, such as public constructors in utility classes, nested blocks, and long lines. It can also catch common sources of bugs and security holes. It can easily be extended. FxCop is its .NET cousin.

- FindBugs is a Java-based system providing an alternative to CheckStyle, including a similar set of validations.

As we have said, for some projects failing the build on any warning may sound too draconian. One approach that we have used to introduce this practice gradually is *ratcheting*. This means comparing the number of things like warnings or TODOs with the number in the previous check-in. If the number increases, we fail the build. Using this approach, you can easily enforce a policy that every commit should reduce the number of warnings or TODOs at least by one.

CheckStyle: The Nagging Is Worth It after All

On one of our projects where we added a CheckStyle test to our collection of commit tests, we all got a little bit tired of it nagging us so much. We were a team of experienced developers and all agreed that it was worth the nagging for a while to get us all into good habits and start the project on a good footing.

After we had been running for a few weeks, we removed the CheckStyle test. This sped up our build and got rid of the nagging. Then the team grew a little, and a few weeks later we started to find more "smells" in the code and found ourselves spending more time doing simple tidy-up refactorings than we had been before.

Eventually we realized that although it came at a cost, CheckStyle was helping our team to stay on top of the almost inconsequential things that together add up to the difference between high-quality code and just code. We turned CheckStyle back on and had to spend some time correcting all of the little complaints it raised, but it was worth it and, at least for that project, we learned to stop complaining about the feeling of being nagged.

Distributed Teams

Using continuous integration with distributed teams is, in terms of process and technology, largely the same as in any other environment. However, the fact that the team is not sitting together in the same room—perhaps they are even working in different time zones—does have an impact in some other areas.

The simplest approach from a technical perspective, and the most effective from a process perspective, is to retain a shared version control system and continuous integration system. If your project uses deployment pipelines as described in later chapters, these too should be simply made available on an equal basis to all members of the team.

When we say that this approach is the most effective, we should emphasize that it is very considerably so. It is worth working hard to achieve this ideal; all other approaches described here are second-best to this by a significant margin.

The Impact on Process

For distributed teams within the same time zone, continuous integration is much the same. You can't use physical check-in tokens of course—although some CI servers support virtual ones—and it is a little more impersonal, so a little easier to cause offense when you remind someone to fix the build. Features such as personal builds become more useful. On the whole, however, the process is the same.

For distributed teams in different time zones, there are more issues to deal with. If the team in San Francisco breaks the build and goes home, this can be a serious handicap for the team in Beijing who are just starting work as the San Francisco team are leaving. The process does not change, but the importance of adhering to it is magnified.

In large projects with distributed teams, tools like VoIP (e.g., Skype) and instant messaging are of enormous importance to enable the fine-grained communications necessary to keep things running smoothly. Everyone associated with development—project managers, analysts, developers, testers—should have access to, and be accessible to, everyone else on IM and VoIP. It is essential for the smooth running of the delivery process to fly people back and forth periodically, so that each local group has personal contact with members from other groups. This is important to build up trust between team members—often the first thing to suffer in a distributed team. It is possible to do retrospectives, showcases, stand-ups, and other regular meetings using videoconferencing. Another great technique is to have each development team record a short video, using screen capture software, that talks through the functionality they've been working on that day.

Naturally, this is a much wider topic than just continuous integration. The point we intend to make is simply to keep the process the same, but be even more disciplined in its application.

Centralized Continuous Integration

Some more powerful continuous integration servers have facilities such as centrally managed build farms and sophisticated authorization schemes that allow you to provide continuous integration as a centralized service to large and distributed teams. These systems make it easy for teams to self-service continuous integration without having to obtain their own hardware. They also allow operations teams to consolidate server resources, control the configuration of continuous integration and testing environments to ensure that they are all consistent and similar to production, and enforce good practices such as managing configuration of third-party libraries and providing preinstalled tools for gathering consistent metrics of code coverage and quality. Finally, they allow standard metrics to be gathered and monitored across projects, providing managers and delivery teams with the ability to create dashboards to monitor code quality at a program level.

Virtualization can also work well in conjunction with centralized CI services, providing the ability to spin up new virtual machines from stored baseline images at the press of a button. You can use virtualization to make provisioning new environments a completely automated process, which can be self-serviced by delivery teams. It also ensures that builds and deployments always run on a consistent, baseline version of these environments. This has the happy effect of removing continuous integration environments that are "works of art," having accumulated software, libraries, and configuration settings over many months that bear no relation to what is present in testing and production environments.

Centralized continuous integration can be a win-win situation. However, in order for this to be the case, it is essential that development teams can easily self-service new environments, configurations, builds, and deployments in an automated fashion. If a team has to send several emails and wait days to get a new CI environment for their latest release branch, they will subvert the process and go back to using spare boxes under their desks to do their real continuous integration—or, worse, not do continuous integration at all.

Technical Issues

Depending on the choice of a version control system, it can be quite painful to share access to version control systems and build and test resources for a globally distributed team when there are slow links between the teams.

When continuous integration is working well, the whole team is committing changes regularly. This means that interaction with the version control system tends to be maintained at a reasonably high level. Although each interaction is usually relatively small in terms of bytes exchanged, because of the frequency of commits and updates, poor communication becomes a significant drag on productivity. It is worth investing in sufficiently high-bandwidth communications between development centers. It is also worth considering to move to a distributed version control system such as Git or Mercurial that allows people to check in even when there is no link to the conventionally designated "master" server.

Distributed Version Control: When Nothing Else Will Work

Some years ago we worked on a project where this was a problem. The communications infrastructure to our colleagues in India was so slow and unreliable that on some days they couldn't check in at all, which would have knock-on effects for days after. Eventually, we did an analysis of the cost of time lost and found that the cost to upgrade the communications would be paid for in a matter of days. On another project, it was simply impossible to get a sufficiently fast and reliable connection. The team moved from using Subversion, a centralized VCS, to Mercurial, a distributed VCS, with noticeable productivity benefits.

It makes sense for the version control system to be reasonably close to the build infrastructure that hosts the running of automated tests. If these tests are being run after every check-in, that implies a fair amount of interaction between the systems across the network.

The physical machines that host the version control system, the continuous integration system, and the various test environments in your deployment pipeline need to be accessible on an equal basis from every development site. The development team in London is going to be at a considerable disadvantage if the version control system in India stops working because the disk is full, everyone in the Indian office has gone home for the evening, and they don't have access to the system. Provide sysadmin-level access to all of these systems from every location. Ensure that the teams at each site not only have access but also the knowledge to manage any problems that may occur on their shift.

Alternative Approaches

If there is some insurmountable problem that prevents spending a little more to get higher-bandwidth communications established between your development centers, then it is possible, but not ideal, to have local continuous integration and test systems, and even local version control systems in extreme circumstances. As you might expect, we really don't advise this approach. Do everything you can to avoid it; it is expensive in terms of time and effort and doesn't work nearly as well as shared access.

The easy stuff is the continuous integration system. It is quite possible to have local continuous integration servers and test environments, even a full-blown local deployment pipeline. This can be of value when there is a significant amount of manual testing being undertaken at a site. Of course, these environments need to be managed carefully to ensure they are consistent across regions. The only caveat is that ideally, binaries or installers should only be built once, and then shipped to all global locations where they are required. However, this is often impractical due to the sheer size of most installers. If you have to build binaries or installers locally, it becomes even more essential to ensure that you manage the configuration of your toolchain rigorously to ensure exactly the same binaries are created everywhere. One approach to enforce this is to automatically generate hashes of your binaries, using md5 or a similar algorithm, and have your CI server automatically check them against the hashes of the "master" binaries to ensure there are no differences.

In certain extreme situations, for example if the version control system is remote and connected via a slow or unreliable link, the value of hosting the continuous integration system locally is seriously compromised. Our oft-stated objective in the use of continuous integration is the ability to identify problems at the earliest opportunity. If the version control system is split, in any manner, we compromise this ability. In circumstances where we are forced to do so, our goal in splitting the version control system must be to minimize the time between an error being introduced and our being able to spot it.

Primarily, there are two options for providing local access to version control systems for distributed teams: division of the application into components and the use of version control systems that are either distributed or support multimaster topologies.

In the component-based approach, both the version control repositories and the teams are divided either by component or by functional boundary. This approach is discussed in much more detail in Chapter 13, "Managing Components and Dependencies."

Another technique that we have seen is to have team-local repositories and build systems with a shared global master repository. The functionally separated teams commit to their local repositories throughout the working day. At a regular time each day, usually after one of the distributed teams in another time zone have finished work for the day, one member of the local team takes responsibility to commit all of the changes for the entire team and takes the pain of merging a whole collection of changes. Clearly, this is much easier if you're using a distributed version control system which is designed for exactly this sort of task. However, this solution is by no means ideal, and we have seen it fail miserably, due to the introduction of significant merge conflicts.

In summary, all of the techniques that we describe in this book have been well proven in distributed teams on many projects. In fact, we would view the use of CI as one of the two or three most important factors in the ability of geographically distributed teams to work effectively together. The continuous part of continuous integration is important; if there really are no other options, there are some workarounds, but our advice is to spend the money on communications bandwidth instead—in the medium and long term, it is cheaper.

Distributed Version Control Systems

The rise of distributed version control systems (DVCSs) is revolutionizing the way teams cooperate. Where open source projects once emailed patches or posted them on forums, tools like Git and Mercurial make it incredibly easy to pull patches back and forth between developers and teams and to branch and merge work streams. DVCSs allow you to work easily offline, commit changes locally, and rebase or shelve them before pushing them to other users. The core characteristic of a DVCS is that every repository contains the entire history of the project, which means that no repository is privileged except by convention. Thus, compared to centralized systems, DVCSs have an additional layer of indirection: Changes to your local working copy must be checked in to your local repository before they can be pushed to other repositories, and updates from other repositories must be reconciled with your local repository before you can update your working copy.

DVCSs offer new and powerful ways to collaborate. GitHub, for example, pioneered a new model of collaboration for open source projects. In the traditional model, committers acted as gatekeepers to the definitive repository for a project, accepting or rejecting patches from contributors. Forks of a project only occurred in extreme circumstances when there were irreconcilable arguments between committers. In the GitHub model, this is turned on its head. Contributions are made by first forking the repository of the project you wish to contribute to, making your changes, and then asking the owners of the original repository to pull your changes. On active projects, networks of forks rapidly proliferate, each with various new sets of features. Occasionally these forks diverge. This model is far more dynamic than the traditional model in which patches languish, ignored, on mailing list archives. As a result, the pace of development tends to be faster on GitHub, with a larger cloud of contributors.

However, this model challenges a fundamental assumption of the practice of CI: That there is a single, canonical version of code (usually called mainline, or trunk) to which all changes are committed. It is important to point out that you can use the mainline model of version control, and do CI perfectly happily, using a DVCS. You simply designate one repository as the master, have your CI server trigger whenever a change is made to that repository, and have everybody push all their changes to this repository in order to share them. This is a perfectly reasonable approach that we have seen used successfully on many projects. It retains the many benefits of DVCS, such as the ability to commit your changes very frequently without sharing them (like saving your game), which comes in very useful while exploring a new idea or performing a complex series of refactorings. However, there are some patterns of use of DVCS that prevent CI. The GitHub model, for example, violates the mainline/trunk model of code sharing, and so prevents true continuous integration.

In GitHub, each user's set of changes exists in a separate repository, and there is no way to easily determine which sets from which users will successfully integrate. You could take the approach of creating a repository to watch all the other repositories and attempt to merge them all together whenever it detects a change to any of them. However, this will almost always fail at the merge stage, let alone when running the automated tests. As the number of contributors, and hence repositories, grows, the problem gets exponentially worse. Nobody will take any notice of what the CI server says, so CI as a method of communicating whether the application is currently working (and if not, who and what broke it) fails.

It is possible to fall back to a simpler model that provides some of the benefits of continuous integration. In this model, you create a CI build for each repository. Every time a change is made, you attempt to merge from the designated master repository and run the build. Figure 3.2 shows CruiseControl.rb building the main repository for the Rapidsms project along with two forks of it.

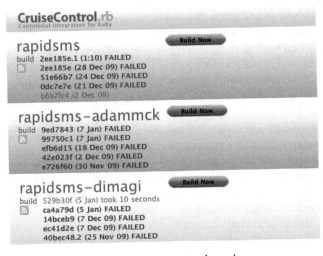

Figure 3.2   *Integrating branches*

In order to create this system, a branch pointing to the main project repository was added to each of CC.rb's Git repositories using the command `git remote add core git://github.com/rapidsms/rapidsms.git`. Every time the build is triggered, CC.rb attempts to merge and run the build:

```
git fetch core
git merge --no-commit core/master
[command to run the build]
```

After the build, CC.rb runs `git reset --hard` to reset the local repository to head of the repository it is pointing at. This system does not provide true continuous integration. However, it *does* tell the maintainers of the forks—and the maintainer of the main repository—whether their fork could in principle be merged with the main repository, and whether the result would be a working version of the application. Interestingly, Figure 3.2 shows that the main repository's build is currently broken, but the Dimagi fork not only merges successfully with it, but also fixes the broken tests (and possibly adds some additional functionality of its own).

At one more step away from continuous integration is what Martin Fowler calls "promiscuous integration" [bBjxbS]. In this model, contributors pull changes not just between forks and the central repository, but also between forks. This pattern is common in larger projects that use GitHub, when some developers are working on what are effectively long-lived feature branches and pull changes from other repositories that are forked off the feature branch. Indeed in this model there need not even be one privileged repository. A particular release of the software could come from any of the forks, provided it passed all the tests and was accepted by the project leaders. This model takes the possibilities of DVCS to their logical conclusion.

These alternatives to continuous integration can create high-quality, working software. However, this is only possible under the following conditions:

- A small and very experienced team of committers who manage pulling patches, tend the automated tests, and ensure the quality of the software.

- Regular pulling from forks, so as to avoid large amounts of hard-to-merge inventory accumulating on them. This condition is especially important if there is a strict release schedule, because the temptation is to leave merging till near the release, at which point it becomes extremely painful—the exact problem that continuous integration is designed to solve.

- A relatively small set of core developers, perhaps supplemented by a larger community which contributes at a relatively slow pace. This is what makes the merges tractable.

These conditions hold for most open source projects, and for small teams in general. However, they very rarely hold for medium or large teams of full-time developers.

To summarize: In general, distributed version control systems are a great advance and provide powerful tools for collaboration, whether or not you are working on a distributed project. DVCSs can be extremely effective as part of a traditional continuous integration system, in which there is a designated central repository to which everybody regularly pushes their changes (at least once a day). They can also be used in other patterns that do not allow for continuous integration, but may still be effective patterns for delivering software. However, we caution against using these patterns when the right conditions, listed above, are not satisfied. Chapter 14, "Advanced Version Control," contains a full discussion of these and other patterns and the conditions under which they are effective.

Summary

If you were to choose just one of the practices in this book to implement on a development team, we would suggest that you choose continuous integration. Time and time again we have seen it make a step change to the productivity of software development teams.

To implement continuous integration is to create a paradigm shift in your team. Without CI, your application is broken until you prove otherwise. With CI, the default state of your application is working, albeit with a level of confidence that depends upon the extent of your automated test coverage. CI creates a tight feedback loop which allows you to find problems as soon as they are introduced, when they are cheap to fix.

Implementing CI forces you to follow two other important practices: good configuration management and the creation and maintenance of an automated build and test process. For some teams, that will seem like a lot to bite off, but they can be achieved incrementally. We discussed the steps to good configuration management in the previous chapter. There is more on build automation in Chapter 6, "Build and Deployment Scripting." We cover testing in more detail in the next chapter.

It should be clear that CI requires good team discipline—but then, any process requires this. What is different about continuous integration is that you have a simple indicator of whether or not discipline is being followed: The build stays green. If you discover that the build is green but there is insufficient discipline, for example poor unit test coverage, you can easily add checks to your CI system to enforce better behavior.

This brings us to our final point. An established CI system is a foundation on which you can build more infrastructure:

- Big visible displays which aggregate information from your build system to provide high-quality feedback

- A system of reference for reports and installers for your testing team

- A provider of data on the quality of the application for project managers

- A system that can be extended out to production, using the deployment pipeline, which provides testers and operations staff with push-button deployments

Chapter 4

Implementing a Testing Strategy

Introduction

Too many projects rely solely on manual acceptance testing to verify that a piece of software conforms to its functional and nonfunctional requirements. Even where automated tests exist, they are often poorly maintained and out-of-date and require supplementing with extensive manual testing. This and the related chapters in Part II of this book aim to help you to plan and implement effective automated testing systems. We provide strategies for automating tests in commonly occurring situations and describe practices that support and enable automated testing.

One of W. Edwards Deming's fourteen points is, "Cease dependence on mass inspection to achieve quality. Improve the process and build quality into the product in the first place" [9YhQXz]. Testing is a cross-functional activity that involves the whole team, and should be done continuously from the beginning of the project. Building quality in means writing automated tests at multiple levels (unit, component, and acceptance) and running them as part of the deployment pipeline, which is triggered every time a change is made to your application, its configuration, or the environment and software stack that it runs on. Manual testing is also an essential part of building quality in: Showcases, usability testing, and exploratory testing need to be done continuously throughout the project. Building quality in also means constantly working to improve your automated testing strategy.

In our ideal project, testers collaborate with developers and users to write automated tests from the start of the project. These tests are written before developers start work on the features that they test. Together, these tests form an executable specification of the behavior of the system, and when they pass, they demonstrate that the functionality required by the customer has been implemented completely and correctly. The automated test suite is run by the CI system every time a change is made to the application—which means the suite also serves as a set of regression tests.

These tests do not just test the functional aspects of the system. Capacity, security, and other nonfunctional requirements are established early on, and automated test suites are written to enforce them. These automated tests ensure that any problems that compromise the fulfillment of these requirements are caught early when the cost of fixing them is low. These tests of the nonfunctional behaviors of the system enable developers to refactor and rearchitect on the basis of empirical evidence: "The recent changes to the search have caused the performance of the application to degrade—we need to modify the solution to ensure that we meet our capacity requirements."

This ideal world is fully achievable in projects that adopt the appropriate discipline early on. If you need to implement them on a project that has already been running for some time, things are a little more difficult. Getting to a high level of automated test coverage will take time and careful planning to ensure that development can continue while teams learn how to implement automated testing. Legacy codebases will certainly benefit from many of these techniques, although it may take a long time until they reach the level of quality of a system built from the start with automated tests. We discuss ways to apply these techniques to legacy systems later on in this chapter.

The design of a testing strategy is primarily a process of identifying and prioritizing project risks and deciding what actions to take to mitigate them. A good testing strategy has many positive effects. Testing establishes confidence that the software is working as it should, which means fewer bugs, reduced support costs, and improved reputation. Testing also provides a constraint on the development process which encourages good development practices. A comprehensive automated test suite even provides the most complete and up-to-date form of application documentation, in the form of an executable specification not just of how the system should work, but also of how it actually does work.

Finally, it's worth noting that we can only scratch the surface of testing here. Our intention is to cover the fundamentals of automated testing, providing enough context for the rest of the book to make sense, and to enable you to implement a suitable deployment pipeline for your project. In particular, we don't dive into the technical details of test implementation, nor do we cover topics such as exploratory testing in detail. For more detail on testing, we suggest you look at one of the companion volumes to this book: Lisa Crispin and Janet Gregory's *Agile Testing* (Addison-Wesley, 2009).

Types of Tests

Many kinds of testing exist. Brian Marick came up with Figure 4.1, which is widely used to model the various types of tests that you should have in place to ensure the delivery of a high-quality application.

In this diagram, he categorized tests according to whether they are business-facing or technology-facing, and whether they support the development process or are used to critique the project.

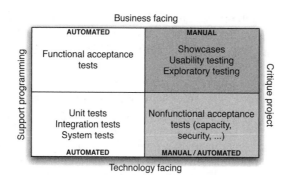

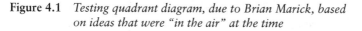

Figure 4.1   *Testing quadrant diagram, due to Brian Marick, based on ideas that were "in the air" at the time*

Business-Facing Tests That Support the Development Process

The tests in this quadrant are more commonly known as functional or acceptance tests. Acceptance testing ensures that the acceptance criteria for a story are met. Acceptance tests should be written, and ideally automated, before development starts on a story. Acceptance tests, like acceptance criteria, can test all kinds of attributes of the system being built, including functionality, capacity, usability, security, modifiability, availability, and so on. Acceptance tests that concern the functionality of the system are known as functional acceptance tests—nonfunctional acceptance tests fall into the fourth quadrant of the diagram. For more on the somewhat blurry and often misunderstood distinction between functional and nonfunctional tests, take a look at our coverage of technology-facing tests that critique the project, below.

Acceptance tests are critical in an agile environment because they answer the questions, "How do I know when I am done?" for developers and "Did I get what I wanted?" for users. When the acceptance tests pass, whatever requirements or stories they are testing can be said to be complete. Thus, in an ideal world, customers or users would write acceptance tests, since they define the success criteria for each requirement. Modern automated functional testing tools, such as Cucumber, JBehave, Concordion, and Twist, aim to realize this ideal by separating the test scripts from the implementation, while providing a mechanism that makes it simple to keep them synchronized. In this way, it is possible for users to write the test scripts, while developers and testers work together on the code that implements them.

In general, for each story or requirement there is a single canonical path through the application in terms of the actions that the user will perform. This is known as the *happy path*. This is often expressed using the form "Given [a few important characteristics of the state of the system when testing begins], when [the user performs some set of actions], then [a few important characteristics of the new state of the system] will result." This is sometimes referred to as the "given-when-then" model for tests.

However, any use case will, in all but the simplest of systems, allow for variations in the initial state, the actions to be performed, and the final state of the application. Sometimes, these variations constitute distinct use cases, which are then known as *alternate paths*. In other cases, they should cause error conditions, resulting in what is called *sad paths*. There are clearly many possible tests that can be performed with different values for these variables. Equivalence partitioning analysis and boundary value analysis will reduce these possibilities to a smaller set of cases that will completely test the requirement in question. However, even then you'll need to use your intuition to pick the most relevant cases.

Acceptance tests should be run when your system is in a production-like mode. Manual acceptance testing is typically done by putting an application in a user acceptance testing (UAT) environment which is as similar as possible to production both in configuration and in terms of the state of the application—although it might use mock versions of any external services. The tester uses the application's standard user interface in order to perform testing. Automated acceptance tests should similarly be run in a production-like environment, with the test harness interacting with the application the same way that a user would.

Automating Acceptance Tests

Automated acceptance tests have a number of valuable properties:

- They make the feedback loop faster—developers can run automated tests to find out if they have completed a particular requirement without having to go to testers.

- They reduce the workload on testers.

- They free testers to concentrate on exploratory testing and higher-value activities instead of boring repetitive tasks.

- Your acceptance tests represent a powerful regression test suite. This is particularly important when writing large applications or working in large teams where frameworks or many modules are being used and changes to one part of the application are likely to affect other features.

- By using human-readable test and test suite names, as advocated by behavior-driven development, it is possible to autogenerate requirements documentation from your tests. Indeed, tools like Cucumber and Twist are designed to allow analysts to write requirements as executable test scripts. The benefit of this approach is that your requirements documentation is never out-of-date—it can be generated automatically with every build.

The question of regression testing is particularly important. Regression tests aren't mentioned on the quadrant diagram because they are a crosscutting category. Regression tests represent the entire corpus of your automated tests. They serve to ensure that when you make a change you don't break existing functionality. They also make it possible to easily refactor code by verifying that you haven't changed any behavior when refactoring is done. When writing automated acceptance tests, you should keep in mind that they will form part of your regression test suite.

However, automated acceptance tests can be costly to maintain. Done badly, they can inflict a significant cost on your delivery team. For this reason, some people recommend against creating large complex suites of automated tests.[1] However, by following good practices and using appropriate tools, it is possible to dramatically reduce the cost of creating and maintaining automated acceptance tests to the point where the benefits clearly exceed the costs. We discuss these techniques in more detail in Chapter 8, "Automated Acceptance Testing."

It's important to remember that not everything needs to be automated. There are many aspects of a system that people are genuinely better at testing. Usability, consistency of look and feel, and so on are difficult things to verify in automated tests. Exploratory testing is also impossible to do automatically—although, of course, testers use automation as part of exploratory testing for things like setting up scenarios and creating test data. In many cases, manual testing can suffice, or indeed can be superior to automated tests. In general, we tend to limit our automated acceptance testing to complete coverage of happy path behaviors and only limited coverage of the most important other parts. This is a safe and efficient strategy, assuming that you already have a comprehensive set of automated regression tests of other kinds. We generally class comprehensive as greater than 80% code coverage, though the quality of the tests is very important and coverage alone is a poor metric. Automated test coverage in this context includes unit, component, and acceptance tests, each of which should cover 80% of the application (we don't subscribe to the naive idea that you can gain 80% coverage with 60% unit test coverage and 20% acceptance test coverage).

As a good litmus test of your automated acceptance test coverage, consider the following scenario. Suppose you swap out some part of our system—such as the persistence layer—and replace it with a different implementation. You complete the replacement, run your automated acceptance tests, and they pass. How confident do you feel that your system is really working? A good automated test suite should give you the confidence necessary to perform refactorings and even rearchitecting of your application knowing that if the tests pass, your application's behavior really hasn't been affected.

As with every other aspect of software development, each project is different, and you need to monitor how much time is being spent on repeating manual

---

1. For example, James Shore [dsyXYv].

tests so you can decide when to automate them. A good rule of thumb is to automate once you have repeated the same test a couple of times, and when you are confident that you won't end up spending a lot of time maintaining the test. For more on when to automate, read Brian Marick's paper "When Should a Test Be Automated?" [90NC1y].

Should Acceptance Tests Hit the UI?

Acceptance tests are generally end-to-end tests that run on a real working environment that is similar to production. This means that in an ideal world, they would be run directly against the UI of the application.

However, most UI testing tools take a naive approach that couples them tightly to the UI, with the result that when the UI changes even slightly, the tests break. This results in many false positives—tests that break not due to any problem with the application's behavior, but rather because some checkbox has had its name changed. Keeping the tests in sync with the application can swallow up huge amounts of time without delivering any value. A good question to ask yourself every now and again is, "How often do my acceptance tests break due to real bugs, and how often due to changes in requirements?"

There are several ways to solve this problem. One is to add an abstraction layer between your tests and your UI so as to reduce the amount of work required when the UI changes. Another is to run acceptance tests against a public API that sits just below the UI—the same API that the UI uses to actually perform actions (it should go without saying that your UI must not contain any business logic). This doesn't obviate the need for UI tests, but it means they can be reduced to a small number of checks of the UI itself, not the business logic. The bulk of your acceptance test suite can then run directly against your business logic.

We deal with this topic at more length in Chapter 8, "Automated Acceptance Testing."

The most important automated test to write is the main happy path test. Every story or requirement should have at least one automated happy path acceptance test. These tests should be used individually by developers as smoke tests to provide rapid feedback on whether they have broken some bit of functionality they are working on. They should be the first target for automation.

When you have time to write and automate further tests, it's hard to choose between alternate happy paths and sad paths. If your application is reasonably stable, then alternate paths should be your priority since they represent all the user-defined scenarios. If your application is buggy and crashes often, strategic application of sad path testing can help you identify problem areas and fix them, and automation can ensure that the application remains stable.

Technology-Facing Tests That Support the Development Process

These automated tests are written and maintained exclusively by developers. There are three kinds of tests that fall into this category: unit tests, component tests, and deployment tests. Unit tests test a particular piece of the code in isolation. For this reason, they often rely on simulating other parts of the system using test doubles (see the "Test Doubles" section on page 91). Unit tests should not involve calling the database, using the filesystem, talking to external systems, or, in general, interaction between components of a system. This enables them to run very fast so you can get early feedback on whether changes have broken any existing functionality. These tests should also cover virtually every code-path in the system (a bare minimum of 80%). Thus they form a key part of your regression test suite.

However, this speed comes at the cost of missing those bugs that occur as a result of interaction between the various pieces of your application. For example, it is very common for objects (in OO programming) or bits of application data to have very different lifecycles. It is only by testing larger chunks of your application that you will find bugs occurring due to the lifecycles of your data or objects not being managed correctly.

Component tests test larger clusters of functionality, so that they can catch problems like these. They are typically slower, since they can require more involved setup and perform more I/O, talking to databases, the filesystem, or other systems. Sometimes, component tests are known as "integration tests"—but the term "integration tests" is overloaded, so we won't use it in this context in the book.

Deployment tests are performed whenever you deploy your application. They check that the deployment worked—in other words, that your application is correctly installed, correctly configured, able to contact any services it requires, and that it is responding.

Business-Facing Tests That Critique the Project

These manual tests verify that the application will in fact deliver to the users the value they are expecting. This is not just a matter of verifying that the application meets its specifications; it is also about checking that the specifications are correct. We have never worked on, or heard of, a project where the application was specified perfectly in advance. Inevitably, when users try an application in real life, they discover that there is room for improvement. They break things because they manage to perform sets of operations that nobody had tried before. They complain that the application could be better at helping them with the tasks that they perform most often. Perhaps they are inspired by the application and identify new features that will give them even more value. Software development is a naturally iterative process that thrives on the establishment of effective feedback loops, and we deceive ourselves if we perceive it any other way.

A particularly important form of business-facing, project-critique tests are showcases. Agile teams perform showcases to users at the end of every iteration to demonstrate the new functionality that they have delivered. Functionality should also be demonstrated to customers as often as possible during development, so as to ensure that any misunderstandings or specification problems are caught as early as possible. Showcases that go well can be both a blessing and a curse—users love getting their hands on new stuff and playing around with it. But they invariably have plenty of suggestions for improvement. At this point, the customer and the project team have to decide how much they want to change the project's plan to incorporate these suggestions. Whatever the outcome, it's much better to get feedback early rather than at the end of the project when it's too late to make changes. Showcasing is the heartbeat of any project: It is the first time that you can say that a piece of work is really done to the satisfaction of the people who are, after all, paying the bills.

Exploratory testing is described by James Bach as a form of manual testing in which "the tester actively controls the design of the tests as those tests are performed and uses information gained while testing to design new and better tests."[2] Exploratory testing is a creative learning process that will not only discover bugs, but also lead to the creation of new sets of automated tests, and potentially feed into new requirements for the application.

Usability testing is done to discover how easy it is for users to accomplish their goals with your software. It is easy to get too close to the problem during development, even for nontechnical people working on specifying the application. Usability testing is therefore the ultimate test that your application is actually going to deliver value to users. There are several different approaches to usability testing, from contextual enquiry to sitting users down in front of your application and filming them performing common tasks. Usability testers gather metrics, noting how long it takes users to finish their tasks, watching out for people pressing the wrong buttons, noting how long it takes them to find the right text field, and getting them to record their level of satisfaction at the end.

Finally, you can give your application to real users using beta testing programs. Indeed, many websites seem to be perpetually in a beta state. Some of the more forward-thinking sites (NetFlix, for example) continually release new features to selected users without them even noticing. Many organizations use canary releasing (see the "Canary Releasing" section on page 263) where several subtly different versions of the application are in production simultaneously and their effectiveness is compared. These organizations gather statistics on how the new functionality gets used, and retire it if it doesn't deliver sufficient value. This provides an evolutionary approach to the adoption of features which is very effective.

---

2.   "Exploratory Testing Explained" by James Bach [9BRHOz], p. 2.

Technology-Facing Tests That Critique the Project

Acceptance testing comes in two categories: functional tests and nonfunctional tests. By nonfunctional tests, we mean all the qualities of a system other than its functionality, such as capacity, availability, security, and so forth. As we mention above, the distinction between functional and nonfunctional testing is in some ways bogus, as is the idea that these tests are not business-facing. This may seem obvious, but many projects do not treat nonfunctional requirements the same way as other requirements or (worse) do not bother to validate them at all. Although users rarely spend a lot of time specifying capacity and security characteristics up front, they will certainly be very upset if their credit card details are stolen or if a website is constantly down due to capacity problems. For this reason, it has been argued by many people that "nonfunctional requirements" is a bad name, with alternatives suggested such as cross-functional requirements or system characteristics. Although we are sympathetic to this position, we have referred to them throughout this book as nonfunctional characteristics so everybody knows what we're talking about. Whatever you call them, nonfunctional acceptance criteria should be specified as part of your application's requirements in exactly the same way as functional acceptance criteria.

The tests used to check whether these acceptance criteria have been met, and the tools used to run the tests tend to be quite different from those used to verify conformance to functional acceptance criteria. These tests often require considerable resources such as special environments to run on and specialized knowledge to set up and implement, and they often take a long time to run (whether or not they are automated). Therefore, their implementation tends to be deferred. Even when they are fully automated, they tend to be run less frequently and further down the deployment pipeline than the functional acceptance tests.

However, things are changing. The tools used to perform these tests are maturing, and the techniques used to develop them are becoming more mainstream. Having been caught short many times by bad performance just before release, we recommend that you set up at least some basic nonfunctional tests towards the start of any project, no matter how simple or inconsequential. For more complex or mission-critical projects, you should consider allocating project time to researching and implementing nonfunctional testing from the start of your project.

Test Doubles

A key part of automated testing involves replacing part of a system at run time with a simulated version. In this way, the interactions of the part of the application under test with the rest of the application can be tightly constrained, so that its behavior can be determined more easily. Such simulations are often known as mocks, stubs, dummies, and so forth. We'll be following the terminology that Gerard Meszaros uses in his book *xUnit Test Patterns*, as summarized by

Martin Fowler [aobjRH]. Meszaros coined the generic term "test doubles" and distinguishes further between the various types of test doubles as follows:

- Dummy objects are passed around but never actually used. Usually they are just used to fill parameter lists.

- Fake objects actually have working implementations, but usually take some shortcut that makes them not suitable for production. A good example of this is the in-memory database.

- Stubs provide canned answers to the calls made during the test, usually not responding at all to anything outside what's programmed in for the test.

- Spies are stubs that also record some information based on how they were called. One form of this might be an email service that records how many messages it was sent.

- Mocks are preprogrammed with expectations that form a specification of the calls they are expected to receive. They can throw an exception if they receive a call they don't expect and are checked during verification to ensure they got all the calls they were expecting.

Mocks are an especially abused form of test doubles. It's very easy to misuse mocks by writing tests that are both pointless and fragile, using them simply to assert the specific details of the workings of some code rather than its interactions with collaborators. Such usage is fragile because if the implementation changes, the test breaks. Examining the distinction between mocks and stubs goes beyond the scope of this book, but you'll find more detail in Chapter 8, "Automated Acceptance Testing." Probably the most comprehensive paper laying out how to use mocks correctly is "Mock Roles, Not Objects" [duZRWb]. Martin Fowler also gives some pointers in his article "Mocks Aren't Stubs" [dmXRSC].

Real-Life Situations and Strategies

Here are some typical scenarios faced by teams who have decided to automate their tests.

New Projects

New projects represent a chance to achieve the ideals that we describe in this book. At this stage, the cost of change is low and, by establishing some relatively simple ground rules and creating some relatively simple test infrastructure, you can give a great start to your process of continuous integration. In this situation, the important thing is to start writing automated acceptance tests from the very beginning. In order to do this, you'll need:

- To choose a technology platform and testing tools.

- To set up a simple, automated build.

- To work out stories that follow the INVEST principles [ddVMFH] (they should be Independent, Negotiable, Valuable, Estimable, Small, and Testable), with acceptance criteria.

You can then implement a strict process:

- Customers, analysts, and testers define acceptance criteria.

- Testers work with developers to automate acceptance tests based on the acceptance criteria.

- Developers code behavior to fulfill the acceptance criteria.

- If any automated tests fail (whether unit, component, or acceptance tests), developers make it a priority to fix them.

It is much simpler to adopt this process at the start of a project than decide a few iterations later that you need acceptance tests. At these later stages, not only will you have to try and to come up with ways to implement the acceptance tests, since support for them won't already exist in your framework—you'll also have to convince skeptical developers of the need to follow the process assiduously. Getting a team addicted to automated testing is simpler to achieve if you start at the beginning of a project.

However, it is also essential that everybody on the team, including customers and project managers, are bought in to these benefits. We have seen projects cancelled because the customer felt that too much time was spent working on automated acceptance tests. If the customer really would rather sacrifice the quality of their automated acceptance test suite in order to get it to market quickly, they are entitled to make that decision—but the consequences should be made quite clear.

Finally, it is important to make sure that your acceptance criteria are carefully written so that they express the business value that the story delivers from the point of view of the user. Blindly automating badly written acceptance criteria is one of the major causes of unmaintainable acceptance test suites. For each acceptance criterion you write, it should be possible to write an automated acceptance test proving that the value described is delivered to the user. This means that testers should be involved in writing requirements from the start, ensuring that a coherent, maintainable automated acceptance test suite is supported throughout the evolution of the system.

Following the process we describe changes the way developers write code. Comparing codebases that have been developed using automated acceptance tests from the beginning with those where acceptance testing has been an afterthought, we almost always see better encapsulation, clearer intent, cleaner separation of concerns, and more reuse of code in the former case. This really is a virtuous circle: Testing at the right time leads to better code.

Midproject

Although it's always pleasant to be starting a project from scratch, the reality is that we often find ourselves working on a large, resource-starved team developing a rapidly changing codebase, under pressure to deliver.

The best way to introduce automated testing is to begin with the most common, important, and high-value use cases of the application. This will require conversations with your customer to clearly identify where the real business value lies, and then defending this functionality against regressions with tests. Based on these conversations you should automate happy path tests that cover these high-value scenarios.

In addition, it is useful to maximize the number of actions that these tests cover. Make them cover slightly broader scenarios than you would normally address with story-level acceptance tests. Fill in as many fields as possible and press as many buttons as possible to satisfy the needs of the test. This approach gives some broad cover for the functionality being tested in these core behavioral tests, even though the tests won't highlight failures or changes in the details of the system. For example, you will know that the basic behavior of you system is working, but may miss the fact that some validations are not. This has the bonus of making manual testing a little more efficient, since you won't have to test every single field. You'll be sure that builds that have passed automated tests will function correctly and deliver business value even if some aspects of their behavior aren't as you would wish.

This strategy means that, since you are only automating the happy path, you will have to perform a correspondingly larger amount of manual testing to ensure that you system is working fully as it should. You should find that the manual tests change rapidly since they'll be testing new or newly changed functionality. The moment you discover you are testing the same function manually more than a couple of times, check and see if that functionality is likely to change. If not, automate the test. Conversely, if you find you are spending a great deal of time fixing particular tests, you can assume that the functionality under test is changing. Again, go and check with the customer and development team if this is the case. If so, it is usually possible to tell your automated testing framework to ignore the test, remembering to give as much detail as possible in the ignore comment so that you know when to get the test working again. If you suspect the test won't be used again in its present form, delete it—you can always retrieve it from version control if you're wrong.

When you are pressed for time, you won't be able to spend a great deal of effort on scripting complex scenarios with a lot of interactions. In this situation it's better to use a variety of sets of test data in order to ensure coverage. Specify clearly the objective of your test, find the simplest possible script which fulfills this objective, and supplement it with as many scenarios as possible in terms of the state of the application at the beginning of the test. We discuss automating the loading of test data in Chapter 12, "Managing Data."

Legacy Systems

Michael Feathers, in his book *Working Effectively with Legacy Code*, provocatively defined legacy systems as systems that do not have automated tests. This is a useful and simple (although controversial) definition. Along with this simple definition comes a simple rule of thumb: Test the code that you change.

The first priority when dealing with such a system is to create an automated build process if one doesn't exist, and then create an automated functional test scaffolding around it. Creating an automated test suite will be easier if documentation, or better still, members of the team who worked on the legacy system are available. However, this is often not the case.

Often, the sponsors of the project are unwilling to allow the development team spend time on what seems to them a low-value activity—creating tests for the behavior of a system that is already in production: "Hasn't this already been tested in the past by the QA team?" So it is important to target the high-value actions of the system. It is easy to explain to the customer the value of creating a regression test suite to protect these functions of the system.

It is important to sit down with users of the system to identify its high-value uses. Using the same techniques described in the previous section, create a set of broad automated tests that cover this core high-value functionality. You shouldn't spend too long doing this, since this is a skeleton to protect the legacy functions. You will be adding new tests incrementally later for the new behavior that you add. These are essentially smoke tests for your legacy system.

Once these smoke tests are in place, you can begin development on stories. It is useful at this point to take a layered approach to your automated tests. The first layer should be very simple and fast-running tests for problems that prevent you from doing useful testing and development on whatever piece of functionality you're working on. The second layer tests the critical functionality for a particular story. As much as possible, new behaviors should be developed and tested in the same way that we described for a new project. Stories with acceptance criteria should be created for the new features, and automated tests should be mandated to represent completion of these stories.

This can sometimes be harder than it sounds. Systems designed to be testable tend to be more modular and easier to test than those that are not. However, this should not divert you from the goal.

A particular problem of such legacy systems is that the code is often not too modular and well structured. Thus it is common for a change in one part of the code to adversely affect behavior in another area. One useful strategy in such circumstances can be to include a careful validation of the state of the application at the completion of the test. If you have time, you can test the alternate paths of the story. Finally, you can write more acceptance tests checking for exception conditions or protecting against common failure modes or undesirable side effects.

It is important to remember that you should only write automated tests where they will deliver value. You can essentially divide your application into two parts. There is the code that implements the features of your application, and there is the support or framework code underneath it. The vast majority of regression bugs are caused by altering framework code—so if you are only adding features to your application that do not require changes to the framework and support code, then there's little value in writing a comprehensive scaffolding.

The exception to this is when your software has to run in a number of different environments. In this case, automated tests combined with automated deployment to production-like environments deliver a great deal of value since you can simply point your scripts at the environments to be tested and save yourself a lot of effort on manual testing.

Integration Testing

If your application is conversing with a variety of external systems through a series of different protocols, or if your application itself consists of a series of loosely coupled modules with complex interactions between them, then integration tests become very important. The line between integration testing and component testing is blurry (not least because integration testing is a somewhat overloaded term). We use the term *integration testing* to refer to tests which ensure that each independent part of your application works correctly with the services it depends on.

Integration tests can be written in the same way as you write normal acceptance tests. Normally, integration tests should run in two contexts: firstly with the system under test running against the real external systems it depends on, or against their replicas controlled by the service provider, and secondly against a test harness which you create as part of your codebase.

It is essential to ensure that you don't hit a real external system unless you are in production, or you have some way of telling the service that you are sending it dummy transactions for testing purposes. There are two common ways to ensure that you can safely test your application without hitting a real external system, and generally you will need to employ both of them:

- Isolate access to the external system in your testing environment with a firewall, which you probably want to do in any case early on in your development process. This is also a useful technique to test the behavior of your application when the external service is unavailable.

- Have a configuration setting in your application that makes it talk to a simulated version of the external system.

In an ideal situation, the service provider will have a replica test service that behaves exactly like the production service, except in terms of its performance characteristics. You can develop your tests against this. However, in the real world, you will often need to develop a test harness of your own. This is the case when:

- The external system is under development but the interface has been defined ahead of time (in these situations, be prepared for the interface to change).

- The external system is developed already but you don't have a test instance of that system available for your testing, or the test system is too slow or buggy to act as a service for regular automated test runs.

- The test system exists, but responses are not deterministic, and so make validation of tests results impossible for automated tests (for example, a stock market feed).

- The external system takes the form of another application that is difficult to install or requires manual intervention via a UI.

- You need to write standard automated acceptance tests for functionality involving external services. These should almost always run against test doubles.

- The load that your automated continuous integration system imposes, and the service level that it requires, overwhelms the lightweight test environment that is only set up to cope with a few manual exploratory interactions.

Test harnesses can be quite sophisticated, depending, in particular, on whether the service it doubles up for remembers state or not. If the external system remembers state, your harness will behave differently according to the requests that you send. The highest-value tests that you can write in this situation are black box tests, in which you consider all the possible responses your external system can give and write a test for each of these responses. Your mock external system needs some way of identifying your request and sending back the appropriate response, or an exception if it gets a request it's not expecting.

It is essential that your test harness replicates not only the expected responses to service calls, but also unexpected ones. In *Release It!*, Michael Nygard discusses creating a test harness which simulates the kinds of pernicious behavior you can expect from remote systems that go wrong or from infrastructural problems.[3]

3. Section 5.7, pp. 136–140.

These behaviors could be due to network transport problems, network protocol problems, application protocol problems, and application logic problems. Examples include such pathological phenomena as refusing network connections, accepting them and then dropping them, accepting connections but never replying, responding extremely slowly to requests, sending back unexpectedly large amounts of data, replying with garbage, refusing credentials, sending back exceptions, or replying with a well-formed response that is invalid given the state of the application. Your test harness should be able to simulate each of these conditions, perhaps by listening on several different ports, each of which corresponds to some failure mode.

You should test your application against as many pathological situations as you can simulate to make sure it can handle them. That other patterns the Nygard describes, such as Circuit Breaker and Bulkheads, can then be used to harden your application against the kinds of unexpected events that are bound to occur in production.

Automated integration tests can be reused as smoke tests during deployment of your system into production. They can also be used as diagnostics to monitor the production system. If you identify integration problems as a risk during development, which they almost inevitably are, developing automated integration tests should be an early priority.

It is essential to incorporate activities concerning integration into your release plan. Integrating with external services is complex and requires time and planning. Every time you have to integrate with an external system, you add risks to your project:

- Will a test service be available, and will it perform well?

- Do the providers of the service have bandwidth to answer questions, fix bugs, and add custom functionality?

- Will I have access to a production version of the system that I can test against to diagnose capacity or availability problems?

- Is the service API accessible easily using the technology my application is developed with, or will we need specialist skills on the team?

- Are we going to have to write and maintain our own test service?

- How will my application perform when the external service doesn't behave as expected?

In addition, you will have to add scope for building and maintaining the integration layer and the associated runtime configuration, as well as any test services required and testing strategies such as capacity testing.

Process

The production of acceptance tests can be an expensive and even laborious task if communication between the team members isn't effective. Many projects rely on testers examining upcoming requirements in detail, going through all possible scenarios, and designing complex test scripts they will follow later. The results of this process might be sent to the customer for approval, following which the tests are implemented.

There are several points at which this process can be very simply optimized. We find that the best solution is to have a single meeting with all of the stakeholders at the beginning of each iteration, or about a week before a story will start development if you're not using iterations. We get customers, analysts, and testers in a room together and come up with the highest-priority scenarios to test. Tools like Cucumber, JBehave, Concordion, and Twist allow you to write acceptance criteria down in natural language in a text editor and then write code to make these tests executable. Refactorings to the test code also update the test specifications. Another approach is to use a domain-specific language (DSL) for testing. This allows acceptance criteria to be entered in the DSL. As a minimum, we will ask the customers to write the simplest possible acceptance tests covering the happy paths of these scenarios there and then. Later, after this meeting, people will often add more sets of data to use to improve the coverage of the tests.

These acceptance tests, and the short descriptions of their objectives, then become the starting point for developers working on the stories concerned. Testers and developers should get together as early as possible to discuss the acceptance tests before starting development. This allows developers to get a good overview of the story and understand what the most important scenarios are. This reduces the feedback cycle between developers and testers that can otherwise occur at the end of development of a story and helps reduce both missed functionality and the number of bugs.

The handover process between developers and testers at the end of the story can easily become a bottleneck. In the worst case, developers can finish a story, begin on another story, and be interrupted halfway through the new story by a tester who has raised bugs on the previous story (or even a story that was completed some time ago). This is very inefficient.

Close collaboration between developers and testers throughout the development of a story is essential to a smooth path to the release. Whenever developers finish some functionality, they should call over the testers to review it. The testers should take over the developers' machine to do this testing. During this time, developers might continue work on an adjacent terminal or laptop, perhaps fixing some outstanding regression bugs. This way they're still occupied (since testing can take some time), but are easily available in case the tester needs to discuss anything.

Managing Defect Backlogs

Ideally, bugs should never be introduced into your application in the first place. If you are practicing test-driven development and continuous integration and have a comprehensive set of automated tests including acceptance tests at the system level as well as unit and component tests, developers should be able to catch bugs before they are discovered by testers or users. However, exploratory testing, showcases, and users will inevitably discover bugs in your system. These bugs will typically end up in a defect backlog.

There are several schools of thought on what constitutes an acceptable defect backlog and how to address it. James Shore advocates having zero defects [b3m55V]. One way to achieve this is to ensure that whenever a bug is found, it is immediately fixed. This of course requires your team to be structured in such a way that testers can find bugs early, and developers can fix them straight away. However, this is not going to help if you already have a defect backlog.

Where a backlog of bugs exists, it is important for the problem to be clearly visible to everyone, and for members of the development team to be responsible for facilitating the process of reducing the backlog. In particular, having the status of your acceptance build displayed as "passed" or "failed" is not good enough if it is always failing. Instead, display the number of tests passed, the number failed, and the number ignored, and put up a graph of these numbers over time somewhere prominent. This focuses the team's attention on the problem.

The scenarios where you decide to continue with a backlog of defects are risky. This is a slippery slope. Many development teams and development processes in the past ignored significant numbers of bugs, deferring the effort to fix them to some more convenient time in the future. After a few months, this almost inevitably leads to a huge list of bugs, of which some will never be fixed, some are no longer relevant since the functionality of the application has changed, and some are critical to some user but have been lost in all the noise.

The problem is even worse when there are no acceptance tests or where acceptance tests are not effective because features are being developed on branches that are not merged regularly to trunk. In this case, it is all too common, once the code is integrated and manual system-level testing starts, for teams to become completely overwhelmed by defects. Arguments break out between testers, developers, and management, release dates slip, and users get landed with poor-quality software. This is a case where many defects could have been prevented by following a better process. See Chapter 14, "Advanced Version Control," for more details.

Another approach is to treat defects the same way as features. After all, working on a bug takes time and effort away from working on some other feature, so it is up to the customer to prioritize the relative importance of a particular bug against that feature. For example, a rare defect with a known workaround in an administrative screen with only a couple of users may not be so important to fix as a new revenue-generating feature for the application as a whole. At the very least, it makes sense to classify bugs as "critical," "blockers," "medium," and "low" priority. A more comprehensive approach might take account of how often the bug occurs, what its effect on the user is, and if there is a workaround.

Given this classification, bugs can be prioritized in your backlog in the same way as stories, and they can appear together. Apart from immediately removing arguments about whether a particular piece of work is a defect or a feature, it means you can see at a glance exactly how much work remains to be done and prioritize it accordingly. Low-priority bugs will go way back in your backlog, and you can treat them the same way you would treat a low-priority story. It is often the case that customers would rather not fix some bugs—so having bugs in the backlog along with features is a logical way to manage them.

Summary

In many projects, testing is treated as a distinct phase carried out by specialists. However, high-quality software is only possible if testing becomes the responsibility of everybody involved in delivering software and is practiced right from the beginning of the project and throughout its life. Testing is primarily concerned with establishing feedback loops that drive development, design, and release. Any plan that defers testing to the end of the project is broken because it removes the feedback loop that generates higher quality, higher productivity, and, most importantly of all, any measure of how complete the project is.

The shortest feedback loops are created through sets of automated tests that are run upon every change to the system. Such tests should run at all levels—from unit tests up to acceptance tests (both functional and nonfunctional). Automated tests should be supplemented with manual testing such as exploratory testing and showcases. This chapter aims to give you a good understanding of the various types of automated and manual tests required to create excellent feedback and how to implement them on various types of projects.

In the principles that we described in the "Introduction" section on page 83, we discuss what defines "done." Incorporating testing into every part of your delivery process is vital to getting work done. Since our approach to testing defines our understanding of "done," the results of testing are the cornerstone of project planning.

Testing is fundamentally interconnected with your definition of "done," and your testing strategy should be focused on being able to deliver that understanding feature by feature and ensuring that testing is pervasive throughout your process.

Part II

The Deployment Pipeline

Chapter 5

Anatomy of the Deployment Pipeline

Introduction

Continuous integration is an enormous step forward in productivity and quality for most projects that adopt it. It ensures that teams working together to create large and complex systems can do so with a higher level of confidence and control than is achievable without it. CI ensures that the code that we create, as a team, works by providing us with rapid feedback on any problems that we may introduce with the changes we commit. It is primarily focused on asserting that the code compiles successfully and passes a body of unit and acceptance tests. However, CI is not enough.

CI mainly focuses on development teams. The output of the CI system normally forms the input to the manual testing process and thence to the rest of the release process. Much of the waste in releasing software comes from the progress of software through testing and operations. For example, it is common to see

- Build and operations teams waiting for documentation or fixes

- Testers waiting for "good" builds of the software

- Development teams receiving bug reports weeks after the team has moved on to new functionality

- Discovering, towards the end of the development process, that the application's architecture will not support the system's nonfunctional requirements

This leads to software that is undeployable because it has taken so long to get it into a production-like environment, and buggy because the feedback cycle between the development team and the testing and operations team is so long.

There are various incremental improvements to the way software is delivered which will yield immediate benefits, such as teaching developers to write production-ready software, running CI on production-like systems, and instituting cross-functional teams. However, while practices like these will certainly improve

105

matters, they still don't give you an insight into where the bottlenecks are in the delivery process or how to optimize for them.

The solution is to adopt a more holistic, end-to-end approach to delivering software. We have addressed the broader issues of configuration management and automating large swathes of our build, deploy, test, and release processes. We have taken this to the point where deploying our applications, even to production, is often done by a simple click of a button to select the build that we wish to deploy. This creates a powerful feedback loop: Since it's so simple to deploy your application to testing environments, your team gets rapid feedback on both the code and the deployment process. Since the deployment process (whether to a development machine or for final release) is automated, it gets run and therefore tested regularly, lowering the risk of a release and transferring knowledge of the deployment process to the development team.

What we end up with is (in lean parlance) a *pull system*. Testing teams deploy builds into testing environments themselves, at the push of a button. Operations can deploy builds into staging and production environments at the push of a button. Developers can see which builds have been through which stages in the release process, and what problems were found. Managers can watch such key metrics as cycle time, throughput, and code quality. As a result, everybody in the delivery process gets two things: access to the things they need when they need them, and visibility into the release process to improve feedback so that bottlenecks can be identified, optimized, and removed. This leads to a delivery process which is not only faster but also safer.

The implementation of end-to-end automation of our build, deploy, test, and release processes has had a number of knock-on effects, bringing some unexpected benefits. One such outcome is that over the course of many projects utilizing such techniques, we have identified much in common between the deployment pipeline systems that we have built. We believe that with the abstractions we have identified, some general patterns have, so far, fit all of the projects in which we have tried them. This understanding has allowed us to get fairly sophisticated build, test, and deployment systems up and running very quickly from the start of our projects. These end-to-end deployment pipeline systems have meant that we have experienced a degree of freedom and flexibility in our delivery projects that would have been hard to imagine a few years ago. We are convinced that this approach has allowed us to create, test, and deploy complex systems of higher quality and at significantly lower cost and risk than we could otherwise have done.

This is what the deployment pipeline is for.

What Is a Deployment Pipeline?

At an abstract level, a deployment pipeline is an automated manifestation of your process for getting software from version control into the hands of your users. Every change to your software goes through a complex process on its way to being released. That process involves building the software, followed by the progress of these builds through multiple stages of testing and deployment. This, in turn, requires collaboration between many individuals, and perhaps several teams. The deployment pipeline models this process, and its incarnation in a continuous integration and release management tool is what allows you to see and control the progress of each change as it moves from version control through various sets of tests and deployments to release to users.

Thus the process modeled by the deployment pipeline, the process of getting software from check-in to release, forms a part of the process of getting a feature from the mind of a customer or user into their hands. The entire process—from concept to cash—can be modeled as a value stream map. A high-level value stream map for the creation of a new product is shown in Figure 5.1.

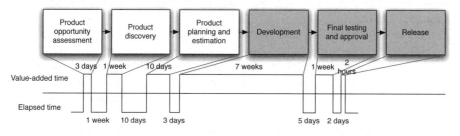

Figure 5.1 *A simple value stream map for a product*

This value stream map tells a story. The whole process takes about three and a half months. About two and a half months of that is actual work being done—there are waits between the various stages in the process of getting the software from concept to cash. For example, there is a five-day wait between the development team completing work on the first release and the start of the testing process. This might be due to the time it takes to deploy the application to a production-like environment, for example. As an aside, it has been left deliberately unclear in this diagram whether or not this product is being developed in an iterative way. In an iterative process, you'd expect to see the development process itself consist of several iterations which include testing and showcasing. The whole process from discovery to release would also be repeated many times[1]

Creating a value stream map can be a low-tech process. In Mary and Tom Poppendieck's classic, *Lean Software Development: An Agile Toolkit*, they describe it as follows.

---

1. The importance of iterative discovery based on customer feedback in the product development process is emphasized in books like *Inspired* by Marty Cagan and *The Four Steps to the Epiphany* by Steven Gary Blank.

With a pencil and pad in hand, go to the place where a customer request comes into your organization. You goal is to draw a chart of the average customer request, from arrival to completion. Working with the people involved in each activity, you sketch all the process steps necessary to fill the request, as well as the average amount of time that a request spends in each step. At the bottom of the map, draw a timeline that shows how much time the request spends in value-adding activities and how much in waiting states and non-value-adding activities.

If you were interested in doing some organizational transformation work to improve the process, you would need to go into even more detail and describe who is responsible for which part of the process, what subprocesses occur in exceptional conditions, who approves the hand-offs, what resources are required, what the organizational reporting structures are, and so forth. However, that's not necessary for our discussion here. For more details on this, consult Mary and Tom Poppendieck's book *Implementing Lean Software Development: From Concept to Cash*.

The part of the value stream we discuss in this book is the one that goes from development through to release. These are the shaded boxes in the value stream in Figure 5.1. One key difference of this part of the value stream is that builds pass through it many times on their way to release. In fact, one way to understand the deployment pipeline and how changes move through it is to visualize it as a sequence diagram,[2] as shown in Figure 5.2.

Notice that the input to the pipeline is a particular revision in version control. Every change creates a build that will, rather like some mythical hero, pass through a sequence of tests of, and challenges to, its viability as a production release. This process of a sequence of test stages, each evaluating the build from a different perspective, is begun with every commit to the version control system, in the same way as the initiation of a continuous integration process.

As the build passes each test of its fitness, confidence in it increases. Therefore, the resources that we are willing to expend on it increase, which means that the environments the build passes through become progressively more production-like. The objective is to eliminate unfit release candidates as early in the process as we can and get feedback on the root cause of failure to the team as rapidly as possible. To this end, any build that fails a stage in the process will not generally be promoted to the next. These trade-offs are shown in Figure 5.3.

There are some important consequences of applying this pattern. First, you are effectively prevented from releasing into production builds that are not thoroughly tested and found to be fit for their intended purpose. Regression bugs are avoided, especially where urgent fixes need releasing into production (such fixes go through the same process as any other change). In our experience, it is also extremely common for newly released software to break down due to some unforeseen interaction between the components of the system and its environment, for example due to a new network topology or a slight difference in the

---

2. Chris Read came up with this idea [9EIHHS].

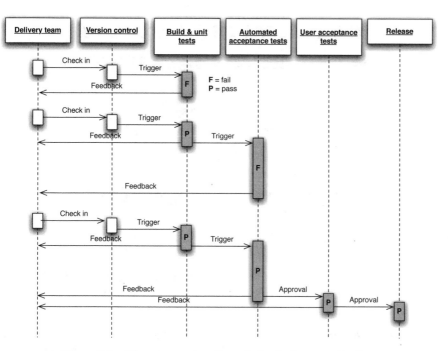

Figure 5.2 *Changes moving through the deployment pipeline*

configuration of a production server. The discipline of the deployment pipeline mitigates this.

Second, when deployment and production release themselves are automated, they are rapid, repeatable, and reliable. It is often so much easier to perform a release once the process is automated that they become "normal" events—meaning that, should you choose, you can perform releases more frequently. This is particularly the case where you are able to step back to an earlier version as well as move forward. When this capability is available, releases are essentially without risk. The worst that can happen is that you find that you have introduced a critical bug—at which point you revert to an earlier version that doesn't contain the bug while you fix the new release offline (see Chapter 10, "Deploying and Releasing Applications").

To achieve this enviable state, we must automate a suite of tests that prove that our release candidates are fit for their purpose. We must also automate deployment to testing, staging, and production environments to remove these manually intensive, error-prone steps. For many systems, other forms of testing and so other stages in the release process are also needed, but the subset that is common to all projects is as follows.

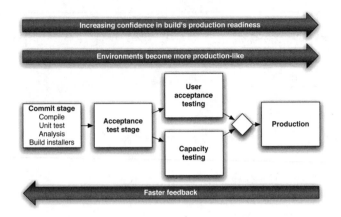

Figure 5.3 *Trade-offs in the deployment pipeline*

- *The commit stage* asserts that the system works at the technical level. It compiles, passes a suite of (primarily unit-level) automated tests, and runs code analysis.

- *Automated acceptance test stages* assert that the system works at the functional and nonfunctional level, that behaviorally it meets the needs of its users and the specifications of the customer.

- *Manual test stages* assert that the system is usable and fulfills its requirements, detect any defects not caught by automated tests, and verify that it provides value to its users. These stages might typically include exploratory testing environments, integration environments, and UAT (user acceptance testing).

- *Release stage* delivers the system to users, either as packaged software or by deploying it into a production or staging environment (a staging environment is a testing environment identical to the production environment).

We refer to these stages, and any additional ones that may be required to model your process for delivering software, as a *deployment pipeline*. It is also sometimes referred to as a continuous integration pipeline, a build pipeline, a deployment production line, or a living build. Whatever it is called, this is, fundamentally, an automated software delivery process. This is not intended to imply that there is no human interaction with the system through this release process; rather, it ensures that error-prone and complex steps are automated, reliable, and repeatable in execution. In fact, human interaction is increased: The ability to deploy the system at all stages of its development by pressing a button encourages its frequent use by testers, analysts, developers, and (most importantly) users.

A Basic Deployment Pipeline

Figure 5.4 shows a typical deployment pipeline and captures the essence of the approach. Of course, a real pipeline will reflect your project's actual process for delivering software.

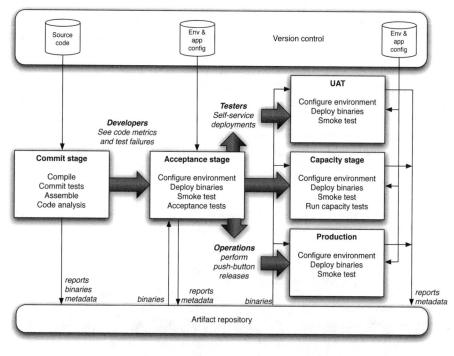

Figure 5.4 *Basic deployment pipeline*

The process starts with the developers committing changes into their version control system. At this point, the continuous integration management system responds to the commit by triggering a new instance of our pipeline. The first (commit) stage of the pipeline compiles the code, runs unit tests, performs code analysis, and creates installers. If the unit tests all pass and the code is up to scratch, we assemble the executable code into binaries and store them in an artifact repository. Modern CI servers provide a facility to store artifacts like these and make them easily accessible both to the users and to the later stages in your pipeline. Alternatively, there are plenty of tools like Nexus and Artifactory which help you manage artifacts. There are other tasks that you might also run as part of the commit stage of your pipeline, such as preparing a test database to use for your acceptance tests. Modern CI servers will let you execute these jobs in parallel on a build grid.

The second stage is typically composed of longer-running automated acceptance tests. Again, your CI server should let you split these tests into suites which can be executed in parallel to increase their speed and give you feedback faster—typically within an hour or two. This stage will be triggered automatically by the successful completion of the first stage in your pipeline.

At this point, the pipeline branches to enable independent deployment of your build to various environments—in this case, UAT (user acceptance testing), capacity testing, and production. Often, you won't want these stages to be automatically triggered by the successful completion of your acceptance test stage. Instead, you'll want your testers or operations team to be able to self-service builds into their environments manually. To facilitate this, you'll need an automated script that performs this deployment. Your testers should be able to see the release candidates available to them as well as their status—which of the previous two stages each build has passed, what were the check-in comments, and any other comments on those builds. They should then be able to press a button to deploy the selected build by running the deployment script in the relevant environment.

The same principle applies to further stages in the pipeline, except that, typically, the various environments you want to be able to deploy to will have different groups of users who "own" these environments and have the ability to self-service deployments to them. For example, your operations team will likely want to be the only one who can approve deployments to production.

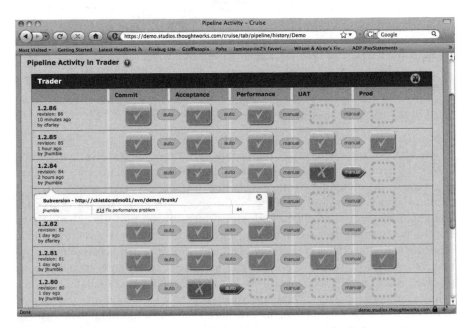

Figure 5.5 *Go showing which changes have passed which stages*

Finally, it's important to remember that the purpose of all this is to get feedback as fast as possible. To make the feedback cycle fast, you need to be able to see which build is deployed into which environment, and which stages in your pipeline each build has passed. Figure 5.5 is a screenshot from Go showing what this looks like in practice.

Notice that you can see every check-in down the side of the page, every stage in the pipeline that each check-in has been through, and whether it passed or failed that stage. Being able to correlate a particular check-in, and hence build, to the stages in the pipeline it has passed through is crucial. It means that if you see a problem in the acceptance tests (for example), you can immediately find out which changes were checked into version control that resulted in the acceptance tests failing.

Deployment Pipeline Practices

Shortly, we'll go into some more detail on the stages in the deployment pipeline. But before we do so, in order to get the benefits of this approach, there are some practices you should follow.

Only Build Your Binaries Once

For convenience, we will refer to the collections of executable code as binaries, although if you don't need to compile your code these "binaries" may be just collections of source files. Jars, .NET assemblies, and .so files are all examples of binaries.

Many build systems use the source code held in the version control system as the canonical source for many steps. The code will be compiled repeatedly in different contexts: during the commit process, again at acceptance test time, again for capacity testing, and often once for each separate deployment target. Every time you compile the code, you run the risk of introducing some difference. The version of the compiler installed in the later stages may be different from the version that you used for your commit tests. You may pick up a different version of some third-party library that you didn't intend. Even the configuration of the compiler may change the behavior of the application. We have seen bugs from every one of these sources reaching production.

 A related antipattern is to promote at the source-code level rather than at the binary level. For more information on this antipattern, see the "ClearCase and the Rebuilding-from-Source Antipattern" section on page 403.

This antipattern violates two important principles. The first is to keep the deployment pipeline efficient, so the team gets feedback as soon as possible. Recompiling violates this principle because it takes time, especially in large systems. The second principle is to always build upon foundations known to be sound. The binaries that get deployed into production should be exactly the same as those that went through the acceptance test process—and indeed in many pipeline implementations, this is checked by storing hashes of the binaries at the time they are created and verifying that the binary is identical at every subsequent stage in the process.

If we re-create binaries, we run the risk that some change will be introduced between the creation of the binaries and their release, such as a change in the toolchain between compilations, and that the binary we release will be different from the one we tested. For auditing purposes, it is essential to ensure that no changes have been introduced, either maliciously or by mistake, between creating the binaries and performing the release. Some organizations insist that compilation and assembly, or packaging in the case of interpreted languages, occurs in a special environment that cannot be accessed by anyone except senior personnel. Once we have created our binaries, we will reuse them without re-creating them at the point of use.

So, you should only build your binaries once, during the commit stage of the build. These binaries should be stored on a filesystem somewhere (not in version control, since they are derivatives of your baseline, not part of its definition) where it is easy to retrieve them for later stages in the pipeline. Most CI servers will handle this for you, and will also perform the crucial task of allowing you to trace back to the version control check-in which was used to create them. It isn't worth spending a lot of time and effort ensuring binaries are backed up—it should be possible to exactly re-create them by running your automated build process from the correct revision in version control.

 If you take our advice, it will initially feel as though you have more work to do. You will need to establish some way of propagating your binaries to the later stages in the deployment pipeline, if your CI tool doesn't do this for you already. Some of the simplistic configuration management tools that come with popular development environments will be doing the wrong thing. A notable example of this is project templates that directly generate assemblies containing both code and configuration files, such as ear and war files, as a single step in the build process.

One important corollary of this principle is that it must be possible to deploy these binaries to every environment. This forces you to separate code, which remains the same between environments, and configuration, which differs between environments. This, in turn, will lead you to managing your configuration correctly, applying a gentle pressure towards better-structured build systems.

> **Why Binaries Should Not Be Environment-Specific**
>
> We consider it a very bad practice to create binary files intended to run in a single environment. This approach, while common, has several serious drawbacks that compromise the overall ease of deployment, flexibility, and maintainability of the system. Some tools even encourage this approach.
>
> When build systems are organized in this way, they usually become very complex very quickly, spawning lots of special-case hacks to cope with the differences and the vagaries of various deployment environments. On one project that we worked on, the build system was so complex that it took a full-time team of five people to maintain it. Eventually, we relieved them of this unpopular job by reorganizing the build and separating the environment-specific configuration from the environment-agnostic binaries.
>
> Such build systems make unnecessarily complex what should be trivial tasks, such as adding a new server to a cluster. This, in turn, forces us into fragile, expensive release processes. If your build creates binaries that only run on specific machines, start planning how to restructure them now!

This brings us neatly to the next practice.

Deploy the Same Way to Every Environment

It is essential to use the same process to deploy to every environment—whether a developer or analyst's workstation, a testing environment, or production—in order to ensure that the build and deployment process is tested effectively. Developers deploy all the time; testers and analysts, less often; and usually, you will deploy to production fairly infrequently. But this frequency of deployment is the inverse of the risk associated with each environment. The environment you deploy to least frequently (production) is the most important. Only after you have tested the deployment process hundreds of times on many environments can you eliminate the deployment script as a source of error.

Every environment is different in some way. If nothing else, it will have a unique IP address, but often there are other differences: operating system and middleware configuration settings, the location of databases and external services, and other configuration information that needs to be set at deployment time. This does not mean you should use a different deployment script for every environment. Instead, keep the settings that are unique for each environment separate. One way to do this is to use properties files to hold configuration information. You can have a separate properties file for each environment. These files should be checked in to version control, and the correct one selected either by looking at the hostname of the local server, or (in a multimachine environment) through the use of an environment variable supplied to the deployment script. Some other ways to supply deploy-time configuration include keeping it in a directory service (like LDAP or ActiveDirectory) or storing it in a database and accessing it through an application like ESCAPE [apvrEr]. There is more on managing software configuration in the "Managing Software Configuration" section on page 39.

It's important to use the same deploy-time configuration mechanism for each of your applications. This is especially true in a large company, or where many heterogeneous technologies are in play. Generally, we're against handing down edicts from on high—but we've seen too many organizations where it was impossibly arduous to work out, for a given application in a given environment, what configuration was actually supplied at deployment time. We know places where you have to email separate teams on separate continents to piece together this information. This becomes an enormous barrier to efficiency when you're trying to work out the root cause of some bug—and when you add together the delays it introduces into your value stream, it is incredibly costly.

It should be possible to consult one single source (a version control repository, a directory service, or a database) to find configuration settings for all your applications in all of your environments.

If you work in a company where production environments are managed by a team different from the team responsible for development and testing environments, both teams will need to work together to make sure the automated deployment process works effectively across all environments, including development environments. Using the same script to deploy to production that you use to deploy to development environments is a fantastic way to prevent the "it works on my machine" syndrome [c29ETR]. It also means that when you come to release, you will have tested your deployment process hundreds of times by deploying to all of your other environments. This is one of the best ways we know to mitigate the risk of releasing software.

We've assumed that you have an automated process for deploying your application—but, of course, many organizations still deploy manually. If you have a manual deployment process, you should start by ensuring that the process is the same for every environment and then begin to automate it bit by bit, with the goal of having it fully scripted. Ultimately, you should only need to specify the target environment and the version of the application to initiate a successful deployment. An automated, standardized deployment process will have a huge positive effect on your ability to release your application repeatably and reliably, and ensure that the process is completely documented and audited. We cover automating deployment in detail in the following chapter.

This principle is really another application of the rule that you should separate what changes from what doesn't. If your deployment script is different for different environments, you have no way of knowing that what you're testing will actually work when you go live. Instead, if you use the same process to deploy everywhere, when a deployment doesn't work to a particular environment you can narrow it down to one of three causes:

- A setting in your application's environment-specific configuration file

- A problem with your infrastructure or one of the services on which your application depends

- The configuration of your environment

Establishing which of these is the underlying cause is the subject of the next two practices.

Smoke-Test Your Deployments

When you deploy your application, you should have an automated script that does a smoke test to make sure that it is up and running. This could be as simple as launching the application and checking to make sure that the main screen comes up with the expected content. Your smoke test should also check that any services your application depends on are up and running—such as a database, messaging bus, or external service.

The smoke test, or deployment test, is probably the most important test to write once you have a unit test suite up and running—indeed, it's arguably even more important. It gives you the confidence that your application actually runs. If it doesn't run, your smoke test should be able to give you some basic diagnostics as to whether your application is down because something it depends on is not working.

Deploy into a Copy of Production

The other main problem many teams experience going live is that their production environment is significantly different from their testing and development environments. To get a good level of confidence that going live will actually work, you need to do your testing and continuous integration on environments that are as similar as possible to your production environment.

Ideally, if your production environment is simple or you have a sufficiently large budget, you can have exact copies of production to run your manual and automated tests on. Making sure that your environments are the same requires a certain amount of discipline to apply good configuration management practices. You need to ensure that:

- Your infrastructure, such as network topology and firewall configuration, is the same.

- Your operating system configuration, including patches, is the same.

- Your application stack is the same.

- Your application's data is in a known, valid state. Migrating data when performing upgrades can be a major source of pain in deployments. We deal more with this topic in Chapter 12, "Managing Data."

You can use such practices as disk imaging and virtualization, and tools like Puppet and InstallShield along with a version control repository, to manage your environments' configuration. We discuss this in detail in Chapter 11, "Managing Infrastructure and Environments."

Each Change Should Propagate through the Pipeline Instantly

Before continuous integration was introduced, many projects ran various parts of their process off a schedule—for example, builds might run hourly, acceptance tests nightly, and capacity tests over the weekend. The deployment pipeline takes a different approach: The first stage should be triggered upon every check-in, and each stage should trigger the next one immediately upon successful completion. Of course this is not always possible when developers (especially on large teams) are checking in very frequently, given that the stages in your process can take a not insignificant amount of time. The problem is shown in Figure 5.6.

In this example, somebody checks a change into version control, creating version 1. This, in turn, triggers the first stage in the pipeline (build and unit tests). This passes, and triggers the second stage: the automated acceptance tests. Somebody then checks in another change, creating version 2. This triggers the build and unit tests again. However, even though these have passed, they cannot trigger a new instance of the automated acceptance tests, since they are already running. In the meantime, two more check-ins have occurred in quick succession. However, the CI system should not attempt to build both of them—if it followed that rule, and developers continued to check in at the same rate, the builds would get further and further behind what the developers are currently doing.

Instead, once an instance of the build and unit tests has finished, the CI system checks to see if new changes are available, and if so, builds off the most recent set available—in this case, version 4. Suppose this breaks the build and unit tests stage. The build system doesn't know which commit, 3 or 4, caused the stage to break, but it is usually simple for the developers to work this out for themselves. Some CI systems will let you run specified versions out of order, in which case the developers could trigger the first stage off revision 3 to see if it passes or fails, and thus whether it was commit 3 or 4 that broke the build. Either way, the development team checks in version 5, which fixes the problem.

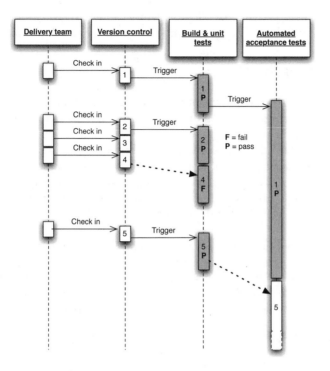

Figure 5.6   *Scheduling stages in a pipeline*

When the acceptance tests finally finish, the CI system's scheduler notices that new changes are available, and triggers a new run of the acceptance tests against version 5.

This intelligent scheduling is crucial to implementing a deployment pipeline. Make sure your CI server supports this kind of scheduling workflow—many do—and ensure that changes propagate immediately so that you don't have to run stages off a fixed schedule.

This only applies to stages that are fully automated, such as those containing automated tests. The later stages in the pipeline that perform deployments to manual testing environments need to be activated on demand, which we describe in a later section in this chapter.

If Any Part of the Pipeline Fails, Stop the Line

As we said in the "Implementing Continuous Integration" section on page 56, the most important step in achieving the goals of this book—rapid, repeatable, reliable releases—is for your team to accept that every time they check code into version control, it will successfully build and pass every test. This applies to the entire deployment pipeline. If a deployment to an environment fails, the whole team owns that failure. They should stop and fix it before doing anything else.

The Commit Stage

A new instance of your deployment pipeline is created upon every check-in and, if the first stage passes, results in the creation of a release candidate. The aim of the first stage in the pipeline is to eliminate builds that are unfit for production and signal the team that the application is broken as quickly as possible. We want to expend a minimum of time and effort on a version of the application that is obviously broken. So, when a developer commits a change to the version control system, we want to evaluate the latest version of the application quickly. The developer who checked in then waits for the results before moving on to the next task.

There are a few things we want to do as part of our commit stage. Typically, these tasks are run as a set of jobs on a build grid (a facility provided by most CI servers) so the stage completes in a reasonable length of time. The commit stage should ideally take less than five minutes to run, and certainly no more than ten minutes. The commit stage typically includes the following steps:

- Compile the code (if necessary).

- Run a set of commit tests.

- Create binaries for use by later stages.

- Perform analysis of the code to check its health.

- Prepare artifacts, such as test databases, for use by later stages.

The first step is to compile the latest version of the source code and notify the developers who committed changes since the last successful check-in if there is an error in compilation. If this step fails, we can fail the commit stage immediately and eliminate this instance of the pipeline from further consideration.

Next, a suite of tests is run, optimized to execute very quickly. We refer to this suite of tests as commit stage tests rather than unit tests because, although the vast majority of them are indeed unit tests, it is useful to include a small selection of tests of other types at this stage in order to get a higher level of confidence that the application is really working if the commit stage passes. These are the same tests that developers run before they check in their code (or, if they have the facility to do so, through a pretested commit on the build grid).

Begin the design of your commit test suite by running all unit tests. Later, as you learn more about what types of failure are common in acceptance test runs and other later stages in the pipeline, you should add specific tests to your commit test suite to try and find them early on. This is an ongoing process optimization that is important if you are to avoid the higher costs of finding and fixing bugs in later pipeline stages.

Establishing that your code compiles and passes tests is great, but it doesn't tell you a lot about the nonfunctional characteristics of your application. Testing nonfunctional characteristics such as capacity can be hard, but you can run analysis tools giving you feedback on such characteristics of your code base as test coverage, maintainability, and security breaches. Failure of your code to meet preset thresholds for these metrics should fail the commit stage the same way that a failing test does. Useful metrics include:

- Test coverage (if your commit tests only cover 5% of your codebase, they're pretty useless)

- Amount of duplicated code

- Cyclomatic complexity

- Afferent and efferent coupling

- Number of warnings

- Code style

The final step in the commit stage, following successful execution of everything up to this point, is the creation of a deployable assembly of your code ready for deployment into any subsequent environment. This, too, must succeed for the commit stage to be considered a success as a whole. Treating the creation of the executable code as a success criteria in its own right is a simple way of ensuring that our build process itself is also under constant evaluation and review by our continuous integration system.

Commit Stage Best Practices

Most of the practices described in Chapter 3, "Continuous Integration," apply to the commit stage. Developers are expected to wait until the commit stage of the deployment pipeline succeeds. If it fails, they should either quickly fix the problem, or back their changes out from version control. In the ideal world—a world of infinite processor power and unlimited network bandwidth—we would like our developers to wait for all tests to pass, even the manual ones, so that they could fix any problem immediately. In reality, this is not practical, as the later stages in the deployment pipeline (automated acceptance testing, capacity testing, and manual acceptance testing) are lengthy activities. This is the reason for pipelining your test process—it's important to get feedback as quickly as possible, when problems are cheap to fix, but not at the expense of getting more comprehensive feedback when it becomes available.

The Origin of the Term "Deployment Pipeline"

When we first used this idea, we named it a pipeline not because it was like a liquid flowing through a pipe; rather, for the hardcore geeks amongst us, it reminded us of the way processors "pipeline" their instruction execution in order to get a degree of parallelism. Processor chips can execute instructions in parallel. But how do you take a stream of machine instructions intended to be executed serially and divide them up into parallel streams that make sense? The way processors do this is very clever and quite complex, but in essence they often come to points where they effectively "guess" the result of an operation in a separate execution pipeline and start executing on the assumption of that guess. If the guess is later found to be wrong, the results of the stream that was based on it are simply dumped. There has been no gain—but no loss either. However, if the guess was good, the processor has just done twice as much work in the time it would take a single stream of execution—so for that spell, it was running twice as fast.

Our deployment pipeline concept works in the same way. We design our commit stage so that it will catch the majority of problems, while running very quickly. As a result, we make a "guess" that all of our subsequent test stages will pass, so we resume work on new features, preparing for the next commit and the initiation of the next release candidate. Meanwhile, our pipeline optimistically works on our assumption of success, in parallel to our development of new features.

Passing the commit stage is an important milestone in the journey of a release candidate. It is a gate in our process that, once passed, frees developers to move on to their next task. However, they retain a responsibility to monitor the progress of the later stages too. Fixing broken builds remains the top priority for the development team even when those breakages occur in the later stages of the pipeline. We are gambling on success—but are ready to pay our technical debts should our gamble fail.

If you only implement a commit stage in your development process, it usually represents an enormous step forward in the reliability and quality of the output of your teams. However, there are several more stages necessary to complete what we consider to be a minimal deployment pipeline.

The Automated Acceptance Test Gate

A comprehensive commit test suite is an excellent litmus test for many classes of errors, but there is much that it won't catch. Unit tests, which comprise the vast majority of the commit tests, are so coupled to the low-level API that it is often hard for the developers to avoid the trap of proving that the solution works in a particular way, rather than asserting that is solves a particular problem.

Why Unit Tests Aren't Enough

We once worked on a large project with around 80 developers. The system was developed using continuous integration at the heart of our development process. As a team, our build discipline was pretty good; we needed it to be with a team of this size.

One day we deployed the latest build that had passed our unit tests into a test environment. This was a lengthy but controlled approach to deployment that our environment specialists carried out. However, the system didn't seem to work. We spent a lot of time trying to find what was wrong with the configuration of the environment, but we couldn't find the problem. Then one of our senior developers tried the application on his development machine. It didn't work there either.

He stepped back through earlier and earlier versions, until he found that the system had actually stopped working three weeks earlier. A tiny, obscure bug had prevented the system from starting correctly.

This project had good unit test coverage, with the average for all modules around 90%. Despite this, 80 developers, who usually only ran the tests rather than the application itself, did not see the problem for three weeks.

We fixed the bug and introduced a couple of simple, automated smoke tests that proved that the application ran and could perform its most fundamental function as part of our continuous integration process.

We learned a lot of lessons from this and many other experiences on this big complex project. But the most fundamental one was that unit tests only test a developer's perspective of the solution to a problem. They have only a limited ability to prove that the application does what it is supposed to from a users perspective. If we want to be sure that the application provides to its users the value that we hope it will, we will need another form of test. Our developers could have achieved this by running the application more frequently themselves and interacting with it. This would have solved the specific problem that we described above, but it is not a very effective approach for a big complex application.

This story also points to another common failing in the development process that we were using. Our first assumption was that there was a problem with our deployment—that we had somehow misconfigured the system when we deployed it to our test environment. This was a fair assumption, because that sort of failure was quite common. Deploying the application was a complex, manually intensive process that was quite prone to error.

So, although we had a sophisticated, well-managed, disciplined continuous integration process in place, we still could not be confident that we could identify real functional problems. Nor could we be sure that, when it came time to deploy the system, further errors would not be introduced. Furthermore, since deployments took so long, it was often the case that the process for deployment would change every time the deployment happened. This meant that every attempt at deployment was a new experiment—a manual, error-prone process. This created a vicious circle which meant very high-risk releases.

Commit tests that run against every check-in provide us with timely feedback on problems with the latest build and on bugs in our application in the small. But without running acceptance tests in a production-like environment, we know nothing about whether the application meets the customer's specifications, nor whether it can be deployed and survive in the real world. If we want timely feedback on these topics, we must extend the range of our continuous integration process to test and rehearse these aspects of our system too.

The relationship of the automated acceptance test stage of our deployment pipeline to functional acceptance testing is similar to that of the commit stage to unit testing. The majority of tests running during the acceptance test stage are functional acceptance tests, but not all.

The goal of the acceptance test stage is to assert that the system delivers the value the customer is expecting and that it meets the acceptance criteria. The acceptance test stage also serves as a regression test suite, verifying that no bugs are introduced into existing behavior by new changes. As we describe in Chapter 8, "Automated Acceptance Testing," the process of creating and maintaining automated acceptance tests is not carried out by separate teams but is brought into the heart of the development process and carried out by cross-functional delivery teams. Developers, testers, and customers work together to create these tests alongside the unit tests and the code they write as part of their normal development process.

Crucially, the development team must respond immediately to acceptance test breakages that occur as part of the normal development process. They must decide if the breakage is a result of a regression that has been introduced, an intentional change in the behavior of the application, or a problem with the test. Then they must take the appropriate action to get the automated acceptance test suite passing again.

The automated acceptance test gate is the second significant milestone in the lifecycle of a release candidate. The deployment pipeline will only allow the later stages, such as manually requested deployments, to access builds that have successfully overcome the hurdle of automated acceptance testing. While it is possible to try and subvert the system, this is so time-consuming and expensive that the effort is much better spent on fixing the problem that the deployment pipeline has identified and deploying in the controlled and repeatable manner it supports. The deployment pipeline makes it easier to do the right thing than to do the wrong thing, so teams do the right thing.

Thus a release candidate that does not meet all of its acceptance criteria will never get released to users.

Automated Acceptance Test Best Practices

It is important to consider the environments that your application will encounter in production. If you're only deploying to a single production environment under your control, you're lucky. Simply run your acceptance tests on a copy of this environment. If the production environment is complex or expensive, you can use a scaled-down version of it, perhaps using a couple of middleware servers while there might be many of them in production. If your application depends on external services, you can use test doubles for any external infrastructure that you depend on. We go into more detail on these approaches in Chapter 8, "Automated Acceptance Testing."

If you have to target many different environments, for example if you're developing software that has to be installed on a user's computer, you will need to run acceptance tests on a selection of likely target environments. This is most easily accomplished with a build grid. Set up a selection of test environments, at least one for each target test environment, and run acceptance tests in parallel on all of them.

In many organizations where automated functional testing is done at all, a common practice is to have a separate team dedicated to the production and maintenance of the test suite. As described at length in Chapter 4, "Implementing a Testing Strategy," this is a bad idea. The most problematic outcome is that the developers don't feel as if they own the acceptance tests. As a result, they tend not to pay attention to the failure of this stage of the deployment pipeline, which leads to it being broken for long periods of time. Acceptance tests written without developer involvement also tend to be tightly coupled to the UI and thus brittle and badly factored, because the testers don't have any insight into the UI's underlying design and lack the skills to create abstraction layers or run acceptance tests against a public API.

The reality is that *the whole team owns the acceptance tests*, in the same way as the whole team owns every stage of the pipeline. If the acceptance tests fail, the whole team should stop and fix them immediately.

One important corollary of this practice is that developers must be able to run automated acceptance tests on their development environments. It should be easy for a developer who finds an acceptance test failure to fix it easily on their own machine and verify the fix by running that acceptance test locally. The most common obstacles to this are insufficient licenses for the testing software being used and an application architecture that prevents the system from being deployed on a development environment so that the acceptance tests can be run against it. If your automated acceptance testing strategy is to succeed in the long term, these kinds of obstacles need to be removed.

It can be easy for acceptance tests to become too tightly coupled to a particular solution in the application rather than asserting the business value of the system. When this happens, more and more time is spent maintaining the acceptance tests as small changes in the behavior of the system invalidate tests. Acceptance tests should be expressed in the language of the business (what Eric Evans calls the "ubiquitous language"[3]), not in the language of the technology of the application. By this we mean that while it is fine to write the acceptance tests in the

3. Evans, 2004.

same programming language that your team uses for development, the abstraction should work at the level of business behavior—"place order" rather than "click order button," "confirm fund transfer" rather than "check fund_table has results," and so on.

While acceptance tests are extremely valuable, they can also be expensive to create and maintain. It is thus essential to bear in mind that automated acceptance tests are also regression tests. Don't follow a naive process of taking your acceptance criteria and blindly automating every one.

We have worked on several projects that found, as a result of following some of the bad practices described above, that the automated functional tests were not delivering enough value. They were costing far too much to maintain, and so automated functional testing was stopped. This is the right decision if the tests cost more effort than they save, but changing the way the creation and maintenance of the tests are managed can dramatically reduce the effort expended and change the cost-benefit equation significantly. Doing acceptance testing right is the main subject of Chapter 8, "Automated Acceptance Testing."

Subsequent Test Stages

The acceptance test stage is a significant milestone in the lifecycle of a release candidate. Once this stage has been completed, a successful release candidate has moved on from something that is largely the domain of the development team to something of wider interest and use.

For the simplest deployment pipelines, a build that has passed acceptance testing is ready for release to users, at least as far as the automated testing of the system is concerned. If the candidate fails this stage, it by definition is not fit to be released.

The progression of the release candidate to this point has been automatic, with successful candidates being automatically promoted to the next stage. If you are delivering software incrementally, it is possible to have an automated deployment to production, as described in Timothy Fitz' blog entry, "Continuous Deployment" [dbnlG8]. But for many systems, some form of manual testing is desirable before release, even when you have a comprehensive set of automated tests. Many projects have environments for testing integration with other systems, environments for testing capacity, exploratory testing environments, and staging and production environments. Each of these environments can be more or less production-like and have their own unique configuration.

The deployment pipeline takes care of deployments to testing environments too. Release management systems such as AntHill Pro and Go provide the ability to see what is currently deployed into each environment and to perform a push-button deployment into that environment. Of course behind the scenes, these simply run the deployment scripts you have written to perform the deployment.

It is also possible to build your own system to do this, based on open source tools such as Hudson or the CruiseControl family, although commercial tools provide visualizations, reporting, and fine-grained authorization of deployments out of the box. If you create your own system, the key requirements are to be able to see a list of release candidates that have passed the acceptance test stage, have a button to deploy the version of your choice into the environment of your choice, see which release candidate is currently deployed in each environment and which version in version control it came from. Figure 5.7 shows a home-brewed system that performs these functions.

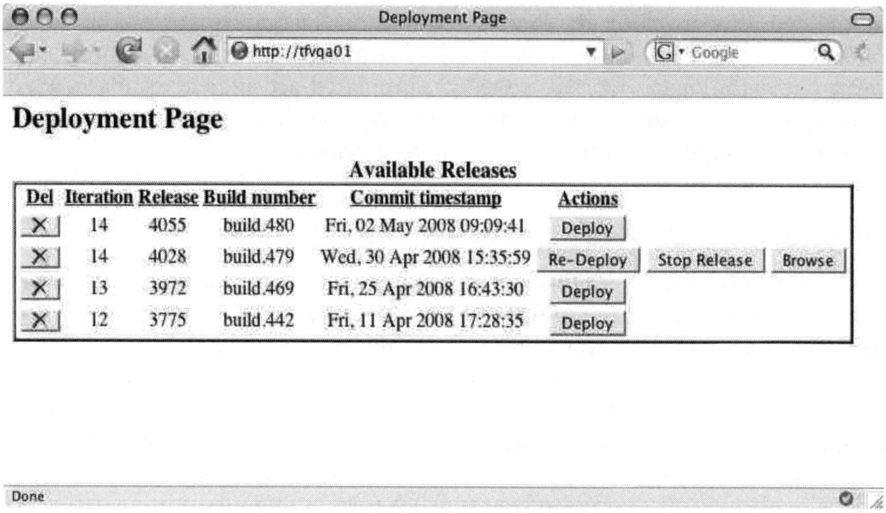

Figure 5.7   *Example deployment page*

Deployments to these environments may be executed in sequence, each one depending on the successful outcome of the one before, so that you can only deploy to production once you have deployed to UAT and staging. They could also occur in parallel, or be offered as optional stages that are manually selected.

Crucially, the deployment pipeline allows testers to deploy any build to their testing environments on demand. This replaces the concept of the "nightly build." In the deployment pipeline, instead of testers being given a build based on an arbitrary revision (the last change committed before everybody went home), testers can see which builds passed the automated tests, which changes were made to the application, and choose the build they want. If the build turns out to be unsatisfactory in some way—perhaps it does not include the correct change, or contains some bug which makes it unsuitable for testing—the testers can redeploy any other build.

Manual Testing

In iterative processes, acceptance testing is always followed by some manual testing in the form of exploratory testing, usability testing, and showcases. Before this point, developers may have demonstrated features of the application to analysts and testers, but neither of these roles will have wasted time on a build that is not known to have passed automated acceptance testing. A tester's role in this process should not be to regression-test the system, but first of all to ensure that the acceptance tests genuinely validate the behavior of the system by manually proving that the acceptance criteria are met.

After that, testers focus on the sort of testing that human beings excel at but automated tests are poor at. They do exploratory testing, perform user testing of the application's usability, check the look and feel on various platforms, and carry out pathological worst-case tests. Automated acceptance testing is what frees up time for testers so they can concentrate on these high-value activities, instead of being human test-script execution machines.

Nonfunctional Testing

Every system has many nonfunctional requirements. For example, almost every system has some kind of requirements on capacity and security, or the service-level agreements it must conform to. It usually makes sense to run automated tests to measure how well the system adheres to these requirements. For more details on how to achieve this, see Chapter 9, "Testing Nonfunctional Requirements." For other systems, testing of nonfunctional requirements need not be done on a continuous basis. Where it is required, in our experience it is still valuable to create a stage in your pipeline for running these automated tests.

Whether the results of the capacity test stage form a gate or simply inform human decision-making is one of the criteria that determine the organization of the deployment pipeline. For very high-performance applications, it makes sense to run capacity testing as a wholly automated outcome of a release candidate successfully passing the acceptance test stage. If the candidate fails capacity testing, it is not usually deemed to be deployable.

For many applications, though, the judgment of what is deemed acceptable is more subjective than that. It makes more sense to present the results at the conclusion of the capacity test stage and allow a human being to decide whether the release candidate should be promoted or not.

Preparing to Release

There is a business risk associated with every release of a production system. At best, if there is a serious problem at the point of release, it may delay the introduction of valuable new capabilities. At worst, if there is no sensible back-out plan in place, it may leave the business without mission-critical resources because they had to be decommissioned as part of the release of the new system.

The mitigation of these problems is very simple when we view the release step as a natural outcome of our deployment pipeline. Fundamentally, we want to

- Have a release plan that is created and maintained by everybody involved in delivering the software, including developers and testers, as well as operations, infrastructure, and support personnel

- Minimize the effect of people making mistakes by automating as much of the process as possible, starting with the most error-prone stages

- Rehearse the procedure often in production-like environments, so you can debug the process and the technology supporting it

- Have the ability to back out a release if things don't go according to plan

- Have a strategy for migrating configuration and production data as part of the upgrade and rollback processes

Our goal is a completely automated release process. Releasing should be as simple as choosing a version of the application to release and pressing a button. Backing out should be just as simple. There is a great deal more information on these topics in Chapter 10, "Deploying and Releasing Applications."

Automating Deployment and Release

The less control we have over the environment in which our code executes, the more potential there is for unexpected behaviors. Thus, whenever we release a software system, we want to be in control of every single bit that is deployed. There are two factors that may work against this ideal. The first is that for many applications, you simply don't have full control of the operational environment of the software that you create. This is especially true of products and applications that are installed by users, such as games or office applications. This problem is generally mitigated by selecting a representative sample of target environments and running your automated acceptance test suite on each of these sample environments in parallel. You can then mine the data produced to work out which tests fail on which platforms.

The second constraint is that the cost of establishing that degree of control is usually assumed to outweigh the benefits. However, usually the converse is true: Most problems with production environments are caused by insufficient control. As we describe in Chapter 11, production environments should be completely locked down—changes to them should only be made through automated processes. That includes not only deployment of your application, but also changes to their configuration, software stack, network topology, and state. Only in this way is it possible to reliably audit them, diagnose problems, and repair them in a predictable time. As the complexity of the system increases, so does the number of different types of servers, and the higher the level of performance required, the more vital this level of control becomes.

The process for managing your production environment should be used for your other testing environments such as staging, integration, and so forth. In this way you can use your automated change management system to create a perfectly tuned configuration in your manual testing environments. These can be tuned to perfection, perhaps using feedback from capacity testing to evaluate the configuration changes that you make. When you are happy with the result, you can replicate it to every server that needs that configuration, including production, in a predictable, reliable way. All aspects of the environment should be managed in this way, including middleware (databases, web servers, message brokers, and application servers). Each can be tuned and tweaked, with the optimal settings added to your configuration baseline.

The costs of automating the provision and maintenance of environments can be lowered significantly by using automated provisioning and management of environments, good configuration management practices, and (if appropriate) virtualization.

Once the environment's configuration is managed correctly, the application can be deployed. The details of this vary widely depending on the technologies employed in the system, but the steps are always very similar. We exploit this similarity in our approach to the creation of build and deployment scripts, discussed in Chapter 6, "Build and Deployment Scripting," and in the way in which we monitor our process.

With automated deployment and release, the process of delivery becomes democratized. Developers, testers, and operations teams no longer need to rely on ticketing systems and email threads to get builds deployed so they can gather feedback on the production readiness of the system. Testers can decide which version of the system they want in their test environment without needing to be technical experts themselves, nor relying on the availability of such expertise to make the deployment. Since deployment is simple, they can change the build under test more often, perhaps returning to an earlier version of the system to compare its behavior with that of the latest version when they find a particularly interesting bug. Sales people can access the latest version of the application with the killer feature that will swing the deal with a client. There are more subtle changes too. In our experience, people begin to relax a little. They perceive the project as a whole as less risky—mainly because it *is* less risky.

An important reason for the reduction in risk is the degree to which the process of release itself is rehearsed, tested, and perfected. Since you use the same process to deploy your system to each of your environments and to release it, the deployment process is tested very frequently—perhaps many times a day. After you have deployed a complex system for the fiftieth or hundredth time without a hitch, you don't think about it as a big event any more. Our goal is to get to that stage as quickly as possible. If we want to be wholly confident in the release process and the technology, we must use it and prove it to be good on a regular basis, just like any other aspect of our system. It should be possible to deploy a single change to production through the deployment pipeline with the minimum possible time and ceremony. The release process should be continuously evaluated and improved, identifying any problems as close to the point at which they were introduced as possible.

Many businesses require the ability to release new versions of their software several times a day. Even product companies often need to make new versions of their software available to users quickly, in case critical defects or security holes are found. The deployment pipeline and the associated practices in this book are what makes it possible to do this safely and reliably. Although many agile development processes thrive on frequent release into production—a process we recommend very strongly when it is applicable—it doesn't always make sense to do so. Sometimes we have to do a lot of work before we are in a position to release a set of features that makes sense to our users as a whole, particularly in the realm of product development. However, even if you don't need to release your software several times a day, the process of implementing a deployment pipeline will still make an enormous positive impact on your organization's ability to deliver software rapidly and reliably.

Backing Out Changes

There are two reasons why release days are traditionally feared. The first one is the fear of introducing a problem because somebody might make a hard-to-detect mistake while going through the manual steps of a software release, or because there is a mistake in the instructions. The second fear is that, should the release fail, either because of a problem in the release process or a defect in the new version of the software, you are committed. In either case, the only hope is that you will be clever enough to solve the problem very quickly.

The first problem we mitigate by essentially rehearsing the release many times a day, proving that our automated deployment system works. The second fear is mitigated by providing a back-out strategy. In the worst case, you can then get back to where you were before you began the release, which allows you to take time to evaluate the problem and find a sensible solution.

In general, the best back-out strategy is to keep the previous version of your application available while the new version is being released—and for some time afterwards. This is the basis for some of the deployment patterns we discuss in Chapter 10, "Deploying and Releasing Applications." In a very simple application, this can be achieved (ignoring data and configuration migrations) by having each release in a directory and using a symlink to point to the current version. Usually, the most complex problem associated with both deploying and rolling back is migrating the production data. This is discussed at length in Chapter 12, "Managing Data."

The next best option is to redeploy the previous good version of your appliation from scratch. To this end, you should have the ability to click a button to release any version of your application that has passed all stages of testing, just as you can with other environments under the control of the deployment pipeline. This idealistic position is fully achievable for some systems, even for systems with significant amounts of data associated with them. However, for some systems, even for individual changes, the cost of providing a full, version-neutral back-out may be excessive in time, if not money. Nevertheless, the ideal is useful, because it sets a target which every project should strive to achieve. Even if it falls somewhat short in some respects, the closer you approach this ideal position the easier your deployment becomes.

On no account should you have a different process for backing out than you do for deploying, or perform incremental deployments or rollbacks. These processes will be rarely tested and therefore unreliable. They will also not start from a known-good baseline, and therefore will be brittle. Always roll back either by keeping an old version of the application deployed or by completely redeploying a previous known-good version.

Building on Success

By the time a release candidate is available for deployment into production, we will know with certainty that the following assertions about it are true:

- The code can compile.

- The code does what our developers think it should because it passed its unit tests.

- The system does what our analysts or users think it should because it passed all of the acceptance tests.

- Configuration of infrastructure and baseline environments is managed appropriately, because the application has been tested in an analog of production.

- The code has all of the right components in place because it was deployable.

- The deployment system works because, at a minimum, it will have been used on this release candidate at least once in a development environment, once in the acceptance test stage, and once in a testing environment before the candidate could have been promoted to this stage.

- The version control system holds everything we need to deploy, without the need for manual intervention, because we have already deployed the system several times.

This "building upon success" approach, allied with our mantra of failing the process or any part of it as quickly as possible, works at every level.

Implementing a Deployment Pipeline

Whether you're starting a new project from scratch or trying to create an automated pipeline for an existing system, you should generally take an incremental approach to implementing a deployment pipeline. In this section we'll set out a strategy for going from nothing to a complete pipeline. In general, the steps look like this:

1. Model your value stream and create a walking skeleton.
2. Automate the build and deployment process.
3. Automate unit tests and code analysis.
4. Automate acceptance tests.
5. Automate releases.

Modeling Your Value Stream and Creating a Walking Skeleton

As described at the beginning of this chapter, the first step is to map out the part of your value stream that goes from check-in to release. If your project is already up and running, you can do this in about half an hour using pencil and paper. Go and speak to everybody involved in this process, and write down the steps. Include best guesses for elapsed time and value-added time. If you're working on a new project, you will have to come up with an appropriate value stream. One way to do this is to look at another project within the same organization that has characteristics similar to yours. Alternatively, you could start with a bare minimum: a commit stage to build your application and run basic metrics and unit tests, a stage to run acceptance tests, and a third stage to deploy your application to a production-like environment so you can demo it.

Once you have a value stream map, you can go ahead and model your process in your continuous integration and release management tool. If your tool doesn't allow you to model your value stream directly, you can simulate it by using dependencies between projects. Each of these projects should do nothing at first—they are just placeholders that you can trigger in turn. Using our "bare minimum" example, the commit stage should be run every time somebody checks in to version control. The stage that runs the acceptance tests should trigger automatically when the commit stage passes, using the same binary created in the commit stage. Any stages that deploy the binaries to a production-like environment for manual testing or release purposes should require you to press a button in order to select the version to deploy, and this capability will usually require authorization.

You can then make these placeholders actually do something. If your project is already well under way, that means plugging in your existing build, test, and deploy scripts. If not, your aim is to create a "walking skeleton" [bEUuac], which means doing the smallest possible amount of work to get all the key elements in place. First of all, get the commit stage working. If you don't have any code or unit tests yet, just create the simplest possible "Hello world" example or, for a web application, a single HTML page, and put a single unit test in place that asserts true. Then you can do the deployment—perhaps setting up a virtual directory on IIS and putting your web page into it. Finally, you can do the acceptance test—you need to do this after you've done the deployment, since you need your application deployed in order to run acceptance tests against it. Your acceptance test can crank up WebDriver or Sahi and verify that the web page contains the text "Hello world."

On a new project, all this should be done before work starts on development—as part of iteration zero, if you're using an iterative development process. Your organization's system administrators or operations personnel should be involved in setting up a production-like environment to run demos from and developing the scripts to deploy your application to it. In the following sections, there's more detail on how to create the walking skeleton and develop it as your project grows.

Automating the Build and Deployment Process

The first step in implementing a pipeline is to automate the build and deployment process. The build process takes source code as its input and produces binaries as output. "Binaries" is a deliberately vague word, since what your build process produces will depend on what technology you're using. The key characteristic of binaries is that you should be able to copy them onto a new machine and, given an appropriately configured environment and the correct configuration for the application in that environment, start your application—without relying on any part of your development toolchain being installed on that machine.

The build process should be performed every time someone checks in by your continuous integration server software. Use one of the many tools listed in the "Implementing Continuous Integration" section on page 56. Your CI server should be configured to watch your version control system, check out or update your source code every time a change is made to it, run the automated build process, and store the binaries on the filesystem where they are accessible to the whole team via the CI server's user interface.

Once you have a continuous build process up and running, the next step is automating deployment. First of all, you need to get a machine to deploy your application on. For a new project, this can be the machine your continuous integration server is on. For a project that is more mature, you may need to find several machines. Depending on your organization's conventions, this environment can be called the staging or user acceptance testing (UAT) environment. Either way, this environment should be somewhat production-like, as described in Chapter 10, "Deploying and Releasing Applications," and its provisioning and maintenance should be a fully automated process, as described in Chapter 11, "Managing Infrastructure and Environments."

Several common approaches to deployment automation are discussed in Chapter 6, "Build and Deployment Scripting." Deployment may involve packaging your application first, perhaps into several separate packages if different parts of the application need to be installed on separate machines. Next, the process of installing and configuring your application should be automated. Finally, you should write some form of automated deployment test that verifies that the application has been successfully deployed. It is important that the deployment process is reliable, as it is also used as a prerequisite for automated acceptance testing.

Once your application's deployment process is automated, the next step is to be able to perform push-button deployments to your UAT environment. Configure your CI server so that you can choose any build of your application and click a button to trigger a process that takes the binaries produced by that build, runs the script that deploys the build, and runs the deployment test. Make sure that when developing your build and deployment system you make use of the principles we describe, such as building your binaries only once and separating configuration from binaries, so that the same binaries may be used in every environment. This will ensure that the configuration management for your project is put on a sound footing.

Except for user-installed software, the release process should be the same process you use to deploy to a testing environment. The only technical differences should be in the configuration of the environment.

Automating the Unit Tests and Code Analysis

The next step in developing your deployment pipeline is implementing a full commit stage. This means running unit tests, code analysis, and ultimately a selection of acceptance and integration tests on every check-in. Running unit tests should not require any complex setup, because unit tests by definition don't rely on your application running. Instead, they can be run by one of the many xUnit-style frameworks against your binaries.

Since unit tests do not touch the filesystem or database (or they'd be component tests), they should also be fast to run. This is why you should start running your unit tests directly after building your application. You can also then run static analysis tools against your application to report useful diagnostic data such as coding style, code coverage, cyclomatic complexity, coupling, and so forth.

As your application gets more complex, you will need to write a large number of unit tests and a set of component tests as well. These should all go into the commit stage. Once the commit stage gets over five minutes, it makes sense to split it into suites that run in parallel. In order to do this, you'll need to get several machines (or one machine with plenty of RAM and a few CPUs) and use a CI server that supports splitting up work and running it in parallel.

Automating Acceptance Tests

The acceptance test phase of your pipeline can reuse the script you use to deploy to your testing environment. The only difference is that after the smoke tests are run, the acceptance test framework needs to be started up, and the reports it generates should be collected at the end of the test run for analysis. It also makes sense to store the logs created by your application. If your application has a GUI, you can also use a tool like Vnc2swf to create a screen recording as the acceptance tests are running to help you debug problems.

Acceptance tests fall into two types: functional and nonfunctional. It is essential to start testing nonfunctional parameters such as capacity and scaling characteristics from early on in any project, so that you have some idea of whether your application will meet its nonfunctional requirements. In terms of setup and deployment, this stage can work exactly the same way as the functional acceptance testing stage. However, the tests of course will differ (see Chapter 9, "Testing Nonfunctional Requirements," for more on creating such tests). When you start off, it is perfectly possible to run acceptance tests and performance tests back-to-back as part of a single stage. You can then separate them in order to be able to distinguish easily which set of tests failed. A good set of automated acceptance tests will help you track down intermittent and hard-to-reproduce problems such as race conditions, deadlocks, and resource contention that will be a good deal harder to discover and debug once your application is released.

The varieties of tests you create as part of the acceptance test and commit test stages of your pipeline will of course be determined by your testing strategy (see Chapter 4, "Implementing a Testing Strategy"). However, you should try and get at least one or two of each type of test you need to run automated early on in your project's life, and incorporate them into your deployment pipeline. Thus you will have a framework that makes it easy to add tests as your project grows.

Evolving Your Pipeline

The steps we describe above are found in pretty much every value stream, and hence pipeline, that we have seen. They are usually the first targets for automation. As your project gets more complex, your value stream will evolve. There are two other common potential extensions to the pipeline: components and branches. Large applications are best built as a set of components which are assembled together. In such projects, it may make sense to have a minipipeline for each component, and then a pipeline that assembles all the components and puts the entire application through acceptance tests, nonfunctional tests, and then deployment to testing, staging, and production environments. This topic is dealt with at length in Chapter 13, "Managing Components and Dependencies." Managing branches is discussed in Chapter 14, "Advanced Version Control."

The implementation of the pipeline will vary enormously between projects, but the tasks themselves are consistent for most projects. Using them as a pattern can speed up the creation of the build and deployment process for any project. However, ultimately, the point of the pipeline is to model your process for building, deploying, testing, and releasing your application. The pipeline then ensures that each change can pass through this process independently in as automated a fashion as possible.

As you implement the pipeline, you will find that the conversations you have with the people involved and the gains in efficiency you realize will, in turn, have an effect on your process. Thus it is important to remember three things.

First of all, the whole pipeline does not need to be implemented at once. It should be implemented incrementally. If there is a part of your process that is currently manual, create a placeholder for it in your workflow. Ensure your implementation records when this manual process is started and when it completes. This allows you to see how much time is spent on each manual process, and thus estimate to what extent it is a bottleneck.

Second, your pipeline is a rich source of data on the efficiency of your process for building, deploying, testing, and releasing applications. The deployment pipeline implementation you create should record every time a process starts and finishes, and what the exact changes were that went through each stage of your process. This data, in turn, allows you to measure the cycle time from committing a change to having it deployed into production, and the time spent on each stage in the process (some of the commercial tools on the market will do this for you). Thus it becomes possible to see exactly what your process' bottlenecks are and attack them in order of priority.

Finally, your deployment pipeline is a living system. As you work continuously to improve your delivery process, you should continue to take care of your deployment pipeline, working to improve and refactor it the same way you work on the applications you are using it to deliver.

Metrics

Feedback is at the heart of any software delivery process. The best way to improve feedback is to make the feedback cycles short and the results visible. You should measure continually and broadcast the results of the measurements in some hard-to-avoid manner, such as on a very visible poster on the wall, or on a computer display dedicated to showing bold, big results. Such devices are known as information radiators.

The important question, though, is: What should you measure? What you choose to measure will have an enormous influence on the behavior of your team (this is known as the Hawthorne effect). Measure the lines of code, and developers will write many short lines of code. Measure the number of defects fixed, and testers will log bugs that could be fixed by a quick discussion with a developer.

According to the lean philosophy, it is essential to optimize globally, not locally. If you spend a lot of time removing a bottleneck that is not actually the one constraining your delivery process, you will make no difference to the delivery process. So it is important to have a global metric that can be used to determine if the delivery process as a whole has a problem.

For the software delivery process, the most important global metric is cycle time. This is the time between deciding that a feature needs to be implemented and having that feature released to users. As Mary Poppendieck asks, "How long would it take your organization to deploy a change that involves just one single line of code? Do you do this on a repeatable, reliable basis?"[4] This metric is hard to measure because it covers many parts of the software delivery process—from analysis, through development, to release. However, it tells you more about your process than any other metric.

Many projects, incorrectly, choose other measures as their primary metrics. Projects concerned with the quality of their software often choose to measure the number of defects. However, this is a secondary measure. If a team using this measure discovers a defect, but it takes six months to release a fix for it, knowing that the defect exists is not very useful. Focusing on the reduction of cycle time encourages the practices that increase quality, such as the use of a comprehensive automated suite of tests that is run as a result of every check-in.

A proper implementation of a deployment pipeline should make it simple to calculate the part of the cycle time corresponding to the part of the value stream from check-in to release. It should also let you see the lead time from the check-in to each stage of your process, so you can discover your bottlenecks.

Once you know the cycle time for your application, you can work out how best to reduce it. You can use the Theory of Constraints to do this by applying the following process.

1. Identify the limiting constraint on your system. This is the part of your build, test, deploy, and release process that is the bottleneck. To pick an example at random, perhaps it's the manual testing process.

2. Exploit the constraint. This means ensuring that you should maximize the throughput of that part of the process. In our example (manual testing), you would make sure that there is always a buffer of stories waiting to be manually tested, and ensure that the resources involved in manual testing don't get used for anything else.

3. Subordinate all other processes to the constraint. This implies that other resources will not work at 100%—for example, if your developers work developing stories at full capacity, the backlog of stories waiting to be tested would

---

4. *Implementing Lean Software Development*, p. 59.

keep on growing. Instead, have your developers work just hard enough to keep the backlog constant and spend the rest of their time writing automated tests to catch bugs so that less time needs to be spent testing manually.

4. Elevate the constraint. If your cycle time is still too long (in other words, steps 2 and 3 haven't helped enough), you need to increase the resources available—hire more testers, or perhaps invest more effort in automated testing.

5. Rinse and repeat. Find the next constraint on your system and go back to step 1.

While cycle time is the most important metric in software delivery, there are a number of other *diagnostics* that can warn you of problems. These include

- Automated test coverage

- Properties of the codebase such as the amount of duplication, cyclomatic complexity, efferent and afferent coupling, style problems, and so on

- Number of defects

- Velocity, the rate at which your team delivers working, tested, ready for use code

- Number of commits to the version control system per day

- Number of builds per day

- Number of build failures per day

- Duration of build, including automated tests

It is worth considering how these metrics are presented. The reports described above produce a huge amount of data, and interpreting this data is an art. Program managers, for example, might expect to see this data analyzed and aggregated into a single "health" metric that is represented in the form of a traffic light that shows red, amber, or green. A team's technical lead will want much more detail, but even they will not want to wade through pages and pages of reports. Our colleague, Julias Shaw, created a project called Panopticode that runs a series of these reports against Java code and produces rich, dense visualizations (such as Figure 5.8) that let you see at a glance whether there is a problem with your codebase and where it lies. The key is to create visualizations that aggregate the data and present them in such a form that the human brain can use its unparalleled pattern-matching skills most effectively to identify problems with your process or codebase.

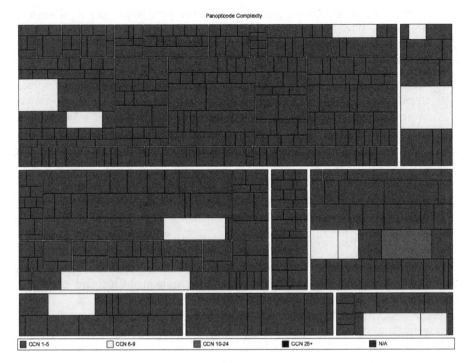

Figure 5.8   *A tree map generated by Panopticode showing cyclomatic complexity for a Java codebase*

Each team's continuous integration server should generate these reports and visualizations on each check-in, and store the reports in your artifact repository. You should then collate the results in a database, and track them across every team. These results should be published on an internal website—have a page for each project. Finally, aggregate them together so that they can be monitored across all of the projects in your development program, or even your whole organization.

Summary

The purpose of the deployment pipeline is to give everyone involved in delivering software visibility into the progress of builds from check-in to release. It should be possible to see which changes have broken the application and which resulted in release candidates suitable for manual testing or release. Your implementation should make it possible to perform push-button deployments into manual testing environments, and to see which release candidates are in those environments. Choosing to release a particular version of your application should also be a push-button task that can be performed with full knowledge that the release candidate being deployed has passed the entire pipeline successfully, and hence has had a battery of automated and manual tests performed on it in a production-like environment.

Once you have a deployment pipeline implemented, inefficiencies in your release process will become obvious. All kinds of useful information can be derived from a working deployment pipeline, such as how long it takes a release candidate to get through the various manual testing stages, the average cycle time from check-in to release, and how many defects are discovered at which stages in your process. Once you have this information, you can work to optimize your process for building and releasing software.

There is no one-size-fits-all solution to the complex problem of implementing a deployment pipeline. The crucial point is to create a system of record that manages each change from check-in to release, providing the information you need to discover problems as early as possible in the process. Having an implementation of the deployment pipeline can then be used to drive out inefficiencies in your process so you can make your feedback cycle faster and more powerful, perhaps by adding more automated acceptance tests and parallelizing them more aggressively, or by making your testing environments more production-like, or by implementing better configuration management processes.

A deployment pipeline, in turn, depends on having some foundations in place: good configuration management, automated scripts for building and deploying your application, and automated tests to prove that your application will deliver value to its users. It also requires discipline, such as ensuring that only changes that have passed through the automated build, test, and deployment system get released. We discuss these prerequisites and the necessary disciplines in Chapter 15, "Managing Continuous Delivery," which includes a maturity model for continuous integration, testing, data management, and so forth.

The following chapters of the book dive into considerably more detail on implementing deployment pipelines, exploring some of the common issues that may arise and discussing techniques that can be adopted within the context of the full lifecycle deployment pipelines described here.

Chapter 6

Build and Deployment Scripting

Introduction

On very simple projects, building and testing the software can be accomplished using the capabilities of your IDE (Integrated Development Environment). However, this is really only appropriate for the most trivial of tasks. As soon as the project extends beyond a single person, spans more than a few days, or produces more than a single executable file as its output, it demands more control if it is not to become complex and unwieldy. It is also vital to script building, testing, and packaging applications when working on large or distributed teams (including open source projects), since otherwise it can take days to get a new team member up and running.

The first step is actually very simple: Pretty much every modern platform has a way to run the build from the command line. Rails projects can run the default Rake task; .NET projects can use MsBuild; Java projects (if set up correctly) can use Ant, Maven, Buildr,[1] or Gradle; and with SCons, not much is required to get a simple C/C++ project going. This makes it straightforward to begin continuous integration—just have your CI server run this command to create binaries. Running tests is also a relatively straightforward process on many platforms, so long as you are using one of the more popular test frameworks. Rails users and Java projects that use Maven or Buildr can just run the relevant command. .NET and C/C++ users will need to do some copy-and-pasting in order to get things up and running. However, once your project gets more complex—you have multiple components, or unusual packaging needs—you'll need to roll up your sleeves and dive into build scripting.

Automating deployment introduces further complexities. Deploying software into testing and production environments is rarely as simple as dropping a single binary file into the production environment and sitting back with a satisfied smile.

---

1. Buildr also handles Scala, Groovy, and Ruby seamlessly at the time of writing—by the time you read this, we expect it to support more languages that target the JVM.

In most cases, it requires a series of steps such as configuring your application, initializing data, configuring the infrastructure, operating systems, and middleware, setting up mock external systems, and so on. As projects get more complex, these steps become more numerous, longer, and (if they are not automated) more error-prone.

Using general-purpose build tools for performing deployments is asking for trouble in all but the simplest of cases. The available deployment mechanisms will be limited to those supporting your target environment and your middleware. More importantly, decisions on how to do automated deployments should be made by developers and operations personnel together, since both of them will need to be familiar with the technology.

This chapter aims to give you an overview of the principles common to all build and deployment tools, information to get you going, some tips and tricks, and pointers to more information. We don't cover managing environments through scripting in this chapter; that will be covered in Chapter 11, "Managing Infrastructure and Environments." Another thing we don't supply in this chapter are code examples and detailed descriptions of tools, since these will rapidly become out-of-date. You'll find much more detail on available tools, along with example scripts, at this book's website [dzMeNE].

Build and deployment systems must be living and breathing things capable of lasting not only during the initial development project but also through its life as a maintainable software system in production. They must therefore be designed and maintained with care—treated the same way you would treat the rest of your source code—and exercised on a regular basis so that we know that they work when we are ready to use them.

An Overview of Build Tools

Automated build tools have been a part of software development for a very long time. Many people will remember Make and its many variants that were the standard build tools used for many years. All build tools have a common core: They allow you to model a dependency network. When you run your tool, it will calculate how to reach the goal you specify by executing tasks in the correct order, running each task that your goal depends on exactly once. For example, say you want to run your tests. In order to do this, it's necessary to compile your code and your tests, and set up your test data. Compiling anything requires initialization of your environment. Figure 6.1 shows an example dependency network.

Your build tool will work out that it needs to perform every task in the dependency network. It can start with either init or setting up test data, since these tasks are independent. Once it has done init, it can then compile the source or the tests—but it must do both, and set up the test data, before the tests can be run. Even though multiple targets depend on init, it will only be performed once.

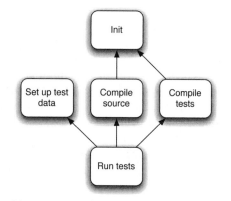

Figure 6.1 *A simple build dependency network*

One small point worth noting is that a task has two essential features: the thing it does and the other things it depends on. These two features are modeled in every build tool.

However, there is one area in which build tools differ: whether they are *task-oriented* or *product-oriented*. Task-oriented build tools (for example, Ant, NAnt, and MsBuild) describe the dependency network in terms of a set of tasks. A product-oriented tool, such as Make, describes things in terms of the products they generate, such as an executable.

This distinction appears somewhat academic at first glance, but it is important in order to understand how to optimize builds and to ensure the correctness of build processes. For instance, a build tool must ensure that for a given goal, each prerequisite must be executed exactly once. If a prerequisite is missed, the result of the build process will be bad. If a prerequisite is executed more than once, the best case scenario is that the build will take longer (if the prerequisite is idempotent), and the worst case is that the result of the build process is again bad.

Typically, build tools will walk the entire network, invoking (but not necessarily executing) each task. So our hypothetical build tool might invoke, in our example, the *Set up test data*, *Init*, *Compile source*, *Init*, *Compile tests*, and then *Run tests* tasks. In a task-oriented tool, each task will know whether or not it has already been executed as part of the build. Thus, even though the *Init* task is invoked twice, it would only be executed once.

However, in a product-oriented tool, the world is modeled as a set of files. So, for example, the *Compile source* and *Compile tests* goals in our example would each result in a single file that contains all the compiled code—let's call them source.so and tests.so. The *Run tests* target, in turn, generates a file called testreports.zip. A product-oriented build system would ensure it invoked *Run tests* after *Compile source* and *Compile tests*, but the *Run tests* target would only actually be executed if the timestamp on either of the .so files is later than the timestamp on testreports.zip.

Product-oriented build tools thus keep their state in the form of timestamps on the files generated by each of the tasks (SCons uses MD5 signatures). This is great when you're compiling C or C++ (for example), because Make will ensure that you only compile those source code files that have changed since the last time the build was run. This feature, known as an incremental build, can save hours over a clean build on large projects. Compilation takes a comparatively long time in C/C++ because the compilers have to do a great deal of work optimizing the code. In languages that run on a virtual machine, the compiler just creates the byte code, and the virtual machine's just-in-time (JIT) compiler does the optimization at run time.

Task-oriented build tools, in contrast, keep no state between builds. This makes them less powerful and entirely unsuitable for compiling C++. However, they work fine for languages such as C# since the compilers for these languages have built-in logic for performing incremental builds.[2] Finally, it is worth noting that Rake can function either as a product-oriented or a task-oriented tool. For more on dependency networks, refer to *Domain-Specific Languages* by Martin Fowler [8ZKox1].

We'll now take a brief survey of current build tools. Again, you can find examples of build scripts using many of these technologies, and further references, at this book's website [dzMeNE].

Make

Make and its variants are still going strong in the world of systems development. It is a powerful product-oriented build tool capable of tracking dependencies within a build and building only those components that are affected by a particular change. This is essential in optimizing the performance of a development team when compile time is a significant cost in the development cycle.

Unfortunately, Make has a number of drawbacks. As applications become more complex and the number of dependencies between their components increases, the complexity of the rules built into Make means that they become hard to debug.

To tame some of this complexity, a common convention adopted by teams working on large codebases is to create a Makefile for each directory, and have a top-level Makefile that recursively runs the Makefiles in each subdirectory. This means that build information and processes can end up spread over many files. When someone checks in a change to the build, it can be quite hard to work out what exactly has changed and how it will affect the final deliverables.

---

2.   Things are slightly more complex in Java. At the time of writing, Sun's Javac compiler did not do incremental builds (hence the Ant task), but IBM's Jikes compiler could. However, the `javac` task in Ant will perform incremental compilation.

Makefiles are also susceptible to a very hard-to-find class of bugs due to the fact that whitespace can be significant under certain circumstances. For example, within a command script, commands to be passed to the shell must be prefaced with a tab. If spaces are used instead, the script will not work.

Another disadvantage of Make is that it relies on the shell to actually do anything. As a result, Makefiles are specific to an operating system (indeed, a great deal of work has gone into the toolchain around Make to enable builds to work across the various UNIX flavors). Since Makefiles are an external DSL which doesn't provide for extensions to the core system (apart from defining new rules), any extensions must reinvent common solutions without access to Make's internal data structures.

These problems, combined with the fact that the declarative programming model at the root of a Make application is not familiar to most developers (who are often more comfortable with imperative programming), mean that Make is rarely used as a primary build tool in newly developed commercial applications.

"This is one of those days when I am not happy with software. It sometimes surprises me how many of those days involve Make." — Mark Dominus, "Suffering from 'make install'" [dyGIMy].

These days, many C/C++ developers are using SCons in preference to Make. SCons itself and its build files are written in Python. This makes it a much more powerful and portable tool than Make. It includes many useful features such as supporting Windows out of the box and parallelized builds.

Ant

With the emergence of Java developers started to do more cross-platform development. The limitations inherent in Make became more painful. In response, the Java community experimented with several solutions, at first porting Make itself to Java. At the same time, XML was coming to prominence as a convenient way to build structured documents. These two approaches converged and resulted in the Apache Ant build tool.

Fully cross-platform, Ant includes a set of tasks written in Java to perform common operations such as compilation and filesystem manipulation. Ant can be easily extended with new tasks written in Java. Ant quickly became the de facto standard build tool for Java projects. It is now widely supported by IDEs and other tools.

Ant is a task-oriented build tool. The runtime components of Ant are written in Java, but the Ant scripts are an external DSL written in XML. This combination gives Ant powerful cross-platform capabilities. It is also an extremely flexible and powerful system, with Ant tasks for most things you could want to do.

However, Ant suffers from several shortcomings:

- You need to write your build scripts in XML, which is neither succinct nor pleasant for humans to read.

- Ant has an anaemic domain model. There are no real domain concepts over and above a task, which means you have to spend a great deal of time writing boilerplate to compile, create JARs, run tests, and so forth.

- Ant is a declarative language, not an imperative one. However, there are just enough imperative-style tags (such as the dreaded `<antcall>`) to allow users to mix their metaphors and create unpleasantness and confusion all round.

- You cannot easily ask questions about Ant tasks, such as "How many tests ran?" and "How long did they take?" All you can do is have a tool print this information out to the command line so you can parse it, or hook into Ant's internals by writing custom Java code to instrument it.

- While Ant supports reuse through the `import` and `macrodef` tasks, these are poorly understood by novice users.

As a result of these limitations, Ant files tend to be long and poorly factored—it is not unusual for Ant files to be thousands of lines long. An invaluable resource when working with Ant files is Julian Simpson's article "Refactoring Ant Build Files," in *The ThoughtWorks Anthology*.

NAnt and MSBuild

When Microsoft first introduced the .NET framework, it had many features in common with the Java language and environment. Java developers who worked on this new platform quickly ported some of their favorite open source Java tools. So instead of JUnit and JMock we have NUnit and NMock—and, rather predictably, NAnt. NAnt uses essentially the same syntax as Ant, with only a few differences.

Microsoft later introduced their own minor variation on NAnt and called it MSBuild. It is a direct descendant of Ant and NAnt, and will be familiar to anyone who has used those tools. However, it is more tightly integrated into Visual Studio, understanding how to build Visual Studio solutions and projects and how to manage dependencies (as a result, NAnt scripts often call out to MSBuild to do compilation). While some users complain that MSBuild provides less flexibility than NAnt, the fact that it is more regularly updated and ships as part of the .NET framework has made NAnt a niche player.

Both of them suffer from many of the limitations of Ant described above.

Maven

For a time, Ant was ubiquitous in the Java community—but innovation did not stop there. Maven attempts to remove the large amount of boilerplate found in Ant files by having a more complex domain that makes many assumptions about the way your Java project is laid out. This principle of favoring convention over configuration means that, so long as your project conforms to the structure dictated by Maven, it will perform almost any build, deploy, test, and release task you can imagine with a single command, without having to write more than a few lines of XML. That includes creating a website for your project which hosts your application's Javadoc by default.

The other important feature of Maven is its support for automated management of Java libraries and dependencies between projects, a problem that is one of the pain points in large Java projects. Maven also supports a complex but rigid software partitioning scheme that allows you to decompose complex solutions into smaller components.

The problem with Maven is threefold. First of all, if your project doesn't conform to Maven's assumptions about structure and lifecycle, it can be extremely hard (or even impossible) to make Maven do what you want. In some shops this is considered a feature—it forces development teams to structure their projects according to Maven's dictates. This can be a good thing with an inexperienced development shop, or if you have a large number of projects. But if you want to do things even slightly off the beaten track (such as loading some custom test data before performing a test), you will have to subvert Maven's lifecycle and domain model—an intensely painful and unmaintainable course of action, but one that is often inevitable. Ant is far more flexible than Maven.

Maven's second problem is that it also uses an external DSL written in XML, which means that in order to extend it, you need to write code. While writing a Maven plugin is not inordinately complex, it is not something you can just knock out in a few minutes; you'll need to learn about Mojos, plugin descriptors, and whatever inversion-of-control framework Maven is using by the time you read this. Fortunately, Maven has plugins for almost everything you'd want to do in the average Java project.

The third problem with Maven is that, in its default configuration, it is self-updating. Maven's core is very small, and in order to make itself functional, it downloads its own plugins from the Internet. Maven will attempt to upgrade itself every time it is run and, as a result of an upgrade or downgrade of one of its plugins, it can fail unpredictably. Perhaps more seriously, it means that you can't reproduce your builds. A related problem is that Maven's library and dependency management functionality allows for the use of snapshots of components to be used across projects, which again makes it hard to reproduce a particular build if it uses snapshot dependencies.

For some teams, the constraints of Maven may be too serious, or it would take too much effort to restructure their build to match Maven's assumptions. As a result, they have stuck with Ant. More recently, a tool called Ivy has been created that lets you manage libraries and dependencies between components without having to use Maven. This makes it possible to gain some of the benefits of Maven if you are, for some reason, tied to using Ant.

Note that while Ivy and Maven are great at managing dependencies between components, their default mechanism for managing external dependencies—downloading them from an Internet archive maintained by the Maven community—is not always the best choice. For a start, there's the fabled problem where kicking off your build for the first time leads to waiting for Maven to download half of the Internet. More problematically, unless you are very disciplined about which version of each dependency you are using, it is easy to end up with diamond dependency problems and breakages due to Maven changing a version of some library without your noticing.

For more on managing libraries and dependencies between components, refer to Chapter 13, "Managing Components and Dependencies."

Rake

Ant and its brethren are external domain-specific languages (DSLs) for building software. However, their choice of XML to represent these languages made them hard to create, read, maintain, and extend. The dominant Ruby build tool, Rake, came about as an experiment to see if Make's functionality could be easily reproduced by creating an internal DSL in Ruby. The answer was "yes," and Rake was born. Rake is a product-oriented tool similar to Make, but it can also be used as a task-oriented tool.

Like Make, Rake has no understanding of anything except tasks and dependencies. However, since Rake scripts are plain Ruby, you can use Ruby's API to carry out whatever tasks you want. As a result, creating powerful, platform-independent build files is straightforward in Rake: You have all the native power of a general-purpose programming language at your disposal.

Of course the use of a general-purpose language means that all of the tools available to you in normal development are available to you when you are maintaining your build scripts. You can refactor and modularize your builds, and you can use your regular development environment. It is straightforward to debug Rake using the standard Ruby debugger. If you hit a bug in the execution of your Rake build script, you will get a stack trace to help you understand what has gone wrong. Indeed, since classes in Ruby are open for extension, you can add methods to Rake's classes from within your build script for debugging purposes. This and many other useful techniques for Rake are described in Martin Fowler's bliki entry "Using the Rake Build Language" [9lfL15].

Just because Rake was developed by Ruby programmers and is widely used for Ruby projects doesn't mean it can't be used for projects that use other technologies (for example, the Albacore project provides a set of Rake tasks for building .NET systems). Rake is a general-purpose build scripting tool. Of course, your development team will need to have (or acquire) some basic programming skills in Ruby, but you can say the same for Ant or NAnt.

There are two general disadvantages of Rake: first, you have to ensure that a decent runtime is available on your platform (JRuby is rapidly gaining momentum as the most portable and reliable platform); and second, you have to interact with RubyGems.

Buildr

The simplicity and power of Rake makes a compelling case that build scripts should be written in a real programming language. The new generation of build tools, such as Buildr, Gradle, and Gantt, have taken this approach. They all feature internal DSLs for building software. However, they attempt to make the more complex challenges of dependency management and multiproject builds just as easy. We'll discuss Buildr in more detail since it's the one we're most familiar with.

Buildr is built on top of Rake, so everything you can do in Rake you can continue to do in Buildr. However, Buildr is also a drop-in replacement for Maven—it uses the same conventions that Maven does, including filesystem layout, artifact specifications, and repositories. It also lets you use Ant tasks (including any custom ones) with zero configuration. It leverages Rake's product-oriented framework to do incremental builds. Astonishingly, it is also faster than Maven. However, unlike Maven, it is extremely simple to customize tasks and create new ones of your own.

If you're starting a new Java project, or looking for a replacement for Ant or Maven, we strongly suggest you consider Buildr, or Gradle if you prefer your DSLs in Groovy.

Psake

Windows users need not miss out on the new wave of internal DSL build tools. Pronounced "saké," Psake is an internal DSL written in PowerShell, which provides task-oriented dependency networks.

Principles and Practices of Build and Deployment Scripting

In this section, we'll lay out some general principles and practices of build and deployment scripting which should apply whichever technology you use.

Create a Script for Each Stage in Your Deployment Pipeline

We are big fans of domain-driven design,[3] and apply these techniques in the design of any software that we create. This is no different when we design our build scripts. That is perhaps a bit of a grandiose way of saying that we want the structure of our build scripts to clearly represent the processes that they are implementing. Taking this approach ensures that our scripts have a well-defined structure that helps us to keep them clean during maintenance and minimizes dependencies between components of our build and deployment system. Luckily, the deployment pipeline provides an excellent organizing principle for dividing up responsibilities between build scripts.

When you first start your project, it makes sense to have a single script containing every operation that will be performed in the course of executing the deployment pipeline, with dummy targets for steps that are not yet automated. However, once your script gets sufficiently long, you can divide it up into separate scripts for each stage in your pipeline. Thus you will have a commit script containing all the targets required to compile your application, package it, run the commit test suite, and perform static analysis of the code.[4] You then need a functional acceptance test script that calls your deployment tool to deploy the application to the appropriate environment, then prepares any data, and finally runs the acceptance tests. You could also have a script that runs any nonfunctional tests such as stress tests or security tests.

 Make sure you keep all your scripts in a version control repository, preferably the same one that your source code lives in. It is essential for developers and operations people to be able to collaborate on build and deployment scripts, and keeping them in the same repository is what enables this.

Use an Appropriate Technology to Deploy Your Application

In a typical deployment pipeline, most stages that follow a successful commit stage, such as the automated acceptance test stage and user acceptance test stage, depend upon the application being deployed to a production-like environment.

---

3. See Evans (2003).
4. There are example commit scripts for Ant, Maven, MSBuild, and Psake at the book's website [dzMeNE].

It is vital that this deployment is automated too. However, you should use the right tool for the job when automating deployment, not a general-purpose scripting language (unless the deployment process is extremely simple). Pretty much every common piece of middleware has tools for configuring it and deploying to it, so you should use those. If you're using the WebSphere Application Server, for example, you'll want to use the Wsadmin tool to configure the container and deploy the application.

Most importantly, deployment of your application will be done both by developers (on their local machines, if nowhere else) and by testers and operations staff. Thus, the decision on how to deploy your application needs to involve all of these people. It also needs to happen towards the start of the project.

Operations and Developers Must Collaborate on the Deployment Process

On one project at a major telecoms company, the developers created an Ant-based system for deploying their application locally. However, when it came time to deploy the application to a production-like UAT environment, not only did the developers' deployment script fail miserably, but the operations team which managed the environment refused to use it, since they had no expertise in Ant.

Partly for this reason, a build team was formed to create a unified process for deploying to every environment. The team had to work closely with both operations staff and developers to create a system that was acceptable to both, and came up with a set of Bash scripts (collectively known as Conan the Deployer) that did things like remoting into application server nodes and reconfiguring Apache and WebLogic.

There were two main reasons for the operations team to be happy to use Conan to deploy to production. First, they were involved in its creation. Second, they got to see the script used throughout the pipeline to deploy to each of the testing environments, and thus came to trust it.

The deployment script should cover the case of upgrading your application as well as installing it from scratch. That means, for example, that it should shut down previously running versions of the application before deploying, and it should be able to create any database from scratch as well as upgrade an existing one.

Use the Same Scripts to Deploy to Every Environment

As described in the "Deployment Pipeline Practices" section on page 113, it is essential to use the same process to deploy to every environment in which your application runs to ensure that the build and deployment process is tested effectively. That means using the same scripts to deploy to each environment and representing the differences between environments—such as service URIs and IP addresses—as configuration information to be managed separately. Separate out configuration information from the script and store it in version control, providing some mechanism for your deployment script to retrieve it as described in Chapter 2, "Configuration Management."

It is essential that both build and deployment scripts work on developers' machines as well as on production-like environments, and that they are used to perform all build and deployment activities by developers. It is all too easy for a parallel build system to spring up that only the developers use—but this removes one of the key forces keeping build and deployment scripts flexible, well factored, and well tested. If your application depends on other components developed in-house, you'll want to make sure it's easy to get the right versions—meaning ones that are known to work reliably together—onto developer machines. This is one area where tools like Maven and Ivy come in very handy.

If your application is complex in terms of its deployment architecture, you will have to make some simplifications to get it working on developer machines. This may involve significant work, such as the ability to replace an Oracle cluster with an in-memory database at deploy time. However, this effort will certainly pay back. When developers have to rely on shared resources in order to run the application, it is necessarily run much less frequently, and the feedback loop is much slower. This, in turn, leads to more defects and a slower pace of development. The question is not "How can we justify the cost?" but rather, "How can we justify not investing in making the application run locally?"

Use Your Operating System's Packaging Tools

We use the term "binaries" throughout this book as a catch-all term for the objects that you put on your target environments as part of your application's deployment process. Most of the time, this is a bunch of files created by your build process, any libraries your application requires, and perhaps another set of static files checked into version control.

However, deploying a bunch of files that need to be distributed across the filesystem is very inefficient and makes maintenance—in the form of upgrades, rollbacks, and uninstalls—extremely painful. This is why packaging systems were invented. If you are targeting a single operating system, or a small set of related operating systems, we strongly recommend using that OS's packaging technology to bundle up everything that needs to be deployed. For example, Debian and Ubuntu both use the Debian package system; RedHat, SuSE, and many other flavors of Linux use the RedHat package system; Windows users can use the Microsoft Installer system, and so forth. All of these packaging systems are relatively simple to use and have great tool support.

Whenever your deployments involve sprinkling files across the filesystem or adding keys to the registry, use a packaging system to do it. This has many advantages. Not only does it become very simple to maintain your application, but you can also then piggyback your deployment process onto environment management tools like Puppet, CfEngine, and Marimba; just upload your packages to an organizational repository, and have these tools install the correct version of your package—the same way you'd have them install the right version of Apache, for example. If you need different things installed on different boxes (perhaps you're using an n-tier architecture), you can create a package for each tier or type of box. Packaging your binaries should be an automated part of your deployment pipeline.

Of course not all deployments can be managed in this way. Commercial middleware servers, for example, often require special tools to perform deployments. In this case, a hybrid approach is necessary. Use packages to get anything in place that doesn't require special tools, and then use the specialized tools to perform the remainder of the deployment.

You can also use platform-specific packaging systems, such as Ruby Gems, Python Eggs, Perl's CPAN, and so on, to distribute your application. However, we tend to prefer the operating system packaging systems when creating packages for deployment. Platform-specific tools work fine if you're distributing libraries for that platform, but they are designed by and for developers, not system administrators. The majority of system administrators dislike these tools because they add another layer of management to deal with, one that doesn't always play nicely with the operating system's package management system. If you are deploying a pure Rails application across multiple operating systems, by all means use RubyGems to package it. Where possible, though, stick to your operating system's standard package management toolchain.[5]

Ensure the Deployment Process Is Idempotent

Your deployment process should always leave the target environment in the same (correct) state, regardless of the state it finds it in when starting a deployment.

The simplest way to achieve this is to start with a known-good baseline environment, provisioned either automatically or through virtualization. This environment should include all the appropriate middleware and anything else your application requires to work. Your deployment process can then fetch the version of the application you specify and deploy it to this environment, using the appropriate deployment tools for your middleware.

If your configuration management procedures are not sufficiently good to achieve this, the next best step is to validate the assumptions your deployment process makes about the environment, and fail the deployment if they are not

---

5.   CPAN is one of the better-designed platform packaging systems, in that it is possible to convert a Perl module into a RedHat or Debian package in a fully automated way. If all platform package formats were designed to allow for automatic conversion to system package formats, this conflict would not exist.

met. You could, for example, validate that the appropriate middleware is installed, running, and is at the correct version. You should, in any case, also validate that any services your application depends on are running and are at the correct version.

If your application is tested, built, and integrated as a single piece, it usually makes sense to deploy it as a single piece. This means that every time you deploy, you should deploy everything from scratch, based on binaries derived from a single revision in version control. This includes multiple-tier systems where, for example, the application and presentation tiers are developed at the same time. When you deploy one tier, you should deploy all tiers.

Many organizations insist that you should deploy only those artifacts that have changed, in order to minimize change. But the process of working out what has changed can be more complex and error-prone than just deploying from scratch. It is also much harder to test; it is, of course, impossible to test every possible permutation of such a process, so the pathological case you didn't consider will be the one that happens during the release, leaving your system in an undefined state.

There are a few exceptions to this rule. Firstly, in the case of clustered systems, it doesn't always make sense to redeploy the whole cluster simultaneously; see the "Canary Releasing" section on page 263 for more details.

Secondly, if your application is componentized and the components are taken from multiple source code repositories, you will need to deploy the binaries created from a tuple of revisions (x, y, z, . . .) from your revision control repositories. In this case, if you know that only one component has changed, and *if you have already tested the combination of component versions you are about to have in production*, then you can deploy only the component that is changing. The crucial distinction here is that the process of upgrading from the previous state to the new state has already been tested. The same principles apply to individual services that form a service-oriented architecture.

Finally, another approach is to use tools for deployment that are idempotent in their own right. At a low level, for example, Rsync will ensure that a target directory on one system is identical to the source directory on another system, whatever the state of the files in the target directory, using a powerful algorithm to transfer over the wire only the differences between the target directory and the source directory. Version control performing directory updates achieves a similar result. Puppet, described in detail in Chapter 11, "Managing Infrastructure and Environments," analyzes the configuration of the target environment and makes only the necessary changes to bring it in sync with the declarative specification of the desired state of the environment. BMC, HP, and IBM produce a whole raft of commercial applications to manage deployments and releases.

Evolve Your Deployment System Incrementally

Everyone can see the appeal of a fully automated deployment process: "Release your software at the push of a button." When you see a large enterprise system that is deployed this way, it looks like magic. The problem with magic is that it can look dauntingly complex from the outside. In fact, if you examine one of our deployment systems, it is merely a collection of very simple, incremental steps that—over time—create a sophisticated system.

Our point here is that you don't have to have completed all of the steps to get value from your work. The first time you write a script to deploy the application in a local development environment and share it with the team, you have saved lots of work of individual developers.

Start by getting the operations team to work with developers to automate deployment of the application into a testing environment. Make sure that the operations people are comfortable with the tools being used to deploy. Ensure that developers can use the same process to deploy and run the application in their development environments. Then, move on to refining these scripts so they can be used in the acceptance test environment to deploy and run the application so that the tests can be run. Then, move further down the deployment pipeline and ensure the operations team can use the same tools to deploy the application into staging and production.

Project Structure for Applications That Target the JVM

Although this book aims to avoid being technology-specific as much as possible, we felt it worth spending a section to describe how to lay out projects that target the JVM. This is because, while there are useful conventions, they aren't enforced outside the Maven world.[6] However, it makes life much easier for developers if they follow the standard layout. It should be possible to abstract the information presented here to other technologies with little additional effort. In particular, .NET projects can fruitfully use the exact same layout, with backslashes substituted for forward slashes of course.[7]

Project Layout

We are going to present the project layout assumed by Maven, known as the Maven Standard Directory Layout. Even if you don't use (or even like) Maven, one of its most important contributions is introducing a standard convention for project layout.

A typical source layout will look like this:

---

6. Unlike Rails, which enforces the directory structure, and the .NET toolchain, which will also handle some of this for you.
7. Check out Jean-Paul Boodhoo's blog entry [ahdDZO].

```
/[project-name]
  README.txt
  LICENSE.txt
  /src
    /main
      /java        Java source code for your project
      /scala       If you use other languages, they go at the same level
      /resources   Resources for your project
      /filters     Resource filter files
      /assembly    Assembly descriptors
      /config      Configuration files
      /webapp      Web application resources
    /test
      /java        Test sources
      /resources   Test resources
      /filters     Test resource filters
    /site          Source for your project website
    /doc           Any other documentation
  /lib
    /runtime       Libraries your project needs at run time
    /test          Libraries required to run tests
    /build         Libraries required to build your project
```

If you use Maven subprojects, they each go in a directory at the project root, with subdirectories that also follow the Maven Standard Directory Layout. Note that the lib directory is not part of Maven—Maven will automatically download dependencies and store them in a local repository it manages. However, if you're not using Maven, it makes sense to check your libraries in as part of your source code.

Managing Source Code

Always follow the standard Java practice and keep your files in directories named after the package that they contain, with one class per file. The Java compiler and all modern development environments will enforce this convention, but we still find places where people violate it. If you don't follow this and other conventions of the language, it can lead to hard-to-find bugs, but more importantly it makes it harder to maintain your project, and the compiler will issue warnings. For the same reasons, be sure to follow Java naming conventions, with package names in PascalCase and classes in camelCase. Use an open source tool such as CheckStyle or FindBugs to enforce adherence to these naming conventions in the code analysis step of your commit stage. For more on naming conventions, see Sun's documentation "Code Conventions for the Java Programming Language" [asKdH6].

Any generated configuration or metadata (e.g., generated by annotations or XDoclet) should not be in the src directory. Instead, put them in the target directory so they can be deleted when you run a clean build, and so they don't get checked in to version control by mistake.

Managing Tests

All source code for tests goes into the directory test/[language]. Unit tests should be stored in a mirror of the package hierarchy of your code—that is, a test for a given class should be in the same package as that class.

Other kinds of tests, such as acceptance tests, component tests, and so forth, can be kept in separate sets of packages, for example com.mycompany.myproject. acceptance.ui, com.mycompany.myproject.acceptance.api, com.mycompany. myproject.integration. However, it is usual to keep them under the same directory as the rest of your tests. In your build scripts, you can use filtering based on package name to ensure they get executed separately. Some people prefer to create separate directories under test for different kinds of tests—but this is a matter of preference since IDEs and build tools are quite capable of coping with both layouts.

Managing Build Output

When Maven builds your project, it puts everything in a directory at the project root called target. This includes generated code, metadata files such as Hibernate mapping files, etc. Putting these into a separate directory makes it easy to clean out artifacts from a previous build, since all you have to do is delete the directory. You should not commit anything from this directory to version control; if you do decide to check in any binary artifacts, copy them to another directory in the repository. The target directory should be ignored by your source control system. Maven creates files in this directory as follows:

```
/[project-name]
  /target
    /classes          Compiled classes
    /test-classes     Compiled test classes
    /surefire-reports Test reports
```

If you're not using Maven, you can just use a directory called reports under target to store test reports.

The build process should ultimately generate binaries in the form of JARs, WARs, and EARs. These go into the target directory to be stored in your artifact repository by your build system. To start with, each project should create one JAR. However, as your project grows, you can create different JARs for different components (for more on components, check out Chapter 13, "Managing Components and Dependencies"). For example, you can create JARs for significant functional chunks of your system that represent whole components or services.

Whatever your strategy, bear in mind that the point of creating multiple JARs is twofold: first, to make it simple to deploy your application, and second, so you can make your build process more efficient and minimize the complexity of your dependency graph. These considerations should guide you in how you package your application.

Instead of storing all your code as one project and creating multiple JARs, an alternative is to create separate projects for each component or subproject. Once your project gets to a certain size, this can be easier to maintain in the long run, though it can also get in the way of navigability of the codebase in some IDEs. This choice really depends upon your development environment and the level of coupling between the code within different components. Creating a separate step in your build process to assemble your application from the various JARs that comprise it can help retain the flexibility to change your mind about the packaging decisions you make.

Managing Libraries

You have several options for managing libraries. One is to completely delegate library management to a tool like Maven or Ivy. In this case, you don't need to check any libraries into version control—just declare the dependencies you require in your project specification. At the other end of the spectrum, you can check into source control all the libraries your project requires to build, test, or run the system, in which case it is common to put them into a directory called lib at the root of your project. We like to separate these libraries into different directories depending on whether they are required at build time, test time, or run time.

There is some debate about how far to take the storage of build-time dependencies, such as Ant itself. We think that a lot depends on the size and duration of the project. On the one hand, tools like the compiler or version of Ant may be used to build many different projects, so storing them inside every project would be wasteful. There is a trade-off here, though: As a project grows, maintaining the dependencies becomes a bigger and bigger problem. One simple solution to this is to store most dependencies in a separate project of its own in your version control system.

A more sophisticated approach is to create a repository within your organization to store all the libraries required in all your projects. Both Ivy and Maven support custom repositories. In organizations where compliance is important, this can be used as a way to make the appropriately blessed libraries available. These approaches are discussed in more detail in Chapter 13, "Managing Components and Dependencies."

You'll need to ensure that any libraries your application depends on are packaged up along with your application's binaries as part of your deployment pipeline, as described in the "Use Your Operating System's Packaging Tools" section on page 154. Ivy and Maven have no place on production boxes.

Deployment Scripting

One of the core principles of environment management is that changes to testing and production environments should only be made through an automated process. That means that you should not log into such systems remotely to perform deployments; they should be entirely scripted. There are three ways to perform scripted deployments. First of all, if your system will run on a single box, you can write a script that will do everything that needs to be done locally on that box.

However, most of the time deployment requires some level of orchestration—that is, running scripts on different computers in order to perform a deployment. In this case, you need to have a set of deployment scripts—one for each independent part of the deployment process—and run them on all the necessary servers. It doesn't follow that there will be one script per server—for example, there might be one script to upgrade your database, one script to deploy a new binary to each of your application servers, and a third script to upgrade a service your application depends on.

You have three options for deploying onto remote machines. The first is to write a script that logs into each box and runs the appropriate commands. The second is to write a script that runs locally, and have agents that run the script on each of the remote machines. The third option is to package your application up using your platform's appropriate packaging technology and have an infrastructure management or deployment tool push out new versions, running any necessary tools to initialize your middleware. The third option is the most powerful, for the following reasons:

- Deployment tools like ControlTier and BMC BladeLogic, and infrastructure management tools like Marionette Collective, CfEngine, and Puppet, are declarative and idempotent, ensuring that the right version of the packages is installed on all necessary boxes even if some of them are down at the time the deployment is scheduled, or if you add a new machine or VM to your environment. See Chapter 11, "Managing Infrastructure and Environments," for more on these tools.

- You can use the same set of tools for both managing application deployment and managing your infrastructure. Since it's the same people—the operations team—that are responsible for both of these things, and the two go hand-in-hand, it makes sense to use a single tool for both purposes.

If this option is not possible, continuous integration servers that have an agent model (that is to say, almost all of them) make it very easy to go with the second option. This approach has several benefits:

- You have to do less work: Just write the scripts as if they were being executed locally, check them into version control, and have your CI server run them on the specified remote machines.

- The CI server provides all the infrastructure for managing jobs, such as rerunning them in the event of a failure, showing console output, and providing a dashboard where you can see the status of your deployments and which versions of your application are currently deployed to each of your environments.

- Depending on your security requirements, it may make sense to have the CI agents on your boxes call into the CI server to get everything they need, without allowing scripts to access testing and production envionments remotely.

Finally, if there is some reason you can't use any of the tools described above, you can script your own deployments. If your remote machines are UNIX, you can use plain old Scp or Rsync to copy over binaries and data, and Ssh to execute the relevant commands to perform deployments. If you're using Windows, there are options for you too: PsExec and PowerShell. There are also higher-level tools such as Fabric, Func, and Capistrano that take care of the nuts and bolts for you, making scripting your own depoyments pretty straightforward.

However, neither using your CI system nor scripting your own deployments will deal with error conditions, such as partially completed deployments, or with the case where a new node is added to the grid and needs to be provisioned and deployed to. For this reason, using a proper deployment tool is preferable.

The tools available in this field are continuously evolving. There are examples of using some of these tools, and updates on newer tools as they come out, at this book's website [dzMeNE].

Deploying and Testing Layers

If there is a fundamental core to our approach to delivery in general and to the building and deployment of complex systems specifically, it is that you should always strive to build on foundations that are known to be good. We don't bother testing changes that don't compile, we don't bother trying to acceptance-test changes that have failed commit tests, and so on.

This is even more true when the time comes to deploy our release candidates into production-like environments. Before we even bother to copy our binary deliverables to the correct place in the filesystem, we want to know that our environment is ready for us. To achieve this, we like to think of deployment as depositing a series of layers, as shown in Figure 6.2.

Apps / services / components	Application configuration
Middleware	Middleware configuration
Operating system	Operating system configuration
Hardware	

Figure 6.2 *Deploying software in layers*

The lowest layer is the operating system. Next is the middleware and any other software your application depends on. Once both these layers are in place, they will need some specific configuration applied to prepare them for the deployment of our application. Only after this has been added, can we deploy our software—the deployable binaries, any services or daemons, and their own associated configuration.

Testing Your Environment's Configuration

Each layer that you deploy may, if deployed incorrectly, prevent the application from functioning as it should. This means that you should test each layer as it is applied, so that you can fail the environment configuration process quickly if a problem occurs. The test should give a clear indication of where the problem lies.

These tests need not be exhaustive. They only need to catch common failures or costly potential failures. They should be very simple "smoke tests" that assert the presence or absence of key resources. The objective is to provide a degree of confidence that the layer that has just been deployed is working.

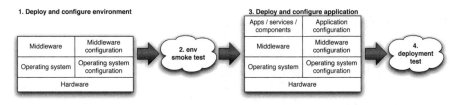

Figure 6.3 *Deployment testing layers*

The infrastructure smoke tests that you write will be unique for any given system. But the intention of the tests is consistent: to prove that the environment's configuration matches our expectations. There is more on infrastructure monitoring in the "Monitoring Infrastructure and Applications" section on page 317. To give you a sense of what we have in mind, here are some examples of tests that we found useful in the past:

- Confirm that we can retrieve a record from our database.

- Confirm that we can contact the website.

- Assert that our message broker has the correct set of messages registered in it.

- Send several "pings" through our firewall to prove that it allows our traffic and provides a round-robin load distribution between our servers.

Smoke-Testing N-Tier Architectures

We were deploying a .NET project to a set of servers. As in many other .NET environments, there were multiple physically separated tiers. On this system, web services were deployed to two servers: a database server and an application server. Each web service had its own port and URI specified in the configuration files of the other tiers. Diagnosing communication problems was very painful and involved trawling through server logs on the machines at each end of the communication channel to find out what the problem was.

We wrote a simple Ruby script that parsed the config.xml files and tried to connect to each URI in turn. It would then print the results on the console, something like this:

```
http://database.foo.com:3002/service1 OK
http://database.foo.com:3003/service2 OK
http://database.foo.com:3004/service3 Timeout
http://database.foo.com:3003/service4 OK
```

This made it very simple to diagnose connection problems.

Tips and Tricks

In this section we will list some solutions and strategies that we have used to solve common build and deployment problems.

Always Use Relative Paths

The most common mistake in a build is to use absolute paths by default. This creates a tight dependency between the configuration of a specific machine and your build process, making it hard to configure and maintain other servers. For example, it makes it impossible to have two check-outs of the same project on one machine—a practice that can be very helpful in lots of different situations, from comparative debugging to parallel testing.

Your default should be to use relative paths for everything. That way, each instance of your build is wholly self-contained and the image that you commit to your version control system automatically ensures that everything is in the right place and works as it should.

Occasionally, the use of absolute paths is hard to avoid. Try to be creative and avoid it where possible. If you are forced to use absolute paths, make sure they are the special case in your build, not the normal approach. Ensure they are kept in properties files or some other configuration mechanism that is independent of your build system. There may be a couple of good reasons for the use of absolute paths to be necessary. The first is if you have to integrate with third-party libraries that rely on hard-coded paths. Isolate these parts of your system as much as possible and don't let them infect the rest of your build.

Even when deploying your application, it is possible to avoid absolute paths. Every operating system and application stack has a convention for installing software, such as UNIX's Filesystem Hierarchy Standard (FHS). Use your system's packaging tools to enforce these conventions. If you must install in some non-standard place, do this through an option in your configuration system. Try to minimize these by making all of the paths in your system relative to one or more well-defined root paths—the deployment root, the configuration root, and so on—and overriding just these roots.

For more information on configuring your application at deployment time, take a look at Chapter 2, "Configuration Management."

Eliminate Manual Steps

It is amazing how many people deploy their software manually or though GUI-driven tools. For many organizations, a "build script" is a printed document with a series of instructions like:

```
...
STEP 14. Copy all the dlls from the CDROM directory E:\web_server\dlls\ into the new
         virtual directory
STEP 15. Open a command prompt and type: regsvr webserver_main.dll
STEP 16. Open the Microsoft IIS Management console and click Create New Application
...
```

This type of deployment is tedious and error-prone. The documentation is always wrong or out-of-date, and therefore requires extensive rehearsal in preproduction environments. Every deployment is unique—a bugfix or a small change to the system may require only one or two parts of the system to be redeployed. So, the deployment procedure must be revised for each release. Knowledge and artifacts from previous deployments cannot be reused. Each deployment is really an exercise of memory and understanding of the system for the individual performing it, and it is fundamentally error-prone.

So, when should you think about automating a process? The simplest answer is, "When you have to do it a second time." The third time you do something, it should be done using an automated process. This fine-grained incremental approach rapidly creates a system for automating the repeated parts of your development, build, test, and deployment process.

Build In Traceability from Binaries to Version Control

It's essential to be able to determine from any given binary which revision in version control was used to generate it. If you have a problem in your production environment, being able to figure out exactly which versions of each component are on that box and where they came from can be a life saver (Bob Aiello tells a great story about this in his book *Configuration Management Best Practices*).

There are various ways to do this. In .NET, you can include versioning meta-data in assemblies—make sure your build scripts always do this, and include the version control revision identifier. JAR files can also include metadata in their manifests, so you can do something analogous here. If the technology you use doesn't support building metadata into your packages, you can go the other way: Take an MD5 hash of each binary your build process generates along with its name and the revision identifier it came from, and store them in a database. That way you can take the MD5 of any binary and determine exactly what it is and where it came from.

Don't Check Binaries into Version Control as Part of Your Build

It can sometimes seem like a good idea to check binaries or reports into version control as part of your build process. However, in general, you should resist this. It is a bad idea in several ways.

First, one of the most important functions of revision control identifiers is to be able to trace what happened to a particular set of check-ins. Usually you will associate a revision control ID with a build label and use that to trace a set of changes through the different environments it passes through into production. If you check in binaries and reports from your build, that means the binaries corresponding to a version control revision identifier will have a different revision identifier of their own—a recipe for confusion.

Instead, put binaries and reports onto a shared filesystem. If you lose them or need to re-create them, the best practice is to get the source and create them again. If you are unable to reliably re-create binaries from your source, it means your configuration management isn't up to scratch and needs to be improved.

The general rule of thumb is not to check in anything *created* as part of your build, test, and deploy cycle into source control. Instead, treat these artifacts as metadata to be associated with the identifier of the revision that triggered the build. Most modern CI and release management servers have artifact repositories and metadata management systems that can help you do this, or you can use tools like Maven, Ivy, or Nexus.

Test Targets Should Not Fail the Build

In some build systems, the default behavior is that the build fails immediately when a task fails. If you have a "test" target, for example, and the tests specified in that target fail, then the whole build will fail immediately after the target is run. This is almost always a Bad Thing—instead, record the fact that the activity has failed, and continue with the rest of the build process. Then, at the end of the process, see if any of the individual tasks failed and, if so, exit with a failure code.

This problem arises because in many projects, it makes sense to have multiple test targets. For example, in a commit test suite there may be a set of unit tests, a couple of integration tests, and a smattering of acceptance smoke tests. If the unit tests run first and fail the build, then we won't know if the integration tests were going to pass until the next time we check in. More wasted time.

A better practice is to make the failure set a flag but fail the build later, after generating more useful reports or running a more complete set of tests. For example, in NAnt and Ant this can be done using a `failure-property` attribute on the test task.

Constrain Your Application with Integrated Smoke Tests

Interaction designers often constrain interfaces to prevent undesirable user input. In the same way, you can constrain your applications so that they do not work if they find themselves in an unfamiliar situation. For example, you can make deployment scripts check that they are running on the correct machine before they deploy anything. This is particularly important for testing and production configurations.

Almost all systems have a "batch processing" piece that runs periodically. In accounting systems, there are components that only run once a month, once a quarter, or once a year. In this case, make sure the deployed version validates its configuration when it is installed. You don't want to be debugging the install you did today at 3 A.M. on January 1st of the next year.

.NET Tips and Tricks

.NET has its own peculiarities—here are a few things you should watch out for.

Solution and project files in .NET contain references to the files they will actually build. If a file is not referenced, it won't get built. This means that it is possible for a file to be removed from the solution but still exist on the filesystem. This can lead to hard-to-diagnose problems, since somewhere, someone will look at this file and wonder what it is for. It is important to keep your project clean by removing these files. One simple way to do this is to turn on the Show Hidden Files feature in all your solutions, and then keep an eye out for files with no icon. When you see one, delete it from your source control system.

Ideally, this would happen automatically when you delete them from the solution, but unfortunately most source control integration tools that integrate with Visual Studio do not do this. While waiting for the tool vendors to implement this, it is important to keep an eye on this problem.

Watch out for bin and obj directories. Make sure your clean deletes all the bin and obj directories in your solution. One way to ensure this is to have your "clean" call Devenv's `clean solution` command.

Summary

We use the term "script" in quite a broad sense. Generally, by this we mean all the automation that helps us build, test, deploy, and release our software. When you approach that broad collection of scripts from the end of the deployment pipeline, it looks dauntingly complex. However, each task in a build or deployment script is simple, and the process itself is not a complex one. Our very strong advice is to use the build and deployment process as a guide to your collection of scripts. Grow your automated build and deployment capabilities step by step, working through the deployment pipeline by iteratively identifying and then automating the most painful steps. Keep the end goal in mind all the time—that is, the goal of sharing the same deployment mechanism between development, testing, and production, but don't get too hung up on that thought early in the creation of your tools. Do, however, involve both operations and developers in the creation of these mechanisms.

These days, a wide variety of technologies exist for scripting your build, test, and deployment process. Even Windows, traditionally the poor relation when it comes to automation, has some enviable tools at its disposal with the arrival of PowerShell and the scripting interfaces in IIS and the rest of the Microsoft stack. We have highlighted the most popular ones in this chapter and provided pointers to further information on these and other resources. Obviously, we can't do more than scratch the surface of this topic in a general book like this. If we have given you a solid understanding of the foundations of build scripting and the various possibilities open to you—and more importantly, inspired you to go forth and automate—then we have achieved our goal.

Finally, it bears reiterating that scripts are first-class parts of your system. They should live for its entire life. They should be version-controlled, maintained, tested, and refactored, and be the *only* mechanism that you use to deploy your software. So many teams treat their build system as an afterthought; in our experience, build and deployment systems are nearly always the poor relation when it comes to design. As a result, such poorly maintained systems are often the barrier to a sensible, repeatable release process, rather than its foundation. Delivery teams should spend time and care to get the build and deployment scripts right. This is not a task for an intern on your team to cut his or her teeth on. Spend some time, think about the goals you want to achieve, and design your build and deployment process to attain them.

Chapter 7

The Commit Stage

Introduction

The commit stage begins with a change to the state of the project—that is, a commit to the version control system. It ends with either a report of failure or, if successful, a collection of binary artifacts and deployable assemblies to be used in subsequent test and release stages, as well as reports on the state of the application. Ideally, a commit stage should take less than five minutes to run, and certainly no more than ten.

The commit stage represents, in more ways than one, the entrance into the deployment pipeline. Not only is it the point at which a new release candidate is created; it is also where many teams start when they begin to implement a deployment pipeline. When a team implements the practice of continuous integration, it creates a commit stage in the process of doing so.

It is the vital first step. Using a commit stage ensures that your project will minimize the time spent on code-level integration. It drives good design practices and has a dramatic effect on the quality of code—and the speed of delivery too.

The commit stage is also the point at which you should begin the construction of your deployment pipeline.

We have already briefly described the commit stage in earlier chapters, "Continuous Integration" and "Anatomy of the Deployment Pipeline." In this chapter, we expand upon that material by describing in more detail how to create an effective commit stage and efficient commit tests. This will primarily be of interest to developers, who are the main consumers of feedback from the commit stage. The commit stage is shown in Figure 7.1.

To refresh your memory, the commit stage works as follows. Somebody checks a change into mainline (trunk) in version control. Your continuous integration server detects the change, checks out the source code, and performs a series of tasks, including

- Compiling (if necessary) and running the commit tests against the integrated source code

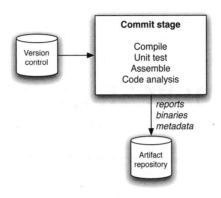

Figure 7.1 *The commit stage*

- Creating binaries that can be deployed into any environment (this will include compiling and assembling if you're using a compiled language)

- Performing any analysis necessary to check the health of the codebase

- Creating any other artifacts (such as database migrations or test data) that will be used later in the deployment pipeline

These tasks are orchestrated by build scripts that are run by your continuous integration server. You can read more about build scripting in Chapter 6, "Build and Deployment Scripting." The binaries (if the stage succeeds) and reports are then stored into your central artifact repository for use by your delivery team and by later stages in the pipeline.

For developers, the commit stage is the most important feedback cycle in the development process. It provides rapid feedback on the most common errors that they, as developers, introduce to the system. The result of the commit stage represents a significant event in the life of every release candidate. Success at this stage is the only way to enter the deployment pipeline and thus initiate the software delivery process.

Commit Stage Principles and Practices

If one of the goals of the deployment pipeline is to eliminate builds that are not fit to make it into production, then the commit stage is the bouncer at the door. Its aim is to ensure that any undesirables are rejected before they cause any trouble. The principal goal of the commit stage is to either create deployable artifacts, or fail fast and notify the team of the reason for the failure.

Here are some principles and practices that make for an effective commit stage.

Provide Fast, Useful Feedback

Failures in the commit tests can usually be attributed to one of the following three causes. Either a syntax error has been introduced into the code, caught by compilation in compiled languages; or a semantic error has been introduced into the application, causing one or more tests to fail; or there is a problem with the configuration of the application or its environment (including the operating system). Whatever the problem, in case of failures, the commit stage should notify the developers as soon as the commit tests are complete and provide a concise summary of the reasons for the failures, such as a list of failed tests, the compile errors, or any other error conditions. The developers should also be able to easily access the console output from the running of the commit stage, which may be split across several boxes.

Errors are easiest to fix if they are detected early, close to the point where they were introduced. This is not only because they are fresh in the minds of those who introduced them to the system, but also because the mechanics of discovering the cause of the error are simpler. If a developer makes a change that results in a failing test and the cause of the failure is not immediately obvious, the natural thing to do is to look at everything that has changed since the last time the system was working to narrow the focus of the search.

If that developer has been following our advice and committing changes frequently, the scope of each change will be small. If the deployment pipeline is able to identify that failure quickly, ideally at the commit stage, then the scope of the change is limited to those changes made personally by the developer. This means that fixing the problems found in the commit stage is significantly simpler than those identified later in the process, in stages that may be testing a larger number of changes batched together.

So, for our deployment pipeline to be efficient, we need to catch errors as early as possible. On most projects we actually begin this process even before the commit stage by maximizing our use of modern development environments—working hard to fix any compile-time warnings (if applicable) or syntax errors as soon as they are highlighted in our development environments. Many modern CI servers also provide the function called *pretested commit,* or *preflight build,* that runs the commit stage against the changes before they are checked in. If you don't have this facility, you must compile and run your commit tests locally before committing.

The commit stage is the first formal step that takes our focus on quality beyond the scope of an individual developer. The first thing that happens in the commit stage is that the committer's changes are integrated with the mainline, and then a kind of automated "proofreading" of the integrated application is performed. If we are to stick to our aim of identifying errors early, we need to focus on failing fast, so we need the commit stage to catch most of the errors that developers are likely to introduce into the application.

A common error early in the adoption of continuous integration is to take the doctrine of "fail fast" a little too literally and fail the build immediately when an error is found. This is nearly right, but is optimized too far. We generally divide our commit stage into a series of tasks (the exact tasks will depend on the project) such as compiling, running unit tests, and so forth. We only stop the commit stage if an error prevents the rest of the stage from running—such as, for example, a compilation error. Otherwise, we run the commit stage to the end and present an aggregated report of all the errors and failures so they can all be fixed at once.

What Should Break the Commit Stage?

Traditionally, the commit stage is designed to fail in one of the circumstances listed above: Compilation fails, tests break, or there is an environmental problem. Otherwise, the commit stage succeeds, reporting that everything is OK. But what if the tests pass because there are only a handful of them? What if the quality of the code is bad? If compilation succeeds but there are hundreds of warnings, should we be satisfied? A green commit stage can easily be a false positive, suggesting that the quality of the application is acceptable when in fact it isn't.

A strong argument can be made that the binary constraint we impose upon the commit stage—either success or a failure—is too limiting. It should be possible to provide richer information, such as a set of graphs representing code coverage and other metrics, upon completion of a commit stage run. This information could be aggregated using a series of thresholds into a traffic lights display (red, amber, green) or a sliding scale. We could, for example, fail the commit stage if the unit test coverage drops below 60%, and have it pass but with the status of amber, not green, if it goes below 80%.

We haven't seen anything this sophisticated in real life. However, we have written commit stage scripts which cause it to fail if the number of warnings increases, or fails to decrease (a practice we call "ratcheting"), as described in the "Failing the Build for Warnings and Code Style Breaches" section on page 73. It is perfectly acceptable to have your scripts fail the commit stage if the amount of duplication increases beyond some preset limit, or for some other violation of code quality.

Remember, though, that if the commit stage fails, the rule is that the delivery team must immediately stop whatever they are doing and fix it. Don't fail the commit test for some reason that hasn't been agreed upon by the whole team, or people will stop taking failures seriously and continuous integration will break down. Do, however, continuously review your application's quality and consider enforcing quality metrics through the commit stage where appropriate.

Tend the Commit Stage Carefully

The commit stage will include both build scripts and scripts to run unit tests, static analysis tools, and so forth. These scripts need to be maintained carefully and treated with the same level of respect as you would treat any other part of your application. Like any other software system, when build scripts are poorly designed and maintained, the effort to keep them working grows in what seems like an exponential manner. This has a double-whammy effect. A poor build system not only draws valuable and expensive development effort away from the important job of creating the business behavior of your application; it also slows down anyone still trying to implement that business behavior. We have seen several projects effectively grind to a halt under the weight of their build problems.

Constantly work to improve the quality, design, and performance of the scripts in your commit stage as they evolve. An efficient, fast, reliable commit stage is a key enabler of productivity for any development team, so a small investment in time and thought to get it working well is nearly always repaid very quickly. Keeping the commit build fast and ensuring that failures, of whatever kind, are caught early requires creativity, such as careful selection and design of test cases. Scripts that are treated as secondary to application code rapidly become impossible to understand and maintain. Our record so far is a project we inherited with an Ant script weighing in at 10,000 lines of XML. Needless to say, this project required an entire team devoted to keeping the build working—a complete waste of resources.

Ensure that your scripts are modular, as described in Chapter 6, "Build and Deployment Scripting." Structure them so as to keep common tasks, used all the time but rarely changing, separate from the tasks that you will be changing often, such as adding a new module to your codebase. Separate the code that runs different stages of your deployment pipeline into separate scripts. Most importantly of all, avoid environment-specific scripts: Separate environment-specific configuration from the build scripts themselves.

Give Developers Ownership

At some organizations, there are teams of specialists who are experts at the creation of effective, modular build pipelines and the management of the environments in which they run. We have both worked in this role. However, we consider it a failure if we get to the point where only those specialists can maintain the CI system.

It is vital that the delivery team have a sense of ownership for the commit stage (and indeed the rest of the pipeline infrastructure). It is intimately tied to their work and their productivity. If you impose any barriers between the developers and their ability to get changes made quickly and effectively, you will slow their progress and store trouble for later.

Run-of-the-mill changes, such as adding new libraries, configuration files, and so on, should be perormed by developers and operations people working together as they find the need to do so. This kind of activity should not be done by a build specialist, except perhaps in the very early days of a project when the team is working to establish the build.

The expertise of specialists is not to be undervalued, but their goal should be to establish good structures, patterns, and use of technology, and to transfer their knowledge to the delivery team. Once these ground rules are established, their specialist expertise should only be needed for significant structural shifts, not regular day-to-day build maintenance.

For very large projects, there is sometimes enough work to keep an environment or build specialist busy full time, but in our experience this is best treated as a temporary stop-gap to solve a thorny problem, with the resulting knowledge to be propagated through the delivery team by developers working with the specialist.

Developers and operations people must feel comfortable with, and responsible for, the maintenance of their build system.

Use a Build Master for Very Large Teams

In small and colocated teams of up to twenty or thirty individuals, self-organization can work very well. If the build is broken, in a team this size it is usually easy enough to locate the person or persons responsible and either remind them of the fact if they are not working on it, or offer to help if they are.

In larger or more widely spread teams, this isn't always easy. Under these circumstances it is useful to have someone to play the role of a "build master." Their job is to oversee and direct the maintenance of the build, but also to encourage and enforce build discipline. If a build breaks, the build master notices and gently—or not gently if it has been a while—reminds the culprit of their responsibility to the team to fix the build quickly or back out their changes.

Another situation where we have found this role useful is in teams new to continuous integration. In such teams, build discipline is not yet ingrained, so reminders are needed to keep things on track.

The build master should never be a permanent role. Team members should rotate through it, perhaps on a weekly basis. It's good discipline—and an important learning experience—for everyone to try this role from time to time. In any case, the kind of people who want to do it full time are few and far between.

The Results of the Commit Stage

The commit stage, like every stage in the deployment pipeline, has both inputs and outputs. The inputs are source code, and the outputs are binaries and reports. The reports produced include the test results, which are essential to work out what went wrong if the tests fail, and reports from analysis of the codebase. Analysis reports can include things like test coverage, cyclomatic complexity, cut and paste analysis, afferent and efferent coupling, and any other useful metrics that help establish the health of the codebase. The binaries generated by the commit stage are precisely the same ones that will be reused throughout the pipeline, and potentially released to users.

The Artifact Repository

The outputs of the commit stage, your reports and binaries, need to be stored somewhere for reuse in the later stages of your pipeline, and for your team to be able to get hold of them. The obvious place might appear to be your version control system. There are several reasons why this is not the right thing to do, apart from the incidental facts that in this way you're likely to work through disk space fast, and that some version control systems won't support such behavior.

- The artifact repository is an unusual kind of version control system, in that it only needs to keep some versions. Once a release candidate has failed some stage in the deployment pipeline, we are no longer interested in it. So we can, if we wish, purge the binaries and reports from the artifact repository.

- It is essential to be able to trace back from your released software to the revisions in version control that were used to create it. In order to do this, an instance of a pipeline should be correlated with the revisions in your version control system that triggered it. Checking anything into source control as part of your pipeline makes this process significantly more complex by introducing further revisions associated with your pipeline.

- One of the acceptance criteria for a good configuration management strategy is that the binary creation process should be repeatable. That is, if I delete the binaries and then rerun the commit stage from the same revision that originally triggered it, I should get exactly the same binaries again. Binaries are second-class citizens in the world of configuration management, although it is worth keeping hashes of your binaries in permanent storage to verify that you can re-create exactly the same thing and to audit back from production to the commit stage.

Most modern continuous integration servers provide an artifact repository, including settings which allow unwanted artifacts to be purged after some length of time. They generally provide a mechanism to specify declaratively which artifacts you want to store in the repository following any jobs that they run, and provide a web interface to allow your team to access the reports and binaries. Alternatively, you could use a dedicated artifact repository like Nexus, or some other Maven-style repository manager, to handle binaries (these are not generally suitable for storing reports). Repository managers make it much easier to access binaries from development machines without having to integrate with your CI server.

Creating Your Own Artifact Repository

It's very simple to create your own artifact repository if you want to. We describe the principles behind artifact repositories in much more detail in Chapter 13, "Managing Components and Dependencies."

Figure 7.2 shows a diagram of the use of an artifact repository in a typical installation. It is a key resource which stores the binaries, reports, and metadata for each of your release candidates.

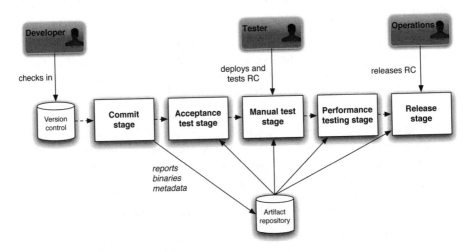

Figure 7.2 *The role of the artifact repository*

The following details each step in the happy path of a release candidate that makes it successfully into production. The numbers refer to the enumerated steps shown in Figure 7.2.

1. Somebody on your delivery team commits a change.

2. Your continuous integration server runs the commit stage.

3. On successful completion, the binary as well as any reports and metadata are saved to the artifact repository.

4. Your CI server then retrieves the binaries created by the commit stage and deploys to a production-like test environment.

5. Your continuous integration server then runs the acceptance tests, reusing the binaries created by the commit stage.

6. On successful completion, the release candidate is marked as having passed the acceptance tests.

7. Testers can obtain a list of all builds that have passed the acceptance tests, and can press a button to run the automated process to deploy them into a manual testing environment.

8. Testers perform manual testing.

9. On successful conclusion of manual testing, testers update the status of the release candidate to indicate it has passed **manual testing**.

10. Your CI server retrieves the latest candidate that has passed acceptance testing, or manual testing depending on the pipeline configuration, from the artifact repository and deploys the application to the production test environment.

11. The capacity tests are run against the release candidate.

12. If successful, the status of the candidate is updated to "capacity-tested."

13. This pattern is repeated for as many stages as the pipeline requires.

14. Once the RC has passed through all of the relevant stages, it is "ready for release," and can be released by anybody with the appropriate authorization, usually a combination of sign-off by QA and operations people.

15. At the conclusion of the release process, the RC is marked as "released."

For simplicity, we described this as a sequential process. For the early stages this is true: They should be executed in order. However, depending on the project, it may make sense to run some of the post-acceptance-stage steps nonsequentially. For example, manual testing and capacity testing can both be triggered by the successful completion of the acceptance tests. Alternatively, the testing team can choose to deploy different release candidates to their environments.

Commit Test Suite Principles and Practices

There are some important principles and practices governing the design of a commit test suite. The vast majority of your commit tests should be comprised of unit tests, and it is these that we focus on in this section. The most important property of unit tests is that they should be very fast to execute. Sometimes we fail the build if the suite isn't sufficiently fast. The second important property is that they should cover a large proportion of the codebase (around 80% is a good rule of thumb), giving you a good level of confidence that when they pass, the application is fairly likely to be working. Of course, each unit test only tests a small part of the application without starting it up—so, by definition, the unit test suite can't give you full confidence that your application works; that's what the rest of the deployment pipeline is for.

Mike Cohn has a good way of visualizing how you should structure your automated test suite. In his test automation pyramid, shown in Figure 7.3, the unit tests form the vast majority of the tests. But since they execute so fast, the unit test suite should still complete in just a few minutes. Even though there are fewer acceptance tests (these are further subdivided into service and UI tests), these will typically take far longer to execute because they run against the full running system. All levels are essential to ensure that the application is working and delivering the expected business value. This test pyramid covers the left-hand side of the testing quadrant diagram ("support programming") shown in the "Types of Tests" section on page 84.

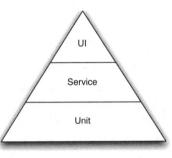

Figure 7.3   *Test automation pyramid (Cohn, 2009, Chapter 15)*

Designing commit tests that will run quickly isn't always simple. There are several strategies that we will describe in the next few paragraphs. Most of them, though, are techniques to achieve a single goal: to minimize the scope of any given test and keep it as focused as possible on testing only one aspect of the system. In particular, running unit tests shouldn't touch the filesystem, databases, libraries, frameworks, or external systems. Any calls to these parts of your environment should be replaced with test doubles, such as mocks and stubs (types of test doubles are defined in the "Test Doubles" section on page 91). A lot has been written about unit testing and test-driven development, so we're only scratching the surface here. Check out the bibliography for more on this topic.[1]

Avoid the User Interface

The user interface is, by definition, the most obvious place where your users will spot bugs. As a result, there is a natural tendency to focus test efforts on it, sometimes at the cost of other types of testing.

---

1.   James Carr has a good blog entry with some TDD patterns [cX6V1k].

For the purposes of commit tests, though, we recommend that you don't test via the UI at all. The difficulty with UI testing is twofold. First, it tends to involve a lot of components or levels of the software under test. This is problematic because it takes effort, and so time, to get all of the pieces ready for the test before executing the test itself. Second, UIs are designed to work at human timescales which, compared to computer timescales, are desperately slow.

If your project or technology choice allows you to avoid both of these issues, perhaps it is worth creating unit-level tests that operate via the UI, but in our experience UI testing is often problematic and usually better handled at the acceptance test stage of the deployment pipeline.

We will discuss approaches to UI testing in much more detail in our chapter on acceptance testing.

Use Dependency Injection

Dependency injection, or inversion of control, is a design pattern that describes how the relationships between objects should be established from outside the objects rather than from within. Obviously, this advice only applies if you're using an object-oriented language.

If I create a `Car` class, I could design it so it creates its own `Engine` whenever I create a new `Car`. Alternately, I can elect to design the `Car` so that it forces me to provide it with an `Engine` when I create it.

The latter is dependency injection. This is more flexible because now I can create `Car`s with different kinds of `Engine` without changing the `Car` code. I could even create my `Car` with a special `TestEngine` that only pretends to be an `Engine` while I'm testing the `Car`.

This technique is not only a great route to flexible, modular software, but it also makes it very easy to limit the scope of a test to just the classes that you want to test, not all of their dependent baggage too.

Avoid the Database

People new to the use of automated testing will often write tests that interact with some layer in their code, store the results in the database, and then confirm that the results were stored. While this has the advantage of being a simple approach to understand, in all other respects it isn't a very effective approach.

First of all, the tests it produces are dramatically slower to run. The statefulness of the tests can be a handicap when you want to repeat them, or run several similar tests in close succession. The complexity of the infrastructure setup makes the whole testing approach more complex to establish and manage. Finally, if it isn't simple to eliminate the database from your tests, it implies poor layering and separation of concerns in your code. This is another area where testability and CI apply a subtle pressure on you and your team to develop better code.

The unit tests that form the bulk of your commit tests should never rely on the database. To achieve this, you should be able to separate the code under test from its storage. This requires good layering in the code, as well as the use of techniques like dependency injection or even an in-memory database as a last resort.

However, you should also include one or two very simple smoke tests in your commit tests. These should be end-to-end tests from your acceptance test suite that test high-value, commonly used functionality and prove that your application actually runs.

Avoid Asynchrony in Unit Tests

Asynchronous behaviors within the scope of a single test case make systems difficult to test. The simplest approach is to avoid the asynchrony by splitting your tests so that one test runs up to the point of the asynchronous break and then a separate test starts.

For example, if your system posts a message and then acts on it, wrap the raw message-sending technology with an interface of your own. Then you can confirm that the call is made as you expect in one test case, perhaps using a simple stub that implements the messaging interface or using mocking as described in the next section. You can add a second test that verifies the behavior of the message handler, simply calling the point that would be normally called by the messaging infrastructure. Sometimes, though, depending on your architecture, this is not possible without a lot of work.

We recommend that you work very hard to eliminate asynchrony in the commit stage testing. Tests which rely on infrastructure, such as messaging (even in-memory), count as component tests, not unit tests. More complex, slower-running component tests should be part of your acceptance test stage, not commit stage.

Using Test Doubles

The ideal unit tests are focused on a small, closely related number of code components, typically a single class or a few closely related classes.

However, in a well-designed system, each class is relatively small in size and achieves its goals through interactions with other classes. This is at the heart of good encapsulation—each class keeping secrets from every other about how it achieves its goals.

The problem is that, in such a nicely designed modular system, testing an object in the middle of a network of relationships may require lengthy setup in all the surrounding classes. The solution is to fake the interactions with a class' dependents.

Stubbing out the code of such dependencies has a long and honorable tradition. We have already described the use of dependency injection and provided a simple example of stubbing when we suggested the use of a `TestEngine` in place of an `Engine`.

Stubbing is the replacement of a part of a system with a simulated version that provides canned responses. Stubs don't respond to anything outside what is programmed. This is a powerful and flexible approach that is useful at every level—from stubbing a single, simple class that your code under test depends upon, to stubbing an entire system.

Using Stubs to Substitute for Messaging Systems

Dave once worked on a trading system that had a requirement to interact, in a fairly complex way, with another system, under development by another team, via a message queue. The conversation was fairly rich, with a collection of messages that to a large extent drove the lifecycle of a trade and kept it in step between the two systems. Without this external system, our system didn't own the full lifecycle of the trade, so it was hard to create meaningful end-to-end acceptance tests.

We implemented a reasonably complex stub that simulated the operation of the live system. This gave us lot of benefits. It allowed us to plug the gap in the lifecycle of our system for testing purposes. It also had the advantage of allowing us to simulate difficult edge cases that would otherwise be difficult to set up in the real systems. Finally, it broke our dependency on the parallel development that was taking place in the other system.

Instead of having to maintain a complex network of distributed systems all talking to one another, we could choose when to interact with the real thing and when to deal with the simpler stub. We managed the deployment of the stub through configuration so we could vary, by environment, whether we were interacting with the real system or the stub.

We tend to use stubbing widely for large-scale components and subsystems, but less so for the components at the programming language level; at this level, we generally prefer mocking.

Mocking is a newer technique. It is motivated by a liking for stubs, and a desire to use them widely, without incurring the work of writing lots of stub code. Wouldn't it be wonderful if, instead of writing tedious code to stub out all the dependencies for the classes we are testing, we could just let the computer build some stubs for us automatically?

Mocking is essentially just that. There are several mocking toolsets, such as Mockito, Rhino, EasyMock, JMock, NMock, Mocha, and so forth. Mocking allows you to effectively say, "Build me an object that can pretend to be a class of type X."

Crucially, it then goes further and allows you to specify, in a few simple assertions, the behavior you expect from the code you are testing. This is the essential difference between mocking and stubbing—with stubs, we don't care about how the stub is called; with mocks, we can verify that our code interacted with the mocks in the way we expected.

Let us return to our `Car` example and consider the two approaches side by side. For the sake of our example, consider a requirement that when we call `Car.drive`, we expect that `Engine.start` followed by `Engine.accelerate` are called.

As we have already described, we will use dependency injection in both cases to associate `Engine`s with `Car`s. Our simple classes might look like this:

```
class Car {
  private Engine engine;

  public Car(Engine engine) {
    this.Engine = engine;
  }

  public void drive() {
    engine.start();
    engine.accelerate();
  }
}

Interface Engine {
  public start();
  public accelerate();
}
```

If we use stubbing, we will create a stub implementation, a `TestEngine` that will record the fact that both `Engine.start` and `Engine.accelerate` were called. Since we require that `Engine.start` should be called first, we should probably throw an exception in our stub, or somehow record the error, if `Engine.accelerate` is called first.

Our test will now consist of the creation of a new `Car` passing a `TestEngine` into its constructor, calling the `Car.drive` method, and confirming that `Engine.start` and `Engine.accelerate` were each called in turn.

```
class TestEngine implements Engine {
  boolean startWasCalled = false;
  boolean accelerateWasCalled = false;
  boolean sequenceWasCorrect = false;

  public start() {
    startWasCalled = true;
  }
  public accelerate() {
    accelerateWasCalled = true;
    if (startWasCalled == true) {
      sequenceWasCorrect = true;
    }
  }
  public boolean wasDriven() {
    return startWasCalled && accelerateWasCalled && sequenceWasCorrect;
  }
}
```

```
class CarTestCase extends TestCase {
  public void testShouldStartThenAccelerate() {
    TestEngine engine = new TestEngine();
    Car car = new Car(engine);

    car.drive();

    assertTrue(engine.wasDriven());
  }
}
```

The equivalent test using mocking tools would be more like this: We create a mock `Engine` by making a call to a mock class, passing a reference to the interface or class that defines the interface to `Engine`.

We declare two expectations specifying, in the correct order, that we expect `Engine.start` and `Engine.accelerate` to be called. Finally, we ask the mock system to verify that what we expected to happen actually happened.

```
import jmock;

class CarTestCase extends MockObjectTestCase {
  public void testShouldStartThenAccelerate() {
    Mock mockEngine = mock(Engine);
    Car car = new Car((Engine)mockEngine.proxy());

    mockEngine.expects(once()).method("start");
    mockEngine.expects(once()).method("accelerate");

    car.drive();
  }
}
```

The example here is based on the use of an open source mock system called JMock, but others are similar. In this case, the final verification step is done implicitly at the end of each test method.

The benefits of mocking are plain. There is considerably less code, even in this trivially oversimplified example. In real use, mocking can save a lot of effort. Mocking is also a great way of isolating third-party code from the scope of your test. You can mock any interfaces to the third-party code and so eliminate the real code from the scope of your test—an excellent move when those interactions use costly remote communications or heavyweight infrastructure.

Finally, compared to the assembly of all the dependencies and state associated with them, tests that use mocking are usually very fast. Mocking is a technique that has lots of benefits: We strongly recommend it to you.

Minimizing State in Tests

Ideally, your unit tests should focus on asserting the behavior of your system. A common problem, particularly with relative newcomers to effective test design, is the accretion of state around your tests. The problem is really twofold. First, it is easy to envisage a test of almost any form where you input some values to one component of your system and get some results returned. You write the test by organizing the relevant data structures so that you can submit the inputs in the correct form and compare the results with the outputs you expect. In fact, virtually all tests are of this form, to a greater or lesser extent. The problem is that without care, systems and their associated tests become more and more complex.

It is too easy to fall into the trap of building elaborate, hard to understand, and hard to maintain data structures in order to support your tests. The ideal test is quick and easy to set up and even quicker and easier to tear down. Well-factored code tends to have neat tests. If your tests look cumbersome and complex, it reflects on the design of your system.

This is a difficult problem to nail, though. Our advice is to work to minimize the dependency on state in your tests. You can never realistically eliminate it, but it is sensible to maintain a constant focus on the complexity of the environment that you need to construct in order to run your test. As the test becomes increasingly complex, it is most likely signaling a need to look at the structure of your code.

Faking Time

Time can be a problem in automated testing for several reasons. Perhaps your system needs to trigger an end-of-day process at 8 P.M. Perhaps it needs to wait 500 milliseconds before progressing with the next step. Perhaps it needs to do something different on February 29th of a leap year.

All of these cases can be tricky to deal with, and potentially disastrous for your unit-testing strategy if you try to tie them to the real system clock.

Our strategy for any time-based behavior is to abstract our need for time information into a separate class that is under our control. We usually apply dependency injection to inject our wrapper for the system-level time behaviors we use.

This way, we can stub or mock the behavior of our Clock class, or whatever suitable abstraction we choose. If we decide, within the scope of a test, that it is a leap year or 500 milliseconds later, it is fully under our control.

For fast builds, this is most important for any behavior that warrants some delay or wait. Structure your code so that all delays during the test run are zero, to keep test performance good. If your unit test needs a real delay, perhaps it is worth reconsidering the design of your code and test to avoid it.

This has become so ingrained in our own development that, if ever we write any code that needs time in almost any capacity, we expect that we will need to abstract our access to the system time services instead of calling them direct from within our business logic.

Brute Force

Developers will always argue for the fastest commit cycle. In reality, though, this need must be balanced with the commit stage's ability to identify the most common errors that you are likely to introduce. This is an optimization process that can only work through trial and error. Sometimes, it is better to accept a slower commit stage than to spend too much time optimizing the tests for speed or reducing the proportion of bugs they catch.

We generally aim to keep our commit stage at under ten minutes. This is pretty much the upper bound as far as we are concerned. It is longer than the ideal, which is under five minutes. Developers working on large projects may balk at the target of ten minutes, thinking it unachievably low. Other development teams will see this as a compromise that goes too far, knowing that the most efficient commit stage is much faster than this. We consider this number to be a useful guide, though, based on our observations of many projects. When this limit is broken, developers start doing two things, both of which have an extremely bad effect on the development process: They start checking in less frequently and, if the commit stage takes *significantly* more than ten minutes to run, they stop caring about whether or not the commit test suite passes.

There are two tricks you can use to make your commit test suite run faster. First of all, split it up into separate suites and run them in parallel on several machines. Modern CI servers have "build grid" functionality that makes it extremely straightforward to do this. Remember that computing power is cheap and people are expensive. Getting feedback on time is much more valuable than the cost of a few servers. The second trick you can use is to push, as part of your build optimization process, those tests that are both long-running and don't often fail out into your acceptance test stage. Note, however, that this results in a longer wait to get feedback on whether a set of changes has broken these tests.

Summary

The commit stage should be focused on one thing: detecting, as fast as possible, the most common failures that changes to the system may introduce, and notifying the developers so they can fix the problems quickly. The value of the feedback that the commit stage provides is such that it is important to invest in keeping it working efficiently, and most of all, quickly.

The commit stage of your deployment pipeline should be run every time someone introduces a change into your application's code or configuration. Thus it will be exercised multiple times each day by each member of your development team. The natural tendency of developers is to complain if the performance of the build falls below an acceptable standard: Let it grow to over five minutes and the complaints will start. It is important to listen to this feedback and to do everything possible to keep this stage fast, while keeping an eye on the real value—which is that it fails fast and so provides feedback on errors that would otherwise be much more costly to fix later.

Thus the establishment of a commit stage—an automated process, launched on every change, that builds binaries, runs automated tests, and generates metrics—is the minimum you can do on the way to your adoption of the practice of continuous integration. A commit stage provides a huge advance in the quality and reliability of your delivery process—assuming you follow the other practices involved in continuous integration, such as checking in regularly and fixing any defects as soon as they are discovered. Though it is only the start of the deployment pipeline, it provides perhaps the biggest bang for your buck: a paradigm shift to knowing the exact moment a change is introduced that breaks your application and being able to get it working again right away.

Chapter 8

Automated Acceptance Testing

Introduction

In this chapter we will explore automated acceptance testing, and its place in the deployment pipeline, in a little more detail. Acceptance tests are a crucial stage in the deployment pipeline: They take delivery teams beyond basic continuous integration. Once you have automated acceptance tests in place, you are testing the business acceptance criteria of your application, that is, validating that it provides users with valuable functionality. Acceptance tests are typically run against every version of your software that passes the commit tests. The workflow of the acceptance test stage of the deployment pipeline is shown in Figure 8.1.

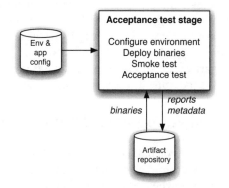

Figure 8.1 *The acceptance test stage*

We begin the chapter by discussing the importance of acceptance tests within the delivery process. Then we discuss in depth how to write effective acceptance tests and how to maintain an efficient acceptance test suite. Finally, we cover the principles and practices that govern the acceptance test stage itself. But before any of that, we should state what we mean by acceptance testing. What is the role of an acceptance test as distinct from a functional test or a unit test?

An individual acceptance test is intended to verify that the acceptance criteria of a story or requirement have been met. Acceptance criteria come in many different varieties; for one thing, they can be functional or nonfunctional. Nonfunctional acceptance criteria include things like capacity, performance, modifiability, availability, security, usability, and so forth. The key point here is that when the acceptance tests associated with a particular story or requirement pass, they demonstrate that its acceptance criteria have been met, and that it is thus both complete and working.

The acceptance test suite as a whole both verifies that the application delivers the business value expected by the customer and guards against regressions or defects that break preexisting functions of the application.

The focus on acceptance testing as a means of showing that the application meets its acceptance criteria for each requirement has an additional benefit. It makes everyone involved in the delivery process—customers, testers, developers, analysts, operations personnel, and project managers—think about what success means for each requirement. We will cover this in more detail in the "Acceptance Criteria as Executable Specifications" section on page 195.

If you are from a test-driven design background, you are perhaps wondering why these aren't the same as our unit tests. The difference is that acceptance tests are business-facing, not developer-facing. They test whole stories at a time against a running version of the application in a production-like environment. Unit tests are an essential part of any automated test strategy, but they usually do not provide a high enough level of confidence that the application can be released. The objective of acceptance tests is to prove that our application does what the customer meant it to, not that it works the way its programmers think it should. Unit tests can sometimes share this focus, but not always. The aim of a unit test is to show that a single part of the application does what the programmer intends it to; this is by no means the same as asserting that a user has what they need.

Why Is Automated Acceptance Testing Essential?

There has always been a great deal of controversy around automated acceptance tests. Project managers and customers often think they are too expensive to create and maintain—which indeed, when done badly, they are. Many developers believe that unit test suites created through test-driven development are enough to protect against regressions. Our experience has been that the cost of a properly created and maintained automated acceptance test suite is much lower than that of performing frequent manual acceptance and regression testing, or that of the alternative of releasing poor-quality software. We have also found that automated acceptance tests catch serious problems that unit or component test suites, however comprehensive, could never catch.

First of all, it is worth pointing out the costs of manual acceptance testing. To prevent defects from being released, acceptance testing of your application needs to be performed every time it is released. We know of one organization that spends $3,000,000 on manual acceptance testing for every release. This is an extremely serious constraint on their ability to release software frequently. Any manual testing effort worth its salt, when performed on an application of any complexity, is going to be very expensive.

Furthermore, to fulfill its role of catching regression defects, such testing needs to be performed as a phase once development is complete and a release is approaching. Thus manual testing usually happens at a time in the project where teams are under extreme pressure to get software out of the door. As a result, insufficient time is normally planned to fix the defects found as part of manual acceptance testing. Finally, when defects are found that require complex fixes, there is a high chance of introducing further regression problems into the application.[1]

An approach advocated by some in the agile community is to do away almost entirely with automated acceptance testing and write comprehensive suites of unit and component tests. These, in combination with other XP practices such as pair programming, refactoring, and careful analysis and exploratory testing by customers, analysts, and testers working together, are regarded by some as providing a superior alternative to the cost of automated acceptance tests.[2]

There are several flaws in this argument. First, no other type of test proves that the application, running more or less as it would in production, delivers the business value its users are expecting. Unit and component tests do not test user scenarios, and are thus incapable of finding the kinds of defects that appear when users put the application through a series of states in the course of interacting with it. Acceptance tests are designed exactly for this. They are also great at catching threading problems, emergent behavior in event-driven applications, and other classes of bugs caused by architectural mistakes or environmental and configuration problems. These kinds of defects can be hard to discover through manual testing, let alone unit or component testing.

Acceptance tests also protect your application when you are making large-scale changes to it. In this scenario, unit tests and component tests will often have to be radically altered along with your domain, limiting their ability to act as defenders of the function of the application. Only acceptance tests are capable of proving your application still works at the end of such a process.

Finally, teams that choose to forgo automated acceptance tests place a much greater burden on testers, who must then spend much more time on boring

---

1. Bob Martin articulates some of the reasons for why automating acceptance testing is important and should not be outsourced [dB6JQ1].
2. Advocates of this approach include J. B. Rainsberger, as described in his "Integrated Tests Are a Scam" blog entry [a0tjh0], and James Shore, in his "The Problems with Acceptance Testing" blog entry [dsyXYv].

and repetitive regression testing. The testers that we know are not in favor of this approach. While developers can take on some of this burden, many developers—who write unit and component tests—are simply not as effective as testers at finding defects in their own work. Automated acceptance tests written with the involvement of testers are, in our experience, a great deal better at finding defects in user scenarios than tests written by developers.

The real reason people don't like automated acceptance testing is that it is perceived as being too expensive. However, it is possible to decrease the cost of automating acceptance testing to well below the level where it becomes efficient and cost-effective. When automated acceptance tests are run against every build that passed the commit tests, the effects on the software delivery process are dramatic. First of all, since the feedback loop is much shorter, defects are found much sooner, when they are cheaper to fix. Second, since testers, developers, and customers need to work closely to create a good automated acceptance test suite, there is much better collaboration between them, and everybody is focused on the business value that the application is supposed to deliver.

There are other positive side effects resulting from an effective acceptance-test-based strategy: Acceptance tests work best with well-factored applications which are properly structured to have a thin UI layer, and carefully designed to be able to run on development machines as well as in production environments.

We have split the problem of creating and maintaining effective automated acceptance tests into four sections: creating acceptance tests; creating an application driver layer; implementing acceptance tests; and maintaining acceptance test suites. We will briefly introduce our approach before we go into detail.

How to Create Maintainable Acceptance Test Suites

Writing maintainable acceptance tests requires, first of all, careful attention to the analysis process. Acceptance tests are derived from acceptance criteria, so the acceptance criteria for your application must be written with automation in mind and must follow the INVEST principles,[3] with a particular reference to being valuable *to the end user* and testable. This is another of those subtle but important pressures that a focus on automated acceptance testing applies to the whole development process: a pressure for better requirements. Automation of badly written acceptance criteria that don't explain how the functionality to be developed is valuable to users is a major source of poor and hard-to-maintain acceptance test suites.

Once you have a set of acceptance criteria describing the value to be delivered to users, the next step is to automate them. Automated acceptance tests should always be layered, as shown in Figure 8.2.

---

3.   That is, they must be independent, negotiable, valuable, estimable, small, and testable.

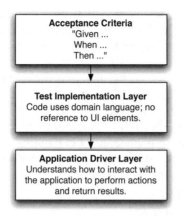

Figure 8.2 *Layers in acceptance tests*

The first layer in acceptance tests is the acceptance criteria. Tools like Cucumber, JBehave, Concordion, Twist, and FitNesse allow you to put acceptance criteria directly in tests and link them to the underlying implementation. However, as described later in this chapter, you can also take the approach of encoding the acceptance criteria in the names of your xUnit tests. You can then run your acceptance tests directly from the xUnit test framework.

It is crucial that your test implementations use your domain language and do not contain details of how to interact with the application. Test implementations that refer directly to the application's API or UI are brittle, and even small changes to the UI will immediately break all the tests referring to the changed UI element. It's not uncommon to see huge swathes of such acceptance test suites break when a single UI element changes.

Unfortunately, this antipattern is very common. Most tests are written at the level of detailed execution: "Poke this, prod that, look here for a result." Such tests are often the output of record-and-playback-style test automation products, which is one of the main reasons automated acceptance tests are perceived as expensive. Any acceptance test suites created with such tools are tightly coupled to the UI and therefore extremely brittle.

Most UI testing systems provide operations that allow you to put data into fields, click buttons, and read results from specified areas of the page. This level of detail is ultimately necessary, but it is a long way from the meaning—the real value—of a test case. The behavior that any given acceptance test case is intended to assert is, inevitably, at a very different level of abstraction. What we really want to know is answers to questions like "If I place an order, is it accepted?" or "If I exceed my credit limit, am I correctly informed?"

Test implementations should call through to a lower layer, which we call the application driver layer, to actually interact with the system under test. The application driver layer has an API that knows how to perform actions and return results. If your tests run against your application's public API, it is the application driver layer that knows the details of this API and calls the right parts of it. If your tests run against the GUI, this layer will contain a window driver. In a well-factored window driver, a given GUI element will only be referenced a handful of times, which mean that if it is changed, only these references to it will need to be updated.

Maintaining acceptance tests over the long term requires discipline. Careful attention must be paid to keep test implementations efficient and well factored, with particular reference to managing state, handling timeouts, and the use of test doubles. Acceptance test suites must be refactored as new acceptance criteria are added to ensure that they remain coherent.

Testing against the GUI

An important concern when writing acceptance tests is whether or not to run tests directly against the application's GUI. Since our acceptance tests are intended to simulate user interactions with the system, ideally we should be working via the user interface of the system, if it has one. If we don't test via the user interface, we are not testing the same code path that the users of our system will invoke in real interactions. However, there are several problems with testing directly against the GUI: its rapid rate of change, the complexity of scenario setup, access to test results, and untestable GUI technologies.

The user interface usually changes frequently during the process of application development. If your acceptance tests are coupled to your UI, small changes to the UI can easily break your acceptance test suites. This is not limited to the period of application development; it can also happen during user tests of the system, due to improvements in usability, spelling corrections, and so on.

Secondly, scenario setup can be complex if the UI is the only way into the system. Setting up a test case can involve many interactions to get the system into a state ready for the test itself. At the conclusion of a test, the results may not be readily evident through the UI which may not provide access to the information you need to validate the test results.

Finally, some UI technologies, especially newer ones, are extremely hard to test automatically.[4] It is important to check that the UI technology you choose can be driven through an automated framework.

There is an alternative to testing through the GUI. If your application is well designed, the GUI layer represents a clearly defined collection of display-only code that doesn't contain any business logic of its own. In this case, the risk associated with bypassing it and writing tests against the layer of code beneath it may be relatively small. An application written with testability in mind will have an API that both the GUI and the test harness can talk to in order to drive the

---

4. At the time of writing, Flex fell into this category—hopefully by the time you read this, new testing frameworks will have sprung up to drive testing through Flex.

application. Running tests against the business layer directly is a reasonable strategy that we recommend if your application can sustain it. It only requires enough discipline in your development team to keep the presentation focused solely on pixel-painting and not straying into the realms of business or application logic.

If your application is not designed in this way, you'll have to test directly against the UI. We'll discuss strategies for managing this later in the chapter, the main strategy being the window driver pattern.

Creating Acceptance Tests

In this section, we will discuss how to create automated acceptance tests. We'll start with the identification of acceptance criteria by analysts, testers, and customers working together, and then talk about representing acceptance criteria in a form that can be automated.

The Role of Analysts and Testers

Your development process should be tailored to suit the needs of your individual project, but as a generalization we recommend that most projects of any size should have a business analyst working as part of each team. The role of the business analyst is primarily to represent the customers and users of the system. They work with the customer to identify and prioritize requirements. They work with the developers to ensure that they have a good understanding of the application from the user's perspective. They guide developers to ensure that stories deliver the business value that they are meant to. They work with testers to ensure that acceptance criteria are specified properly, and to ensure that functionality developed meets these acceptance criteria and delivers the expected value.

Testers are essential on any project. Their role is ultimately to ensure that the current quality and production-readiness of the software being developed is understood by everybody on the delivery team, including the customer. They do this through working with customers and analysts to define acceptance criteria for stories or requirements, working with developers to write automated acceptance tests, and performing manual testing activities such as exploratory testing, manual acceptance testing, and showcases.

Not every team has separate individuals who perform these roles 100% of the time. Sometimes, developers act as analysts, or analysts act as testers. Ideally, the customer is sitting with the team performing the analyst role. The important point is that these roles should always exist on the team.

Analysis on Iterative Projects

In general, in this book we have attempted to avoid any presupposition of the development process that you are using. We believe that the patterns we describe are of benefit to any delivery team, whatever process they use. However, we believe that iterative development processes are essential to the creation of quality software. So, we hope that you will forgive us if it seems relevant to us to give a little more detail of iterative development processes here, because it helps to delineate the roles of the analyst, tester, and developer.

In iterative approaches to delivery, analysts spend much of their time defining acceptance criteria. These are the criteria by which teams can judge if a particular requirement has been met. Initially, the analysts will work closely with testers and the customer to define acceptance criteria. Encouraging analysts and testers to collaborate at this stage helps both parties and makes for a more effective process. The analyst gains because the tester can provide the benefit of their experience of what sorts of things can and should be usefully measured to define when a story is done. The tester benefits by gaining an understanding of the nature of the requirements before the testing of those requirements becomes their primary focus.

Once the acceptance criteria have been defined, just before the requirement is to be implemented, the analyst and tester sit with the developers who will do the implementation, along with the customer if available. The analyst describes the requirement and the business context in which it exists, and goes through the acceptance criteria. The tester then works with the developers to agree on a collection of automated acceptance tests that will prove that the acceptance criteria have been met.

These short kick-off meetings are a vital part of the glue that binds the iterative delivery process together, ensuring that every party to the implementation of a requirement has a good understanding of that requirement and of their role in its delivery. This approach prevents analysts from creating "ivory tower" requirements that are expensive to implement or test. It prevents testers from raising defects that aren't defects but are instead a misunderstanding of the system. It prevents developers from implementing something that bears little relationship to what anyone really wants.

While the requirement is being implemented, the developers will consult with the analyst if they find an area that they don't understand well enough, or if they have discovered a problem or a more efficient approach to solving the problem that the requirement poses. This interactivity is at the heart of iterative delivery processes that are enormously facilitated by the ability provided by the deployment pipeline to run our application whenever we need to on the environment of our choice.

When the developers believe that they have completed the work—which means all of the associated unit and component tests pass, and the acceptance tests have all been implemented and show that the system has fulfilled the requirement—they will demonstrate it to the analyst, the tester, and the customer. This review allows the analyst and customer to see the working solution to the requirement, and gives them an opportunity to confirm that it does indeed fulfill the requirement as intended. Often at this review a few small issues will be picked up, which are addressed immediately. Sometimes, such reviews trigger a discussion of alternatives or the implications of the change. This is a good opportunity for the team to test their shared understanding of the direction in which the system is evolving.

Once the analyst and the customer are happy that the requirement has been fulfilled, it moves on to testing by the testers.

Acceptance Criteria as Executable Specifications

As automated testing has become more central to the delivery of projects that use iterative processes, many practitioners have realized that automated testing is not just about testing. Rather, acceptance tests are executable specifications of the behavior of the software being developed. This is a significant realization which has spawned a new approach to automated testing, known as behavior-driven development. One of the core ideas of behavior-driven development is that your acceptance criteria should be written in the form of the customer's expectations of the behavior of the application. It should then be possible to take acceptance criteria thus written, and execute them directly against the application to verify that the application meets its specifications.

This approach has some significant advantages. Most specifications begin to become out-of-date as the application evolves. This is not possible for executable specifications: If they don't specify what the application does accurately, they will raise an exception to that effect when run. The acceptance test stage of the pipeline will fail when run against a version of the application that does not meet its specifications, and that version will therefore not be available for deployment or release.

Acceptance tests are business-facing, which means they should verify that your application delivers value to its users. Analysts define acceptance criteria for stories—criteria that must be fulfilled for the story to be recognized as done. Chris Matts and Dan North came up with a domain-specific language for writing acceptance criteria, which takes the following form:

Given some initial context,
When an event occurs,
Then there are some outcomes.

In terms of your application, "given" represents the state of your application at the beginning of the test case. The "when" clause describes an interaction between a user and your application. The "then" clause describes the state of the application after this interaction has completed. The job of your test case is to get the application into the state described in the "given" clause, perform the actions described in the "when" clause, and verify that the application's state is as described in the "then" clause.

For example, consider a financial trading application. We can write an acceptance criterion in the following format:

```
Feature: Placing an order

  Scenario: User order should debit account correctly
  Given there is an instrument called bond
  And there is a user called Dave with 50 dollars in his account
  When I log in as Dave
  And I select the instrument bond
  And I place an order to buy 4 at 10 dollars each
  And the order is successful
  Then I have 10 dollars left in my account
```

Tools like Cucumber, JBehave, Concordion, Twist, and FitNesse allow you to write acceptance criteria like these as plain text and keep them synchronized with the actual application. For example, in Cucumber, you would save the acceptance criterion described above in a file called something like features/placing_an_order.feature. This file represents the acceptance criteria in Figure 8.2. You would then create a Ruby file, listing the steps required for this scenario, as features/step_definitions/placing_an_order_steps.rb. This file represents the test implementation layer in Figure 8.2.

```ruby
require 'application_driver/admin_api'
require 'application_driver/trading_ui'

Before do
  @admin_api = AdminApi.new
  @trading_ui = TradingUi.new
end

Given /^there is an instrument called (\w+)$/ do |instrument|
  @admin_api.create_instrument(instrument)
end

Given /^there is a user called (\w+) with (\w+) dollars in his account$/ do
    |user, amount|
  @admin_api.create_user(user, amount)
end

When /^I log in as (\w+)$/ do |user|
  @trading_ui.login(user)
end

When /^I select the instrument (\w+)$/ do |instrument|
  @trading_ui.select_instrument(instrument)
end

When /^I place an order to buy (\d+) at (\d+) dollars each$/ do |quantity, amount|
  @trading_ui.place_order(quantity, amount)
end

When /^the order for (\d+) of (\w+) at (\d+) dollars each is successful$/ do
    |quantity, instrument, amount|
  @trading_ui.confirm_order_success(instrument, quantity, amount)
end
```

```
Then /^I have (\d+) dollars left in my account$/ do |balance|
  @trading_ui.confirm_account_balance(balance)
end
```

To support this and other tests, you would need to create the `AdminApi` and `TradingUi` classes in the directory `application_driver`. These classes form part of the application driver layer in Figure 8.2. They might call Selenium, Sahi, or WebDriver, if your application is web based, or White if it's a rich client .NET application, or use HTTP POST or GET if your application has a REST API. Running cucumber on the command line delivers the following output:

```
Feature: Placing an order

  Scenario: User order debits account correctly
            # features/placing_an_order.feature:3
  Given there is an instrument called bond
            # features/step_definitions/placing_an_order_steps.rb:9
  And there is a user called Dave with 50 dollars in his account
            # features/step_definitions/placing_an_order_steps.rb:13
  When I log in as Dave
            # features/step_definitions/placing_an_order_steps.rb:17
  And I select the instrument bond
            # features/step_definitions/placing_an_order_steps.rb:21
  And I place an order to buy 4 at 10 dollars each
            # features/step_definitions/placing_an_order_steps.rb:25
  And the order for 4 of bond at 10 dollars each is successful
            # features/step_definitions/placing_an_order_steps.rb:29
  Then I have 10 dollars left in my account
            # features/step_definitions/placing_an_order_steps.rb:33

1 scenario (1 passed)
7 steps (7 passed)
0m0.016s
```

This approach to creating executable specifications is the essence of behavior-driven design. To recap, this is the process:

- Discuss acceptance criteria for your story with your customer.

- Write them down in the executable format described above.

- Write an implementation for the test which uses only the domain language, accessing the application driver layer.

- Create an application driver layer which talks to the system under test.

Using this approach represents a significant advance over the traditional method of keeping acceptance criteria in Word documents or tracking tools and using record-and-playback to create acceptance tests. The executable specifications form the system of record for tests—they really are executable specifications. There is no more need for testers and analysts to write Word documents that are thrown over the wall to developers—analysts, customers, testers, and developers can collaborate on executable specifications during the development process.

For readers working on projects with particular regulatory constraints, it is worth noting that these executable specifications can generally be turned into a document suitable for auditing using a simple, automated process. We have worked in several teams where this was done successfully and the auditors were very happy with the results.

The Application Driver Layer

The application driver layer is the layer that understands how to talk to your application—the system under test. The API for the application driver layer is expressed in a domain language, and indeed can be thought of as a domain-specific language in its own right.

What Is a Domain-Specific Language?

A domain-specific language (DSL) is a computer programming language that is targeted at solving a problem specific to a particular problem domain. It differs from general-purpose programming languages by having many classes of problems it will be unable to address because it is designed to work only within its particular problem area.

DSLs can be classified into two types: internal and external. An external domain-specific language is one which requires explicit parsing before the instructions in it can be executed. The acceptance criteria scripts that form the top layer in the Cucumber example in the previous section demonstrate an external DSL. Other examples include the XML build scripts of Ant and Maven. External DSLs need not be Turing-complete.

An internal DSL is one that is expressed directly in code. The example in Java below is an internal DSL. Rake is another example. In general, internal DSLs are more powerful because you have the power of the underlying language at your disposal but, depending on the syntax of the underlying language, they can be less readable.

There is some very intriguing work going on in the area of executable specifications which crosses over with a couple of other themes in modern computing: intentional programming and domain-specific languages. You can begin to view your test suite, or rather your executable specifications, as defining the intent of your application. The manner in which you state that intent can be thought of as a domain-specific language, where the domain is application specification.

With a well-designed application driver layer, it becomes possible to completely dispense with the acceptance criteria layer and express the acceptance criteria in the implementation of the test. Here is the same acceptance test we wrote in

Cucumber above, expressed as a simple JUnit test. This example is very lightly adapted from Dave's current project.

```java
public class PlacingAnOrderAcceptanceTest extends DSLTestCase {
  @Test
  public void userOrderShouldDebitAccountCorrectly() {
    adminAPI.createInstrument("name: bond");
    adminAPI.createUser("Dave", "balance: 50.00");
    tradingUI.login("Dave");

    tradingUI.selectInstrument("bond");
    tradingUI.placeOrder("price: 10.00", "quantity: 4");
    tradingUI.confirmOrderSuccess("instrument: bond", "price: 10.00", "quantity: 4");

    tradingUI.confirmBalance("balance: 10.00");
  }
}
```

This test creates a new user, registering them successfully and ensuring that they have sufficient funds to trade. It also creates a new instrument for them to trade upon. Both of these activities are complex interactions in their own right, but the DSL abstracts them to a degree that makes the task of initializing this test as simple as a couple of lines of code. The key characteristics of tests written in this way is that they abstract the tests from the details of their implementation.

One key characteristic of these tests is the use of aliases to represent key values. In the example above we create an instrument named bond and a user of the system called Dave. What the application driver does behind the scenes is create real instruments and users, each with its own unique identifier generated by the application. The application driver will alias these values internally so that we can always refer to Dave or bond, even though the real user is probably called something like testUser11778264441. That value is randomized and will change every time the test is run because a new user is created each time.

This has two benefits. First, it makes acceptance tests completely independent of each other. Thus you can easily run acceptance tests in parallel without worrying that they will step on each other's data. Second, it allows you to create test data with a few simple high-level commands, freeing you from the need to maintain complex seed data for collections of tests.

In the style of DSL shown above, each operation (placeOrder, confirmOrderSuccess, and so on) is defined with multiple string parameters. Some parameters are required, but most are optional with simple defaults. For example, the login operation allows us to specify, in addition to the alias for a user, a specific password and a product code. If our test doesn't care about these details, the DSL will supply defaults that work.

To give you an indication of the level of defaulting going on here, the full set of parameters for our createUser instruction are:

- name (required)

- password (defaults to password)

- `productType` (defaults to `DEMO`)

- `balance` (defaults to `15000.00`)

- `currency` (defaults to `USD`)

- `fxRate` (defaults to `1`)

- `firstName` (defaults to `Firstname`)

- `lastName` (defaults to `Surname`)

- `emailAddress` (defaults to `test@somemail.com`)

- `homeTelephone` (defaults to `02012345678`)

- `securityQuestion1` (defaults to `Favourite Colour?`)

- `securityAnswer1` (defaults to `Blue`)

One of the consequences of a well-designed application driver layer is improved test reliability. The system this example is taken from is in reality highly asynchronous, meaning that our tests often have to wait for results before progressing to the next step. This can lead to intermittent or fragile tests that are sensitive to slight changes in the timing of things. Because of the high degree of reuse that is implicit in the use of a DSL, complex interactions and operations can be written once and used in many tests. If intermittent problems appear when the tests are run as part of your acceptance test suite, they will be fixed in a single place, that ensuring future tests that reuse these features will be equally reliable.

We start the construction of an application driver layer very simply—by establishing a few cases and building some simple tests. From then on, the team works on requirements and adds to the layer whenever they find that it is lacking some feature a particular test requires. Over a relatively short time, the application driver layer, along with the DSL represented by its API, tends to become quite extensive.

How to Express Your Acceptance Criteria

It is instructive to compare the example acceptance test in JUnit, above, to the one expressed in Cucumber in the previous section. Either of these approaches will work just fine, and each has its pros and cons. Both approaches represent a significant improvement over the traditional approaches to acceptance testing. Jez is using the Cucumber-style approach in his current project (although using Twist, rather than Cucumber), while Dave is using JUnit directly (like the example above).

The benefit of the external DSL approach is that you can round-trip your acceptance criteria. Instead of having acceptance criteria in your tracking tool and then reexpressing them in your xUnit test suite, your acceptance criteria—and your stories—simply *are* your executable specifications. However, while modern tools reduce the overhead of writing executable acceptance criteria and keeping them synchronized with the acceptance test implementation, there is inevitably some overhead.[5]

If your analysts and customers are sufficiently technical to work with xUnit tests written using the internal DSL, using the direct xUnit approach works great. It requires less complex tooling, and you can use the autocomplete functionality that is built into regular development environments. You also have direct access to the DSL from your tests instead of having to go through a level of indirection—with all the power of the aliasing approach, described above, at your fingertips. However, while you can use a tool like AgileDox to turn your class and method names into a plain text document that lists the features ("Placing an order" in the example above) and scenarios ("User order should debit account correctly"), it's harder to convert the actual test into a set of plain text steps. Furthermore, the conversion is one-way—you have to make changes in the tests, not in the acceptance criteria.

The Window Driver Pattern: Decoupling the Tests from the GUI

The examples in this chapter are designed to clearly illustrate the separation of acceptance tests into three layers: executable acceptance criteria, test implementation, and the application driver layer. The application driver layer is the only layer which understands how to interact with the application—the two other layers use only the domain language of the business. If your application has a GUI, and you have decided that your acceptance tests should run against the GUI, the application driver layer will understand how to interact with this. The part of your application driver layer that interacts with the GUI is known as the window driver.

The window driver pattern is designed to make tests that run against the GUI less brittle, by providing a layer of abstraction that reduces the coupling between the acceptance tests and the GUI of the system under test. It thus helps to insulate our tests from the effect of changes to the GUI of the system. In essence, we write an abstraction layer that pretends to be the user interface to our tests. All of the tests interact with the real UI solely via this layer. Thus if changes are made to the GUI, we can make corresponding changes to the window driver which leaves the window driver's interface, and therefore the tests, unchanged.

The FitNesse open source testing tool takes a very similar approach, allowing Fit fixtures to be created as the "drivers" to whatever it is that you need to test. This is an excellent tool that comes into its own in this context.

---

5. Twist, a commercial tool created by Jez' employer, allows you to use Eclipse's auto-complete functionality and parameter lookup on your acceptance criteria scripts directly, and allows you to refactor the scripts and the underlying test implementation layer while keeping the two synchronized.

When implementing the window driver pattern, you should write the equivalent of a device driver for each part of your GUI. Acceptance test code only interacts with the GUI through an appropriate window driver. The window driver provides a layer of abstraction, which forms part of your application driver layer, to insulate your test code from changes in the specifics of the UI. When the UI changes, you change the code in the window driver, and all of the tests that depend upon it are fixed. The window driver pattern is shown in Figure 8.3.

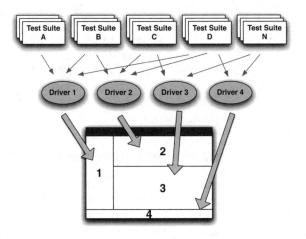

Figure 8.3 *The use of the window driver pattern in acceptance testing*

The distinction between the application driver and the window driver is this: It is the window driver that understands how to interact with the GUI. If you provided a new GUI for your application—for example, a rich client in addition to the web interface—you would just create a new window driver plugged into the application driver.

Using the Window Driver Pattern to Create Maintainable Tests

In one very large project we had chosen to use an open source GUI test scripting tool. During the development of the first release, we almost managed to keep pace with development: Our automated acceptance test suite was running, although lagging on the versions of the software by a week or two.

In the second release, our acceptance test suite fell behind more and more rapidly. By the end of that release it was so far behind that none of the tests from the first release were runnable at all—not one!

We implemented the window driver pattern in the third release, and changed some aspects of the process of test creation and maintenance, most notably making developers responsible for test maintenance. By the end of that release we had a working deployment pipeline, which included our automated tests being run immediately after each successful commit.

Here is an example of an acceptance test written without any of the layering described in this chapter:

```
@Test
public void shouldDeductPaymentFromAccountBalance() {
  selectURL("http://my.test.bank.url");
  enterText("userNameFieldId", "testUserName");
  enterText("passwordFieldId", "testPassword");
  click("loginButtonId");
  waitForResponse("loginSuccessIndicator");

  String initialBalanceStr = readText("BalanceFieldId");

  enterText("PayeeNameFieldId", "testPayee");
  enterText("AmountFieldId", "10.05");
  click("payButtonId");

  BigDecimal initialBalance = new BigDecimal(initialBalanceStr);
  BigDecimal expectedBalance = initialBalance.subtract(new BigDecimal("10.05"));
  Assert.assertEquals(expectedBalance.toString(), readText("BalanceFieldId"));
}
```

Here is the same example refactored into two layers: test implementation and window driver. The `AccountPanelDriver` in this example is the window driver. This is a good start to decomposing your tests.

```
@Test
public void shouldDeductPaymentFromAccountBalance() {
  AccountPanelDriver accountPanel = new AccountPanelDriver(testContext);

  accountPanel.login("testUserName", "testPassword");
  accountPanel.assertLoginSucceeded();

  BigDecimal initialBalance = accountPanel.getBalance();
  accountPanel.specifyPayee("testPayee");
  accountPanel.specifyPaymentAmount("10.05");
  accountPanel.submitPayment();

  BigDecimal expectedBalance = initialBalance.subtract(new BigDecimal("10.05"));

  Assert.assertEquals(expectedBalance.toString(), accountPanel.getBalance());
}
```

We can see a much clearer separation between the semantics of the test and the details of interacting with the UI that underlies it. If you consider the code that underpins this test, the code in the window driver, there is more code overall in this test, but the level of abstraction is higher. We will be able to reuse the window driver across many different tests that interact with the page, enhancing it as we go.

If, for the sake of our example, the business decided that instead of a web-based user interface, our product would be more effective with a gesture-based user interface on a touch screen, the fundamentals of this test would remain the same. We could create a new window driver to interact with the gesture-based UI instead of the boring old web page, substitute it with the original driver inside the application driver layer, and the test would continue to work.

Implementing Acceptance Tests

There is more to the implementation of acceptance tests than layering. Acceptance tests involve putting the application in a particular state, performing several actions on it, and verifying the results. Acceptance tests must be written to handle asynchrony and timeouts in order to avoid flakiness. Test data must be managed carefully. Test doubles are often required in order to allow any integration with external systems to be simulated. These topics are the subject of this section.

State in Acceptance Tests

In the preceding chapter we discussed the problems of stateful unit tests and offered advice to try and minimize your tests' reliance on state. This is an even more complex problem for acceptance testing. Acceptance tests are intended to simulate user interactions with the system in a manner that will exercise it and prove that it meets its business requirements. When users interact with your system, they will be building up, and relying upon, the information that your system manages. Without such state your acceptance tests are meaningless. But establishing a known-good starting state, the prerequisite of any real test, and then building a test to rely on that state can be difficult.

When we speak of stateful tests we are using a bit of a shorthand. What we mean to imply by the use of the term "stateful" is that in order to test some behavior of the application, the test depends upon the application being in a specific starting state (the "given" clauses of behavior-driven development). Perhaps the application needs an account with specific privileges, or a particular collection of stock items to operate against. Whatever the required starting state, getting the application ready to exhibit the behavior under test is often the most difficult part of writing the test.

Although we can't realistically eliminate state from any test, let alone an acceptance test, it is important to focus on minimizing the test's dependency on a complex state.

First of all, avoid the lure of obtaining a dump of production data to populate your test database for your acceptance tests (although this can occasionally be useful for capacity testing). Instead, maintain a controlled, minimal set. A key aspect of testing is to establish a known-good starting point. If you attempt to track the state of a production system in your test environment—an approach we have seen many times in a variety of organizations—you will spend more time trying to get the dataset working than you will testing. After all, the focus of your testing should be the behavior of the system, not the data.

Maintain the minimum coherent set of data that allows you to explore the system's behavior. Naturally, this minimal starting state should be represented as a collection of scripts, stored in your version control system, that can be applied at the commencement of your acceptance test run. Ideally, as we describe in Chapter 12, "Managing Data," the tests should use your application's public API to put it in the correct state to begin tests. This is less brittle than running data directly into the application's database.

The ideal test should be atomic. Having atomic tests means that the order in which they execute does not matter, eliminating a major cause of hard-to-track bugs. It also means that the tests can be run in parallel, which is essential to getting fast feedback once you have an application of any size.

An atomic test creates all it needs to execute and then tidies up behind itself, leaving no trace except a record of whether it passed or failed. This can be difficult, though not impossible, to achieve in acceptance tests. One technique that we use regularly for component tests when dealing with transactional systems, particularly relational databases, is to establish a transaction at the beginning of a test, and then roll it back at the conclusion of the test. Thus the database is left in the same state it was before the test ran. Unfortunately, if you take another of our pieces of advice, which is to treat acceptance tests as end-to-end tests, this approach isn't usually available to you.

The most effective approach to acceptance testing is to use the features of your application to isolate the scope of the tests. For example, if your software supports multiple users who have independent accounts, use the features of your application to create a new account at the start of every test, as shown in the example in the previous section. Create some simple test infrastructure in your application driver layer to make the creation of new accounts trivially simple. Now when your test is run, any activities and resulting state belonging to the account associated with the test is independent of activities taking place in other accounts. Not only does this approach ensure that your tests are isolated, but it also tests that isolation, particularly when you run acceptance tests in parallel. This effective approach is only problematic if the application is unusual enough to have no natural means of isolating cases.

Sometimes, though, there is no alternative to sharing state between test cases. In these circumstances, tests must be designed very carefully indeed. Tests like these have a tendency to be fragile because they are not operating in an environment where the starting point is known. Simplistically, if you write a test that writes four records to the database and then retrieves the third for the next step, you had better be certain that no one else added any rows before your test started, or you will pick the wrong record. You also should be careful that you don't run your tests repeatedly without a tear-down process being executed between runs. These are nasty tests to maintain and keep running. Sadly, they are sometimes hard to avoid, but it is worth the effort to try to avoid them as much as you can. Think carefully about how to design the test differently so that it won't leave any state behind.

When you reach the last resort and find that you must create tests whose starting state cannot be guaranteed and that cannot be cleaned up, we recommend that you focus on making such tests *very* defensive. Verify that the state at the beginning of the test is what you expect, and fail the test immediately if anything seems untoward. Protect your test with precondition assertions that ensure that the system is ready to run your test. Make such tests work in relative rather than absolute terms; for example, don't write a test that adds three objects to a collection and then confirms that there are only three objects in it, but instead get an initial count and assert that there are $x + 3$.

Process Boundaries, Encapsulation, and Testing

The most straightforward tests, and therefore the tests that should be your model for all acceptance tests, are those that prove requirements of the system without the need for any privileged access to it. Newcomers to automated testing recognize that to make their code testable they will have to modify their approach to its design, which is true. But often, they expect that they will need to provide many secret back doors to their code to allow results to be confirmed, which is not true. As we have described elsewhere, automated testing does apply a pressure on you to make your code more modular and better encapsulated, but if you are breaking encapsulation to make it testable you are usually missing a better way to achieve the same goal.

In most cases, you should treat a desire to create a piece of code that only exists to allow you to verify the behavior of the application with a great deal of suspicion. Work hard to avoid such privileged access, think hard before you relent, take a hard line with yourself—and don't give in to the easy option until you are absolutely certain that you can't find a better way.

However, sometimes inspiration fails and you are forced to provide a back door of some kind. These may be the calls allowing you to modify the behavior of some part of the system, perhaps to return some key results, or to switch that part of the system into a specific test mode. This approach works if you really have no other choice. However, we would advise you to only do this for components that are external to your system, replacing the code responsible for interacting with the external component with a controllable stub or some other test double. We would recommend that you never add test-only interfaces to remote system components that will be deployed into production.

> **Using Stubs to Simulate External Systems**
>
> The most obvious example of this problem that we have run into is when we hit a process boundary in the middle of our test. We wanted to write an acceptance test that involved communicating with a service representing a gateway to another system, a system outside the scope of our testing. However, we needed to be sure that our system worked up to that point. We also needed to be sure that our system responded appropriately to any problems with that communication.
>
> We already had a stub to represent the foreign system, and our service interacted with that. In the end, we implemented a what-to-do-on-the-next-call method that our test could use to switch the stub into a waiting mode, triggered to respond, as we had defined, to the next call.

As an alternative to special interfaces, you can provide test-time components that react to "magic" data values. Again, this strategy works, but should be reserved for components that will not be deployed as part of your production system. This is a useful strategy for test doubles.

Both of these strategies tend to result in high-maintenance tests that frequently need tinkering with. The real solution is to try and avoid these kinds of compromises wherever you can and rely on the actual behavior of the system itself to verify successful completion of any test. Save these strategies only for when you run out of other options.

Managing Asynchrony and Timeouts

Testing asynchronous systems presents its own collection of problems. For unit tests, you should avoid any asynchrony within the scope of a test, or indeed across the boundaries of tests. The latter case can cause hard-to-find intermittent test failures. For acceptance testing, depending on the nature of your application, asynchrony may be impossible to avoid. This problem can occur not just with explicitly asynchronous systems but also with any system that uses threads or transactions. In such systems, the call you make may need to wait for another thread or transaction to complete.

The problem here boils down to this: Has the test failed, or are we just waiting for the results to arrive? We have found that the most effective strategy is to build fixtures that isolate the test itself from this problem. The trick is, as far as the test itself is concerned, to make the sequence of events embodying the test *appear* to be synchronous. This is achieved by isolating the asynchrony behind synchronous calls.

Imagine a that we are building a system that collects files and stores them. Our system will have an inbox, a location on a filesystem, which it will poll at regular intervals. When it finds a file there, it will store it safely and then send an email to someone to say that a new file has arrived.

When we are writing unit tests to be run at commit time, we can test each component of our system in isolation, asserting that each interacts with its neighbors appropriately in this little cluster of objects using test doubles. Such tests will not actually touch the filesystem, but will use a test double to simulate the filesystem. If we run into time as a concept during the course of our testing—which we will because of the polling—we will fake the clock, or just force the poll to be "now."

For our acceptance test, we need to know more. We need to know that our deployment has worked effectively, that we have been able to configure the polling mechanism, that our email server is correctly configured, and that all of our code works seamlessly together.

There are two problems for our test here: the polling interval that the system waits for before checking to see if a new file has arrived, and the length of time it takes for an email to arrive.

The outline of our ideal test (using C# syntax) would look something like this:

```
[Test]
public void ShouldSendEmailOnFileReceipt() {
  ClearAllFilesFromInbox();
  DropFileToInbox();
  ConfirmEmailWasReceived();
}
```

However, if we write the code of this test naively, simply checking that we have the email we expect when we get to that line in the test, our test will almost certainly outpace the application. The email won't have been received by the time we check for its arrival. Our test will fail, although actually it was just quicker at getting to the assertion than our application was at delivering the email.

```
// THIS VERSION WON'T WORK
private void ConfirmEmailWasReceived() {
  if (!EmailFound()) {
    Fail("No email was found");
  }
}
```

Instead, our test must pause, giving the application an opportunity to catch up before deciding on failure.

```
private void ConfirmEmailWasReceived() {
  Wait(DELAY_PERIOD);

  if (!EmailFound()) {
    Fail("No email was found in a sensible time");
  }
}
```

If we make the DELAY_PERIOD long enough, this will work as a valid test.

The drawback with this approach is that these DELAY_PERIODs quickly add up. We once reduced the time of our acceptance tests from 2 hours to 40 minutes by changing from this strategy to something a little more tuned.

The new strategy was based, principally, on two ideas. One was to poll for results, and the other was to monitor intermediate events as a gate to the test. Instead of simply waiting for the longest acceptable period before timing out, we implemented some retries.

```
private void ConfirmEmailWasReceived() {
  TimeStamp testStart = TimeStamp.NOW;
  do {
    if (EmailFound()) {
      return;
    }
    Wait(SMALL_PAUSE);
  } while (TimeStamp.NOW < testStart + DELAY_PERIOD);
  Fail("No email was found in a sensible time");
}
```

In this example, we have retained a small pause, because otherwise we waste valuable CPU cycles checking for the email that could have been spent processing the incoming email. But even with this SMALL_PAUSE, this test is much more efficient than the preceding version, providing that SMALL_PAUSE is small compared to DELAY_PERIOD (typically two or more orders of magnitude smaller).

The final enhancement is a little more opportunistic, and will depend very much on the nature of your application. We have found that in systems that use asynchrony a lot, there are usually other things going on that can help. In our example, imagine for a moment that we have a service that handles incoming emails. When an email arrives, it generates an event to that effect. Our test becomes quicker (if more complex) if we wait for that event instead of polling for the arrival of the email.

```
private boolean emailWasReceived = false;

public void EmailEventHandler(...) {
  emailWasReceived = true;
}

private boolean EmailFound() {
  return emailWasReceived;
}

private void ConfirmEmailWasReceived() {
  TimeStamp testStart = TimeStamp.NOW;
  do {
    if (EmailFound()) {
      return;
    }
    Wait(SMALL_PAUSE);
  } while(TimeStamp.NOW < testStart + DELAY_PERIOD);
  Fail("No email was found in a sensible time");
}
```

As far as any client of `ConfirmEmailWasRecived` is concerned, the confirmation step looks as though it is synchronous for all of the versions we show here. This makes the high-level test that uses it much simpler to write, particularly if there are actions in the test that follow this check. This sort of code should exist in the application driver layer so it can be reused by many different test cases. Its relative complexity is worth the effort because it can be tuned to be efficient and completely reliable, making all of the tests that depend upon it tuned and reliable too.

Using Test Doubles

Acceptance testing relies on the ability to execute automated tests in a production-like environment. However, a vital property of such a test environment is that it is able to successfully support automated testing. Automated acceptance testing is not the same as user acceptance testing. One of the differences is that automated acceptance tests should not run in an environment that includes integration to all external systems. Instead, your acceptance testing should be focused on providing a controllable environment in which the system under test can be run. "Controllable" in this context means that you are able to create the correct initial state for our tests. Integrating with real external systems removes our ability to do this.

You should work to minimize the impact of external dependencies during acceptance testing. However, our objective is to find problems as early as we can, and to achieve this, we aim to integrate our system continuously. Clearly there is a tension here. Integration with external systems can be difficult to get right and is a common source of problems. This implies that it is important to test such integration points carefully and effectively. The problem is that if you include the external systems themselves within the scope of your acceptance testing, you have less control over the system and its starting state. Further, the intensity of your automated testing can place significant and unexpected loads on those external systems much earlier in the life of the project than the people responsible for them may have expected.

This balancing act usually results in a compromise of some sort that the team establishes as part of their testing strategy. As with any other aspect of your development process, there are few "right" answers, and projects will vary. Our strategy is two-pronged: We usually create test doubles that represent the connection to all external systems that our system interacts with, as shown in Figure 8.4. We also build small suites of tests around each integration point, intended to run in an environment that does have real connections to these external systems.

In addition to providing us with the ability to establish a known starting point on which we can base tests, creating test doubles to use instead of external systems has another advantage: It provides us with additional points in the application where we can control behavior, simulate communications failures, simulate error responses or responses under load, and so on—all completely under our control.

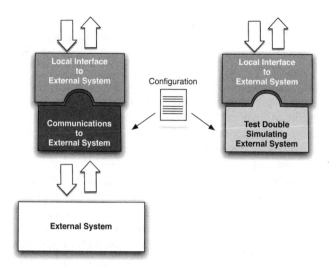

Figure 8.4 *Test doubles for external systems*

Good design principles should guide you to minimize the coupling between external systems and the one that you are developing. We usually aim to have one component of our system to represent all interactions with an external system—that is, one component (a gateway or adapter) per external system. This component concentrates the communications and any problems associated with it into one place and isolates the technical details of that communication from the rest of the system. It also allows you to implement patterns to improve the stability of your application, such as the circuit breaker pattern described in *Release It!*[6]

This component represents an interface to the external system. Whether the interface that is exposed belongs to the external system itself or is part of your codebase, this interface represents the contract that you need to prove works. This interface needs to be proven both from the perspective of your system's interactions with it and as a genuine point of communication with the external system. Stubs allow you to assert that your system interacts correctly with the remote system. Integration tests, which we describe next, allow you to assert that the external system behaves as you expect for your interactions. In this sense, test doubles and interaction tests work together to eliminate the chance of errors.

Testing External Integration Points

Integration points to external systems are a common source of problems for a variety of reasons. The code that your team is working on may change something relevant to successful communication. A change in the data structures shared

---

6. Nygard, 2007, p. 115.

between your system and the external system, or in the frequency of message exchange, or in the configuration of addressing mechanisms—almost any kind of difference could be a problem. The code at the other end of the communication may change too.

The tests that we write to assert the behavior of such integration points should be focused on the likely problems, and these will depend heavily upon the nature of the integration and where the external system is in its lifecycle. If the external system is mature and in production, the problems will be different to those you will face if it is in active development. These factors will dictate to some extent where and when we will run these tests.

If the external system is under active development, there are likely to be changes in the nature of the interface between the two systems. Schemas, contracts, and so on may change, or, more subtly, the way in which the content of the information you exchange may change. Such a scenario needs careful testing on a regular basis to identify points at which the two teams diverge. In our experience, there are usually a few obvious scenarios to simulate in most integrations. We recommend that you cover these obvious scenarios with a small number of tests. This strategy will miss some problems. Our approach is to address breakages as we find them by writing a test to catch each case. Over time, we build a small suite of tests for each integration point that will catch most problems very quickly. This strategy is not perfect, but attempting to get perfect coverage in such scenarios is usually very difficult and the returns of effort versus reward diminish very quickly.

Tests should always be scoped to cover the specific interactions that your system has with an external system. They should not aim to test the external system interface fully. Again, this is based on the law of diminishing returns: If you don't care about the presence or absence of a particular field, don't test for it. Also, follow the guidelines that we provide in the "Integration Testing" section on page 96.

As we have said, the timing of when to run integration tests can't be fixed. It varies from project to project, and from integration point to integration point. Occasionally, integration points can sensibly be run at the same time as acceptance tests, but more often this is not the case. Think carefully about the demands that you will place on the external system. Remember that your tests will be running many times each day. If every interaction test with the external system results in a real interaction, your automated tests may create production-like load on the external system. This may not always be welcome, particularly if the providers of your external system don't do much automated testing themselves.

One strategy to alleviate this is to implement your test suite so that it doesn't run every time the acceptance tests run, but perhaps once a day, or once a week. You can run these tests as a separate stage in your deployment pipeline, or as part of the capacity test stage, for example.

The Acceptance Test Stage

Once you have a suite of acceptance tests, they need to be run as part of your deployment pipeline. The rule is that the acceptance test suite should be run against every build that passes the commit tests. Here are some practices applicable to running your acceptance tests.

A build that fails the acceptance tests will not be deployable. In the deployment pipeline pattern, only release candidates that have passed this stage are available for deployment to subsequent stages. Later pipeline stages are most commonly treated as a matter of human judgment: If a release candidate fails to pass capacity testing, on most projects someone decides whether the failure is important enough to end the journey of the candidate there and then, or whether to allow it to proceed despite the performance problem. Acceptance testing offers no room for such fudged results. A pass means that the release candidate can progress, a fail means that it never can.

Because of this hard line, the acceptance test gate is an extremely important threshold and must be treated as such if your development process is to continue smoothly. Keeping the complex acceptance tests running will take time from your development team. However, this cost is in the form of an investment which, in our experience, is repaid many times over in reduced maintenance costs, the protection that allows you to make wide-ranging changes to your application, and significantly higher quality. This follows our general principle of bringing the pain forward in the process. We know from experience that without excellent automated acceptance test coverage, one of three things happens: Either a lot of time is spent trying to find and fix bugs at the end of the process when you thought you were done, or you spend a great deal of time and money on manual acceptance and regression testing, or you end up releasing poor-quality software.

Recording Acceptance Tests for Debugging

A common problem with automated UI tests is understanding why exactly a test failed. Since these tests are necessarily of very high level, there are many potential points of failure. Sometimes these may not be related to the project at all. At other times there may be a failure early in a test suite, in a different window or dialog, that leads to the problem later on. Often the only way to find out what went wrong is to rerun the test and watch it as it proceeds.

On one project we found a way to make this much easier. Before the tests started, we would start a screen capture recording on the test machine with an open source tool called Vnc2swf. After the tests finished, in case of failure we would publish the video as an artifact. Only after this video was created would we fail the build. Then it became very simple to debug the acceptance tests.

> At one stage we found that someone had logged on to the machine and looked at the task manager, probably to check on memory usage or performance. They had left the window open, and since it is a modal window, it obscured the application window. Hence the UI tests could not click on some of the buttons. The bug as reported by the build page was "Could not find button 'X'"—but the video revealed the true cause.

It is difficult to enumerate the reasons that make a project warrant such an investment in automated acceptance testing. For the type of projects that we usually get involved in, our default is that automated acceptance testing and an implementation of the deployment pipeline are usually a sensible starting point. For projects of extremely short duration with a small team, maybe four or fewer developers, it may be overkill—you might instead run a few end-to-end tests as part of a single-stage CI process. But for anything larger than that, the focus on business value that automated acceptance testing gives to developers is so valuable that it is worth the costs. It bears repeating that large projects start out as small projects, and by the time a project gets large, it is invariably too late to retro-fit a comprehensive set of automated acceptance tests without a Herculean level of effort.

We recommend that the use of automated acceptance tests created, owned, and maintained by the delivery team should be the default position for all of your projects.

Keeping Acceptance Tests Green

Because of the time taken to run an effective acceptance test suite, it often makes sense to run them later in the deployment pipeline. The problem with this is that if the developers are not sitting there waiting for the tests to pass, as they are for the commit tests, so they often ignore acceptance test failures.

This inefficiency is the trade-off we accept for a deployment pipeline that allows us to catch most failures very quickly at the commit test gate, while also maintaining good automated test coverage of our application. Let's address this antipattern quickly: Ultimately it is an issue of discipline, with the whole delivery team responsible for keeping the acceptance tests passing.

When an acceptance test breaks, the team needs to stop and immediately triage the problem. Is it a fragile test, a poorly configured environment, an assumption that is no longer valid because of a change in the application, or a real failure? Then somebody needs to take immediate action to make the tests pass again.

Who Owns Acceptance Tests?

For a while, we used the fairly traditional model that acceptance tests are the responsibility of the testing team. This strategy proved very troublesome, particularly on large projects. The test team was always at the end of the chain of development, so our acceptance tests spent most of their lives failing.

Our development teams would be working away, making changes that would break swathes of acceptance tests without realizing the impact of their changes. The test team would find out about the change relatively late in the process, after it had been developed and checked in. Since the test team had so many automated tests to repair, it would take some time to get around to fixing the most recent breakages, meaning the developers had often moved on to some other task and so were not ideally placed to fix the problem. The test team rapidly became snowed under with tests to repair, as well as the work to implement new tests for the new requirements that the developers were implementing.

This is not a trivial problem. Acceptance tests are often complex. Determining the root cause of an acceptance test failure can often take time. It was precisely this set of circumstances that led us to try our first pipelined build. We wanted to improve the time between a change in the code highlighting a problem and someone knowing that there was a problem with an acceptance test.

We changed the ownership of the automated acceptance tests. Instead of the test team being responsible for their development and maintenance, we made our whole delivery team, including developers and testers, responsible. This had many positive benefits: It focused the developers on achieving the acceptance criteria of the requirement. It made them more immediately aware of the impact of the changes that they made, since they became responsible for tracking the acceptance test build. It also meant that, now that the developers were thinking in terms of the acceptance tests, they were often more successful at predicting which areas of the acceptance test suite their new changes might affect, and so could better target their work.

In order to keep your acceptance tests working and to maintain the focus of the developers on the behavior of the application, it is important that the acceptance tests are owned and maintained by the delivery team as a whole, not by a separate testing team.

What happens if you let your acceptance tests rot? As you approach release time, you try to get your acceptance tests green so that you can feel confident about the quality of your software. Going through the acceptance tests, you discover that it is extremely hard to tell the difference between an acceptance test that is failing because the acceptance criteria changed, one that fails because the code has been refactored and the test was previously too tightly coupled to the implementation, or one that fails because the behavior of the application is now wrong. In these circumstances, it is common for tests to end up being deleted or ignored as there is not enough time for the code archaeology necessary to find out the reasons for the failure. You end up in the same situation that continuous integration was supposed to address—a rush at the end to get everything working, but without any indication of how long it will take, plus a lack of clarity about the actual state of the code.

It is essential to fix acceptance test breakages as soon as possible, otherwise the suite will deliver no real value. The most important step is to make the failure visible. We have tried various approaches, such as build masters who track down the people whose changes are most likely to have caused the failure, emails to possible culprits, even standing up and shouting, "Who is fixing the acceptance test build?" (this works quite well). The most effective approach that we have found is through gimmicks, such as lava lamps, a large build monitor, or one of the other techniques described in the "Bells and Whistles" section on page 63. Here are some ways to keep your tests in good shape.

Identify Likely Culprits

Determining what may have caused a specific acceptance test failure is not as simple as for a unit test. A unit test will have been triggered by a single check-in by a single developer or a developer pair. If you check something in and the build fails when it was working before, there should be little doubt that it was you who broke it.

However, since there can be several commits in between two acceptance test runs, there are more opportunities for the build to have been broken. Designing your build pipeline so that you are able to trace which changes are associated with each acceptance test run is a valuable step. Some modern continuous integration systems make it simple to be able to track pipelined builds through their lifecycle, and thus make it relatively straightforward to solve this problem.

Acceptance Testing and the Build Master

On the first project in which we implemented a complex build pipeline, we wrote some simple scripts that were run as part of our multistage CruiseControl build process. The scripts would collate the check-ins since the last successful acceptance test run, identify all of the commit tags, and hence all of the developers who made them, so that we could send emails to everyone who had made a commit as yet untested by an acceptance test run. This worked fairly well in this very large team, but we still needed someone to play the role of a build master to enforce discipline and to get the failures addressed.

Deployment Tests

As we have described, a good acceptance test is focused on proving that a specific acceptance criterion for a specific story or requirement has been met. The best acceptance tests are atomic—that is, they create their own start conditions and tidy up at their conclusion. These ideal tests minimize their dependency on state and test the application only through publicly accessible channels with no back door access. However, there are some types of test that don't qualify on this basis but that are, nevertheless, very valuable to run at the acceptance test gate.

When we run our acceptance tests, we design the test environment to be as close as reasonably achievable to the expected production environment. If it's not expensive to do so, they should be identical. Otherwise use virtualization to simulate your production environment as far as possible. The operating system and any middleware you use should certainly be identical to production, and the important process boundaries that we may have simulated or ignored in our development environment will certainly be represented here.

This means that in addition to testing that our acceptance criteria have been met, this is the earliest opportunity for us to confirm that our automated deployment to a production-like environment works successfully and that our deployment strategy works. We often choose to run a small selection of new smoke tests designed to assert that our environment is configured as we expect and that the communications channels between the various components of our system are correctly in place and working as intended. We sometimes refer to these as infrastructure tests or environment tests, but what they really are is deployment tests intended to show that the deployment has been successful and to establish a known-good starting point for the execution of the more functional acceptance tests.

As usual, our objective is to fail fast. We want the acceptance test build to fail as quickly as possible if it is going to fail. For this reason, we often treat the deployment tests as a special suite. If they fail, we will fail the acceptance test stage as a whole immediately and won't wait for the often lengthy acceptance test suite to complete its run. This is particularly important in testing asynchronous systems where, if your infrastructure is not correctly set up, your tests will execute to their maximum time-outs at every point. This failure mode on one of our projects once resulted in a wait of more than 30 hours for an acceptance test run to fail comprehensively—a test run that under normal circumstances would have completed in about 90 minutes.

This prioritized, fail-fast collection of tests is also a convenient place for any intermittent tests or tests that regularly catch common problems. As we have said before, you should find commit-level tests that can catch common failure modes, but sometimes this strategy can work as an interim step while you are thinking of how to catch a common, but awkward to test, problem.

> **The Aardvark Roll Call**
>
> On one of our projects we were using JUnit-based acceptance tests. The only convenient control we had over which test suites ran when was the name of the suite—they were ordered alphabetically. We constituted a collection of environment tests and called them our "aardvark roll call tests" to ensure they ran before any other suite.
>
> Always remember to do a roll call of your aardvarks before you start to depend upon them.

Acceptance Test Performance

Since our automated acceptance tests are there to assert that our system delivers the expected value to our users, their performance is not our primary concern. One of the reasons for creating a deployment pipeline in the first place is the fact that acceptance tests usually take too long to run to wait for their results during a commit cycle. Some people are philosophically opposed to this point of view, arguing that a poorly performing acceptance test suite is a symptom of a poorly maintained acceptance test suite. Let us be clear: We think it is important to constantly tend your acceptance test suite to keep it well factored and coherent, but ultimately it is more important to have a comprehensive automated test suite than one that runs in ten minutes.

Acceptance tests must assert the behavior of the system. They must do that, as far as possible, from an external user's viewpoint and not just by testing the behavior of some hidden layer within it. This automatically implies performance penalties even for relatively simple systems. The system and all of its appropriate infrastructure must be deployed, configured, started, and stopped, before we even consider the time it takes to run a single test.

However, once you start down the path of implementing a deployment pipeline, fail-fast systems and rapid feedback cycles begins to show their value. The longer the time between the point where a problem is introduced and the point of discovering it, the more difficult it will be to find the source of the problem and fix it. Typically, acceptance test suites take several hours to complete rather than a few minutes. This is certainly a workable state; many projects work very well with multihour acceptance test stages. But you can be more efficient. There is a spectrum of techniques that you can apply to improve the overall efficiency of the team by cutting down the time it takes to get a result from the acceptance test stage.

Refactor Common Tasks

The obvious first step is to look for quick wins by keeping a list of the slowest tests and regularly spending a little time on them to find ways to make them more efficient. This is precisely the same strategy that we advised for managing unit tests.

One step up from this is to look for common patterns, particularly in the test setup. In general, by their nature, acceptance tests are much more stateful than unit tests. Since we recommend that you take an end-to-end approach to acceptance tests and minimize shared state, this implies that each acceptance test should set up its own start conditions. Frequently, specific steps in such test setup are the same across many tests, so it is worth spending some extra time on ensuring that these steps are efficient. If there is a public API that can be used instead of performing such setup through the UI, then that is ideal. Sometimes, prepopulating the application with "seed data" or using some back door into the application to populate it with test data is a valid approach, but you should treat such back doors with a degree of skepticism, since it is all too easy for this test data to not be quite the same as that created by the normal operation of the application, which invalidates the correctness of subsequent testing.

Whatever the mechanism, refactoring tests to ensure that the code that they execute for common tasks is the same through the creation of test helper classes is an important step toward better performance and greater reliability in tests.

Share Expensive Resources

We have already described some techniques to achieve a suitable starting state for tests in commit stage testing in earlier chapters. These techniques can be adapted to acceptance testing, but the black box nature of acceptance tests rules some options out.

The straightforward approach to this problem is to create a standard blank instance of the application at the start of the test and discard it at the end. The test is then wholly responsible for populating this instance with any start data it needs. This is simple and very reliable, having the valuable property that each test is starting from a known, completely reproducible starting point. Unfortunately, for most systems that we create it is also very slow, because for anything but the simplest software systems it takes a significant amount of time to clear any state and start the application in the first place.

It is therefore necessary to compromise. We need to pick which resources we will share between tests and which we will manage within the context of a single test. Typically, for most server-based applications, it is possible to start by sharing an instance of the system itself. Create a clean running instance of the system under test at the beginning of the acceptance test run, run all of the acceptance tests against that instance, and shut it down at the end. Depending on the nature of the system under test, there are sometimes other time-consuming resources that can be optimized to make the acceptance test suite as a whole run faster.

Speeding up Selenium Tests

On Dave's current project, he uses the excellent open source Selenium tool for testing web applications. He uses Selenium remoting and writes acceptance tests as JUnit tests using the DSL techniques described earlier in this chapter, the DSL sitting on top of a layer of window drivers. Initially, these window drivers would start and stop instances of Selenium and a test browser as needed. This is convenient, robust, and reliable, but it is slow.

Dave could modify his code to share the running instances of Selenium and the browser between tests. This would make the code a little more complex, and may create some complexities with session state, but ultimately could be an option to speed up the three hour acceptance test build.

Instead, Dave ended up choosing a different strategy: parallelizing acceptance testing and running it on a compute grid. Later, he optimized each test client to run its own Selenium instance, as described in the following section.

Parallel Testing

When the isolation of your acceptance tests is good, another possibility to speed things up presents itself: running the tests in parallel. For multiuser, server-based systems this is an obvious step. If you can divide your tests so that there is no risk of interaction between them, then running the tests in parallel against a single instance of the system will provide a significant decrease in the duration of your acceptance test stage overall.

Using Compute Grids

For systems that are not multiuser, for tests that are expensive in their own right, or for tests where it is important to simulate many concurrent users, the use of compute grids is of enormous benefit. When combined with the use of virtual servers, this approach becomes exceedingly flexible and scalable. At the limit, you could allocate each test its own host, so the acceptance test suite would only take as long as its slowest test.

In practice, more constrained allocation strategies usually make more sense. This advantage has not been lost on some of the vendors in this space. Most modern CI servers provide the facility to manage a grid of test servers for just this purpose. If you are using Selenium, another alternative is to use the open source Selenium Grid, which allows for the use of unmodified acceptance tests written to use Selenium Remoting to be executed in parallel on a compute grid.

Using Cloud Computing for Acceptance Tests

One of Dave's projects increased the sophistication of its acceptance test environment over time. We began testing using Java-based acceptance tests written in JUnit and interacting with our web applications via Selenium Remoting. This worked very well, but the time to run our acceptance test suite kept increasing as more and more tests were added.

We began with our regular optimization approach by identifying and refactoring common patterns in our acceptance tests. We ended up with some very useful helper classes that abstracted and simplified much of our test setup. This improved the performance somewhat, but primarily it improved the reliability of our tests with a hard-to-test, highly asynchronous application.

Our application had a public API as well as several distinct web applications that interact, via the API, with the back-end system. So the next optimization we made was to separate out our API tests and to run them first, ahead of the UI-based tests. If the API acceptance test suite (which ran much faster than the UI tests) failed, we failed the acceptance test run there and then. This gave us faster failure and improved our ability to catch silly mistakes and fix them quickly.

Still, our acceptance test time crept up as more tests were added.

Our next step was to do some course-grained parallel running of tests. We divided them up into a couple of batches. For simplicity we organized the groups alphabetically. We then ran both batches of tests, each with its own instance of the application, on separate virtual machines in our development environment. By this time we were already heavy users of virtualization in our development environment, to the extent that all of our servers, both development and production, were virtual.

This halved our acceptance test time at a stroke, and we could easily extend this approach with very little configuration overhead. This approach has the distinct advantage of requiring less test isolation than full parallel running. Each partial acceptance test suite can have its own distinct application instance; within the scope of each suite the tests run serially as before. This advantage comes at the cost of needing as many additional hosts, be they virtual or physical, as there are partial acceptance test suites.

However, at this point we decided to change tack a little. We switched to the use of the Amazon EC2 compute cloud to allow us easy access to wider scalability. Figure 8.5 shows a diagram of the logical organization of our test virtual machines. One set of VMs was hosted in-house; the other, running simulated clients interacting with the system under test, was distributed in the Amazon EC2 cloud.

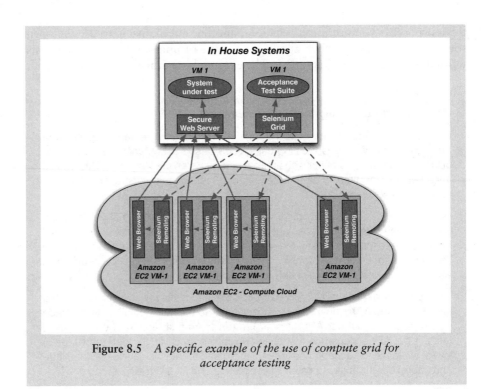

Figure 8.5   *A specific example of the use of compute grid for acceptance testing*

Summary

The use of acceptance testing is an important addition to the effectiveness of your development process. It acts to focus the attention of all members of a delivery team on what really counts: the behavior that the users need from the system.

Automated acceptance tests are usually more complex than unit tests. They take more time to maintain, and they will probably spend more of their life being broken than unit tests do because of the inherent lag between fixing a failure and having the acceptance test suite pass. However, when used as a guarantee of the behavior of the system from a user's perspective, they offer an invaluable defense against regression problems that will arise during the life of any application of any complexity.

The extreme difficulty, if not impossibility, of measuring one software project against another in any meaningful way makes it hard for us to supply you with any data that backs our assertion—that the use of automated acceptance testing will pay for itself many times over. We can only assure you that, despite having worked on many projects where keeping the acceptance tests running was hard work and exposed us to some complex problems, we have never regretted their use. Indeed, they have often saved us by providing the facility to change large parts of our system safely. We still strongly believe that the focus that such testing encourages within a development team is a powerful ingredient of successful software delivery. We recommend that you try adopting the focus on acceptance testing that we describe in this chapter and see for yourself if it is worthwhile.

Adopting the discipline to reject any release candidate that is unable to pass the acceptance test gate is another practice that in our opinion represents a significant step forward in the quality of the output of a delivery team.

Our experience of the software industry is that manual testing is the norm and often represents the only form of testing adopted by a team. We have found that manual testing is both prohibitively expensive and rarely good enough on its own to ensure a high-quality result. Manual testing, of course, has its place: exploratory testing, usability testing, user acceptance testing, showcasing. But human beings are simply not equipped to work effectively at the mundane, repetitive but complex tasks that manual regression testing requires of them—at least without feeling miserable. Poor-quality software is the inevitable outcome of such a poor-quality process.

In recent years, an increased focus on unit testing has helped raise the game for some teams. This is a significant step beyond reliance on only manual testing, but in our experience it can still result in code that doesn't do what the users wanted it to do. Unit testing is not business-focused. We believe that the adoption of tests driven by acceptance criteria represents a further step forward, by

- Increasing confidence that the software is fit for purpose

- Providing protection against large-scale changes to the system

- Significantly improving quality through comprehensive automated regression testing

- Providing fast and reliable feedback whenever a defect occurs so that it can be fixed immediately

- Freeing up testers to devise testing strategies, develop executable specifications, and perform exploratory and usability testing

- Reducing cycle time and enabling continuous deployment

Chapter 9

Testing Nonfunctional Requirements

Introduction

We have described various aspects of automating the testing of an application as part of the process of implementing a deployment pipeline. However, so far our focus has been mostly on testing those behaviors of the application commonly described as functional requirements. In this chapter, we will describe our approach to testing nonfunctional requirements, with a specific focus on testing capacity, throughput, and performance.

First of all, let's clear up some confusion around the terms. We'll use the same terminology as Michael Nygard.[1] To paraphrase, *performance* is a measure of the time taken to process a single transaction, and can be measured either in isolation or under load. *Throughput* is the number of transactions a system can process in a given timespan. It is always limited by some bottleneck in the system. The maximum throughput a system can sustain, for a given workload, while maintaining an acceptable response time for each individual request, is its *capacity*. Customers are usually interested in throughput or capacity. In real life, "performance" is often used as a catch-all term; we will try to be rather more careful in this chapter.

Nonfunctional requirements (NFRs) are important because they present a significant delivery risk to software projects. Even when you are clear about what your nonfunctional requirements are, it is very difficult to hit the sweet spot of doing just enough work to ensure that they are met. Many systems fail because they weren't able to cope with the load applied to them, were not secure, ran too slowly, or, perhaps most common of all, became unmaintainable because of poor code quality. Some projects fail because they go to the other extreme and worry so much about the NFRs that the development process is too slow, or the system becomes so complex and over-engineered that no one can work out how to develop efficiently or appropriately.

---

1. Nygard, 2007, p. 151.

225

Thus, in many ways, the division of requirements into functional and non-functional is an artificial one. Nonfunctional requirements such as availability, capacity, security, and maintainability are every bit as important and valuable as functional ones, and they are essential to the functioning of the system. The name is misleading—alternatives such as cross-functional requirements and system characteristics have been suggested—and, in our experience, the way in which they are commonly dealt with rarely works very well. The stakeholders in a project should be able to make a priority call on whether to implement the feature that allows the system to take credit card payments as opposed to the feature that allows 1,000 concurrent users to access it. One may genuinely be of more value to the business than the other.

It's essential to identify which nonfunctional requirements are important at the beginning of the project. Then, the team needs to find a way to measure them and incorporate regular testing of them into the delivery schedule and, where appropriate, the deployment pipeline. We start off this chapter by discussing the analysis of nonfunctional requirements. We then talk about how to develop your application in such a way as to meet its capacity requirements. Next, we cover how to measure capacity and how to create an environment in which to conduct the measurements. Finally, we discuss the strategies for creating capacity tests from your automated acceptance test suite and for incorporating nonfunctional testing into the deployment pipeline.

Managing Nonfunctional Requirements

In one sense, nonfunctional requirements (NFRs) are the same as any others: They can have real business value. In another sense, they are different, in that they tend to cross the boundaries of other requirements. The crosscutting nature of many NFRs makes them hard to handle both in terms of analysis and in terms of implementation.

The difficulty with treating nonfunctional requirements of the system differently from functional requirements is that it makes it easy to drop them off the project plan or to pay insufficient attention to their analysis. This may be disastrous because NFRs are a frequent source of project risk. Discovering late in the delivery process that an application is not fit for purpose because of a fundamental security hole or desperately poor performance is all too frequent—and may cause projects to be late or even to get cancelled.

In terms of implementation, NFRs are complex because they usually have a very strong influence on the architecture of the system. For example, any system that requires high performance should not involve requests traversing several tiers. Since the architecture of the system is hard to change later on in the delivery process, it is essential to think about nonfunctional requirements at the beginning of the project. This means doing just enough analysis up front to make an informed decision on what architecture to choose for the system.

In addition, NFRs tend to interact with one another in an unhelpful manner: Very secure systems often compromise on ease of use; very flexible systems often compromise on performance, and so forth. Our point here is that, while in an ideal world everyone wants their systems to be highly secure, very high-performance, massively flexible, extremely scalable, easy to use, easy to support, and simple to develop and maintain, in reality every one of these characteristics comes at a cost. Every architecture involves some trade-off between nonfunctional requirements—hence the Software Engineering Institute's Architectural Tradeoff Analysis Method (ATAM) designed to help teams decide upon a suitable architecture by a thorough analysis of its NFRs (referred to as "quality attributes").

In summary, at the beginning of the project, everybody involved in delivery—developers, operations personnel, testers, and the customer—need to think through the application's NFRs and the impact they may have on the system architecture, project schedule, test strategy, and overall cost.

Analyzing Nonfunctional Requirements

For a project that is in flight, we sometimes capture NFRs as regular acceptance criteria for functional stories where we don't anticipate that a significant additional effort will be required to meet them. But this can often be an awkward and inefficient way of managing them. It often makes sense, instead, to create specific sets of stories or tasks for nonfunctional requirements as well, especially at the beginning of a project. Since our aim is to minimize the degree to which we have to deal with crosscutting concerns, a blend of both approaches—creating specific tasks to manage nonfunctional requirements as well as adding nonfunctional acceptance criteria to other requirements—is needed.

For example, one approach to managing an NFR, such as auditability, is to say something like "All important interactions with the system should be audited," and perhaps create a strategy for adding relevant acceptance criteria to the stories involving the interactions that need to be audited. An alternative approach is to capture requirements from the perspective of an auditor. What would a user in that role like to see? We simply describe the auditor's requirements for each report they want to see. This way, auditing is no longer a crosscutting nonfunctional requirement; instead, we treat it the same as any other so it may be tested and prioritized on par with other requirements.

The same is true of characteristics like capacity. It makes sense to define your expectations of the system as stories, quantitatively, and specify them in enough detail so you can perform a cost-benefit analysis and thus prioritize them accordingly. In our experience, it also tends to result in the requirement being much more efficiently managed, and therefore in happier users and customers. This strategy can take you quite far for most common classes of nonfunctional requirements: security, auditability, configurability, and so on.

It is essential to supply a reasonable level of detail when analyzing NFRs. It is not enough to say that your requirement for response time is "as fast as possible."

"As fast as possible" puts no cap on the effort or budget that can sensibly be applied. Does "as fast as possible" mean being careful about how and what you cache, or does it mean manufacturing your own CPU, as Apple did for the iPad? All requirements, whether functional or not, must be assigned a value so it is possible to estimate and prioritize them. This approach forces teams to do the thinking about where the development budget is best spent.

Many projects face the problem of the acceptance criteria of the application being not particularly well understood. They will have apparently well-defined statements like "All user interactions will take less than two seconds to respond" or "The system will process 80,000 transactions per hour." Such definitions are too general for our needs. Wooly talk about "application performance" is often used as a shorthand way of describing performance requirements, usability requirements, and many others. If we state that our application should respond in under two seconds, does that mean in all circumstances? If one of our datacenters fails, do we still need to meet the two second threshold? Is that threshold still relevant for rarely used interactions, or just the common ones? When we say two seconds, does that mean two seconds to successful conclusion of the interaction, or just two seconds before the user receives some kind of feedback? Do we need to respond within two seconds with an error message if something goes wrong, or is it just for the success cases? Is the two seconds requirement to be met when the system is under stress, dealing with its peak load, or an average response time?

Another common misuse of performance requirements is as a lazy way to describe the usability of the system. What many people often mean when they say "Respond in two seconds" is "I don't want to sit in front of a computer without any feedback for too long." Usability problems are best dealt with when they are recognized as such, not disguised as performance requirements.

Programming for Capacity

The problem with poorly analyzed nonfunctional requirements is that they tend to constrain thinking and often lead to overdesign and inappropriate optimization. It is too easy to spend excessive amounts of time on writing "performant" code. Programmers are fairly poor at predicting where the performance bottlenecks in an application are. They tend make code unnecessarily complex, and thus costly to maintain, in an effort to achieve doubtful performance gains. It is worth quoting in full Donald Knuth's famous dictum:

> We should forget about small efficiencies, say, about 97% of the time: Premature optimization is the root of all evil. Yet we should not pass up our opportunities in that critical 3%. A good programmer will not be lulled into complacency by such reasoning, he will be wise to look carefully at the critical code; but only after that code has been identified.

The crucial phrase is the last one. Before a solution can be found, the source of the problem has to be identified. Before that happens, we need to know that we have a problem at all. The point of the capacity testing stage is to tell us whether we have a problem, so that we can go on to fix it. Don't guess; measure.

> **Premature Optimization In Action**
>
> One of our projects involved "enhancing" a legacy system. This system had been written for a relatively small population of users, and had been used by even fewer because it performed so poorly. For one set of interactions, it was necessary to display an error message that originated from a message queue. The errors were picked up from the queue and put into a list in memory. This list was polled asynchronously in a separate thread before being forwarded on to another module where it was placed in a second list, which was then polled. This pattern was repeated seven times before the message was finally displayed in the user interface.
>
> You may be thinking that this was bad design—and it was. But the intent behind the design was to avoid performance bottlenecks. The asynchronous polling pattern was intended to deal with surges of load without compromising the overall capacity of the application. Clearly, doing this seven times was an overkill, but in theory it wasn't a bad strategy to protect the application if the load became heavy. The real problem was that it was a complex solution to a problem that wasn't there. The situation simply never arose, since the message queue was never flooded with errors. Even if it was, it couldn't swamp the application unless the application asked for the information too often. Someone had invented seven hand-crafted queues that sat in front of a commercial message queue.
>
> Such almost paranoid focus on capacity is a frequent cause of over-complicated—and hence poor—code. Designing high-capacity systems is difficult, but it is made more difficult by worrying about capacity at the wrong points in the development process.

Focusing too early and too heavily on optimizing the capacity of the application is inefficient, expensive, and rarely delivers a high-performance system. At its most extreme, it can prevent a project from delivering altogether.

In fact, code written for high-capacity systems is, by necessity, simpler than that written for everyday systems. Complexity adds delays, but most programmers find this difficult to understand, let alone act upon. This book is not really a place for a treatise on the design of high-performance systems, but here is a broad outline of the approach that we have used—presented here in order to put capacity testing into context in the delivery process.

In the design of any system, bottlenecks will exist where performance of the system is constrained. Sometimes, these bottlenecks are easy to predict, but more often they are not. At the initiation of a project, it is sensible to recognize the most common causes of capacity problems and work to avoid running into them. The most costly things that most modern systems do is communicate across a network or store data on a disk. Communication across process and network boundaries is very costly in terms of performance and impacts application stability, so such communication should be minimized.

Writing high-capacity software requires more discipline than other types of systems and a degree of mechanical sympathy for how the underlying hardware and software supporting your application works. High performance comes at an extra cost, and this additional cost must be understood and weighed against the business value that added performance brings. A focus on capacity often panders to the mindset of technical people. It can bring out the worst in us, becoming the most likely cause of over-engineered solutions and so inflated project costs. It is extremely important to try and place decisions on the capacity characteristics of a system into the hands of the business sponsors. We would like to reiterate the fact that high-performance software is in fact simpler, not more complex. The trouble is that it can take extra work to find a simple solution to a problem.

There is a balance to be struck. Building high-capacity systems is tricky, and making the naive assumption that you will be able to fix all of the problems later is also not a great strategy for success. Once the initial, likely broad, performance issues of the application are dealt with at the level of defining an architecture to minimize cross-process-boundary interactions, more detailed "optimizations" during development should be avoided unless they are fixing a clearly identified and measurable problem. This is where experience pays. In order to succeed, you must avoid two extremes: at one end, the assumption that you will be able to fix all capacity issues later; at the other end, writing defensive, overcomplex code in fear of future capacity problems.

Our strategy is to address capacity problems in the following ways:

1. Decide upon an architecture for your application. Pay particular attention to process and network boundaries and I/O in general.

2. Understand and use patterns and avoid antipatterns that affect the stability and capacity of your system. Michael Nygard's excellent volume *Release It!* describes these in detail.

3. Keep the team working within the boundaries of the chosen architecture but, other than applying patterns where appropriate, ignore the lure to optimize for capacity. Encourage clarity and simplicity in code over esoterica. Never compromise readability for capacity without an explicit test that demonstrates the value.

4. Pay attention to the data structures and algorithms chosen, making sure that their properties are suitable for your application. For example, don't use an $O(n)$ algorithm if you need $O(1)$ performance.

5. Be extremely careful about threading. Dave's current project is the highest performance system he has worked on — his trading system can process tens of thousands of transactions per second — and one of the key ways to achieve this was by keeping the core of the application single-threaded. As Nygard

says, "The blocked threads antipattern is the proximate cause of most failures . . . leading to chain reactions and cascading failures."[2]

6. Establish automated tests that assert the desired level of capacity. When these tests fail, use them as a guide to fixing the problems.

7. Use profiling tools as a focused attempt to fix problems identified by tests, not as a general "make it as fast as possible" strategy.

8. Wherever you can, use real-world capacity measures. Your production system is your only real source of measurement. Use it and understand what it is telling you. Pay particular attention to the number of users of the system, their patterns of behavior, and the size of the production data set.

Measuring Capacity

Measuring capacity involves investigating a broad spectrum of characteristics of an application. Here are some types of measurements that can be performed:

- *Scalability testing.* How do the response time of an individual request and the number of possible simultaneous users change as we add more servers, services, or threads?

- *Longevity testing.* This involves running the system for a long time to see if the performance changes over a protracted period of operation. This type of testing can catch memory leaks or stability problems.

- *Throughput testing.* How many transactions, or messages, or page hits per second can the system handle?

- *Load testing.* What happens to capacity when the load on the application increases to production-like proportions and beyond? This is perhaps the most common class of capacity testing.

All of these represent interesting and valid measurements of the behavior of the system, but can require different approaches. The first two types of testing are fundamentally different from the other two in that they imply relative measurements: How does the performance profile of the system change as we change attributes of the system? The second group, though, are only useful as absolute measures.

In our view, an important aspect of capacity testing is the ability to simulate realistic use scenarios for a given application. The alternative to this approach is to benchmark specific technical interactions in the system: "How many transactions per second can the database store?", "How many messages per second

---

2. Nygard, 2007, p. 76.

can the message queue convey?", and so on. While there are times in a project when such benchmark measurements can be of value, they are academic when compared to the more business-focused questions like "How many sales per second can I handle, given regular usage patterns?" or "Can my predicted user base use the system effectively at times of peak load?"

Focused, benchmark-style capacity tests are extremely useful for guarding against specific problems in the code and optimizing code in a specific area. Sometimes, they can be useful by providing information to help with technology selection processes. However, they form only a part of the picture. If performance or throughput is an important issue for an application, then we need some tests that assert the system's ability to meet its business needs, not our guess as technicians as to what the throughput of a particular component should be.

Because of this, we believe it is vital to include scenario-based testing into our capacity testing strategy. We represent a specific scenario of use of the system as a test, and evaluate that against our business predictions of what it must achieve in the real world. We describe this in more detail in the "Automating Capacity Testing" section on page 238.

In the real world, though, most modern systems—at least the type that we generally work on—are not doing one thing at a time. While the point of a sale system is processing sales, it is also updating stock positions, handling orders for services, recording timesheets, supporting an in-store audit, and so on. If our capacity tests don't test such complex combinations of interactions, there are many classes of problems that they will be unable to defend against. The implication of this is that each of our scenario-based tests should be capable of running alongside other capacity tests involving other interactions. To be most effective, capacity tests should be composable into larger-scale suites which will run in parallel.

Working out how much and what kind of load to apply, and taking care of alternative-path scenarios such as unauthorized indexing services scraping your system is, as Nygard says, "both an art and a science. It is impossible to duplicate real production traffic, so you use traffic analysis, experience, and intuition to achieve as close a simulation of reality as possible."[3]

How Should Success and Failure Be Defined for Capacity Tests?

Much capacity testing that we have seen has definitely been more measurement than testing. Success or failure is often determined by a human analysis of the collected measurements. The drawback with a capacity measurement strategy over a capacity testing strategy is that it can be a lengthy exercise to analyze the results. However, it is an extremely useful property of any capacity test system if it is also able to generate measurements, providing insight into what happened, not just a binary report of failure or success. A graph is really worth a thousand

---

3.   Nygard, 2007, p. 142.

words in the context of capacity testing—trends can be as important to decision making as absolute values. For this reason, we always create graphs as part of our capacity testing and make sure they are easily accessible from our deployment pipeline dashboard.

However, if we are using our capacity environment for testing as well as measurement, then, for each test that we run, we need to define what it means for it to pass. Setting the level at which capacity tests should pass is tricky. On one hand, if you set the level too high, so that your application can only just pass when everything is in its favor, you are likely to suffer regular, intermittent test failures. Your tests may fail when the network is in use for other tasks, or when your capacity test environment is simultaneously working on another task.

Conversely, if your test asserts that your application must handle 100 transactions per second (tps) while it can actually handle 200, then your test won't spot introducing a change that almost halves the throughput. That means you will defer a potentially difficult problem to some unpredictable later time, long after you have forgotten the details of the guilty change. Some time later you might make an otherwise innocent change that reduces the capacity for a good reason, and the test fails even if the reduction was only a few percent.

There are two strategies to adopt here. First, aim for stable, reproducible results. As far as practically possible, isolate capacity test environments from other influences and dedicate them to the task of measuring capacity. This minimizes the impact of other, non-test-related, tasks and so makes the results more consistent. Capacity testing is one of the few situations where virtualization is not appropriate (unless your production environment is virtual) because of the performance overhead it introduces. Next, tune the pass threshold for each test by ratcheting it up once the test is passing at a minimum acceptable level. This provides you with protection from the false-positive scenario. If the test begins to fail following a commit, and the threshold is set well above your requirement, then you can always decide to simply lower the threshold if the capacity degradation is for a well-understood and acceptable reason, but the test will retain its value as a protection against inadvertent capacity-damaging changes.

Setting Initial Capacity Thresholds

Let's consider as an example an imaginary system for processing documents. The system will need to accept 100,000 documents per day. Each document will pass through a series of five validation steps over a period of three days. For the purposes of our example, let us assume that this application will run in a single time zone, and by its nature will have its peak load during business hours.

Starting from the documents, we could assume that if the load is fairly evenly spread, we will need to process approximately 100,000 documents every 8 hours per working day. That is 12,500 documents per hour. If we are primarily interested in the throughput of the application, we don't really need to run for a whole day, or even a whole hour—we will treat longevity testing as a separate exercise. 12,500 documents per hour is a little under 210 documents per minute or 3.5 documents per second. We could run our test for 30 seconds and, if we can accept 105 documents, we can be fairly confident that all is well.

Well, almost. In the real world, while all of these documents are being accepted, there is other work going on in the system. If we want a test that is representative of reality, we need to simulate the other loads that the system will be under while accepting the documents. Each document will be in play for three days, each undergoing its five-step validation process. So on any given day, in addition to the load applied to the system by coping with accepting the documents, we must add a load that represents these validations. On any given day, we will be processing 5/3 of the validations from two days earlier, 5/3 from one day earlier and 5/3 from today. So on average, for every document that the system accepts, we must simulate each of the five validation steps during the same time.

So, a pass for our 30 second test now looks something like, "Accept 105 documents and perform each validation step 105 times within 30 seconds."

This example is based on tests that we performed in a real project—and for that project, this extrapolation was accurate. However, it is important to remember that many systems have a much spikier load profile, where the load varies significantly, so any calculations for a representative test should be based on estimates of peak load.

For our tests to be genuine tests, rather than performance measurements, each must embody a specific scenario and must evaluate against a threshold beyond which the test is deemed to pass.

The Capacity-Testing Environment

Absolute measurements of the capacity of a system should ideally be carried out in an environment that, as closely as possible, replicates the production environment in which the system will ultimately run.

While it is possible to learn useful information from differently configured environments, unless they are based on measurement, any extrapolation from capacity in the test environment to capacity in the production environment is highly speculative. The behavior of high-performance computer systems is a specialist and complex area. Configuration changes tend to have a nonlinear effect on capacity characteristics. Simple things like altering the ratio of permitted UI sessions to the number of application server connections and database connections can increase the overall throughput of a system by an order of magnitude (so these are some of the important variables to play with).

If capacity or performance is a serious issue for your application, make the investment and create a clone of your production environment for the core parts of your system. Use the same hardware and software specifications, and follow our advice on how to manage configuration to ensure that you are using the same configuration for each environment, including networking, middleware, and operating system configuration. In most circumstances, if you are building a high-capacity system, any strategy other than this is a compromise which comes with additional risk—that when it is in its production environment, connected to real external systems, and with a real load and production-sized data sets, your application will not be able to meet your capacity requirements.

Capacity Testing on a Cluster of iPods

A team of our colleagues was working on a project for a well-known web-based company. This was a long-established company with enough history to have developed their own legacy of problems. Our team was building a wholly new system for this client, but the client was trying to save money by using very old production hardware as a performance testing environment.

The client was, justifiably, concerned about the capacity of the system and spent a lot of time, and thus money, trying to focus the development team on the issue of capacity. In many conversations, our team pointed out that the hardware in the test environment was old, which alone was making a significant contribution to the perceived poor capacity of the application.

After one especially poor test result, the team did some comparisons and demonstrated that the capacity testing environment could be out-performed by a cluster of iPods. Upon presenting these findings, the client bought some more up-to-date test hardware.

In the real world, the ideal of capacity testing in an exact replica of the production environment isn't always possible. Sometimes it is not even sensible, for example when the project is small enough, or when the performance of the application is of insufficient concern to warrant the expense of duplicating production hardware.

A replica of production is equally inappropriate for projects at the other extreme. Big software-as-a-service providers will often have hundreds or thousands of servers running in their production environments, so it is impractical to sustain the maintenance overhead, let alone hardware costs, that fully replicating their production environment would entail. Even if they did, the complexity of generating the load to stress such environments and a representative data set would be a mammoth enterprise. In situations like this, capacity testing can be performed as part of a canary release strategy (see the "Canary Releasing" section on page 263 for more on this). The risk of new changes altering the application's capacity can be mitigated by more frequent releases.

Most projects, though, sit somewhere between these extremes, and such projects should try to run capacity tests in environments as similar to production as possible. Even if the project is too small to warrant the expense of replicating the production environment, you should remember that, while capacity testing on lower-specification hardware will highlight any serious capacity problems, it won't be able to demonstrate that the application can fully meet its goals. This is a risk that must be evaluated for the project—but don't be naive in your calculations.

Don't fool yourself by counting on your application scaling linearly with some particular parameter of your hardware. For example, it is naive to assume that an application will be twice as fast in production if your test processor has half the clock rate of the production servers. That assumes not only that your application is CPU-bound, but also that as CPU speed increases, it still remains the bottleneck. Complex systems very rarely behave in such a linear fashion, even when they are designed to do so.

If you have no other choice, try to get a number of scaling runs to benchmark the variance between the test and production environments, if at all possible.

The Shortcomings of Scaling Factors

In one of our projects, the client did not want to spend money on two sets of production-standard hardware and instead provided significantly less powerful machines on which we hosted our capacity tests. Fortunately, we managed to convince them that if they could defer the commissioning of their upgraded production servers by a week, we could better mitigate the capacity risks that, we had told them, they were running. During that week, we worked furiously to run our capacity tests and to collect lots of data. We then reran precisely the same tests in our lower-powered capacity test environment and established a series of scaling factors that we could use to extrapolate future capacity test results.

This is a good story, but in reality, when our system made it into production, we still found several unanticipated capacity problems that we would have found had we had production-standard hardware. For this particular project, not replicating the production environment for capacity testing was a false economy, because we were building a high-performance system and the problems that we found exhibited themselves at loads that we simply couldn't apply in our lower-spec capacity test environment. These subsequent problems were costly to fix.

One obvious strategy to limit the test environment costs and to provide some sensibly accurate performance measures is available where the application is to be deployed into production on a farm of servers, as shown in Figure 9.1. Replicate one slice of the servers, as shown in Figure 9.2, not the whole farm.

For example, if your application is deployed to four web servers, eight application servers, and four database servers, have one each of the web and database servers and two application servers in your performance test environment. This will give you fairly accurate measurements of performance for a single leg, and

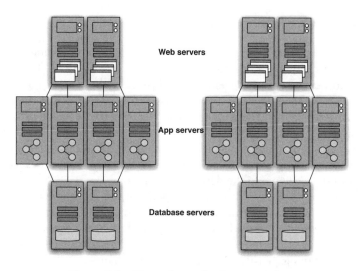

Figure 9.1   *Example production server farm*

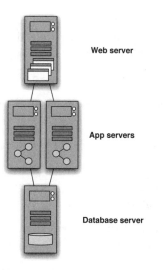

Figure 9.2   *Example capacity test environment*

it may reveal some of the problems arising when two or more servers are in contention for resources from another tier, such as database connections.

Extrapolating capacity is a heuristic that will vary widely, both in how to best practice it and in whether it is successful, from project to project. We can only advise that you treat assumptions about extrapolating results with a healthy degree of skepticism.

Automating Capacity Testing

On projects in the past, we have mistakenly treated capacity testing as a wholly separate exercise: a phase of the delivery process in its own right. This approach was a reaction to the cost of developing and running those tests. Ignoring costs for a moment, when capacity is a specific issue for a project, it is as important to know that you have introduced a change affecting the system's capacity as it is to know that you have introduced a functional problem. You need to know about a reduction in capacity as soon as possible after the corresponding change was introduced, so you can fix it quickly and efficiently. This argues for adding capacity testing as a stage to the deployment pipeline.

If we're adding capacity testing to the pipeline, an automated capacity test suite should be created and run against every change to the system that passes the commit stage and (optionally) the acceptance test stage. This can be difficult because, even more than other types of acceptance tests, capacity tests may be fragile, complex things, easily broken with minor changes to the software—not with the useful breaks indicative of a capacity problem, but those resulting from a change in the interface that the capacity tests interact with.

Capacity tests should

- Test specific real-world scenarios, so we don't miss important bugs in real-world use through overly abstract testing

- Have a predefined threshold for success, so we can tell that they have passed

- Be of short duration, so that capacity testing can take place in a reasonable length of time

- Be robust in the face of change, to avoid constant rework to keep up with changes to the application

- Be composable into larger-scale complex scenarios, so that we can simulate real-world patterns of use

- Be repeatable, capable of running sequentially and in parallel, so that we can both build suites of tests to apply load and run longevity tests

Achieving all of these goals in a manner that does not cripple development progress with over-engineered testing is not easy. A good strategy is to take some existing acceptance tests and adapt them to become capacity tests. If your acceptance tests are effective, they will represent realistic scenarios of interaction with your system, and will be robust in the face of change in the application. The properties that they lack are: the ability to scale up so you can apply serious load to the application, and a specification of a measure of success.

In most other respects, the advice that we have given in previous chapters about writing and managing effective acceptance tests means that they will, to a significant degree, already fulfill most of the criteria outlined above for good capacity tests. Our goal is two-fold: creating a realistic production-like load, and choosing and implementing scenarios that represent realistic but pathological real-life loading situations. The last point is essential: We don't just test the happy path in acceptance tests, and the same is true of capacity testing. For example, one useful technique for testing how your system scales is suggested by Nygard: "Identify whatever your most expensive transactions are, and double or triple the proportion of those transactions."[4]

If you can record the interactions that these tests perform with the system, duplicate them many times over, and then replay the duplicates, you can apply various kinds of load to the system under test and thus test various scenarios.

We have seen this general strategy work on several projects, each using very different technologies and each having very different capacity testing needs. The details of how the information for the tests themselves was recorded, how it was scaled up, and how it was replayed, varied enormously between the projects. What was consistent were the fundamentals of recording the output of functional acceptance tests, postprocessing it to scale up the requests, adding success criteria for each test, and then replaying the tests to apply very high volumes of interaction with the system.

The first strategic decision to be made is at which point in the application should recording, and the subsequent playback, take place. Our goal is to simulate realistic use of the system as closely as we can; however, there are costs to this. For some systems, simply recording interactions performed via the user interface and playing them back will be sufficient. However, if you are developing a system to be used by tens of thousands of users or more, do not attempt to apply load to the system by interacting through the UI. For this to be a realistic simulation, you would need thousands of client machines dedicated to the task of injecting load to the system. Compromises must sometimes be made.

Systems built using modern service-oriented architectures, or those using asynchronous communications as primary inputs, are particularly amenable to one of our common strategies: record and playback.

Depending on a lot of variables of the system's behavior and its fundamental architecture, the choices boil down to recording and playing back at several points (Figure 9.3):

1. Through the user interface.

2. Through a service or public API—for example, making HTTP requests directly into a web server.

3. Through a lower-level API—for example, making direct calls to a service layer or perhaps the database.

---

4. Nygard, 2007, p. 61.

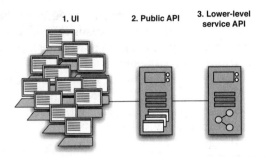

Figure 9.3   *Potential injection points for capacity testing*

Capacity Testing via the User Interface

The most obvious point at which to record and subsequently play back inter-actions with the system is via the user interface. This is the point at which most commercial load-testing products operate. Such tools provide the ability to either script or directly record interactions via the user interface, and then to duplicate and scale up these test interactions so that the test can simulate hundreds or thousands of interactions for each test case.

As we have already mentioned, for high-volume systems this is not always a practical approach, despite the significant advantage of fully exercising the system. Such an approach has another significant disadvantage: In distributed architec-tures, where servers host significant business logic—and thus are where capacity problems are more likely to be concentrated—it may not be possible to apply sufficient load to the system to test it appropriately. This can be true for such systems when the clients are either too complex, with significant logic of their own, or too thin, such as lightweight UIs for the centralized services. In these cases, the real measure is the ratio of clients to servers.

For some systems, UI-based testing is the right thing to do, but realistically, it is an appropriate strategy only for systems that handle moderate volumes. Even then, the cost of managing and maintaining the UI-centered tests can be very high.

There is a fundamental problem at play with UI-based testing. Any well-designed system will comprise components that focus on different concerns. In most applications, the role of the UI is to provide, by definition, an interface ap-propriate for the user of the system to interact with it. This interface usually takes a broad set of interactions and condenses them into more targeted interactions with other components of the system: For example, a sequence of text entries, list selections, button clicks, and so forth often results in a single event passed to another component. This second component will have a more stable API, and the tests that run against this API will therefore be less fragile than those written to a GUI.

For capacity testing in a distributed application, whether or not we are inter-ested in the performance of UI clients depends on the nature of the system. For simple, thin web-based clients, we are often less interested in the performance of the client itself than that of the centralized resources at the server end of the conversation. If our acceptance tests were written to exercise the UI and ensure that interactions through it operate in a functionally correct manner, recording at one of the later points in the application for capacity test purposes may be a more effective option. Conversely, however, some capacity problems only manifest themselves as interactions between clients and a server, especially in the case of thick clients.

For distributed systems with complex client applications and centralized server-based components, it often makes sense to separate out capacity testing, finding an intermediate record and injection point, as we described earlier, to test the servers, and defining independent UI client tests where the UI operates against a stubbed version of the back-end system. We recognize that this advice goes against our earlier recommendation to use end-to-end "whole system" tests for capacity testing, but we consider the UI, in capacity-testing distributed systems, to be a special case, best treated as such. In this instance, more than others, it depends on the nature of the system under test.

To summarize, although it is the most common approach to capacity testing, certainly as embodied in off-the-shelf capacity test products, we generally prefer to avoid capacity testing through the UI. The exception is when it is important to prove that the UI itself, or alternatively the interactions between clients and a server, are not a performance bottleneck.

Recording Interactions against a Service or Public API

This strategy can be used in applications that provide a public API other than a graphical user interface, such as a web service, message queues, or some other event-driven communication mechanism. This can be an ideal point to record interactions, allowing you to sidestep the issues of client scale-out, the complexity of managing hundreds or thousands of client processes, and the relative fragility of interacting with the system via the user interface. Service-oriented architectures are particularly suited to this approach.

Figure 9.4 shows a diagram of a capacity-test recorder component making a record of the interactions as they happen.

Using Recorded Interaction Templates

Our objective in recording interactions in the first place is to achieve a kind of template of the interactions with the system that an acceptance test embodies. These interaction templates will be used later to generate the capacity test data for a subsequent capacity test run.

Our ideal is to perform a special run of the acceptance tests, or a subset of them representing capacity test scenarios. During this special run, we will instrument the code in some manner by injecting an additional piece of code that will

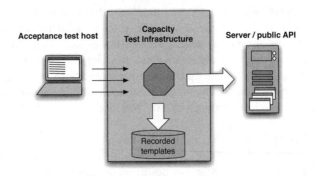

Figure 9.4 *Recording interactions against a public API*

record the interactions, save them to disk, and forward them to the system proper. From the rest of the system's perspective, there is no difference in the interactions that take place—the recording is transparent: We simply divert a copy of all inputs and outputs to disk.

Figure 9.5 shows a diagram of a simple example of this process. In this example, some values are tagged for future replacement and some are left alone, since they don't affect the meaning of the test. Clearly, as much or as little tagging within the message can be done as needed. On the whole, though, we tend toward less rather than more replacement; we should aim to replace as little as we can get away with. This will limit the coupling between the test and the test data, thus making our tests more flexible and less fragile.

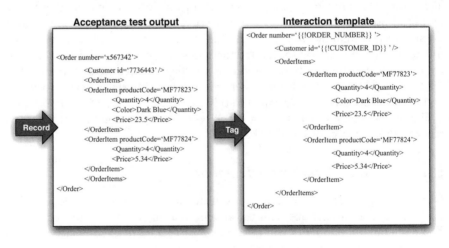

Figure 9.5 *Creating interaction templates*

Once the interaction templates have been recorded, we will create the test data to accompany them. This data is generated to complement the interaction templates, with each collection of test data representing, when combined with an appropriate template, a valid instance of interaction with the system under test. Figure 9.6 shows a diagram representing this step in the process.

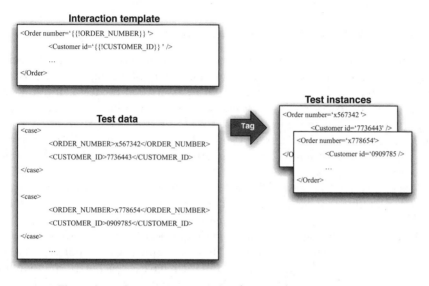

Figure 9.6 *Creating test instances from interaction templates*

In addition to the recorded content of the template, we add a success criteria for the test that the template represents. We haven't got enough experience of testing this way yet to recommend it as the best and only way; we have only tried it on one project so far, but for that project this was very successful and helped us to create a very simple yet very powerful capacity test system. Once established, this system took a very small effort to record new tests and no effort at all to prepare for and perform capacity test runs.

Finally, when it is time to execute the capacity test, the separate test instances are fed back into the system at the same point.

Interaction templates and test data can also be used as inputs to open source performance test tools, such as Apache's JMeter, Marathon, or Bench. It is also possible to write a simple test harness to manage and run tests in this way. Building your own capacity test harness is neither as silly nor as difficult as it may sound; it allows the capacity test harness to be tailored to measure precisely what you need for your project.

We have one caveat to the advice presented in this section. For seriously high-capacity and high-performance systems, the highest performance part of the whole system is, necessarily, the test, not the production code. The test has to operate fast enough to apply load and confirm results. Modern hardware is so fast that the levels of performance that we are talking about are extremely unusual, but if you are down to the level of counting clock cycles and tweaking the machine code that the compilers are creating, interaction templates are just too costly. At least, we haven't yet found a way for them to be efficient enough to test the application.

Using Capacity Test Stubs to Develop Tests

For capacity testing in very high-performance systems, the complexity of writing the capacity test can often outweigh the complexity of writing code that is fast enough to pass it. It is therefore essential to assert that the test can test at the rates necessary to assert a pass. Whenever you are writing capacity tests, it is important to start by implementing a simple no-op stub of the application, interface, or technology under test so you can show that your test can run at the speeds that it needs to and correctly assert a pass when the other end is doing no work.

This may sound like overkill, but we assure you that we have seen many capacity tests asserting that the application fails when in fact it was the test itself that couldn't keep up. Dave is, at the time of writing, working in a very high-performance computing environment. In that project, we run a battery of capacity and performance tests at all levels. These tests run as part of our deployment pipeline, as you would expect, and most of them have a benchmark run that first executes each test against a test stub, asserting that the test itself is valid before we trust its results. The results of these benchmark runs are reported alongside our other capacity test results, so we have a clear indication where any failure lies.

Adding Capacity Tests to the Deployment Pipeline

Most applications need to meet some minimum capacity threshold. Most modern commercial applications will be servicing many concurrent users, and will therefore be required to scale to meet their peak demand profile while delivering acceptable performance. During development, what we need is the ability to assert that our application will achieve the capacity required by the customer.

While capacity-related nonfunctional requirements are an important facet of the development of a project, it is important to specify what "good enough" means in some quantifiable measure. These measures should be evaluated by automated tests of some kind that are run as part of the deployment pipeline. That means that every change that passes the commit tests and acceptance tests should have automated capacity tests run against it. Thus it becomes possible to identify the moment of introducing a change that significantly affects the application's capacity.

Passing the automated capacity tests, with the sweet spot clearly delineated by their success criteria, ensures that the capacity requirements are met. In this way, we guard against over-engineered solutions to the capacity problem. We always apply the dictum that we will do the minimum amount of work to achieve the result we are aiming for, as implied by the YAGNI ("You Ain't 'Gonna Need It") principle. YAGNI reminds us that any behavior we add defensively is potentially wasted effort. Applying Knuth's dictum, optimizations should be deferred to the point when it is clear that they are required, deferred until the last responsible moment, and targeted based on runtime application profiling so as to attack bottlenecks in descending order of importance.

As ever, our goal with any testing is to fail as quickly as possible after a change breaking our assumptions is introduced. In this way, the change is easily identified and quickly fixed. However, capacity tests are often relatively complex and can take a long time to run.

If you are lucky enough to be able to prove that your application meets its performance goals within a few seconds, add your capacity tests to the commit testing stage so you can get immediate feedback on any problems. However, in this case beware of any technology that relies on runtime optimizing compilers. The runtime optimizations in .NET and Java take many iterations to stabilize, and sensible results can only be gathered after several minutes of "warm-up."

A similar strategy can be useful for protecting known performance hot spots from getting worse over time as the code develops. When such a hot spot is identified, create a "guard test" that runs very quickly as part of you commit test cycle. Such tests act as a kind of performance smoke test—they aren't going to tell you that your application meets all of its performance criteria, but they may highlight trends in the wrong direction and let you tackle them before they become a problem. However, watch out that you don't introduce untrustworthy tests that fail intermittently with this strategy.

Most capacity tests, though, aren't candidates for the commit stage of your deployment pipeline. They usually take too long and require too many resources to run. Adding capacity tests to the acceptance stage is feasible if the capacity tests remain fairly simple and don't take too long to run. On the whole, though, we don't recommend adding capacity tests to the acceptance test stage of your deployment pipeline. There are several reasons:

- To be really effective, capacity tests need to be run in their own special environment. Trying to figure out why the latest release candidate failed its capacity requirements so badly can be quite costly if the real reason was that some other automated tests were running simultaneously on the same environment. Some CI systems allow you to specify target environments for tests. You can use this feature to partition capacity tests and run them in parallel with acceptance tests.

- Some types of capacity test can take a very long time to run, resulting in an untenable delay before getting an acceptance test result.

- Many activities downstream from acceptance testing can be done in parallel with capacity testing, such as demonstrating the latest working software, manual testing, integration testing, and so forth. Gating these on a successful capacity test run is unnecessary and, for many projects, inefficient.

- For some projects, it does not make sense to run capacity tests as frequently as acceptance tests.

In general, apart from the performance smoke tests we have described, we prefer to add automated capacity testing as a wholly separate stage in our deployment pipeline.

How this capacity stage of the pipeline is treated differs somewhat from project to project. For some projects, it makes sense to treat it in a way similar to the acceptance test stage—as a fully automated deployment gate. That is, unless the tests in the capacity test stage all pass, you can't deploy the application without a manual override. This is most appropriate for high-performance or large-scale applications that are simply not fit for purpose if they do not meet a well-understood threshold of capacity. This is the most rigorous model for capacity testing that, on the face of it, seems optimal to most projects. However, this is not always the case.

If there are real issues of throughput or latency, or information that is only relevant or accurate for specific windows of time, automated tests can act very effectively as executable specifications that can assert that the requirement is met.

At a high level, the acceptance test stage in the deployment pipeline is a template for all subsequent testing stages, including capacity testing, as shown in Figure 9.7. For capacity tests, as for others, the stage begins by preparing for deployment, deploying, then verifying that the environment and application are correctly configured and deployed. Only then are the capacity tests run.

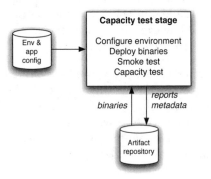

Figure 9.7   *The capacity test stage of the deployment pipeline*

Additional Benefits of a Capacity Test System

The capacity test system is usually the closest analog to your expected production system. As such, it is a very valuable resource. Further, if you follow our advice and design your capacity tests as a series of composable, scenario-based tests, what you really have is a sophisticated simulation of your production system.

This is an invaluable resource for a whole variety of reasons. We have discussed already why scenario-based capacity testing is of importance, but given the much more common approach of benchmarking specific, technically focused interactions, it is worth reiterating. Scenario-based testing provides a simulation of real interactions with the system. By organizing collections of these scenarios into complex composites, you can effectively carry out experiments with as much diagnostic instrumentation as you wish in a production-like system.

We have used this facility to help us perform a wide variety of activities:

- Reproducing complex production defects

- Detecting and debugging memory leaks

- Longevity testing

- Evaluating the impact of garbage collection

- Tuning garbage collection

- Tuning application configuration parameters

- Tuning third-party application configuration, such as operating system, application server, and database configuration

- Simulating pathological, worst-day scenarios

- Evaluating different solutions to complex problems

- Simulating integration failures

- Measuring the scalability of the application over a series of runs with different hardware configurations

- Load-testing communications with external systems, even though our capacity tests were originally intended to run against stubbed interfaces

- Rehearsing rollback from complex deployments.

- Selectively failing parts or the application to evaluate graceful degradation of service

- Performing real-world capacity benchmarks in temporarily available production hardware so that we could calculate more accurate scaling factors for a longer-term, lower-specification capacity test environment

This is not a complete list, but each of these scenarios comes from a real project.

Fundamentally, your capacity test system is an experimental resource in which you can effectively speed up or slow down time to suit your needs. You can use it to design and execute all manner of experiments to help diagnose problems, or to predict issues and work out strategies to cope with them.

Summary

Designing systems to meet their nonfunctional requirements is a complex topic. The crosscutting nature of many NFRs means that it is hard to manage the risks that they pose to any given project. This, in turn, can lead to two paralyzing behaviors: not paying enough attention to them from the start of the project or, at the other extreme, defensive architecture and over-engineering.

Technical people are lured towards complete, closed solutions—that is, solutions that are fully automated for as many cases as they can imagine. For them, this is usually the default approach to solving a problem. For example, operations people will want systems that can be redeployed and reconfigured without shutting down, whereas developers will want to defend themselves against every possible future evolution of the application, whether or not it will ever be required. NFRs are a difficult area because, compared to functional requirements, they forse technical people to provide more input into their analysis, which may detract them from the business value they are asked to deliver.

Nonfunctional requirements are the software equivalent of a bridge builder making sure that the chosen beams are strong enough to cope with the expected traffic and weather. These requirements are real, they have to be considered, but they aren't what is in the mind of the business people paying for the bridge: They want something that can get them from one side of the river to the other, and looks nice. This means that, as technical people, we must guard carefully against our own tendency to see technical solutions first. We must work closely with customers and users to determine the sensitivity points of our application and define detailed nonfunctional requirements based upon real business value.

Once this work has been done, the delivery team can decide upon the correct architecture to use for the application and create requirements and acceptance criteria capturing the nonfunctional requirements in the same way that functional requirements are captured. It thus becomes possible to estimate the effort involved in meeting nonfunctional requirements and prioritize them in the same way as functional requirements.

Once this work is done, the delivery team needs to create and maintain automated tests to ensure that these requirements are met. These tests should be run as part of your deployment pipeline every time a change to your application, infrastructure, or configuration passes the commit test and acceptance test stages. Use your acceptance tests as a starting point for broader scenario-based testing of NFRs—this is a great strategy to get comprehensive, maintainable coverage of the characteristics of the system.

Chapter 10

Deploying and Releasing Applications

Introduction

There are differences between releasing software into production and deploying it to testing environments—not least, in the level of adrenaline in the blood of the person performing the release. However, in technical terms, these differences should be encapsulated in a set of configuration files. When deployment to production occurs, the same process should be followed as for any other deployment. Fire up your automated deployment system, give it the version of your software to deploy and the name of the target environment, and hit go. This same process should also be used for all subsequent deployments and releases.

Since the same process is used for both, this chapter deals with both deploying and releasing software. We will describe how to create and follow a strategy for releasing software, including deployments to testing environments. The main difference between deploying and releasing is the ability to roll back, and we deal with this problem at length in this chapter. We also introduce two extremely powerful techniques that can be used to perform zero-downtime releases and rollbacks on even the largest of production systems: blue-green deployments and canary releasing.

All of these processes—deploying to testing and production environments and rolling back—need to form part of your deployment pipeline implementation. It should be possible to see a list of builds available for deployment into each of these environments and run the automated deployment process by pressing a button or clicking a mouse to select the version to deploy and the environment to deploy it to. This, in fact, should be the only way to make changes to these environments of any kind—including the configuration of the operating system and third-party software. Thus it becomes possible to see exactly which versions of your application are in which environments, who authorized the deployment, and what changes have been made to the application since the last time it was deployed.

We will be concentrating in this chapter on the problem of deploying application software to environments shared by multiple users, although the same principles will apply to user-installed software. In particular, we discuss releasing products and ensuring continuous delivery of client-installed software.

Creating a Release Strategy

The most important part of creating a release strategy is for the application's stakeholders to meet up during the project planning process. The point of their discussions should be working out a common understanding concerning the deployment and maintenance of the application throughout its lifecycle. This shared understanding is then captured as the release strategy. This document will be updated and maintained by the stakeholders throughout the application's life.

When creating the first version of your release strategy at the beginning of the project, you should consider including the following:

- Parties in charge of deployments to each environment, as well as in charge of the release.

- An asset and configuration management strategy.

- A description of the technology used for deployment. This should be agreed upon by both the operations and development teams.

- A plan for implementing the deployment pipeline.

- An enumeration of the environments available for acceptance, capacity, integration, and user acceptance testing, and the process by which builds will be moved through these environments.

- A description of the processes to be followed for deployment into testing and production environments, such as change requests to be opened and approvals that need to be granted.

- Requirements for monitoring the application, including any APIs or services the application should use to notify the operations team of its state.

- A discussion of the method by which the application's deploy-time and runtime configuration will be managed, and how this relates to the automated deployment process.

- Description of the integration with any external systems. At what stage and how are they tested as part of a release? How do the operations personnel communicate with the provider in the event of a problem?

- Details of logging so that operations personnel can determine the application's state and identify any error conditions.

- A disaster recovery plan so that the application's state can be recovered following a disaster.

- The service-level agreements for the software, which will determine whether the application will require techniques like failover and other high-availability strategies.

- Production sizing and capacity planning: How much data will your live application create? How many log files or databases will you need? How much bandwidth and disk space will you need? What latency are clients expecting?

- An archiving strategy so that production data that is no longer needed can be kept for auditing or support purposes.

- How the initial deployment to production works.

- How fixing defects and applying patches to the production environment will be handled.

- How upgrades to the production environment will be handled, including data migration.

- How application support will be managed.

The act of creating a release strategy is useful: It will usually be a source of both functional and nonfunctional requirements for both software development and for the design, configuration, and commissioning of hardware environments. These requirements should be recognized as such and added to the development plan as they are discovered.

Creating the strategy is of course just the beginning; it will be added to and changed as the project progresses.

A vital component of the release strategy is the *release plan* describing how releases are performed.

The Release Plan

The first release is usually the one that carries the highest risk; it needs careful planning. The results of this planning may be automated scripts, documentation, or other procedures needed to reliably and repeatedly deploy the application into the production environment. In addition to the material in the release strategy, it should include

- The steps required to deploy the application for the first time

- How to smoke-test the application and any services it uses as part of the deployment process

- The steps required to back out the deployment should it go wrong

- The steps required to back up and restore the application's state

- The steps required to upgrade the application without destroying the application's state

- The steps to restart or redeploy the application should it fail

- The location of the logs and a description of the information they contain

- The methods of monitoring the application

- The steps to perform any data migrations that are necessary as part of the release

- An issue log of problems from previous deployments, and their solutions

There are sometimes other considerations to add. For example, if your new software is taking over from a legacy system, you should document the steps to transfer users to the new system and decommission the old system, not forgetting a rollback process if things go wrong.

Again, this plan will need to be maintained as the project progresses and new insights are gained.

Releasing Products

The strategies and plans listed above are fairly generic. They are worth considering for all projects, even if, after some consideration, you decide to only use a few of the sections.

One class of software projects where you must consider other issues is software destined to be released as a commercial product. Here's a list of additional deliverables that should be considered if the output of your project is a software product:

- Pricing model

- Licensing strategy

- Copyright issues around third-party technologies used

- Packaging

- Marketing materials—print, web-based, podcasts, blogs, press releases, conferences, etc.

- Product documentation

- Installers

- Preparing sales and support teams

Deploying and Promoting Your Application

The key to deploying any application in a reliable, consistent manner is constant practice: Use the same process to deploy to every environment, including production. Automating the deployment should start with the very first deployment to a testing environment. Instead of manually pulling the pieces of software into shape, write a simple script that does the job.

The First Deployment

The first deployment of any application should happen in the first iteration when you showcase your first stories or requirements to the customer. Choose one or two stories or requirements that are of high priority but very simple to deliver in your first iteration (assuming your iterations are one or two weeks and you have a small team—you should choose more if these conditions do not apply). Use this showcase as a reason to make the application deployable to a production-like showcase environment (UAT). In our minds, one of the principal goals of the first iteration of a project is to get the early stages of our deployment pipeline running and to be able to deploy and demonstrate *something*, no matter how small, at the end. This is one of the very few situations where we recommend prioritizing technical value over business value. You can think of this strategy as priming the pump of your development process.

At the end of this pump-priming iteration, you should have the following in place:

- Your deployment pipeline's commit stage

- A production-like environment to deploy to

- An automated process that takes the binaries created by your commit stage and deploys them into the environment

- A simple smoke test that verifies that the deployment worked and the application is running

This shouldn't be too much trouble for an application that has only been under active development for a few days. The tricky bit here is working out how production-like the environment should be. Your deployment target does not need to be a clone of the eventual production environment, but there are some aspects of the production environment that are more important than others.

A good question to ask is, "How different is the production environment from my development environment?" If the production environment runs on a different operating system, you should use the same operating system that will be used in production for your UAT environment. If your production environment is a cluster, you should build a small, limited cluster for your staging environment. If your production environment is a distributed one with many different nodes, make sure your production-like test environment has at least one separate process to represent each class of process boundary.

Virtualization and chicken-counting (0, 1, many) are your friends here. Virtualization makes it easy to create an environment that represents the important aspects of your production environment, while being able to run on a single physical machine. Chicken-counting means that if your production site has 250 web servers, 2 should be enough to represent the significant process boundaries. Later on, as development progresses, you can get more sophisticated.

In general, a production-like environment has the following characteristics.

- It should run the same operating system as the production system will.

- It should have the same software installed as the production system will—and in particular, none of the development toolchain (such as compilers or IDEs) should be installed on it.

- This environment should, as far as is reasonable, be managed the same way as the production environment, using the techniques described in Chapter 11, "Managing Infrastructure and Environments."

- In the case of client-installed software, your UAT environment should be representative of your clients' hardware statistics, or at least someone else's real-world statistics.[1]

Modeling Your Release Process and Promoting Builds

As your application grows and becomes more complex, so will your deployment pipeline implementation. Since your deployment pipeline should model your test and release process, you need first to work out what this process is. While this is often expressed in terms of promoting builds between environments, there are more details that we care about. In particular, it is important to capture

- What stages a build has to go through in order to be released (for example, integration testing, QA acceptance testing, user acceptance testing, staging, production)

- What the required gates or approval are

- For each gate, who has the authority to approve a build passing through that gate

At the end of this exercise, you might end up with a diagram similar to Figure 10.1. Of course, your process may be more or less complex than this. Creating a diagram like this is, in fact, the first step to creating a value stream

---

1. The Unity 3D web player software publishes statistics on its site [cFI7XI].

map for your release process. We discussed value stream mapping as a way to optimize your release process in Chapter 5, "Anatomy of the Deployment Pipeline."

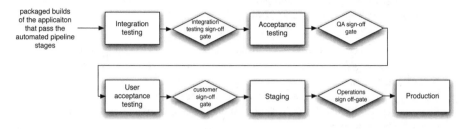

Figure 10.1 *An example test and release process diagram*

Once you've created this diagram, you can create placeholders for each part of your release process in the tool you use for managing deployments. Go and AntHill Pro both allow you to do this out of the box, and most continuous integration tools can model and manage this process with some work. Once this is done, it should be possible for the people responsible for approvals to approve, using your tool, a particular build moving through a gate in the release process.

The other essential facility that must be provided by the tool you use to manage your deployment pipeline is the ability, for each stage, to see which builds have passed all the previous stages in the pipeline and are hence ready for the next stage. It should then be possible to choose one of these builds and press a button to have it deployed. This process is known as promotion. Promoting builds at the press of a button is what turns the deployment pipeline into a pull system, giving everybody involved in the delivery process the ability to manage their own work. Analysts and testers can self-service deployments for exploratory testing, showcasing, or usability testing. Operations personnel can deploy any version of their choice to staging or production at the press of a button.

An automated deployment mechanism makes promotion a simple matter of selecting the desired release candidate and waiting for it to deploy to the correct environment. This automated deployment mechanism should be usable by anyone who needs to deploy the application. It should not require any knowledge or understanding of the technicalities of the deployment itself. To this end, it is very helpful to include automated smoke tests that run once the deployment system thinks that the system is ready. This way, we can assure the person requesting a deployment—whether it is an analyst, tester, or operations person—that the system is ready for use and working as it should be, or make it easy to diagnose the cause if it is not.

Continuous Demos for Product Development

One of the projects we worked on was for a start-up company. It was a greenfield development in a wholly new business area. It was extremely important to be able to demonstrate to potential customers, partners, and investors, what they were signing up for. In the very early days of the project, these tasks were performed by mock-ups, slideshows, and simple prototypes.

Fairly soon, though, the application began to outstrip the prototypes, and so we began to use one of our manual test environments for such demonstrations, often at quite short notice. Our deployment pipeline was good, so we could be confident that any build that had passed our acceptance test gate was viable for a demonstration. We could also be confident of being able to deploy any candidate very easily and quickly.

Our business analysts could control the deployments into testing environments. They could choose which release candidate to show and coordinate with the test team which test environment to use without disrupting testing.

Each stage in your test and release process involves basically the same workflow: testing a particular version of the application to determine its fitness to be released according to a set of acceptance criteria. In order to perform this testing, the chosen build of the application needs to be deployed into an environment. This environment might be the tester's desktop machine, if your application is user-installed software that needs to be manually tested. In the case of embedded software, this might require a specialized, dedicated hardware environment. In the case of a hosted software service, it might be a set of boxes that resemble production. Or it might be a combination of these.

In any of these cases, the workflow for any of the testing stages in the process will be similar.

1. The person or team doing the testing should have a way to select which version of the application they want to deploy into their testing environment. This list will include all versions of the application that have passed all the prior stages of the deployment pipeline. Selecting a particular build should cause the following steps, up to the actual testing, to be performed automatically.

2. Prepare the environment and associated infrastructure (including middleware) so it is in a clean state, ready for deployment of the application. This should be done in a fully automated fashion, as described in Chapter 11, "Managing Infrastructure and Environments."

3. Deploy the application's binaries. These binaries should always be fetched from the artifact repository, never built from scratch for each deployment.

4. Configure the application. Configuration information should be managed in a consistent way across all applications and applied at deployment time or run time, using a tool like Escape [apvrEr]. There's more information on this subject in Chapter 2, "Configuration Management."

5. Prepare or migrate any data managed by the application, as described in Chapter 12, "Managing Data."

6. Smoke-test the deployment.

7. Perform the testing (this might be manual or automated).

8. If this version of the application passes the tests, approve its promotion to the next environment.

9. If this version of the application does not pass the tests, record why.

Promoting Configuration

It is not just the binaries that need to be promoted. The configuration of the environment and of the application also need to be promoted at the same time. To make things more complex, you don't want to promote all of the configuration. For example, you need to make sure that any new configuration settings get promoted, but you won't want to promote to production a setting that points your application at your SIT database or a test double of an external service. Managing the promotion of certain bits of configuration associated with an application — but not others which are associated instead with an environment — is a complex problem.

One way to attack this problem is to make your smoke tests verify that you are pointing at the right things. For example, you could have a test double service return the environment it expects to talk to as a string, and have the smoke tests check that the string your application gets back from an external service matches the environment it is deploying to. In the case of middleware configuration, such as thread pools, you can monitor these settings using a tool like Nagios. You can also write infrastructure tests that check any key settings and report them to your monitoring software. The "Behavior-Driven Monitoring" section on page 323 provides more detail.

In the case of service-oriented architectures and componentized applications, all the services or components forming the application need to be promoted together. As we discussed in the previous section, it is usually in the system integration testing environment that a good combination of versions of the application's services and components is found. Your deployment system needs to enforce that this combination is then promoted as a whole, to avoid a situation where someone deploys a wrong version of one of the services, causing the application to fail — or worse, introducing an intermittent and hard-to-track-down defect.

Orchestration

Environments are often shared between several applications. This can cause complications in two ways. First, it means you have to take extra care when preparing the environment for a new deployment of an application so as to not disturb the operation of any other applications in this environment. This normally means ensuring that changes to the configuration of the operating system or any middleware don't cause the other applications to misbehave. If the production environment is shared between the same applications, then this work serves a useful purpose: ensuring that there are no conflicts between the chosen versions of the applications. If this turns out to be a complex exercise, you might consider using some form of virtualization technology to isolate the applications from each other.

Second, the applications sharing the environment may depend on each other. This is common when using a service-oriented architecture. In this situation, the integration testing (also called systems integration testing, or SIT) environment is the first time that the applications will be talking to each other rather than to a test double of some kind. Thus, much of the work in the SIT environment involves deploying new versions of each of the applications until they all cooperate. In this situation the smoke test suite is usually a fully fledged set of acceptance tests that run against the whole application.

Deployments to Staging Environments

Before you let your application loose on unsuspecting users, you should perform some final tests in a staging environment that is very similar to production. If you managed to get a capacity testing environment that is a close replica of production, it may sometimes make sense to skip the staging step: You can employ the capacity testing environment for both capacity testing and staging. In general, though, we would recommend against this for anything other than simple systems. If your application includes any integration with external systems, staging is the point where you get a final confirmation that all aspects of integration work between the intended production versions of each system.

You should have started to put your staging environment together at the beginning of your project. If you have the hardware for production and it is not being used for anything else, use it as a staging environment until you perform your first release. Here are some things to plan from the beginning of the project:

- Ensure your production, capacity testing, and staging environments are commissioned. In particular, on a green field project, have your production environment ready some time before the release, and deploy to it as part of your pipeline.

- Have an automated process for configuring your environment, including networks, external services, and infrastructure.

- Ensure the deployment process is adequately smoke-tested.

- Measure the warm-up period for your application. This is especially applicable if your application uses caching. Incorporate this into your deployment plan.

- Test integration with external systems. You don't want your application's release to be the first time you run against the real external systems.

- If possible, get your application into its production environment well before release. If "release" can be as simple as reconfiguring some router to direct traffic from a holding page to your production environment, so much the better. This technique, known as blue-green deployment, is described a little later in this chapter.

- If possible, try rolling your system out to a small group of users before you roll it out to everybody. This technique is known as canary releasing, and is also described later in this chapter.

- Deploy every change that passes acceptance tests to your staging environment (although not necessarily to production).

Rolling Back Deployments and Zero-Downtime Releases

It is essential to be able to roll back a deployment in case it goes wrong. Debugging problems in a running production environment is almost certain to result in late nights, mistakes with unfortunate consequences, and angry users. You need to have a way to restore service to your users when things go wrong, so you can debug the failure in the comfort of normal working hours. There are several methods of performing a rollback that we will discuss here. The more advanced techniques—blue-green deployments and canary releasing—can also be used to perform zero-downtime releases and rollbacks.

Before we start, there are two important constraints. The first is your data. If your release process makes changes to your data, it can be hard to roll back. Another constraint is the other systems you integrate with. With releases involving more than one system (known as orchestrated releases), the rollback process becomes more complex too.

There are two general principles you should follow when creating a plan for rolling back a release. The first is to ensure that the state of your production system, including databases and state held on the filesystem, is backed up before doing a release. The second is to practice your rollback plan, including restoring from the backup or migrating the database back before every release to make sure it works.

Rolling Back by Redeploying the Previous Good Version

This is often the simplest way to roll back. If you have an automated process for deploying your application, the simplest way to get back to a good state is to redeploy the previous good version from scratch. This will also include reconfiguring the environment it runs on, so it becomes configured precisely the same way that it was before. This is one of the reasons it is so important to be able to re-create environments from scratch.

Why create the environment and do the deployment from scratch? There are a few good reasons:

- If you do not have an automated rollback process but you do have an automated deployment process, then redeploying the last version is a fixed-time operation that poses a lower risk (because there is less to go wrong).

- It is the same process you have tested (hopefully) hundreds of times before. Rollbacks are performed much less frequently, and therefore are more likely to contain bugs.

We can't think of any situations where this will not work. However, there are some disadvantages:

- Even though the time it takes to redeploy the old version is fixed, it is nonzero. It will thus lead to a downtime.

- It makes it harder to debug what went wrong. Redeploying the old version often overwrites the new version, thereby removing the opportunity to work out what happened. This can be mitigated if your production environment is virtual, which we describe later on. With relatively simple applications, it's often easy to keep the old version around by deploying each version to a new directory and using symbolic links to point to the current version.

- If you restore from the database backup you took before deploying the latest version, you will lose any data created following the deployment. This may not be a big deal if you roll back reasonably quickly, but in some situations this is not acceptable.

Zero-Downtime Releases

A zero-downtime release, also known as hot deployment, is one in which the actual process of switching users from one release to another happens nearly instantaneously. Crucially, it must also be possible to back users out to the previous version nearly instantaneously too, if something goes wrong.

The key to zero-downtime releases is decoupling the various parts of the release process so they can happen independently as far as possible. In particular, it should be possible to put in place new versions of shared resources your applications depend on, such as databases, services, and static resources, before you upgrade your applications.

With static resources and web-based services, this is relatively easy. You just include the version of the resource or service in the URI, and you can have multiple versions of them available simultaneously. For example, Amazon Web Services has a date-based versioning system, with the latest version of the EC2 API (at the time of writing) available at `http://ec2.amazonaws.com/doc/2009-11-30/AmazonEC2.wsdl`. Of course, they keep the earlier versions of the API working as well at the old URIs. For resources, when you push a new version of your website out, you put the static resources such as images, Javascript, HTML, and CSS to a new directory—for example, you could put the images for version 2.6.5 of your application under `/static/2.6.5/images`.

Things are a little harder with databases. There is a section dedicated to managing databases in a zero-downtime scenario in Chapter 12, "Managing Data."

Blue-Green Deployments

This is one of the most powerful techniques we know for managing releases. The idea is to have two identical versions of your production environment, which we'll call blue and green.

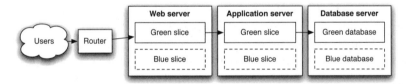

Figure 10.2 *Blue-green deployments*

In the example in Figure 10.2, users of the system are routed to the green environment, which is the currently designated production. We want to release a new version of the application. So we deploy it to the blue environment, and let the application warm up (you can do this as much as you like). This does not in any way affect the operation of the green environment. We can run smoke tests against the blue environment to check it is working properly. When we're ready, moving to the new version is as simple as changing the router configuration to point to the blue environment instead of the green environment. The blue environment thus becomes production. This switchover can typically be performed in much less than a second.

If something goes wrong, we simply switch the router back to the green environment. We can then debug what went wrong on the blue environment.

It can be seen that this approach yields several improvements over the redeployment approach. However, some care is needed when managing databases with blue-green deployments. It is usually not possible to switch over directly from the green database to the blue database because it takes time to migrate the data from one release to the next if there are schema changes.

One way to approach this problem is to put the application into read-only mode shortly before switchover. You can then take a copy of the green database, restore it into the blue database, perform the migration, and then switch over to the blue system. If everything checks out, you can put the application back into read-write mode. If something goes wrong, you can simply switch back to the green database. If this happens before the application goes back into read-write mode, nothing more needs to be done. If your application has written data you want to keep to the new database, you will need to find a way to take the new records and migrate them back to the green database before you try the release again. Alternatively, you could find a way to feed transactions to both the new and old databases from the new version of the application.

Another approach is to design your application so that you can migrate the database independently of the upgrade process, which we describe in detail in Chapter 12, "Managing Data."

If you can only afford a single production environment, you can still use blue-green deployments. Simply have two copies of your application running side by side on the same environment. Each copy has its own resources—its own ports, its own root on the filesystem, and so forth—so they can both be running simultaneously without interfering with each other. You can deploy to each environment independently. Another approach would be to use virtualization, although you should first test the effect of virtualization on the capacity of your application.

If you have a sufficient budget, your blue and green environments can be completely separate replicas of each other. This requires less configuration, but is of course more expensive. One variant of this approach, known as *shadow domain releasing*, *shadow environment releasing*, or *live-live releasing*, is to use your staging and production environments as your blue and green environments. Deploy the new version of your application to staging, and then switch users from production to the staging environment to send the new version of your application live. At this point, staging becomes production, and production becomes staging.

 We worked with one very large organization that had five parallel production environments. They used this technique, but also kept multiple versions of the production system running in parallel, allowing them to migrate different areas of their business at different rates. This approach also has some characteristics of canary releasing, described below.

Canary Releasing

It is usually a safe assumption that you only have one version of your software in production at a time. This makes it much easier to manage bugfixes, and indeed your infrastructure in general. However, it also presents an impediment to testing your software. Even with a solid and comprehensive testing strategy, defects pop up in production. And even with a low cycle time, development teams could still benefit from faster feedback on the new features and whatever they could be doing to make their software more valuable.

Furthermore, if you have an extremely large production environment, it's impossible to create a meaningful capacity testing environment (unless your application's architecture employs end-to-end sharing). How do you ensure a new version of your application won't perform poorly?

Canary releasing aims to address these challenges. Canary releasing, as shown in Figure 10.3, involves rolling out a new version of an application to a subset of the production servers to get fast feedback. Like a canary in a coal mine, this quickly uncovers any problems with the new version without impacting the majority of users. This is a great way to reduce the risk of releasing a new version.

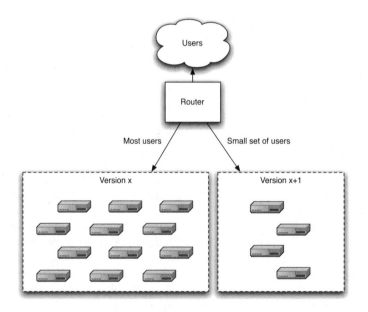

Figure 10.3 *Canary releasing*

Like blue-green deployments, you need to initially deploy the new version of the application to a set of servers where no users are routed to. You can then do smoke tests and, if desired, capacity tests, on the new version. Finally, you can start to route selected users to the new version of the application. Some companies select "power users" to hit the new version of the application first. You can even have multiple versions of your application in production at the same time, routing different groups of users to different versions as required.

There are several benefits to canary releasing:

1. It makes rolling back easy: Just stop routing users to the bad version, and you can investigate the logs at your leisure.

2. You can use it for A/B testing by routing some users to the new version and some to the old version. Some companies measure the usage of new features, and kill them if not enough people use them. Others measure the actual revenue generated by the new version, and roll back if the revenue for the new version is lower.[2] If your software generates search results, you might compare the quality of the results obtained by real users in the new version versus the old version. You don't need to route a large number of users to the new version to do A/B testing; a representative sample is sufficient.

3. You can check if the application meets capacity requirements by gradually ramping up the load, slowly routing more and more users to the application and measuring the application's response time and metrics like CPU usage, I/O, and memory usage, and watching for exceptions in logs. This is a relatively low-risk way to test capacity if your production environment is too large to create a realistic production-like capacity testing environment.

There are also some variations on the theme. Canary releasing is not the only way to do A/B testing—you can, instead, use switches in your application to route different users to different behavior. Alternatively, you could use runtime configuration settings to change behavior. However, these alternatives don't provide the other benefits of canary releasing.

Canary releasing is not for everyone, though. It is harder to use it where the users have your software installed on their own computers. There is a solution to this problem (one used in grid computing)—enable your client software or desktop application to automatically update itself to a known-good version hosted by your servers.

Canary releasing imposes further constraints on database upgrades (which also apply to other shared resources, such as shared session caches or external services): Any shared resource needs to work with all versions of the application you want to have in production. The alternative approach is to use a shared-nothing architecture where each node is truly independent of other nodes, with no shared database or services,[3] or some hybrid of the two approaches.

---

2. For a great analysis of the evolution of Amazon's shopping cart, check out [blrMWp].
3. Google created a framework called Protocol Buffers for all its internal services, designed to handle versioning [beffuK].

Canary Releasing for Point-of-Sale Systems

Canary releasing may sound a little theoretical, but we assure you that it is here only because we have seen it used in real projects (long before Google, NetFlix, and IMVU came up with the idea). On a project to deliver a high volume point-of-sale system, we used this strategy for all of the reasons outlined above. Our application was a highly distributed, rich-client system. There were tens of thousands of clients. When it came time to deploy changes to the client systems, sometimes we simply didn't have sufficient network bandwidth to get all of the changes out to all of the clients during the time when all of the stores were closed. Instead, we would roll new versions the system out over a period of several days, sometimes weeks.

This meant that different collections of stores would be operating with different versions of the client system, talking to different versions of the server-side system but all sharing a common underlying database.

The stores that used our system were divided into several different brands. Our incremental roll-out strategy meant that the different groups of stores could decide when to take the risk of updating their system. If a release had new features that were crucial to their operation, they would be keen to take it early, but if it was largely focused on features that were more relevant to one of their sibling store groups, they could defer the release until it had been proven elsewhere.

Finally, it is important to keep as few versions of your application in production as possible—try to limit it to two. Supporting multiple versions is painful, so keep the number of canaries to a minimum.

Emergency Fixes

In every system, there comes a moment when a critical defect is discovered and has to be fixed as soon as possible. In this situation, the most important thing to bear in mind is: Do not, under any circumstances, subvert your process. Emergency fixes have to go through the same build, deploy, test, and release process as any other change. Why do we say this? Because we have seen so many occasions where fixes were made by logging directly into production environments and making uncontrolled changes.

This has two unfortunate consequences. The first is that the change is not tested properly, which can lead to regressions and patches that do not fix the problem and may even exacerbate it. Secondly, the change is often not recorded (and even if it is, the second and third changes made to fix the problems you introduced with the first change do not get recorded). Hence the environment ends up in an unknown state that makes it impossible to reproduce, and breaks further deployments in unmanageable ways.

The moral of the story is: Run every emergency fix through your standard deployment pipeline. This is just one more reason to keep your cycle time low.

Sometimes it is not actually worth fixing a defect through an emergency fix. You should always consider how many people the defect affects, how often it occurs, and how severe the defect is in terms of its impact on users. If the defect affects few people, occurs infrequently, and has a low impact, it may not make sense to fix it immediately if the risks associated with deploying a new version are relatively high. Of course this is a great argument for reducing the risks associated with deployment through effective configuration management and an automated deployment process.

One alternative to making an emergency fix is to roll back to the previous known good version, as described earlier.

Here are some considerations to take into account when dealing with a defect in production:

- Never do them late at night, and always pair with somebody else.

- Make sure you have tested your emergency fix process.

- Only under extreme circumstances circumvent the usual process for making changes to your application.

- Make sure you have tested making an emergency fix using your staging environment.

- Sometimes it's better to roll back to the previous version than to deploy a fix. Do some analysis to work out what the best solution is. Consider what happens if you lose data or face integration or orchestration problems.

Continuous Deployment

Following the motto of Extreme Programming—if it hurts, do it more often—the logical extreme is to deploy every change that passes your automated tests to production. This technique is known as continuous deployment, a term popularized by Timothy Fitz [aJA8lN]. Of course it's not just continuous deployment (I can continuously deploy to UAT all I like: no big deal). The crucial point is that it is continuous deployment *to production*.

The idea is simply this: I take my pipeline and make the final step—deployment to production—automatic. That way, if a check-in passes all the automated tests, it gets deployed directly to production. In order for this not to cause breakages, your automated tests have to be fantastic—there should be automated unit tests, component tests, and acceptance tests (functional and nonfunctional) covering your entire application. You have to write all your tests—including acceptance tests—first, so that only when a story is complete will check-ins pass the acceptance tests.

Continuous deployment can be combined with canary releasing by using an automated process that rolls out a new version to a small group of users first, rolling it out to all users once it has been determined (probably as a manual step) that there are no problems with the new version. The added safeguards provided by a good canary releasing system make continuous deployment an even less risky proposition.

Continuous deployment isn't for everyone. Sometimes, you don't want to release new features into production immediately. In companies with constraints on compliance, approvals are required for deployments to production. Product companies usually have to support every release they put out. However, it certainly has the potential to work in a great many places.

The intuitive objection to continuous deployment is that it is too risky. But, as we have said before, more frequent releases lead to lower risk in putting out any particular release. This is true because the amount of change between releases goes down. So, if you release every change, the amount of risk is limited just to the risk inherent in that one change. Continuous deployment is a great way to *reduce* the risk of any particular release.

Perhaps most importantly, continuous deployment forces you to do the right thing (as Fitz points out in his blog post). You can't do it without automating your entire build, deploy, test, and release process. You can't do it without a comprehensive, reliable set of automated tests. You can't do it without writing system tests that run against a production-like environment. That's why, even if you can't *actually* release every set of changes that passes all your tests, you should aim to create a process that would let you do so if you choose to.

Your authors were really delighted to see the continuous deployment article cause such a stir in the software development community. It reinforces what we've been saying about the release process for years. Deployment pipelines are all about creating a repeatable, reliable, automated system for getting changes into production as fast as possible. It is about creating the highest quality software using the highest quality process, massively reducing the risks of the release process along the way. Continuous deployment takes this approach to its logical conclusion. It should be taken seriously, because it represents a paradigm shift in the way software is delivered. Even if you have good reasons for not releasing every change you make—and there are less such reasons than you might think—you should behave as if you were going to do so.

Continuously Releasing User-Installed Software

Releasing a new version of your application to a production environment you control is one thing. Releasing a new version of software installed by users on their own machines—client-installed software—is another. There are several issues to consider:

- Managing the upgrade experience

- Migrating binaries, data, and configuration

- Testing the upgrade process

- Getting crash reports from users

A serious issue with client-installed software is managing the large number of versions of your software that, over time, end up in the wild. This can cause a support nightmare: In order to debug any problems, you have to revert your source to the correct version and cast your mind back to the peculiarities of the application at that point in time, along with any known issues. Ideally, you want everyone to use the same version of your software: the latest stable version. In order to achieve this, it is essential to make the upgrade experience as painless as possible.

There are several ways in which clients can handle the upgrade process:

1. Have your software check for new versions and prompt the user to download and upgrade to the latest version. This is the easiest to implement, but the most painful to use. Nobody wants to watch a download progress bar.

2. Download in the background and prompt for installation. In this model, your software periodically checks for updates while running and downloads them silently. After the download is successful, it keeps prompting the user to upgrade to the latest version.

3. Download in the background and silently upgrade the next time the application is restarted. Your application might also prompt you to restart now if you'd like to upgrade (as Firefox does).

If you want to be conservative, options 1 and 2 may look more attractive. However, they are, in almost every case, the wrong choice. As an application developer, you want to give your users options. However, in the case of upgrading, users have no understanding of why they might want to delay the upgrade. It forces them to think about upgrading without providing any information to help them decide one way or the other. As a result, the rational choice is usually not to upgrade, simply because any upgrade might break the application.

In fact, exactly the same thought process is going on in the development team's head. The upgrade process might break the application, thinks the development team, so we should give the user a choice on this matter. But, if the upgrade process is indeed flaky, the user would of course be correct never to upgrade. If the upgrade process is not flaky, then there is no point in providing the choice: The upgrade should happen automatically. So in fact, giving users a choice simply tells them that the developers have no confidence in the upgrade process.

The correct solution is to make the upgrade process bullet proof—and to upgrade silently. In particular, if the upgrade process fails, the application should automatically revert to the previous version and report the failure to the development team. They can then fix the problem and roll out a new version which will (hopefully) upgrade correctly. All this can happen without the user even having to know anything. The only good reason for prompting the user is if there is some corrective action that needs to be taken.

Of course, there are reasons why you might not want your software to silently upgrade. Perhaps you don't want it to phone home, or you are part of the operations team of a corporate network which only allows the new versions of applications to be deployed after they have been exhaustively tested with the rest of the approved applications to ensure a rock-solid desktop. These are both reasonable use cases, and they can be accommodated with a configuration option to turn off automatic upgrades.

In order to provide a rock-solid upgrade experience, you need to handle migrating binaries, data, and configuration. In each case, the upgrade process should keep copies of the old ones around until it is absolutely sure the upgrade has been successful. If the upgrade fails, it should restore the old binaries, data, and configuration silently. One easy way to do this is to have a directory inside the install directory with the current versions of all of these things, and to create a new directory with the new ones. Then, switching versions is simply a matter of renaming directories or putting a reference to the current version's directory somewhere (on UNIX systems, this is commonly accomplished using symbolic links).

Your application should be able to upgrade from any version to any other version. In order to do this, you need to version your data store and your configuration file. Every time you change the schema of your data store or your configuration, you need to create a script to roll them forward from one version to the next and, if you want to support downgrades, a script to roll back from the new version to the old version. Then, when your upgrade script runs, it determines the current version of the data store and configuration, and applies the relevant scripts to migrate them to the latest version. This technique is described in much more detail in Chapter 12, "Managing Data."

You should test the upgrade process as part of your deployment pipeline. You can have a stage in your pipeline just for this purpose, which takes a selection of initial states with real data and configuration, taken from friendly users, and runs the upgrade to the latest version. This should be done automatically on a representative selection of target machines.

Finally, it is essential for client-installed software to be able to report crashes back to the development team. In his blog entry on continuous deployment for client software [amYycv], Timothy Fitz describes the wide range of hostile events encountered by client software: "broken hardware, out-of-memory conditions, foreign-language operating systems, random DLLs, other processes inserting their code into yours, drivers fighting for first-to-act in the event of crashes, and other progressively more esoteric and unpredictable integration issues."

This makes a crash reporting framework essential. Google has open-sourced its framework [b84QtM] for C++ on Windows, which can be called from inside .NET if required. A discussion of how to do crash reporting well and what metrics it is useful to report depends on the technology stack you are using and is beyond the scope of this book. Fitz' blog entry provides some useful discussion as a starting point.

Tips and Tricks

The People Who Do the Deployment Should Be Involved in Creating the Deployment Process

Often, deployment teams are asked to deploy systems that they have not had any hand in developing. They are given a CD and a sheaf of photocopied papers, with vague instructions like "Install SQL Server."

This kind of thing is symptomatic of a bad relationship between operations and the development teams, and it is certain that when it comes to the actual deployment to production, the process will be painful and drawn out with many recriminations and short tempers.

The first thing developers should do when starting a project is to seek out the operations people informally and involve them in the development process. That way, the operations people will have been involved in the software from the very beginning, and both sides will know, and have practiced many times, exactly what is going to happen long before the release, which will thus be as smooth as a newborn baby's bottom.

Things Go Better When Development and Operations Are Friends

We wanted to deploy a system on a very aggressive timetable. In the meeting between the operations and the development teams, the operations team was very strongly pushing back on the schedule. After the meeting, some of the technical people hung around for a chat, and swapped phone numbers. In the next few weeks, their communication continued, and the system was deployed to a production server and a small group of users one month later.

A member of the deployment team came and worked with the development team to create the deployment scripts, at the same time writing the installation documentation on the wiki. This meant that there were no surprises at deployment time. In operations team meetings where many systems were discussed and scheduled for deployment, this system was hardly discussed, since the operations team was confident of their ability to deploy it and of the quality of the software itself.

Log Deployment Activities

If your deployment process isn't completely automated, including the provisioning of environments, it is important to log all the files that your automated deployment process copies or creates. That way, it's easy to debug any problems that occur—you know exactly where to look for configuration information, logs, and binaries.

In the same way, it is important to keep a manifest of every piece of hardware in your environments, which bits you touched during deployment, and the logs of actual deployments.

Don't Delete the Old Files, Move Them

When you do a deployment, make sure you keep a copy of the previous version around. Then, ensure that you clear out the old files before deploying the new version. If a stray file from the old deployment is still lying around in the newly deployed version, it can cause hard-to-track-down bugs. At worst, it could lead to corrupted data if, for example, an old administration interface page is left in place.

A good practice in the UNIX world is to deploy each version of the application into a new directory and have a symbolic link that points to the current version. Deploying and rolling back versions is simply a matter of changing the symbolic link to point to the previous version. The network version of this is to have different versions sitting on different servers or different port ranges on the same server. Switch between them using a reverse proxy, as we describe in the "Blue-Green Deployments" section on page 261.

Deployment Is the Whole Team's Responsibility

A "build and deployment expert" is an antipattern. Every member of the team should know how to deploy, and every member of the team should know how to maintain the deployment scripts. This can be achieved by making sure that every time you build the software, even on a developers machine, it uses the real deployment scripts.

A broken deployment script should break the build.

Server Applications Should Not Have GUIs

It used to be common to see server applications with GUIs. This was particularly common with PowerBuilder and Visual Basic applications. These applications often had other problems we have mentioned, such as configuration that is not scriptable, applications that are sensitive to where they are installed, etc. The main problem, though, was that to work, the machine must have had a user logged in and the UI showing. This means that a reboot, either accidental or due to upgrades, will log the user out, and the server will stop. A support engineer would then have to log into the machine and manually start the server.

Chris Stevenson's PowerBuilder Bottleneck

At one client, there was a PowerBuilder application that processed all incoming trades for a major commodity broker. The application had a GUI and had to be manually started every day. It was also a single-threaded application, and if an error happened while processing a trade, the application would throw up a dialog box with a message saying "Error. Continue?" and a single "OK" button.

When this dialog appeared on the screen, all processing of trades would stop. It would take a call from a frustrated trader for the support people to go and look at the machine, and press the "OK" button to let processing continue. At one stage, someone wrote another VB application whose job was to watch for the dialog and programmatically click the "OK" button.

Much later, when other parts of the system had been improved, we found another peculiarity. At some stage, the application had been deployed on an old version of Windows 3.x that would not reliably close saved files. The application worked around this by incorporating a hard-coded five-second pause for every trade. Along with the single-threading constraint, this meant that if a lot of trades came in at the same time, the system would take a very long time to process them all. Levels of frustration would rise, and traders would reenter trades into the system, causing duplicate entries and a decrease in the reliability of the system.

This was in 2003. Don't underestimate how long your applications will be used.

Have a Warm-Up Period for a New Deployment

Don't switch on your eBay-killer website at the prearranged hour. By the time the site is officially "live," it should have been running for some time, long enough for the application servers and databases to fill their caches, make all their connections, and "warm up."

With websites, this can be accomplished through canary releasing. Your new servers and new release can start by serving some small proportion of requests; then, when the environment is bedded in and proven, you can switch more load over to the new system.

Many applications have internal caches that are eagerly filled at deployment time. Until the caches are full, the application will often have a poor response time and may even fail. If your application behaves like this, ensure you make a note of it in your deployment plan, including the length of time it takes to fill the cache (which you will of course have tested on a production-like environment).

Fail Fast

Deployment scripts should incorporate tests to ensure that the deployment was successful. These should be run as part of the deployment itself. They shouldn't be comprehensive unit tests, but simple smoke tests that make sure the deployed units are working.

Ideally, the system should perform these checks as it initializes, and if it encounters an error, it should fail to start.

Don't Make Changes Directly on the Production Environment

Most downtime in production environments is caused by uncontrolled changes. Production environments should be completely locked down, so that only your deployment pipeline can make changes to it. That includes everything from the configuration of the environment to the applications deployed on it and their data. Many organizations have strict access management processes in place. Schemes that we have seen used to manage access to production include limited-lifetime passwords created by an approval process and two-phase authentication systems that require a code to be typed in from an RSA fob. In one organization, changes to production could only be authorized from a terminal in a locked room with a CCTV camera monitoring the screen.

These authorization processes should be baked into your deployment pipeline. Doing so gains you a considerable benefit: It means that you have a system of record for every change made to production. There is no better audit trail than a record of exactly which change was made to production, when, and who authorized it. The deployment pipeline provides exactly such a facility.

Summary

The latter stages of the deployment pipeline are all concerned with deploying into testing and production environments. These stages are different from the previous stages of the pipeline in that there are no automated tests run as part of the latter stages. That means these stages don't pass or fail. But they still form an integral part of the pipeline. Your implementation should make it possible to deploy any version of your application that has made it past the automated tests into any of your environments at the push of a button, given the correct credentials. It should be possible for everyone on your team to see exactly what is deployed where, and what changes are included in that version.

The best way to lower the risk of your releases is, of course, to rehearse them. The more frequently you release the application into a variety of test environments, the better. Specifically, the more frequently you release the application into new test environments for the first time, the more reliable your process will be and the less likely you are to encounter a problem in a production release.

Your automated deployment system should be able to commission a new environment from scratch, as well as update a preexisting environment.

Nevertheless, for a system of any size and complexity, the first release into production will always be a momentous occasion. It is vital to have thought about the process and planned for it sufficiently to make it as straightforward as possible. However agile your team, the release strategy is one of those aspects of the software project where the last responsible moment to make decisions is not a few days, or even a few iterations, before the release. This should be part of your planning and, at least in part, be influencing your development decisions from early on in the life of the project. The release strategy will, and should, evolve over time, becoming more accurate and more detailed as the time of the first release approaches.

The most crucial part of release planning is assembling representatives from every part of your organization involved in delivery: build, infrastructure, and operations teams, development teams, testers, DBAs, and support personnel. These people should continue to meet throughout the life of the project and continually work to make the delivery process more efficient.

Part III

The Delivery Ecosystem

Chapter 11

Managing Infrastructure and Environments

Introduction

As we describe in Chapter 1, there are three steps to deploying software:

- Creating and managing the infrastructure in which your application will run (hardware, networking, middleware, and external services)

- Installing the correct version of your application into it

- Configuring the application, including any data or state that it requires

This chapter deals with the first of these steps. Since our goal is that all testing environments (including continuous integration environments) should be production-like, particularly in the way they are managed, this chapter will also, by extension, cover the management of testing environments.

Let's start by defining what we mean by environment in this context. An *environment* is all of the resources that your application needs to work and their configuration. The following attributes describe the environment:

- The hardware configuration of the servers that form the environment (such as the number and type of CPUs, amount of memory, spindles, NICs, and so on) and the networking infrastructure that connects them

- The configuration of the operating system and middleware (such as messaging systems, application and web servers, database servers) required to support the applications that will run within it

The general term *infrastructure* represents all environments in your organization, along with the services that support them, such as DNS servers, firewalls, routers, version control repositories, storage, monitoring applications, mail servers, and so on. Indeed, the boundary between an application's environment and the rest of your organization's infrastructure can vary from very clearly defined (in the case of embedded software, for example) to extremely fuzzy (in the case of service-oriented architectures, in which much infrastructure is shared and relied upon by applications).

The process of preparing environments for deployment and managing them after deployment is the main focus of this chapter. However what enables this is a holistic approach to managing all infrastructure, based upon the following principles.[1]

- The desired state of your infrastructure should be specified through version-controlled configuration.

- Infrastructure should be autonomic—that is, it should correct itself to the desired state automatically.

- You should always know the actual state of your infrastructure through instrumentation and monitoring.

While infrastructure should be autonomic, it is also essential that it should be simple to re-create, so that, in the case of a hardware failure for example, you can quickly reestablish a new known-good configuration. This means that infrastructure provisioning should also be an automated process. This combination of automated provisioning and autonomic maintenance ensures that infrastructure can be rebuilt in a predictable amount of time in the event of failure.

There are several things that need to be managed carefully to reduce the risk of deployment to any production-like environment:

- The operating system and its configuration, for both testing and production environments

- The middleware software stack and its configuration, including application servers, messaging systems, and databases

- Infrastructural software, such as version control repositories, directory services, and monitoring systems

- External integration points, such as external systems and services

- Network infrastructure, including routers, firewalls, switches, DNS, DHCP, and so on

- The relationship between the application development team and the infrastructure management team

We shall start with the last item in the list. It may seem out of context in this otherwise technical enumeration. However, everything else becomes a great deal easier if these two teams work closely together to solve problems. They should

---

1.   Some of these are inspired by James White [9QRI77].

collaborate on all aspects of environment management and deployment from the beginning of the project.

This focus on collaboration is one of the central principles of the DevOps movement, which aims to bring an agile approach to the world of system administration and IT operations. The other core principle of the movement is that agile techniques can be usefully brought to bear on managing infrastructure. Many of the techniques discussed in this chapter, such as autonomic infrastructure and behavior-driven monitoring, were developed by people involved in founding this movement.

As you read this chapter, keep in mind the guiding principle that testing environments should be production-like. This means that they should be similar (although not necessarily identical) in most of the technical aspects listed above. The goal is to catch environmental problems early and to rehearse critical activities like deployment and configuration before you get to production, so as to reduce the risk of releases. Test environments should be similar enough to achieve this. Crucially, the techniques to manage them should be identical.

This approach can be hard work and potentially expensive, but there are tools and techniques to help, such as virtualization and automated data center management systems. The benefits of this approach are so great, in terms of catching obscure and hard-to-reproduce configuration and integration problems early in the development process, that your effort will be repaid many times over.

Finally, although this chapter assumes that your application's production environment is under the control of an operations team, the principles and issues are the same for software products. For example, although a software product doesn't necessarily have someone backing up its data regularly, data recovery will be an important concern for any user. The same applies to other nonfunctional requirements such as recoverability, supportability, and auditability.

Understanding the Needs of the Operations Team

It is axiomatic that most projects fail due to people problems rather than technical problems. Nowhere is this more true than when it comes to deploying code to testing and production environments. Almost all medium and large companies separate the activities of development and infrastructure management (or operations as it is often known) into different groups or silos.[2] It is often the case that these two groups of stakeholders have an uneasy relationship. This is because development teams are incentivized to deliver software as rapidly as possible, whereas operations teams aim for stability.

Probably the most important thing to keep in mind is that all stakeholders have a common goal: making the release of valuable software a low-risk activity. In our experience, we have found that the best way to do this is by releasing as

---

2. For the purposes of this chapter, we will consider support to be part of the work of operations, although this is not always the case.

frequently as possible (hence *continuous delivery*). This ensures that there is as little change as possible between releases. If you work in an organization where releases take several days, with sleepless nights and long working hours, you will no doubt recoil in horror at this idea. Our response is that releasing can and should be an activity that can be performed in a few minutes. This may seem unrealistic. However, we have seen many large projects in large companies where release has gone from a sleep deprivation experiment driven by Gantt charts to a low-risk activity performed in minutes several times a day.

In small organizations, the development team is often responsible for operations. However, in most medium and large organizations these are independent groups. Each will have its own lines of reporting: There will be a head of operations and a head of software development. Every time a production release occurs, these teams and their managers work to ensure that any problems that arise are not their fault. This is clearly a potential cause of tension between the groups. Each group wants to minimize deployment risk, but each has its own approach.

Operations teams measure their effectiveness in terms of the key quality-of-service metrics such as mean time between failures (MTBF) and mean time to repair failures (MTTR). Often operations teams have service-level agreements (SLAs) they have to meet. Any change, including a change in process, which has an effect on operations teams' ability to meet these and any other targets (such as conformance to legal regulation), represents a risk. Given this context, here are some of the most important high-level concerns of operations teams.

Documentation and Auditing

Operations managers want to ensure that any change to any environment they control is documented and audited, so that, if things go wrong, they can find the relevant changes that caused the problem.

There are other reasons why operations managers are concerned about their ability to track changes; for example, the conformance to Sarbanes-Oxley, the US legislation intended to encourage good corporate auditing and responsibility, and the desire to ensure that environments remain consistent. But principally it's so that they can work out what happened between the last known good state of the environment and any breakage.

One of the most important processes an organization will have in place is a change management process, which is used to manage every change made to any controlled environments—and often operations will control both production and production-like testing environments. This usually means that any time anybody wants to make a change to any testing or production environment, a change must be requested. Many types of low-risk configuration changes can be made by operations on their own (in ITIL, these are "standard" changes).

However, deploying a new version of your application will usually be a "normal" change which will require approval by the change manager, advised by the change advisory board (CAB). A request for change needs to include details on the risk and impact of the change, and how it will be remediated if it fails. The request should be submitted before work starts on the new version to be deployed, not a couple of hours before the business expects it to go live. The first time you go through this process, expect to answer a lot of questions.

Member of the software development team have a *responsibility* to familiarize themselves with any such systems and processes that the operations team has in place, and comply with them. Identifying the procedures that need to be followed to release your software should be part of your development team's release plan.

Alerts for Abnormal Events

Operations managers will have systems in place to monitor their infrastructure and the applications running, and will want to be alerted when an abnormal condition occurs in any of the systems they manage so that they can minimize any downtime.

Every operations team has some way of monitoring their production environments. They might have OpenNMS, or one of the alternatives such as Nagios or HP's Operations Manager. Perhaps they have created their own custom monitoring system. Whichever system they use, they will want your application to hook into it so that they know the moment any error condition occurs, and where to look for more details to determine what has gone wrong.

It is important to find out, right at the beginning of the project, how the operations team expects to monitor your application, and make it part of your release plan. What do they want to monitor? Where are they expecting your logs to be? What hooks should your application use to notify operations staff of malfunctions?

For example, one of the most common coding mistakes that inexperienced developers make is to swallow errors. A quick chat with your operations team should convince you of the necessity to log every error condition to a single well-known location, with the appropriate severity, so they know exactly what the problem is. A corollary of this is that if your application fails for some reason, it should be easy for operations to restart or redeploy it.

Again, it is the development team's responsibility to determine the operations team's monitoring requirements and make them part of the release plan. The best way to tackle these requirements is to treat them in the same way as any other requirements. Actively consider the use of your application from the perspective of operations personnel—they are an important constituency of users. You will need to update the release plan with the procedure to restart and redeploy your application as the first release approaches.

The first release is just the beginning of the life of any application. Every new version of your application will behave differently, including the kinds of errors and log messages it produces, and perhaps the way it is monitored. It may fail in new ways, too. It's important to keep operations people in the loop when you release new versions of your application, so that they can prepare for these changes.

IT Service Continuity Planning

Operations managers will be involved in the creation, implementation, testing, and maintenance of their organization's IT service continuity plan. Each service the operations team manages will have a recovery point objective (RPO)—a measure of the length of time prior to a disaster for which data loss is acceptable, and a recovery time objective (RTO)—the maximum length of time allowed before services are restored.

The RPO governs the data backup and restore strategy, since data must be backed up frequently enough that the RPO can be achieved. Of course data is no good without the applications operating on it and the environments and infrastructure it lives in, so you need to be able to redeploy the correct versions of the applications and their environments and infrastructure. This, in turn, means that all of these things must have their configuration carefully managed so they can be reproduced by the operations team.

In order to meet the business' desired RTO, it might be necessary to establish a copy of the production environments and infrastructure in a second location that can be used if the primary systems fail. Applications should be able to deal with this eventuality. For high-availability applications, this means replicating data and configuration while the application is live.

A related requirement is for archiving: The amount of data generated by an application in production may become very large very quickly. There should be some simple method of archiving production data so it can be kept for auditing or support purposes while not filling up the disk or slowing down the application.

You should have tested performing backups, recovery, and archiving of your application's data as part of business continuity testing, as well as retrieving and deploying of any given version of your application, and provided the operations team with the process for performing each of these activities as part of your release plan.

Use the Technology the Operations Team Is Familiar With

Operations managers want changes to be made to their environments using technology that is familiar to their team, so they can own and maintain their environments.

It is quite common for operations teams to be well versed in Bash or PowerShell, but less likely that they will be Java or C# ninjas. However, it is almost certain that they will want to review changes being made to the configuration of their environments and infrastructure. If the operations team cannot understand the deployment process because it uses technologies and languages they are not familiar with, there is inevitably an increased risk of making changes. Operations teams may veto deployment systems they don't have the skills to maintain.

The development team and operations team should sit down at the beginning of every project and decide how deployment of the application will be performed. It may be necessary for either the operations team or the software development team to learn an agreed-upon technology—perhaps a scripting language such as Perl, Ruby, or Python, or a packaging technology such as the Debian packaging system or WiX.

It is important that both teams understand the deployment system, because the same process must be used to deploy changes to every environment—development, continuous integration, testing, and production—and the developers will initially be responsible for creating them. At some point, they will be handed over to the operations team which will be responsible for maintaining them, which means that they should be involved from the start in writing them. The technologies to be used for deploying and making other changes to environments and infrastructure should form part of the release plan.

The deployment system forms an integral part of the application—it should be tested and refactored with the same care and attention as the rest of the application, and kept in version control. When this is not the case (and we have seen many projects where it is not), the result is always a set of poorly tested, brittle, and badly understood scripts that make change management risky and painful.

Modeling and Managing Infrastructure

With the exception of stakeholder management, everything else in this chapter can be broadly considered a branch of configuration management. However, implementing full configuration management of your testing and production environments is nontrivial, which explains the amount of space we devote to this topic. Even so, we will only be covering the high-level principles of environment and infrastructure management.

There are many different classes of configuration information at play in any environment, all of which should be provisioned and managed in an automated fashion. Figure 11.1 shows some examples of types of servers, divided up by level of abstraction.

If you have full control over the technology choices for the system you are creating, you should ask, as part of your procurement and inception process, how easy it will be to automate the deployment and configuration of the hardware and software infrastructure itself. Having underlying technology that can be configured and deployed in an automated fashion is a necessary condition for automating the processes of integration, testing, and deployment of your system.

Even if you don't have control over the selection of your infrastructure, if you intend to fully automate your build, integration, testing, and deployment, you must address each of the following questions:

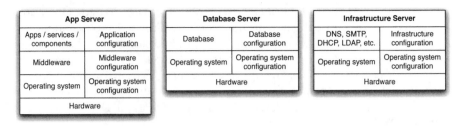

Figure 11.1 *Types of servers and their configuration*

- How will we provision our infrastructure?

- How will we deploy and configure the various bits of software that form part of our infrastructure?

- How do we manage our infrastructure once it is provisioned and configured?

A modern operating system has thousands of ways in which one installation may differ from another: different device drivers, different system configuration settings, and a vast array of parameters that will influence the way in which your software will run. Some software systems are much more tolerant than others to differences at this level. Most commercial off-the-shelf software (COTS) is expected to run in a wide variety of software and hardware configurations, and so should not care too much about differences at this level—although you should always check the system requirements of your COTS as part of the procurement or upgrade process. However, a very high-performance web application may be sensitive to even tiny changes, such as variations in packet sizes or filesystem configuration.

For most multiuser applications that run on servers, it is not appropriate to simply accept the default settings of operating systems and middleware. Operating systems will need to have access control, firewalls, and other hardening measures (such as disabling nonessential services) configured. Databases will need to be configured and have users set up with the correct permissions, application servers will need to have components deployed, message brokers will need to have messages defined and subscriptions registered, and so on.

As with every other aspect of your delivery process, you should keep everything you need to create and maintain your infrastructure under version control. At the least, that means

- Operating system install definitions (such as those used by Debian Preseed, RedHat Kickstart, and Solaris Jumpstart)

- Configuration for data center automation tools like Puppet or CfEngine

- General infrastructure configuration, such as DNS zone files, DHCP and SMTP server configuration files, firewall configuration files, and so forth

- Any scripts you use for managing your infrastructure

These files in version control form inputs to the deployment pipeline the same way the source code does. The job of the deployment pipeline in the case of infrastructural changes is threefold. First, it should verify that all applications will work with any infrastructural changes before they get pushed out to production environments, ensuring that every affected application's functional and nonfunctional tests pass against the new version of the infrastructure. Second, it should be used to push changes out to operations-managed testing and production environments. Finally, the pipeline should perform deployment tests to ensure that the new infrastructure configuration has been deployed successfully.

Referring back to Figure 11.1, it is worth observing that the scripts and tools used to deploy and configure applications, services, and components are often distinct from those used to provision and manage the rest of the infrastructure. Sometimes, the process created for deploying applications also performs the task of deploying and configuring middleware as well. These deployment processes are generally created by the development teams responsible for the application in question, but they of course have an implicit dependency on the rest of the infrastructure being in place and in the correct state.

An important consideration when dealing with infrastructure is the extent to which it is shared. If a particular piece of infrastructural configuration is relevant only to a particular application, then it should be part of the deployment pipeline of the application and have no separate lifecycle of its own. However, if some infrastructure is shared between applications, then you are faced with a problem of managing dependencies between applications and the versions of infrastructure they depend on. That means recording which version of the infrastructure each version of the application requires in order to work. You then need to set up a separate pipeline to push out infrastructural changes, ensuring that changes affecting multiple applications move through the delivery process in a way that obeys the dependency rules.

Controlling Access to Your Infrastructure

If your organization is small or new, you have the luxury of devising a strategy for the configuration management of all of your infrastructure. If you have an existing system that is not under good control, you'll need to work out how to get it under control. There are three parts to this:

- Controlling access to prevent anyone from making a change without approval

- Defining an automated process for making changes to your infrastructure

- Monitoring your infrastructure to detect any issues as soon as they occur

While in general we are not fans of locking things down and establishing approval processes, when it comes to your production infrastructure it is essential. As a corollary of that, since we believe that you should treat your testing environments the same way you treat your production environments, the same process should apply to both.

It is essential to lock down the production environments to prevent unauthorized access not only from people outside your organization, but also from people within it—even operations staff. Otherwise it is just too tempting, when something goes wrong, to log into the environment in question and poke around to resolve problems (a process sometimes politely called a *problem-solving heuristic*). This is almost always a terrible idea for two reasons. First, it usually leads to service disruptions (people tend to try rebooting or applying service packs at random). Second, if something goes wrong later, there is no record of who did what when, which means it's impossible to work out the cause of whatever problem you're facing. In this situation, you may as well re-create the environment from scratch so it is in a known state.

If your infrastructure is not capable of being re-created from scratch via an automated process, the first thing to do is implement access control so that changes cannot be made to any infrastructure without going through an approval process. *The Visible Ops Handbook* calls this "stabilizing the patient." This will undoubtedly cause much annoyance, but it is a prerequisite for the next step: creating an automated process for managing infrastructure. Without turning off access, operations staff end up spending all of their time firefighting because unplanned changes break things all the time. A good way to set the expectations of when work will be done and enforce access control is to create maintenance windows.

Requests to make changes to your production and testing environments should go through a change management process. This need not be bureaucratic: As is pointed out in *The Visible Ops Handbook*, many organizations which perform best in terms of the MTBF (mean time between failures) and MTTR (mean time to repair) "were doing 1000–1500 changes per week, with a change success rate of over 99%."

However, the approval for changes to your testing environments should of course be easier to get than the approval to change production. Often, changes to production environments have to be approved by heads of departments or your CTO (depending on the size of your organization and its regulatory environment). Most CTOs, however, would be upset if asked to approve changes to the UAT environment. The important point is that you are going through the same process for your testing environments as you do for production.

Making Changes to Infrastructure

Of course sometimes it is necessary to make changes to infrastructure. There are several essential characteristics of an effective change management process.

- Every change, whether it's updating firewall rules or deploying a new version of your flagship service, should go through the same change management process.

- This process should be managed using a single ticketing system that everybody can log into and which generates useful metrics such as average cycle time per change.

- The exact change that is made should be logged so it can be easily audited later.

- It should be possible to see a history of changes made to every environment, including deployments.

- The change you want to make should first have been tested on one of your production-like testing environments, and automated tests should be run to ensure that it doesn't break any of the applications that use the environment.

- The change should be made to version control and then applied through your automated process for deploying infrastructural changes.

- There should be a test to verify that the change has worked.

Creating an automated process for deploying infrastructural changes from version control is at the core of good change management. The most effective way to do this is to require all changes to be made to your environments via a central system. Use a testing environment to work out the change you want to make, test it in a fresh, production-like staging environment, put it into configuration management so that future rebuilds incorporate it, have it approved, and then have the automated system roll out the change. Many organizations have built their own solutions to this problem, but if you do not have one, you can use a data center automation tool like Puppet, CfEngine, BladeLogic, Tivoli, or HP Operations Center.

The best way to enforce auditability is to have all changes made by automated scripts which can be referenced later in case anybody needs to find out exactly what was done. In general, we prefer automation over documentation for this reason. Written documentation is never a guarantee that the documented change was performed correctly, and the differences between what somebody claims they did and what they actually did are sufficient to cause a problem that may take hours or days to track down.

Managing Server Provisioning and Configuration

Provisioning servers and managing their configuration is often overlooked in small and even medium-sized operations for the simple reason that it seems complicated. Almost everybody's initial experience of getting a server up and running comes from taking the install media, putting it into the computer, and doing an interactive install, followed by an uncontrolled configuration management process. However, this quickly leads to servers that are "works of art," which leads to inconsistent behavior between servers and systems that cannot be re-created easily in the event of a failure. Furthermore, provisioning new servers is a manual, repetitive, resource-intensive, and error-prone process—exactly the kind of problem that can be solved with automation.

At a high level, provisioning servers—whether for testing or production environments—starts with putting a new box in your data center and wiring it in. Once that's done, pretty much every part of its lifecycle, including powering it up for the first time, can be done remotely in a fully automated fashion. You can use out-of-band management systems such as IPMI or LOM to turn on the box and have it network-boot to install a base operating system via PXE (described below), which should include an agent for your data center management tool. Your data center management tool (Puppet in the diagram below) then manages the configuration of the box from then onwards. This fully automated process is shown in Figure 11.2.

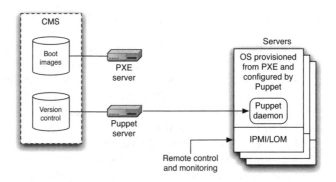

Figure 11.2 *Automated provisioning and configuration of servers*

Provisioning Servers

There are several ways to create operating system baselines:

- A fully manual process
- Automated remote installation

- Virtualization

We won't consider the fully manual process, except to note that it is not reliably repeatable and therefore doesn't scale. However, this is how development teams often manage their environments. It is often the case that developer workstations and even continuous integration environments managed by development teams are works of art that have accumulated cruft over long periods of time. These environments bear no relation to the environment your application will actually live in. This in itself can be a huge source of inefficiency. Really, these systems should be managed the same way you manage testing and production environments.

Virtualization as a way of creating operating system baselines and managing environments will be considered later, in the "Virtualization" section on page 303.

Automated remote installation is the best option to take a new physical machine and get it up and running (even if you plan to later use it as a virtual host). The best place to start with this is PXE (Preboot eXecution Environment) or Windows Deployment Services.

PXE is a standard for booting boxes over Ethernet. When you choose to boot via the network in your BIOS, what happens under the hood is PXE. The protocol uses a modified version of DHCP to find servers that offer images to boot from. When the user has selected the image to boot from, the client then loads the appropriate image into RAM via TFTP. The standard Internet Services Consortium DHCP server, dhcpd, which ships with all Linux distributions, can be configured to provide PXE services, and you'll then need to configure a TFTP server to provide the actual images. If you're using RedHat, an application called Cobbler will serve a selection of Linux operating system images via PXE. It will also let you (if you are running a RedHat box) spin up new virtual machines with your chosen OS image. There is also a plugin for Hudson which provides PXE services. BMC's BladeLogic includes a PXE server.

Pretty much every common UNIX flavor provides images suitable for PXE. Of course you can also create your own custom images—both the RedHat and Debian package management systems allow you to save the state of an installed system in a file which can then be used to initialize other systems.

Once you've got your base system provisioned, you'll want to configure it. One way to do this is to use your operating system's unattended install process: RedHat's Kickstart, Debian's Preseed, or Solaris' Jumpstart. These can be used to perform postinstall activities such as installing operating system patches and deciding which daemons to run. The next step after installation is to get an agent for your infrastructure management system installed on the box, and have those tools manage your operating system's configuration from then on.

The Windows analog of PXE is known as Windows Deployment Services—and indeed, it uses PXE under the hood. WDS comes on Windows Server 2008 Enterprise Edition, and can also be installed on Windows Server 2003. It can be used to boot versions of Windows from Windows 2000 onwards (not including

ME)—although things have been streamlined considerably from Vista forwards. In order to use WDS, you'll need an ActiveDirectory domain, a DHCP server, and a DNS server. You can then install (if required) and enable WDS. To set up a profile to boot off in WDS, you need two things: a boot image and an install image. The boot image is what is loaded into RAM by PXE—in the case of Windows, this is a bit of software called WinPE (Windows Preinstallation Environment), which is what you run when you boot a Vista (or later) installation DVD. The install image is the actual full install image which the boot image loads onto your machine. From Vista onwards, both of these images are available in the Sources directory in the installation DVD as BOOT.WIM and INSTALL.WIM. Given these two files, WDS will do all the configuration necessary to make them available over the network for booting.

You can also create your own custom install images for WDS. This is most easily done using Microsoft Hyper-V, as described by Ben Armstrong [9EQDL4]. Simply start a virtual machine based off the operating system you want to create an image from. Configure it the way you want it, run Sysprep on it, and then use ImageX to turn the drive image into a WIM file that you can register with WDS.

Ongoing Management of Servers

Once you have got the operating system installed, you will need to ensure that its configuration doesn't change in an uncontrolled manner. That means ensuring, first, that nobody is able to log into the boxes except the operations team, and second, that any changes are performed using an automated system. That includes applying OS service packs, upgrades, installing new software, changing settings, or performing deployments.

The goal of your configuration management process is to ensure that configuration management is declarative and idempotent—which means you configure the desired state of your infrastructure and a system ensures that this configuration is applied so that, whatever the initial state of the infrastructure, the end result is the same, even if the same configuration is reapplied. This is possible in both the Windows and UNIX worlds.

Once this system is in place, it becomes possible to manage all the testing and production environments within your infrastructure from a central, versioned configuration management system. You can then reap the following benefits:

- You can ensure consistency across all environments.

- You can easily provision new environments that match the configuration of existing ones, for example to create staging environments that match production.

- If you have a hardware failure on one of your boxes, you can put in a new box and have it configured the same way as the old one using a fully automated process.

Bad Configuration Management Means Debugging on Release Day

In one of our projects, we had a deployment to production fail mysteriously. The deployment script just hung. We traced the problem to the login shell being set to sh on the production server and bash on the staging server. This meant that when we tried to detach a process on production, we were unable to. It was a simple problem to fix, but only an inspired guess prevented us from rolling back the deployment. Such subtle differences can be much trickier than this to spot; comprehensive configuration management is vital.

On Windows, Microsoft provides (in addition to Windows Deployment Services) a solution for managing your Microsoft infrastructure: System Center Configuration Manager. SCCM uses ActiveDirectory and Windows Software Update Services to manage operating system configuration, including updates and settings on each of the boxes in your organization. You can also deploy applications using SCCM. SCCM also talks to Microsoft virtualization technologies, allowing you to manage virtual servers the same way you manage physical ones. Access control is managed using Group Policy, which integrates with ActiveDirectory and is built into all Microsoft servers since Windows 2000.

Back in the UNIX world, LDAP along with the usual UNIX access controls are used to control who can do what on which boxes. There are a number of solutions for managing operating system configuration, including which software and updates are installed, on an ongoing basis. Perhaps the most popular are CfEngine, Puppet, and Chef, but several other similar tools exist, such as Bcfg2 and LCFG [9bhX9H]. At the time of writing, the only such tool which supports Windows is WPKG, which does not support UNIX platforms. However, work was being done on both Puppet and Chef to add Windows support. Also worth mentioning is the fantastic Marionette Collective (mcollective for short), a tool that uses a message bus to query and manage large numbers of servers. It has plugins to remotely control other services, and can talk to Puppet and Facter.

Alternatively, there are, as you might expect, powerful and expensive commercial tools to manage your server infrastructure. Apart from Microsoft, the main players are BMC, with their BladeLogic suite, IBM, with Tivoli, and HP, with their Operations Center suite.

All of these tools—whether open source or commercial—operate in a similar way. You specify what you want the state of your boxes to be, and the tool ensures that your infrastructure is in the specified state. This is done by having agents run on each of your boxes to pick up the configuration and alter the state of the other boxes to match it, performing tasks such as installing software and making configuration changes. The key characteristic of such systems is that they enforce idempotence—that is, whatever state the box is in when the agent finds it, and however many times the agent applies the configuration, the box will always end up in the desired end state. In short, you can just specify the desired end state, fire up the tool, and it will continually make the appropriate adjustments. This achieves the higher goal of making your infrastructure autonomic—in other words, self-healing.

You should be able to take a vanilla set of servers and deploy everything to them from scratch. Indeed, a great way to introduce automation or virtualization into your build, deploy, test, and release strategy is to make it a test of your environment provisioning process. A good question to ask, and to test, is: How long would it take to provision a new copy of my production environment if it failed catastrophically?

In the case of most open source tools, your environments' configuration information is stored as a series of text files that can be kept in version control. This in turn means your infrastructure's configuration is self-documenting—you can just go to version control to see its current expected state. The commercial tools typically include databases to manage configuration information and clicky UIs for editing it.

We'll go into a bit more detail on Puppet, because it is one of the most popular open source systems currently available (along with CfEngine and Chef). The underlying principles are the same for the other tools. Puppet manages configuration through a declarative, external domain-specific language (DSL) tailored to configuration information. This allows for complex enterprise-wide configurations with common patterns extracted into modules that can be shared. Thus you can avoid duplicating configuration information.

Puppet configuration is managed by a central master server. This server runs the Puppet master daemon (puppetmasterd) which has a list of machines that it controls. Each of the controlled machines run the Puppet agent (puppetd). It communicates with the server to ensure that the servers under Puppet's control are synchronized with the latest version of the configuration.

Test-Driven Changes to Your Environments

Matthias Marschall describes how to put out changes to your environments using a test-driven approach [9e23My]. The idea is this:

1. In your monitoring system, write a service that monitors the problem you are trying to solve, and make sure the service shows red on your dashboard.

2. Implement the configuration change, and have Puppet roll it out to your test system.

3. Once the service shows green on your dashboard, have Puppet roll out the change to production.

When a configuration changes, the Puppetmaster will propagate that change to all the clients that need to be updated, install and configure the new software, and restart the servers where necessary. The configuration is declarative, and describes the desired end state of each server. This means they can be configured from any starting state, including a fresh copy of a VM or a newly provisioned machine.

An Automated Approach to Provisioning

The power of this approach should be obvious from an example.

Ajey is maintaining a large number of servers for a global IT consultancy. These servers are located in machine rooms in Bangalore, Beijing, Sydney, Chicago, and London.

He logs into the change management ticket system and sees that there is a request for a new UAT environment from one of the project teams. They are about to enter the UAT process for the latest release, and will keep developing new features on the trunk. The new environment will require three machines, and Ajey quickly locates three servers of the requisite specifications. Since the project already has a testing environment, he can simply reuse the definitions from that environment.

He adds three lines to the Puppet master's definitions and checks the file back into source control. The Puppet master picks up the changes and configures the machines, emailing Ajey when the task is complete. Ajey closes the ticket, adding the machine names and IP addresses as a comment. The ticket system emails the team, telling them that their environment is now ready.

Let's take installing Postfix as an example of how to use Puppet. We're going to write a module defining how we want Postfix to be configured on our mail server. Modules consist of manifests and, optionally, templates and other files. We're going to create a new module called postfix to hold our new manifest, which defines how Postfix should be installed. This means creating a directory called postfix/manifests under the modules root (/etc/puppet/modules), and creating a manifest in a file called init.pp there:

```
# /etc/puppet/modules/postfix/manifests/init.pp
class postfix {

  package { postfix: ensure => installed }
  service { postfix: ensure => running, enable => true }

  file { "/etc/postfix/main.cf":
    content => template("postfix/main.cf.erb"),
    mode => 755,
  }
}
```

This file defines a class which describes how to install Postfix. The `package` statement ensures that the `postfix` package is installed. Puppet can talk to all popular packaging systems, including Yum, Aptitude, RPM, Dpkg, Sun's package manager, Ruby Gems, and BSD and Darwin ports. The `service` statement ensures that the Postfix service is enabled and running. The `file` statement creates the file /etc/postfix/main.cf on the box, taking it from an erb template. The erb template is fetched from /etc/puppet/modules/[module name]/templates on the Puppetmaster's filesystem, so you'd create the main.cf.erb file in /etc/puppet/modules/postfix/templates.

Which manifests are to be applied to which hosts is defined in Puppet's main site.pp file:

```
# /etc/puppet/manifests/site.pp
  node default {
    package { tzdata: ensure => installed }
    file { "/etc/localtime":
      ensure => "file:///usr/share/zoneinfo/US/Pacific"
    }
  }

  node 'smtp.thoughtworks.com' {
    include postfix
  }
```

In this file, we tell Puppet to apply the Postfix manifest to the host smtp.thoughtworks.com. There is also a definition for the default node, which gets applied to every box with Puppet installed on it. We've used this target to ensure that all boxes are set to the Pacific timezone (this syntax creates a symbolic link).

Here's a more advanced example. In many organizations, it makes sense to have applications packaged up and stored on an organizational package server. However, you don't want to have to configure each of your servers to look at the organization's package server by hand. In this example, we have Puppet tell our boxes where our custom Apt repository is, add the correct Apt GPG key to these boxes, and add a crontab entry to run an Apt update every night at midnight.

```
# /etc/puppet/modules/apt/manifests/init.pp
class apt {
  if ($operatingsystem == "Debian") {
    file { "/etc/apt/sources.list.d/custom-repository":
      source => "puppet:///apt/custom-repository",
      ensure => present,
    }
    cron { apt-update:
      command => "/usr/bin/apt-get update",
      user => root,
      hour => 0,
      minute => 0,
    }
  }
}
```

```
define apt::key(keyid) {
  file { "/root/$name-gpgkey":
    source => "puppet:///apt/$name-gpgkey"
  }

  exec { "Import $keyid to apt keystore":
    path => "/bin:/usr/bin",
    environment => "HOME=/root",
    command => "apt-key add /root/$name-gpgkey",
    user => "root",
     group => "root",
    unless => "apt-key list | grep $keyid",
  }
}
```

The main apt class, first of all, checks that the node the manifest is being applied to is running Debian. This is an example of using a fact about the client—the variable $operatingsystem is one of several that are automatically predefined based on what Puppet knows about the client. Run facter on the command line to list all the facts known by Puppet. We then copy the file custom-repository from Puppet's internal file server to the right place on the box, and add an entry to root's crontab which runs apt-get update every night. The crontab action is idempotent—that is, the entry won't be re-created if it already exists. The apt::key definition copies the GPG key from Puppet's fileserver, and runs the apt-key add command on it. We ensure idempotence by telling the command not to run if Apt already knows about the key (this is the unless line).

You need to ensure that the files custom-repository, defining the custom Apt repositories, and custom-repository-gpgkey, containing the GPG key for it, are placed on the Puppet master server in the directory /etc/puppet/modules/apt/files. Then, include the definitions as follows, substituting in the correct key ID:

```
# /etc/puppet/manifests/site.pp

node default {
  apt::key { custom-repository: keyid => "<KEY_ID>" }
  include apt
}
```

Note that Puppet is designed to work with version control: everything under /etc/puppet should be kept under version control and changed only through version control.

Managing the Configuration of Middleware

Once your operating system's configuration is properly managed, you need to think about the management of the middleware that sits on top of it. Middleware—whether web servers, messaging systems, or commercial off-the-shelf software (COTS)—can be decomposed into three parts: binaries, configuration, and data. The three have different lifecycles which makes it important to treat them independently.

Managing Configuration

Database schemas, web server configuration files, application server configuration information, message queue configuration, and every other aspect of the system that needs to be changed for your system to work should be under version control.

For most systems, the distinction between the operating system and the middleware is a fairly hazy one. If you're using an open source stack built on Linux, for example, pretty much all the middleware can be managed in the same way as the operating system, using Puppet or one of the other similar tools. In this case, you don't have to do anything special to manage your middleware. Simply follow the same model as in the Postfix example in the previous section for the rest of your middleware: tell Puppet to ensure the right packages are installed, and update the configuration from templates on the Puppet master server checked into version control. Operations like adding new websites and new components can be managed in this way too. In the Microsoft world, you can use System Center Configuration Manager, or one of the commercial tools like BladeLogic or Operations Center.

If your middleware isn't part of the standard operating system install, the next best thing is to package it up using your operating system's package management system and put it on your organization's internal package server. Then you can use your chosen server management system to manage this middleware using the same model.

However, there are some bits of middleware that are not susceptible to this treatment—usually those which are not designed with scripting and silent installation in mind. We will tackle this scenario in the following section.

Applying Configuration Management to Recalcitrant Middleware

One very large project that we worked on had many different test and production environments. Our application was hosted by a well-known commercial Java application server. Each server was manually configured using the administration console supplied with the application server. Every one was different.

We had a team of people dedicated to maintaining this configuration. When we needed to deploy the application to a new environment, it took planning to ensure that the hardware was ready, to get the OS configured, deploy the application server, configure it, deploy the application, and then test it manually to confirm that it works. The whole process would take several days for a new environment, and at least one day just to deploy a new version of the software.

We tried detailing the manual steps in documents, expending a lot of effort to capture and record the ideal configuration, but still small differences remained. We often had bugs in one environment that we couldn't reproduce in another. We still don't know why, in some cases.

In order to fix this problem, we took the application server's installation directory and put it into source control. We then wrote a script that checked it out of source control and remotely copied it to the right place on the environment of our choice.

We also took note of where it stored its configuration. We created a directory in a separate version control repository for each environment we had to deploy to. In the directory for each environment, we put the application server's configuration file relevant to that environment.

Our automated deployment process ran the script that deployed the application server's binaries, checked out the relevant configuration file for the environment we were deploying to, and copied that to the relevant place on the filesystem. This process proved to be robust, reliable, and repeatable as a way of setting up application servers for our deployments.

The project we describe in the preceding sidebar was completed a few years ago. If we were starting it now, we would be much more careful at the outset to manage the configuration information associated with the various test and production environments. We would also carry out the necessary work early in the project to eliminate manual steps in this process as far as possible and save everyone a lot of work.

Configuration information associated with middleware is as much a part of the system as the programs written in your favorite programming language. Much modern middleware supports scriptable methods of configuration: XML configuration is common, and some supply simple command-line tools suitable for scripting. Learn about and utilize these facilities. Version-control the files in the same way as you version-control all the other code in your system.

If you have a choice, select middleware with these features. In our experience, these facilities are much more important than the sexiest administration tool or even the most recent level of standards compliance.

Sadly, there remain many (often expensive) middleware products that, while aiming to provide "enterprise-level services," fall down in the ease of deployment and configuration management. In our experience, the success of a project can often turn on its ability to be deployed cleanly and reliably.

In our view, no technology can be considered genuinely enterprise-ready unless it is capable of being deployed and configured in an automated way. If you can't keep vital configuration information in versioned storage and thus manage changes to in a controlled manner, the technology will become an obstacle to delivering high-quality results. We have been burnt by this many times in the past.

When it is two o'clock in the morning, and you have a critical bugfix to send into production, it is far too easy to make a mistake when entering data into a GUI-based configuration tool. It is at times like this that an automated deployment procedure will save you.

Often, open source systems and components lead the way in scriptable configuration. As a result, open source solutions to infrastructural problems are usually easy to manage and integrate. Disappointingly, some parts of the software industry take a different view. We are often asked to work on projects where we don't have a free choice. So what are the strategies to employ when faced with a monolithic block of a system in the midst of your nice modular, configurable, versioned, automated build and deployment process?

Research the Product

When looking for a low-cost, low-energy solution, the obvious starting point is to be absolutely certain that the product in question doesn't have a poorly advertised automated configuration option. Read the documentation carefully, looking specifically for such options, search the web for advice, talk to your product's support representatives, check on forums or groups. In short, make sure that there isn't a better option before you move on to the other strategies described below.

Strangely, we have found the product support route surprisingly unhelpful. After all, all we are asking for is the ability to version-control the work that we invest in their product. Our favorite response from one large vendor was, "Oh yes, we are going to build our own version control into the system in the release after next." Even if they had done so, and even if having the feature a year or two later could make any difference to the project we were working on at the time, integrating to a crude, proprietary version control system wouldn't have helped us manage a consistent configuration set.

Examine How Your Middleware Handles State

If you are certain that your middleware does not support any form of automated configuration, the next step is to see if you can cheat by version-controlling its storage behind its back. Many products these days use XML files to store their configuration information. Such files work extremely well with modern version control systems and present few problems. If the third-party system stores its state in binary files, consider revision-controlling these binaries. They will usually change frequently as the development progresses.

In most cases, where flat files of any kind are used to supply configuration information to your product, the principal issue that you will face is how and when the product reads the relevant configuration information. In a few automation-friendly cases, simply copying the new versions of the files into the correct location will suffice. If this works, you can go further and separate your product's binaries from their configuration. In this case, it is necessary to reverse-engineer the installation process and, essentially, write your own installer. You will need to look and see where the application installs its binaries and libraries.

You then have two options. The simplest option is to store the relevant binaries in version control along with a script that installs them to the relevant environment. Option two is to really go ahead and write your own installer (or a package such as an RPM if you're using a RedHat-derived Linux distribution, for example). Creating RPMs (or other installers, for that matter) is not that hard, and it might be well worth the trouble, depending on your circumstances. You can then deploy your product to a new environment using your installers, and apply the configuration from version control.

Some products use databases to store their configuration information. Such products usually have sophisticated administration consoles that hide the complexities of the information that they store. These products present particular difficulties for automated environment management. You basically have to treat the database as a blob. However, at the very least your vendor should provide instructions for backing up and restoring the database. If so, you should certainly create an automated process to do this. It may then be possible to take the backup, work out how to manipulate its data, and then restore it back with your changes.

Look for a Configuration API

Many products in the class we're discussing here support programming interfaces in one form or another. Some may allow you to configure the system sufficiently to meet your needs. One strategy is to define your own simple configuration file for the system that you are working with. Create custom build tasks to interpret those scripts and to use the API to configure the system. This strategy of "invent your own" configuration files puts configuration management back into your hands—allowing you to version-control the configuration files and automate their use. Microsoft's IIS is one system where we have used this approach in the past, using its XML metabase. However, newer versions of IIS allow for scripting via PowerShell.

Use a Better Technology

Theoretically, you could try some other approaches—for example, creating your own version-control-friendly configuration information and writing code to map it into the native configuration of you product via whatever means present themselves, such as playing back user interactions through the admin console or reverse-engineering the database structure. In reality, we haven't yet reached this point. We came close a couple of times, but then usually found APIs allowing us to do what we need.

While it is possible to reverse-engineer the binary file formats or even database schemas of your infrastructure products, you should check if doing so will breach the terms of your license agreement. If you find yourselves at this extreme, it is worth asking the vendors if they can help, perhaps offering to share any technology that you produce to offer them some benefit in return. Some vendors (particularly smaller ones) are reasonably enlightened about this kind of thing, so it's worth a try. However, many will not be interested because of the difficulty of supporting such a solution. If so, at this point we would strongly recommend adopting an alternate technology which is more tractable.

Many organizations are wary about changing the software platform that they use because they have already spent a great deal of money on it. However, this argument, known as the sunk cost fallacy, does not take into account the lost opportunity cost of moving to a superior technology. Try to get someone sufficiently senior, or a friendly auditor, to understand the financial ramifications of the loss of efficiency that you are suffering and get them to invest in a superior alternative. On one of our projects, we kept a "pain-register," a diary of time lost on inefficient technology, which after a month easily demonstrated the cost of struggling with technology that slowed down delivery.

Managing Infrastructure Services

It is extremely common for problems with infrastructure services—such as routers, DNS, and directory services—to break software in production environments that worked perfectly all through the deployment pipeline. Michael Nygard wrote an article for InfoQ in which he tells the story of a system which died mysteriously at the same time every day [bhc2vR]. The problem turned out to be a firewall which dropped inactive TCP connections after one hour. As the system was idle at night, when activity started in the morning, the TCP packets from the pooled database connections would be dropped silently by the firewall.

Problems like this will happen to you, and when they do, they will be maddeningly difficult to diagnose. Although networking has a long history, very few people really understand the ins and outs of the entire TCP/IP stack (and how some infrastructure, such as firewalls, can break the rules), especially when several different implementations coexist on the same network. This is the usual situation in production environments.

We have several pieces of advice for you.

- Every part of your networking infrastructure's configuration, from DNS zone files to DHCP to firewall and router configurations to SMTP and other services your applications rely on, should be version-controlled. Use a tool like Puppet to push configuration out from version control to your systems so that they are autonomic, and you know that there is no other way to introduce changes except via changing a configuration file in version control.

- Install a good network monitoring system such as Nagios, OpenNMS, HP Operations Manager, or one of their brethren. Make sure that you know when network connectivity is broken, and monitor every port on every route that your application uses. Monitoring is discussed at more length in the "Monitoring Infrastructure and Applications" section on page 317.

- Logging is your friend. Your applications should log at WARNING level every time a network connection times out or is found to be unexpectedly closed. You should log at INFO or, if the logs are too verbose, DEBUG level every time you close a connection. You should log at DEBUG level every connection that you open, including as much information as possible on the endpoint of the connection.

- Make sure that your smoke tests check all of the connections at deployment time to flush out any routing or connectivity problems.

- Make your integration testing environment's network topology as similar as possible to production, including using the same pieces of hardware with the same physical connections between them (down to the level of using exactly the same sockets and the same part number of cable). An environment so constructed can usefully serve as a backup environment should a hardware failure occur. Indeed, many enterprises have an environment known as staging which serves the dual purpose of both exactly replicating production, so that the production deployment can be tested, and acting as a failover. The blue-green deployment pattern, described in the "Blue-Green Deployments" section on page 261, allows you to do this even if you have only one physical environment.

Finally, when something does go wrong, have forensic tools available. Wireshark and Tcpdump are both fantastically useful tools that make it easy to see packets flying past, and filter them so you can isolate exactly the packets you're looking for. The UNIX tool Lsof and its Windows cousins Handle and TCPView (part of the Sysinternals suite) also come in very handy to see what files and sockets are open on your machine.

Multihomed Systems

One important piece of hardening on production systems is the use of multiple, isolated networks for different types of traffic, in conjunction with multihomed servers. Multihomed servers have multiple network interfaces, each of which talks to a different network. At a minimum, you might have a network for monitoring and administering production servers, a network for running backups, and a network for production data to move to and from your servers. Such a topology is shown in Figure 11.3.

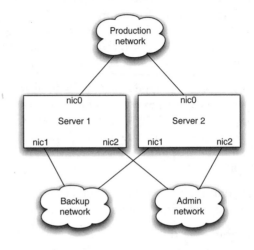

Figure 11.3   *Multihomed servers*

The administration network is physically separated from the production network for security reasons. Typically, any services such as ssh or SNMP required to control and monitor production servers would be configured to bind only to the nic2, so it is impossible to access these services from the production network. The backup network is physically separated from the production network, so that the large volumes of data that move during backups don't affect the performance or administration networks. High-availability and high-performance systems sometimes use multiple NICs for production data, either for failover or for dedicated services—for example, you might have a separate, dedicated network for your organization's message bus or database.

First, it's important to ensure that each service and application running on a multihomed box binds only to the relevant NICs. In particular, application developers need to make the IP addresses that their application listens on configurable at deploy time.

Second, all the configuration (including routing) for a multihomed network configuration should be managed and monitored centrally. It's very easy to make mistakes that require a visit to the data center—such as when Jez, early on in his career, brought down an administration NIC on a production box, forgetting that he was sshed in rather than on a physical tty. As Nygard points out,[3] it's

---

3.   Nygard, 2007, p. 222.

also possible to make more serious routing errors, such as allowing traffic from one NIC on a multihomed box through to another, potentially creating security breaches such as exposing customer data.

Virtualization

We have already discussed the problems that occur when environments differ because servers are works of art. Virtualization provides a way to amplify the benefits of the techniques, already described in this chapter, for automating the provisioning of servers and environments.

What Is Virtualization?

In general, virtualization is a technique that adds a layer of abstraction on top of one or more computer resources. However, in this chapter we're mostly concerned with platform virtualization.

Platform virtualization means simulating an entire computer system so as to run multiple instances of operating systems simultaneously on a single physical machine. In this configuration, there is a virtual machine monitor (VMM), or hypervisor, which has full control of the physical machine's hardware resources. Guest operating systems run on virtual machines, which are managed by the VMM. Environment virtualization involves simulating one or more virtual machines as well as the network connections between them.

Virtualization was originally developed by IBM in the 1960s as an alternative to creating a multitasking time-sharing operating system. The main application for virtualization technology is server consolidation. Indeed there was a period when IBM *avoided* recommending its VM family to its customers, since it would result in lower hardware sales. However, there are many other applications of this powerful technology. It can be used in a wide range of situations, such as simulating historical computer systems on modern hardware (a common practice in the retro-games community), or as a mechanism to support disaster recovery, or as part of a configuration management system to support software deployment.

Here we will describe the use of environment virtualization to help provide a controlled, fully repeatable deployment and release process. Virtualization can help reduce the time it takes to deploy software, and the risks associated with it, in a variety of ways. The use of virtual machines in deployment is an enormous aid to achieving effective configuration management across the breadth and depth of your systems.

In particular, virtualization provides the following benefits:

- *Fast response to changing requirements*. Need a new testing environment? A new virtual machine can be provisioned in seconds at no cost, versus days or weeks to obtain a new physical environment. Obviously, you cannot run an infinite number of VMs on a single host—but using virtualization can in some situations decouple the need to buy new hardware from the lifecycle of the environments that they run.

- *Consolidation.* When organizations are relatively immature, each team will often have its own CI servers and testing environments sitting on physical boxes under their desks. Virtualization makes it easy to consolidate CI and testing infrastructure so it can be offered as a service to delivery teams. It is also more efficient in terms of hardware usage.

- *Standardizing hardware.* Functional differences between components and subsystems of your application no longer force you to maintain distinct hardware configurations, each with its own specification. Virtualization allows you to standardize on a single hardware configuration for physical environments but run a variety of heterogeneous environments and platforms virtually.

- *Easier-to-maintain baselines.* You can maintain a library of baseline images—operating system plus application stacks—or even environments, and push them out to a cluster at the click of a button.

It is the simplicity of maintaining and provisioning new environments that is most useful when applied to the deployment pipeline.

- Virtualization provides a simple mechanism to create a baseline for the environments in which your systems operate. You can create and tune the environments that host your applications as virtual servers, and once you are happy with the result, you can save the images and configuration and then go on to create as many copies as you wish, knowing that what you're getting are faithful clones of the original.

- Since the server images from which your hosts are built are stored in a library and can be associated with a particular build of your application, it is simple to revert any environment back to a previous state—not just the application but every aspect of the software that you deploy.

- The use of virtual servers to baseline host environments makes it simple to create copies of production environments, even where a production environment consists of several servers, and to reproduce them for testing purposes. Modern virtualization software offers a significant degree of flexibility, allowing some aspects of the system, like network topology, to be controlled programmatically.

- It is the last missing piece that allows for true push-button deployments of *any* build of your application. If you need a new environment to demonstrate the latest features for a potential customer, you can create the new environment in the morning, run the demonstration at lunchtime, and delete it in the afternoon.

Virtualization also improves our ability to test both functional and nonfunctional requirements.

- VMMs provide programmatic control of features of your system, such as network connectivity. This makes the testing of nonfunctional requirements, such as availability, much easier and capable of automation. For example, it is relatively straightforward to test the behavior of a cluster of servers by disconnecting one or more of the nodes programmatically and observing the effect on system.

- Virtualization also provides the capability to significantly speed up long-running tests. Instead of running them on a single box, you can run them in parallel on a build grid of virtual machines. We routinely do this on our projects. On one of our larger ones, it reduced the time to run our tests from 13 hours to 45 minutes.

Managing Virtual Environments

One of the most important characteristics of VMMs is that a virtual machine image is a single file. Such a file is called a disk image. The useful thing about disk images is that you can copy them and version them (probably not in version control, unless your VCS can handle lots of very large binary files). You can then use them as templates, or baselines (in configuration management terminology). Some VMMs treat templates as something different from disk images, but ultimately they're the same thing. Many VMMs even allow you to create templates from running VMs. You can then create as many running instances as you want from these templates in seconds.

Another useful tool some VMM vendors provide is taking a snapshot of a physical box and turning it into a disk image. This is incredibly useful, because it means you can take a copy of the boxes in your production environment, save them as templates, and fire up copies of your production environment to do continuous integration and testing on.

Earlier in this chapter, we discussed how to provision new environments using a completely automated process. If you have a virtualized infrastructure, you can create a disk image of a server thus provisioned and use it as a template for every server that uses the same configuration. Alternatively, you could use a tool like rPath's rBuilder to create and manage baselines for you. Once you have templates for every type of machine you need in your environment, you can use your VMM software to start up new environments from your templates as needed. Figure 11.4 demonstrates this.

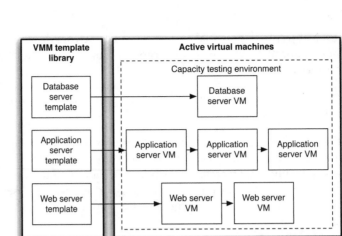

Figure 11.4   *Creating virtual environments from templates*

These templates form the baselines, known-good versions of your environments, on which the rest of your configuration and deployment can be made. We trivially satisfy our requirement that it should be quicker to provision a new environment than debug and fix one that's in an unknown state due to uncontrolled changes—you just pull down the defective VM and start a new one from the baseline template.

It now becomes possible to implement an automated process for environment provision in an incremental way. Instead of always starting from scratch, you can start your provisioning process from a known-good baseline image, which may have only the base operating system installed. You should still install an agent for your data center automation tool (Puppet in Figure 11.5 below) on every template so that your virtual machines are autonomic, and so that changes can be rolled out consistently across your entire system.

You can then run your automated process to configure the operating system and install and configure any software required by your applications. Once again, at this point, save a copy of each type of box in your environment as a baseline. This workflow is described in Figure 11.5.

Virtualization also makes two other intractable scenarios, discussed earlier in the chapter, much easier to manage: dealing with environments that have evolved in an uncontrolled way, and dealing with software in your stack that can't be managed in an automated fashion.

Environments that have evolved through undocumented or poorly documented manual changes, including legacy systems, present a problem in every organization. If these works of art malfunction, it is extremely hard to debug them, and it is virtually impossible to make copies of them for testing purposes. If the people who set them up and manage them leave or go on holiday and something goes wrong, you are in trouble. It is also very risky to make changes to such systems.

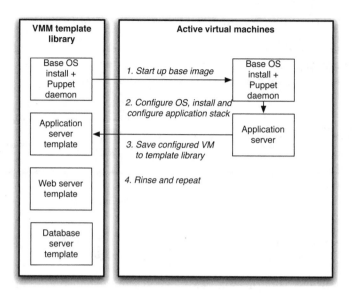

Figure 11.5   *Creating VM templates*

Virtualization provides a way to mitigate this risk. Use your virtualization software to take a snapshot of the running machine or machines that comprise the environment and turn them into VMs. You can then easily create copies of the environment for testing purposes.

This technique provides a valuable way to move incrementally from managing environments manually to an automated approach. Instead of automating your provisioning process from scratch, create templates based on your current known-good systems. Again, you can replace the real environments with the virtual ones to confirm that your templates are good.

Finally, virtualization provides a way to deal with software that your application relies on that cannot be installed or configured in an automated way, including COTS. Simply install and configure the software manually on a virtual machine, and then create a template from it. This can then serve as a baseline that you can replicate as and when you require.

If you manage environments in this way, it is essential to keep track of baseline versions. Every time you make a change to a baseline, you need to store it as a new version, and as we have said previously, to rerun all of the pipeline stages that are based on that baseline against the most recent release candidate. You also need to be able to correlate the use of specific baseline versions with the versions of your applications that are known to run on them for every environment, which brings us to the next section.

Virtual Environments and the Deployment Pipeline

The purpose of the deployment pipeline is to put every change you make to your application through your automated build, deploy, and test process to verify its fitness for release. A simple pipeline is shown in Figure 11.6.

Figure 11.6 *A simple pipeline*

There are some features of the pipeline approach that are worth revisiting to consider how to use them in the context of virtualization.

- Each instance of a pipeline is associated with a change in version control that triggered it.

- Every stage of the pipeline subsequent to the commit stage should be run in a production-like environment.

- Exactly the same deployment process using exactly the same binaries should be run in every environment—differences between environments should be captured as configuration information.

It can be seen that what is being tested in the pipeline is not just the application. Indeed when there is a test failure in the pipeline, the first thing that happens is triage to determine the cause of the failure. The five most likely causes of a failure are

- A bug in the application's code

- A bug or invalid expectation in a test

- A problem with the application's configuration

- A problem with the deployment process

- A problem with the environment

Thus the configuration of the environment represents one of the degrees of freedom in configuration space. It follows that a known-good version of your application is not just correlated with the revision numbers in the version control system that were the source of the binary code, automated tests, deployment scripts, and configuration. A known-good version of your application is also correlated with the configuration of the environment that the pipeline instance ran on. Even if it ran on multiple environments, they should all have had exactly the same production-like configuration.

When releasing to production, you should use precisely the same environment that you ran all of your tests in. The corollary of all this is that a change in configuration to your environment should trigger a new pipeline instance the same way as any other change (to source code, tests, scripts, and so on). Your build and release management system should be able to remember the set of VM templates that you used to run the pipeline and be able to start exactly from that set of templates when you deploy to production.

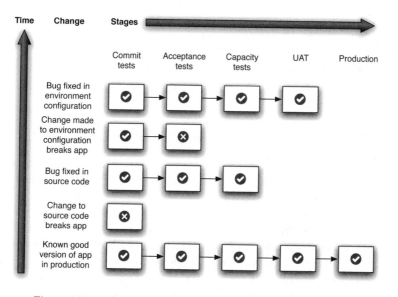

Figure 11.7 *Changes passing through the deployment pipeline*

In this example, you can see changes triggering a new release candidate, and the release candidate's progression through the deployment pipeline. First, a change is made to the source code; perhaps a developer checks in a bugfix or part of the implementation of a new feature. The change breaks the application; a test in the commit stage fails, notifying the developers of the defect. The developer fixes the defect and checks in again. This triggers a new build, which passes the automated tests (commit stage, acceptance test stage, capacity test stage). Next, an operations person wishes to test an upgrade to a piece of software in the production environment. She creates a new VM template with the upgraded software. This triggers a new pipeline instance, and the acceptance tests fail. Our operations person works with the developer to find the source of the problem (perhaps some configuration setting) and fixes it. This time, the application works with the new environment, passing all of its automated and manual tests. The application, *along with the environment baseline it was tested on*, is ready to be deployed into production.

Of course when the application is deployed to UAT and production, it uses exactly the same VM template that was used to run the acceptance and capacity tests. This verifies that this precise configuration of the environment with this version of the application have an acceptable capacity and are defect-free. Hopefully, this example demonstrates the power of using virtualization.

However, it is not a good idea to make every change to your staging and production environments by taking a copy of a virtual baseline and creating a new one. Not only will you get through disk space very quickly if you do this; you will lose the benefits of autonomic infrastructure managed through declarative, version-controlled configuration. It is better to keep a relatively stable VM baseline image—a basic operating system image with the latest service packs, any bits of middleware or other software dependencies, and an agent for your data center management tool installed. Then, the tool is used to complete the provisioning process and bring the baseline to exactly the right configuration required.

Highly Parallel Testing with Virtual Environments

Things are somewhat different in the case of user-installed software, particularly outside of a corporate environment. In this case, you normally don't have much control over the production environment, because it is the user's computer. In this case, it becomes important to test your software on a wide variety of "production-like" environments. For example, desktop applications often have to be multiplatform, running on Linux, Mac OS, and Windows, and usually on several different versions and configurations of each of these platforms.

Virtualization provides an excellent way to handle multiplatform testing. Simply create virtual machines with examples of each of the potential environments that your application targets, and create VM templates from them. Then run all of the stages in your pipeline (acceptance, capacity, UAT) on all of them in parallel. Modern continuous integration tools make this approach straightforward.

You can use the same technique to parallelize tests to shorten the vital feedback cycle of expensive acceptance and capacity tests. Assuming that your tests are all independent (see our advice in the "Acceptance Test Performance" section on page 218), you can run them in parallel on multiple virtual machines (of course you could also run them in parallel as separate threads, but there is a limit to how well this scales). This approach to creating a dedicated compute grid for your build can vastly speed up running your automated tests. Ultimately, the performance of your tests is only limited by the time it takes for your single slowest test case to run and the size of your hardware budget. Again, modern CI tools and software like Selenium Grid make this very simple.

Virtual Networks

Modern virtualization tools have powerful networking configurations which make it straightforward to set up private virtual networks. Using these tools, it is possible to make your virtual environments even more production-like by replicating the exact network topology (right down to the IP and MAC addresses) you use in production. We have seen this technique used to create multiple versions of large, complex environments. On one project, the production environment had five servers: a web server, an application server, a database server, a server to run Microsoft BizTalk, and a server to host a legacy application.

The delivery team created baseline templates of each of these servers, and used their virtualization tool to create multiple copies of this environment for doing UAT, capacity testing, and running automated tests simultaneously. The setup is shown in Figure 11.8.

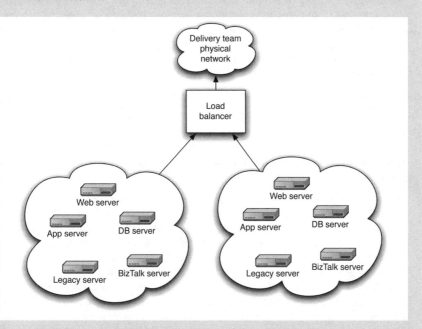

Figure 11.8   *Using virtual networks*

Each of the environments was connected to the outside world via virtual LANs. It was possible to programmatically simulate the connection between the application server and the database server dropping using the virtualization API as part of the automated nonfunctional tests. Needless to say, doing this kind of thing is orders of magnitude harder without virtualization.

Cloud Computing

Cloud computing is an old idea, but in recent years it has become ubiquitous. In cloud computing, information is stored on the Internet and accessed and manipulated through software services also available on the Internet. The defining characteristic of cloud computing is that the computing resources you use, such as CPU, memory, storage, and so on, can expand and contract to meet your need, and you pay only for what you use. Cloud computing can refer to both the software services themselves, and the hardware and software environments that they run on.

Utility Computing

A concept commonly connected with cloud computing is that of utility computing. This is the idea that computing resources (resources like CPU, memory, storage, and bandwidth) are provided as a metered service in the same way that gas or electricity are provided to your home. This concept was first proposed in 1961 by John McCarthy, but it has taken several decades for computing infrastructure to mature sufficiently so that cloud-based services could be provided reliably to large numbers of users. HP, Sun, and Intel had been offering cloud solutions for a while, but it was only with the launch of Amazon's EC2 service in August of 2006 that things really took off. One simple reason for the popularity of Amazon's web services was that Amazon had been using them internally for some time—which means they already knew the service was useful. Since then, the cloud computing ecosystem has exploded, with large numbers of vendors supplying cloud services and tools to help manage them.

The main benefit of utility computing is that it requires no capital investment in infrastructure. Many start-ups began to use Amazon Web Services (AWS) to host their services because that requires no minimum contract or up-front payment. As a result, start-ups are able to bill their AWS fees onto a credit card and pay them after they had received service charges from their users. Utility computing is also attractive to larger businesses because it appears as recurring costs rather than capital expenditure on a balance sheet. Since the costs are relatively low, purchases don't require approval by senior management. It also allows you to manage scaling extremely simply—assuming that your software is already capable of running on a grid of boxes, starting up a new box (or 1,000, for that matter) is just a single API call away. You can start with a single box, and if your new idea isn't wildly successful, your losses are low.

Thus cloud computing encourages entrepreneurship. In most organizations, one of the main barriers to the adoption of compute clouds is a feeling of nervousness about putting the company's information assets into the hands of a third party and the security implications of that move. However, with the advent of technologies like Eucalyptus, it has become possible to run your own compute cloud in-house.

It is common to distinguish three categories of cloud computing [9i7RMz]: applications in the cloud, platforms in the cloud, and infrastructure in the cloud. Applications in the cloud are services like WordPress, SalesForce, Gmail, and Wikipedia—traditional web-based services that are hosted on cloud infrastructure. SETI@Home was perhaps the earliest mainstream example of an application in the cloud.

Infrastructure in the Cloud

At the highest level of configurability is infrastructure in the cloud, such as Amazon Web Services (AWS). AWS provides many infrastructural services, including message queues, static content hosting, streaming video hosting, load balancing, and storage, in addition to its well-known utility VM hosting service called EC2. With these offerings, you have almost complete control over the systems, but you also have to do most of the work to tie everything together.[4]

Many projects are using AWS for their production systems. Assuming your software is architected properly, with the ideal being a shared-nothing architecture, scaling your application is fairly straightforward in terms of infrastructure. There are many providers of services which you can use to simplify the management of your resources, and a bewildering array of specialized services and applications built on top of AWS. However, the more you use these services, the more you lock yourself in to their proprietary architecture.

Even if you don't use AWS for your production infrastructure, it can still be an extremely useful tool for your software delivery process. EC2 makes it easy to fire up new testing environments on demand. Other uses include running tests in parallel to speed them up, capacity testing, and multiplatform acceptance testing, as descibed earlier in this chapter.

There are two important issues that are raised by people migrating to cloud infrastructure: security and service levels.

Security is often the first blocker mentioned by medium and large companies. With your production infrastructure in someone else's hands, what's to stop people compromising your service or stealing your data? Cloud computing providers are aware of this issue, and have established various mechanisms to address them, such as highly configurable firewalls and private networks which connect to your organization's VPN. Ultimately, there is no fundamental reason why cloud-based services should be less secure than public-accessible services hosted on infrastructure that you own, although the risks with cloud-based infrastructure are different and you need to plan for a cloud-based rollout.

---

4. Microsoft's Azure provides some services that count as infrastructure in the cloud. However, their virtual machine offering has some of the characteristics of platforms in the cloud, since at the time of writing you do not have administrator access to VMs and thus cannot change their configuration or install software that requires elevated privileges.

Compliance is often mentioned as a constraint on using cloud computing. However, the problem is usually not that regulations forbid the use of cloud computing so much as the fact they haven't caught up with them. As many regulations ignore cloud computing, the implications of the regulations for cloud-hosted services are sometimes not sufficiently well understood, or require inter-pretation. Given careful planning and risk management, it is usually possible to reconcile the two. The healthcare company TC3 encrypted its data in order to be able to host its service on AWS, and was thus able to remain HIPAA-compliant. Some cloud vendors provide a level of PCI DSS compliance, and some also provide payment services that are PCI-compliant so you don't have to handle credit card payments. Even large organizations that require level 1 compliance can use a heterogeneous approach where the payment system is hosted in-house and the rest of the system is hosted in the cloud.

Service levels are particularly important when your entire infrastructure is outsourced. As with security, you'll need to do some research to ensure that your provider can meet your requirements. This is particularly the case when it comes to performance. Amazon offers services at different levels of performance depend-ing upon your needs—but even the highest level they offer is no match for high-performance servers. If you need to run an RDBMS with a large dataset and a high load, you probably don't want to put it in a virtualized environment.

Platforms in the Cloud

Examples of platforms in the cloud include services, such as Google App Engine and Force.com, where the service provider gives you a standardized application stack to use. In return for your using their stack, they take care of things like scaling the application and infrastructure. Essentially, you sacrifice flexibility so that the provider can easily take care of nonfunctional requirements such as capacity and availability. The advantages of platforms in the cloud are the following:

- You get all the same benefits of infrastructure in the cloud in terms of cost structure and flexibility of provisioning.

- The service provider will take care of nonfunctional requirements such as scalability, availability, and (to some extent) security.

- You deploy to a completely standardized stack, which means there is no need to worry about configuring or maintaining testing, staging, or produc-tion environments, and no messing around with virtual machine images.

The last point is especially revolutionary. We spend a good chunk of this book discussing how to automate your deploy, test, and release process and how to set up and manage your testing and deployment environments. Using platforms in the cloud almost completely dispenses with many of these considerations. Typically you can just run a single command to deploy your application to the Internet. You can go from nothing to a released application in literally minutes, and push-button deployments come with practically zero investment on your part.

The very nature of platforms in the cloud means that there will always be pretty severe constraints on your application. This is what allows these services to provide simple deployment and high scalability and performance. For example, Google App Engine only provides an implementation of BigTable, not a standard RDBMS. You can't start new threads, call out to SMTP servers, and so forth.

Platforms in the cloud also suffer from the same issues that can make infrastructure in the cloud unsuitable. In particular, it is worth pointing out that concerns over portability and vendor lock-in are considerably more severe with platforms in the cloud.

Nevertheless, we expect that for many applications this type of cloud computing will be a large step forward. Indeed, we expect the availability of these types of services to change the way people architect applications.

One Size Doesn't Have to Fit All

Of course, you can mix and match different services to implement your system. For example, you might have static content and streaming video hosted on AWS, your application hosted on Google App Engine, and a proprietary service running on your own infrastructure.

To achieve this, applications have to be designed to work in these kinds of heterogeneous environments. This kind of deployment requires that you implement a loosely coupled architecture. The value of a heterogeneous solution in terms of cost and the ability to satisfy nonfunctional requirements makes a compelling business case for a loosely coupled architecture. Actually designing one that works is hard, and beyond the scope of this book.

Cloud computing is at a relatively early stage in its evolution. In our opinion, this is not just a latest overhyped, must-have technology—it is a genuine step forward that will grow in importance over the coming years.

DIY Cloud Computing

Cloud computing doesn't have to involve swanky new technology. We know of several organizations that use spare capacity on desktop computers to perform system functions during times when the desktop machines are little used.

One bank that we worked with halved their capital costs for computer hardware by using the capacity of the desktop computers of staff members who had gone home for the evening to perform overnight batch operations. The hardware that had previously been needed to perform these overnight calculations was no longer needed and the calculations ran faster when broken down into discrete chunks that could be allocated to the cloud.

This was a large multinational organization, so at any given time of day there were always thousands of people on the opposite side of the world who were asleep, but their computers were busy contributing a relatively small chunk of computing capacity to the cloud. In total, the computing capacity of the cloud at any given time was enormous; all that was required was the ability to divide problems up into small enough chunks that could allocated to discrete elements of it.

Criticisms of Cloud Computing

Although we are convinced cloud computing will continue to grow, it is worth bearing in mind that not everybody is overjoyed by the incredible potential of cloud computing as sold to us by the likes of Amazon, IBM, or Microsoft.

Larry Ellison notably commented that "The interesting thing about cloud computing is that we've redefined cloud computing to include everything that we already do . . . I don't understand what we would do differently in the light of cloud computing other than change the wording of some of our ads." (Wall Street Journal, September 26, 2008). He found an unlikely ally in Richard Stallman, who was even more trenchant: "It's stupidity. It's worse than stupidity: it's a marketing hype campaign. Somebody is saying this is inevitable—and whenever you hear somebody saying that, it's very likely to be a set of businesses campaigning to make it true." (The Guardian, September 29, 2008).

First of all, "the Cloud" is not, of course, the Internet—a system with an open architecture designed from the ground up for interoperability and resilience. Each vendor offers a different service, and you are to some extent tied to your choice of platform. For some time, peer-to-peer services seemed like the most likely paradigm for building large, distributed, scalable systems. However, the vision of peer-to-peer has not yet been realized, perhaps because it is so hard for vendors to make money from peer-to-peer services, and cloud computing still very much follows the utility computing model whose revenue characteristics are well understood. Essentially, that means that your application and your data are ultimately at the mercy of the vendors. This may or may not be an improvement over your current infrastructure.

At the moment, there is no common standard even for the basic virtualization platforms used by utility computing services. It seems even less likely that there will be standardization at the API level. The Eucalyptus project has created an implementation of parts of AWS' API to allow people to create private clouds, but the APIs presented by Azure or Google AppEngine will be considerably harder to reimplement. This makes it hard to make applications portable. Vendor lock-in is as much, or more of, a reality in the cloud as it is elsewhere.

Finally, depending on your application, the economics may simply make it unreasonable to use cloud computing. Project the costs and savings of moving to utility computing versus owning your own infrastructure, and run a proof of concept to validate your assumptions. Consider factors such as the break-even point of the two models, taking into account depreciation, maintenance, disaster recovery, support, and the benefits of not spending on the capital account. Whether or not cloud computing is the right model for you depends as much on your business model and organizational constraints as it does on technical concerns.

There is a detailed discussion on the pros and cons of cloud computing, including some interesting economic modeling, in Armbrust et al.'s paper, "Above the Clouds: A Berkeley View of Cloud Computing" [bTAJ0B].

Monitoring Infrastructure and Applications

It is essential to have insight into what is going on in your production environments for three reasons. First, businesses can get feedback on their strategies much faster if they have real-time business intelligence, such as how much revenue they are generating and where that revenue is coming from. Second, when something goes wrong, the operations team needs to be informed immediately that there is an incident, and have the necessary tools to track down the root cause of the incident and fix it. Finally, historical data is essential for planning purposes. If you don't have detailed data on how your systems behaved when there was an unexpected spike in demand, or when new servers were added, it's impossible to plan evolving your infrastructure to meet your business requirements.

There are four areas to consider when creating a monitoring strategy:

- Instrumenting your applications and your infrastructure so you can collect the data you need

- Storing the data so it can easily be retrieved for analysis

- Creating dashboards which aggregate the data and present it in a format suitable for operations and for the business

- Setting up notifications so that people can find out about the events they care about

Collecting Data

First, it is important to decide what data you want to gather. Monitoring data can come from the following sources:

- Your *hardware*, via out-of-band management (also known as lights-out management or LOM). Almost all modern server hardware implements the Intelligent Platform Management Interface (IPMI) which lets you monitor voltages, temperatures, system fan speeds, peripheral health, and so forth, as well as perform actions such as power cycling or lighting an identification light on the front panel, even if the box is powered off.

- The *operating system* on the servers comprising your infrastructure. All operating systems provide interfaces to get performance information such as memory usage, swap usage, disk space, I/O bandwidth (per disk and NIC), CPU usage, and so forth. It's also useful to monitor the process table to work out the resources each process is consuming. On UNIX, Collectd is the standard way to gather this data. On Windows, it's done using a system called performance counters, which can also be used by other providers of performance data.

- Your *middleware*. This can provide information on the usage of resources such as memory, database connection pools, and thread pools, as well as information on the number of connections, response time, and so forth.

- Your *applications*. Applications should be written so that they have hooks to monitor things that both operations and business users care about, such as the number of business transactions, their value, conversion rate, and so forth. Applications should also make it easy to analyze user demographics and behavior. They should record the status of connections to external systems that they rely on. Finally, they should be able to report their version number and the versions of their internal components, if applicable.

There are various ways data can be gathered. First of all, there are many tools—both commercial and open source—that will gather everything described above across your whole data center, store it, produce reports, graphs, and dashboards, and provide notification mechanisms. The leading open source tools include Nagios, OpenNMS, Flapjack, and Zenoss, although there are many more [dcgsxa]. The leading commercial players are IBM with Tivoli, HP with Operations Manager, BMC, and CA. A relatively new commercial entrant to the field is Splunk.

Splunk

One of the killer tools to hit the IT operations world in recent years is Splunk. Splunk indexes log files and other textual data that includes timestamps (which most of the data sources we describe above can be configured to provide) across your whole data center. You can then perform real-time searches that let you pinpoint unusual events and do root-cause analysis of what's going on. Splunk can even used as an operations dashboard, and be configured to send notifications.

Under the hood, these products use various open technologies for monitoring. The main ones are SNMP, its successor CIM, and JMX (for Java systems).

SNMP is the most venerable and ubiquitous standard for monitoring. SNMP has three main components: *managed devices*, which are physical systems such as servers, switches, firewalls, and so forth, *agents* that talk to the individual applications or devices that you want to monitor and manage via SNMP, and a *network management system* which monitors and controls managed devices. Network management systems and agents communicate via the SNMP network protocol, which is an application-layer protocol that sits on top of the standard TCP/IP stack. SNMP's architecture is shown in Figure 11.9.

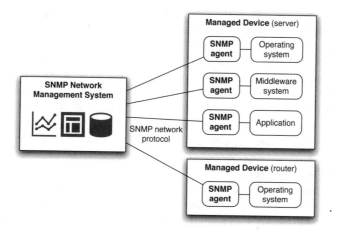

Figure 11.9 *SNMP architecture*

In SNMP, everything is a variable. You monitor systems by watching variables and control them by setting variables. Which variables are available for any given type of SNMP agent, with their descriptions, their types, and whether they can be written to or are read-only, is described in a MIB (Management Information Base), an extensible database format. Each vendor defines MIBs for the systems it provides SNMP agents for, and the IANA maintains a central registry [aMiYLA]. Pretty much every operating system, most common middleware (Apache, WebLogic, and Oracle, for example), as well as many devices have SNMP built-in. Of course, you can also create SNMP agents and MIBs for your own applications, although it's a nontrivial undertaking that will require close collaboration between the development and operations teams.

Logging

Logging also has to form a central part of your monitoring strategy. Operating systems and middleware produce logs which are tremendously useful both for understanding user behavior and for tracking down the source of problems.

Your applications also need to produce good quality logs. In particular, it's important to pay attention to log levels. Most logging systems have several levels, such as DEBUG, INFO, WARNING, ERROR, and FATAL. By default, your application should only show WARNING-, ERROR-, and FATAL-level messages, but be configurable at run time or deploy time to show other levels when debugging is necessary. Since logs are only available to operations teams, it's acceptable to print underlying exceptions in log messages. This can significantly help the debugging process.

Bear in mind that the operations team is the main consumer of log files. It's instructive for developers to spend time working with support solving problems reported by users, or with operations solving problems in production. Developers will quickly learn that recoverable application errors, such as a user being unable to log in, should not belong anywhere above DEBUG level, whereas a timeout on an external system your application depends on should be at ERROR or FATAL level (depending on whether your application can still process transactions without the external service).

Logging, which is part of auditability, should be treated as a first-level set of requirements, the same as any other nonfunctional requirements. Talk to your operations team to work out what they need, and build these requirements in from the beginning. Consider, in particular, the tradeoff between logs being comprehensive and human-readable. It's essential for humans to be able to either page through a log file or grep it easily to get the data they want—which means that each entry should use a single line in a tabular or column-based format that exposes at a glance the timestamp, the log level, where in the application the error came from, and the error code and description.

Creating Dashboards

As with continuous integration for the development team, it's essential that the operations team has a big visible display where they can see at a high level if there are any incidents. They then need to be able to dive into the detail when things go wrong to work out what the problem is. All the open source and commercial tools offer this kind of facility, including the ability to view historical trends and do some kind of reporting. A screenshot from Nagios is shown in Figure 11.10. It's also extremely useful to know which version of each application is in which environment, and that will require some additional instrumentation and integration work.

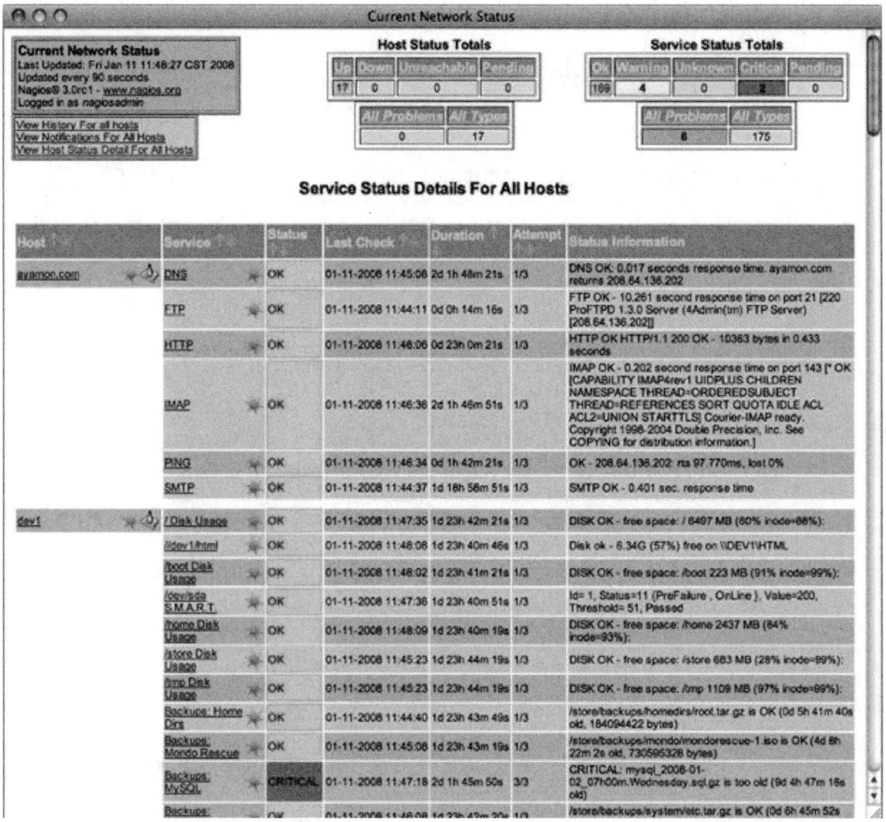

Figure 11.10   *Nagios screenshot*

There are potentially thousands of things that you could monitor, and it is essential to plan ahead so your operations dashboard isn't drowned in noise. Come up with a list of risks, categorized by probability and impact. Your list might include generic risks, like running out of disk space or unauthorized access to your environments, as well as specific risks to your business, such as transactions that couldn't be completed. You then need to work out what to actually monitor, and how to display that information.

In terms of aggregating data, the red-amber-green traffic light aggregation is well understood and commonly used. First of all, you need to work out which entities to aggregate up to. You could create traffic lights for environments, for applications, or for business functions. Different entities will be appropriate for different target audiences. Once you've done this, you need to set thresholds for the traffic lights. Nygard provides the following guidelines (Nygard, 2007, p. 273).

Green means all of the following are true:

- All expected events have occurred.

- No abnormal events have occurred.

- All metrics are nominal (within two standard deviations for this time period).

- All states are fully operational.

Amber means at least one of the following is true:

- An expected event has not occurred.

- At least one abnormal event, with a medium severity, has occurred.

- One or more parameters are above or below the nominal values.

- A noncritical state is not fully operational (for example, a circuit breaker has cut off a noncritical feature).

Red means at least one of the following is true:

- A required event has not occurred.

- At least one abnormal event, with a high severity, has occurred.

- One or more parameters are far above or below the nominal values.

- A critical state is not fully operational (for example, "accepting requests" is false where it should be true).

Behavior-Driven Monitoring

In the same way that developers perform behavior-driven development by writing automated tests to verify the behavior of their applications, operations personnel can write automated tests to verify the behavior of their infrastructure. You can start by writing the test, verifying that it fails, and then defining a Puppet manifest (or whatever your configuration management tool of choice is) that puts your infrastructure into the expected state. You then run the test to verify that the configuration worked correctly and your infrastructure behaves as expected.

Martin Englund, who came up with the idea, uses Cucumber to write tests. Here's an example from his blog entry [cs9LsY]:

```
Feature: sendmail configure
  Systems should be able to send mail

  Scenario: should be able to send mail # features/weblogs.sfbay.sun.com/mail.feature:5
  When connecting to weblogs.sfbay.sun.com using ssh # features/steps/ssh_steps.rb:12
  Then I want to send mail to "martin.englund@sun.com" # features/steps/mail_steps.rb:1
```

Lindsay Holmwood wrote a program called Cucumber-Nagios [anKH1W] which allows you to write Cucumber tests that output the format expected of Nagios plugluginins, so that you can write BDD-style tests in Cucumber and monitor the results in Nagios.

You can also use this paradigm to plug smoke tests for your applications into your monitoring application. Simply take a selection of your application's smoke tests and plug them into Nagios with Cucumber-Nagios, and you can verify not just that your web server is up, but that your application is in fact working as expected.

Summary

We can understand if, having read this chapter, you feel that we are taking things too far—are we seriously suggesting that your infrastructure should be completely autonomic? Do we really think that you should try to subvert the use of the administration tools supplied with your expensive enterprise software? Well, actually, yes; we are suggesting those things, within what we consider to be reasonable limits.

As we have said, the degree to which you need to take the configuration management of your infrastructure will depend on its nature. A simple command-line tool may have few expectations of the environment in which it runs, whereas a tier 1 website will need to consider all of these things and more. In our experience, most enterprise applications should consider configuration management much more seriously than they do, and their failure to do so results in many delays, losses of efficiency in development, and increased cost of ownership on an ongoing basis.

The recommendations we have made and the strategies we have described in this chapter certainly add complexity to the deployment systems that you must create. They may challenge you to come up with creative workarounds for the poor support for configuration management in your third-party products. But if you are creating a large and complex system with many configuration points, and perhaps relying on many technologies, this approach can save your project.

If it were cheap and easy to accomplish, we would all want autonomic infrastructure, making it straightforward to create copies of our production environments. This fact is so obvious that it is almost not worth stating. However, if we would all take it if it was free, then our only objection to having the ability to perfectly reproduce any environment at any time is that of cost. So, somewhere on the spectrum of costs, between free and too expensive, is a cost that is worth bearing.

We believe that using the techniques described in this chapter, as well as the broader strategic choice of the deployment pipeline, you can manage these costs to a degree. While undoubtedly adding something to the cost of creating your version control, build, and deployment systems, these costs are dramatically outweighed by the costs of manual environment management not only across the lifecycle of your applications, but even across the initial development phase.

If you are evaluating third-party products for use in your enterprise system, making sure that they fit into your automated configuration management strategy should be very high on your list or priorities. Oh, and please do us all a favor and give any vendors of such products a hard time if their product is lacking in this regard. Too many are sloppy and half-hearted in their support of serious configuration management.

Finally, make sure that you have an infrastructure management strategy in place right from the beginning of your project, and engage stakeholders from the development and operations teams at that stage.

Chapter 12

Managing Data

Introduction

Data and its management and organization pose a particular set of problems for testing and deployment processes for two reasons. First, there is the sheer volume of information that is generally involved. The bytes allocated to encoding the behavior of our application—its source code and configuration information—are usually vastly outweighed by the volume of data recording its state. Second is the fact that the lifecycle of application data differs from that of other parts of the system. Application data needs to be preserved—indeed, data usually outlasts the applications that were used to create and access it. Crucially, data needs to be preserved and migrated during new deployments or rollbacks of a system.

In most cases, when we deploy new code, we can erase the previous version and wholly replace it with a new copy. In this way we can be certain of our starting position. While that option is possible for data in a few limited cases, for most real-world systems this approach is impossible. Once a system has been released into production, the data associated with it will grow, and it will have significant value in its own right. Indeed, arguably it is the most valuable part of your system. This presents problems when we need to modify either the structure or the content.

As systems grow and evolve, it is inevitable that such modifications will be required, so we must put mechanisms into place that allow changes to be accomplished while minimizing disruption and maximizing the reliability of the application and of the deployment process. The key to this is automating the database migration process. A number of tools now exist that make automating of data migration relatively straightforward, so that it can be scripted as part of your automated deployment process. These tools also allow you to version your database and migrate it from any version to any other. This has the positive effect of decoupling the development process from the deployment process—you can create a migration for each database change required, even if you don't deploy every schema change independently. It also means that your database administrators (DBAs) don't need a big up-front plan—they can work incrementally as the application evolves.

The other important area we cover in this chapter is the management of test data. When performing acceptance testing or capacity testing (or even, sometimes, unit testing), the default option for many teams is to take a dump of the production data. This is problematic for many reasons (not least the size of the dataset), and we provide alternative strategies here.

One caveat for the rest of this chapter: The vast majority of applications rely on relational database technology to manage their data. This isn't the only way of storing data, and is certainly not the best choice for all uses, as the rise of the NoSQL movement demonstrates. The advice that we offer in this chapter is relevant to any system of data storage, but where we discuss details, we will be talking about RDBMS systems, since they still represent the vast majority of storage systems for applications.

Database Scripting

As with any other change to your system, any changes to any databases used as part of your build, deploy, test, and release process should be managed through automated processes. That means that database initialization and all migrations need to be captured as scripts and checked into version control. It should be possible to use these scripts to manage every database used in your delivery process, whether it is to create a new local database for a developer working on the code, to upgrade a systems integration testing (SIT) environment for testers, or to migrate production databases as part of the release process.

Of course, the schema of your database will evolve along with your application. This presents a problem because it is important that the database has the correct schema to work with a particular version of your application. For example, when deploying to staging, it is essential to be able to migrate the staging database to the correct schema to work with the version of the application being deployed. Careful management of your scripts makes this possible, as described in the "Incremental Change" section on page 327.

Finally, your database scripts should also be used as part of your continuous integration process. While unit tests should not, by definition, require a database in order to run, any kind of meaningful acceptance tests running against a database-using application will require the database to be correctly initialized. Thus, part of your acceptance test setup process should be creating a database with the correct schema to work with the latest version of the application and loading it with any test data necessary to run the acceptance tests. A similar procedure can be used for later stages in the deployment pipeline.

Initializing Databases

An extremely important aspect of our approach to delivery is the ability to repro-duce an environment, along with the application running in it, in an automated fashion. Without this ability, we can't be certain that the system will behave in the way we expect.

This aspect of database deployment is the simplest to get right and to maintain as your application changes through the development process. Almost every data management system supports the ability to initialize a data store, including schemas and user credentials, from automated scripts. So, creating and maintain-ing a database initialization script is a simple starting point. Your script should first create the structure of the database, database instances, schemas, and so on, and then populate the tables in the database with any reference data required for your application to start.

This script, along with all other scripts involved in maintaining the database, should of course be stored in version control along with your code.

For a few simple projects, this can be enough. For projects where the opera-tional dataset is in some manner transient—or where it is predefined, such as systems that use a database as a read-only resource at run time—simply erasing the previous version and replacing it with a fresh new copy, re-created from versioned storage, is a simple and effective strategy. If you can get away with it, do this!

At its simplest, then, the process for deploying a database afresh is as follows:

- Erase what was there before.

- Create the database structure, database instances, schemas, etc.

- Load the database with data.

Most projects use databases in more sophisticated ways than this. We will need to consider the more complex, but more common, case where we are making a change after a period of use. In this case, there is existing data that has to be migrated as part of the deployment process.

Incremental Change

Continuous integration demands that we are able to keep the application working after every change made to it. This includes changes to the structure or content of our data. Continuous delivery demands that we must be able to deploy any successful release candidate of our application, including the changes to the database, into production (the same is also true for user-installed software that contains a database). For all but the simplest of systems, that means having to update an operational database while retaining the valuable data that is held in it. Finally, due to the constraint that the data in the database must be retained during a deployment, we need to have a rollback strategy should a deployment go wrong for some reason.

Versioning Your Database

The most effective mechanism to migrate data in an automated fashion is to version your database. Simply create a table in your database that contains its version number. Then, every time you make a change to the database, you need to create two scripts: one that takes the database from a version x to version $x + 1$ (a roll-forward script), and one that takes it from version $x + 1$ to version x (a roll-back script). You will also need to have a configuration setting for your application specifying the version of the database it is designed to work with (this can be kept as a constant in version control and updated every time a database change is required).

At deployment time, you can then use a tool which looks at the version of the database currently deployed and the version of the database required by the version of the application that is being deployed. The tool will then work out which scripts to run to migrate the database from its current version to the required version, and run them on the database in order. For a roll forward, it will apply the correct combination of roll-forward scripts, from oldest to newest; for a roll back, it will apply the relevant roll-back scripts in reverse order. This technique is already built in if you're using Ruby on Rails, in the form of ActiveRecord migrations. If you're using Java or .NET, some of our colleagues developed a simple open source application called DbDeploy (the .NET version is DbDeploy.NET) to manage this process for you. There are also several other solutions that do similar things, including Tarantino, Microsoft's DbDiff, and IBatis' Dbmigrate.

Here's a simple example. When you first start writing your application, you write your first SQL file, 1_create_initial_tables.sql:

```
CREATE TABLE customer (
  id      BIGINT GENERATED BY DEFAULT AS IDENTITY (START WITH 1) PRIMARY KEY,
  firstname  VARCHAR(255)
  lastname  VARCHAR(255)
);
```

In a later version of your code, you discover you need to add the customer's date of birth to the table. So you create another script, 2_add_customer_date_of_birth.sql, that describes how to add this change and how to roll it back:

```
ALTER TABLE customer ADD COLUMN dateofbirth DATETIME;

--//@UNDO

ALTER TABLE customer DROP COLUMN dateofbirth;
```

The part of the file before the `- -//@UNDO` comment represents how to roll forward from version 1 to version 2 of the database. The part of the file after the comment represents how to roll back from version 2 to version 1. This syntax is the one used by DbDeploy and DbDeploy.NET.

Writing roll-back scripts isn't too hard if your roll-forward scripts add new structures to your database. Your roll-back scripts can simply delete them, remembering to remove any referential constraints first. It is usually also possible to create corresponding roll-back scripts for changes that alter existing structures. However, in some cases it is necessary to delete data. In this situation, it is still possible to make your roll-forward script nondestructive. Have your script create a temporary table into which the data to be destroyed is copied before it is deleted from the main table. It is essential, when doing this, to also copy over the table's primary keys so that the data can be copied back, and the referential constraints reestablished, by the roll-back script.

There are sometimes practical limits to the degree to which you can easily step databases back and forward. In our experience, the commonest problem that causes difficulty is changing the database schema. If such changes are additive, in that they create new relationships, you are mostly fine—unless you do things like adding constraints that existing data violates, or adding new objects without default values. If schema changes are subtractive, problems arise because once you have lost information on how one record is related to another, it is harder to reconstitute that relationship again.

The technique of managing database changes achieves two goals: First, it allows you to continuously deploy your application without worrying about the current state of the database in the environment you're deploying to. Your deployment script simply rolls the database back or forward to the version your application is expecting.

However, it also allows you to decouple, to some extent, changes to the database from changes to the application. Your DBA can work on scripts to migrate your database and check them into version control without having to worry that they might break your application. To achieve this, your DBA simply ensures they are part of a migration to a newer version of the database, which won't actually run until the code is written to use it and the developers set the version of the database required to the newer version.

We recommend Scott Ambler and Pramod Sadalage's excellent book *Refactoring Databases*, and the accompanying minibook *Recipes for Continuous Database Integration*, for more detail on managing incremental changes to databases.

Managing Orchestrated Changes

In many organizations, it is common to integrate all applications through a single database. This is not a practice we recommend; it's better to have applications talk to each other directly and factor out common services where necessary (as, for example, in a service-oriented architecture). However, there are situations in which it either makes sense to integrate via the database, or it is simply too much work to change your application's architecture.

In this case, making a change to a database can have a knock-on effect on other applications that use the database. First of all, it is important to test such changes in an orchestrated environment—in other words, in an environment in which the database is reasonably production-like, and which hosts versions of the other applications that use it. Such an environment is often known as a systems integration testing (SIT) environment, or alternatively staging. In this way, assuming tests are frequently run against the other applications that use the database, you will soon discover if you have affected another application.

> ### Managing Technical Debt
>
> It is worth considering how Ward Cunningham's concept of "technical debt" applies to database design. There is an inevitable cost to any design decision. Some costs are obvious, for example the amount of time it takes to develop a feature. Some costs are less obvious, such as the cost of maintaining code in the future. Where poorer design choices are made to expedite the delivery of a system, the cost is usually paid in terms of the number of bugs in the system. This inevitably affects the quality of the design, and, more importantly, the cost of maintenance of the system. So the analogy of debt is a good one.
>
> If we make design choices that are suboptimal, we are in effect borrowing from the future. As with any debt, there are interest payments to be made. For technical debt, the interest is paid in the form of maintenance. In exactly the same way as financial debt, those projects that accrue significant technical debt will reach the point at which they are only paying off interest and are never paying off the original loan. Such projects are in constant maintenance just to keep them working, but do not gain any new functionality that could improve the value they bring to their owners.
>
> In general, it is an axiom of an agile approach to development that you should try to minimize your technical debt by refactoring designs after every change to optimize the design. In reality, there is a tradeoff; sometimes, it is useful to borrow from the future. The important thing is to stay on top of the payments. Our experience has been that most projects tend to accrue technical debt very quickly and pay it off very slowly, so it is better to err on the side of caution and refactor after every change. Where a point is reached that taking out some technical debt is deemed worthwhile to achieve some shorter-term objective, it is important to devise a payment plan first.
>
> Technical debt is an important consideration when managing data, as databases are frequently used as integration points in a system (this is not a recommended architectural pattern, but a common one). As a result, the database frequently represents a point at which changes in design can have widespread effects.

In such environments, it is also useful to keep a registry of which applications use which database objects, so you know which changes will affect which other applications.

One approach we have seen used is to autogenerate a list of database objects touched by each application through static analysis of the codebase. This list is generated as part of the build process for every application, and the results are made available to everybody else, so it is easy to work out if you are going to affect somebody else's application.

Finally, you need to ensure that you work with the teams maintaining the other applications to agree on which changes can be made. One way to manage incremental change is to make applications work with multiple versions of your database, so that the database can be migrated independently of the applications it depends on. This technique is also useful for zero-downtime releases, which we describe in more detail in the next section.

Rolling Back Databases and Zero-Downtime Releases

Once you have roll-forward and roll-back scripts for each version of your application, as described in the previous section, it is relatively easy to use an application like DbDeploy at deploy time to migrate your existing database to the correct version required by the version of the application you are deploying.

However, there is a special case: deployment to production. There are two common requirements which impose extra constraints on a deployment to production: the ability to roll back without losing transactions that have been performed since the upgrade, and the necessity to keep the application available according to a demanding SLA, known as hot deployment or zero-downtime releases.

Rolling Back without Losing Data

In the case of a rollback, your roll-back scripts (as described in the previous section) can usually be designed to preserve any transactions that occur after the upgrade took place. In particular, there should be no problem if your roll-back scripts satisfy the following criteria:

- They involve schema changes that do not lose any data (such as a normalization or denormalization, or moving a column between tables, for example). In this case, you simply run the roll-back scripts.

- They delete some data that only the new system understands, but it is not critical if this data is lost. In this case, again, simply run the roll-back scripts.

However, there are some circumstances in which just running the roll-back scripts will not be possible.

- Rolling back involves adding back in data from temporary tables. In this case, integrity constraints could be violated by the new records that have been added since the upgrade.

- Rolling back involves deleting data from new transactions that it is unacceptable for the system to lose.

In this case, there are a few solutions that can be used to roll back to a previous version of the application.

One solution is to cache transactions that you do not want to lose, and provide a way to replay them. When you upgrade your database and application to the new version, ensure you take a copy of each transaction that goes into the new system. This can be done by recording the events that come through the user interface, by intercepting the more coarse-grained messages that pass between the components of your system (relatively easy if your application uses an event-driven paradigm), or by actually copying each database transaction that occurs from the transaction log. These events can be played back once the application has been successfully redeployed. Of course this approach requires careful design and testing to work, but that can be an acceptable tradeoff if you really need to ensure there is no data loss in the event of a rollback.

A second solution can be employed if you are using blue-green deployments (see Chapter 10, "Deploying and Releasing Applications"). To refresh your memory, in blue-green deployments both the old and the new versions of your application are run side by side, one in the blue environment, the other in the green environment. "Releasing" simply means switching user requests from the old version to the new version, and "rolling back" means switching them back to the old version.

In blue-green deployments, a backup of the production database (let's assume it's the blue database) needs to be scheduled at release time. If your database doesn't allow hot backups, or there is some other constraint that prevents this, you will need to put your application into read-only mode so the backup can be performed. This backup is then restored onto the green database, and the migration performed on it. Users are then switched to the green environment as part of the release process.

If a rollback needs to be performed, users are simply switched back to the blue environment. New transactions from the green environment's database can then be recovered, either to be reapplied to the blue database before another upgrade is attempted, or to be reapplied once the upgrade is performed again.

Some systems have so much data that such backup and restore operations are simply not possible without incurring unacceptable levels of downtime. In this case, this approach cannot be used—while blue-green environments are still possible, they switch which database they run against at release time, instead of having independent databases of their own.

Decoupling Application Deployment from Database Migration

However, there is a third approach that can be used to manage hot deployments. It is to decouple the database migration process from the application deployment process and perform them independently, as shown in Figure 12.1. This solution is also applicable to managing orchestrated changes, as well as to the blue-green deployment and canary releasing patterns described in Chapter 10, "Deploying and Releasing Applications."

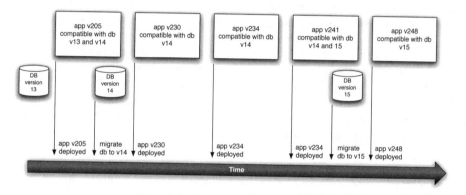

Figure 12.1   *Decoupling database migration from application deployment*

If you are releasing frequently, you do not need to migrate your database for every release of your application. When you do need to migrate your database, instead of having the application work only with the new version of the database, you must ensure it works with both the new version and the current version. In the diagram, version 241 of the application is designed to work with both the currently deployed version of the database, version 14, and the new version, version 15.

You deploy this transitional version of your application and have it work against the current version of the database. When you're sure the new version of the application is stable and doesn't need to be rolled back, you can upgrade the database to the new version (version 15 in the diagram). Of course, you need to back it up before you do so. Then, when the next version of the application to be deployed is ready (version 248 in the diagram), you can deploy it without having to migrate the database. This version of the application just needs to work with version 15 of the database.

This approach can also be useful in circumstances where reverting your database to an earlier version is difficult. We have used it in a situation where the new version of the database made some significant changes, including changes to the database schema that lost information. As a result, the upgrade would compromise our ability to revert to an earlier version of the software if a problem occurred. We deployed the new version of our application which, being backward-compatible, could run against the database schema of the old version without deploying the new database changes. We could then observe the behavior of the new version, confirming that it didn't introduce any problems that warranted reversion to the previous one. Finally, once we were confident, we deployed the database changes too.

Forward compatibility is also not a generic solution, though for the run-of-the-mill, normal changes it is a useful strategy to adopt. Forward compatibility, in this context, is the ability of an earlier version of an application to work against the database schema of a later version. Naturally, if there are additional fields or tables in the new schema, these will be ignored by the application versions that aren't designed to work with them. Nevertheless, those parts of the database schema that are common to the two versions remain the same.

It is best to adopt this as the default approach for most changes. That is, most changes should be additive, adding new tables or columns to our database, but not changing existing structures, where possible.

Another approach to managing database changes and refactorings is to use an abstraction layer, in the form of stored procedures and views [cVVuV0]. If the application accesses the database through such an abstraction layer, it is possible to make changes to the underlying database objects while keeping the interface presented to the application by the views and stored procedures constant. This is an example of "branch by abstraction," described in the "Branch by Abstraction" section on page 349.

Managing Test Data

Test data is important for all tests, whether manual or automated. What data will allow us to simulate common interactions with the system? What data represents edge cases that will prove that our application works for unusual inputs? What data will force the application into error conditions so that we can evaluate its response under those circumstances? These questions are relevant at every level at which we test our system, but pose a particular set of problems for tests that rely on our test data being in a database somewhere.

There are two concerns that we will highlight in this section. First is test performance. We want to make sure our tests run as fast as possible. In the case of unit tests, that means either not running against a database at all, or running against an in-memory database. For other types of tests, it means managing test data carefully, and certainly not using a dump of the production database except in a few limited cases.

A second issue is test isolation. An ideal test runs in a well-defined environment whose inputs are controlled so that we can easily evaluate its outputs. A database, on the other hand, is a durable store of information that allows changes to persist between test invocations—unless you explicitly do something to prevent it. This can make the starting conditions unclear, particularly when you may have no direct control over the execution order of your tests, which is usually the case.

Faking the Database for Unit Tests

It is important that unit tests do not run against a real database. Usually unit tests will inject test doubles in place of services that talk to databases. However, if this is not possible (for example, if you want to test these services), there are two other strategies that you can apply.

One is to replace your database access code with a test double. It is good practice to encapsulate code that accesses the database within your application. A commonly used pattern to achieve this objective is the repository pattern [blIgdc]. In this pattern, you create an abstraction layer above your data access code which decouples your application from the database being used (this is actually an application of the branch by abstraction pattern described in Chapter 13, "Managing Components and Dependencies"). Once this is done, you can swap out your data access code for a test double. This approach is shown in Figure 12.2.

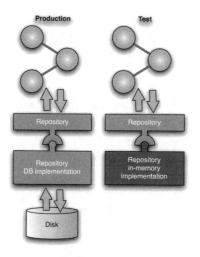

Figure 12.2 *Abstracting database access*

This strategy not only provides a mechanism to support testing, as we have described, but also encourages a focus on the business behavior of the system separately from its data storage needs. It also tends to ensure that all data access code is kept together, thus making maintaining the codebase easier. This combination of benefits usually outweighs the relatively small cost of maintaining a separate layer to provide the relevant abstraction.

Where this approach is not used, it is still possible to fake the database. There are several open source projects that provide an in-memory relational database (take a look at H2, SqlLite, or JavaDB). By making the database instance that the application interacts with configurable, you can organize your unit tests to run against the in-memory database. Then the acceptance tests can run against the more usual disk-based database. Again, this approach has some subsidiary benefits: It encourages code to be written in a slightly more decoupled way, at least to the degree that it will work against two different database implementations. This, in turn, ensures that future changes—to a newer version, or even perhaps to a different RDBMS vendor—will be easier to accomplish.

Managing the Coupling between Tests and Data

When it comes to test data, it is important that each individual test in a test suite has some state on which it can depend. In the "given, when, then" format for writing acceptance criteria, the initial state when the test starts is the "when." Only when the starting state is known can you compare it against the state after the test has finished, and thus verify the behavior under test.

This is simple for a single test, but requires some thought to achieve for suites of tests, particularly for tests that rely upon a database.

Broadly, there are three approaches to managing state for tests.

- **Test isolation:** Organize tests so that each test's data is only visible to that test.

- **Adaptive tests:** Each test is designed to evaluate its data environment and adapt its behavior to suit the data it sees.

- **Test sequencing:** Tests are designed to run in a known sequence, each depending, for inputs, on the outputs of its predecessors.

In general, we strongly recommend the first of these approaches. Isolating tests from one another makes them more flexible as well as, importantly, capable of being run in parallel to optimize test suite performance.

Both of the other approaches are possible but, in our experience, don't scale up well. As the suite of tests becomes larger and the interactions it embodies more complex, both of these strategies tend to result in failures that are very hard to detect and correct. Interactions between tests become increasingly obscure, and the cost of maintaining a working suite of tests begins to grow.

Test Isolation

Test isolation is a strategy for ensuring that each individual test is atomic. That is, it should not depend on the outcome of other tests to establish its state, and other tests should not affect its success or failure in any way. This level of isolation is relatively simple to achieve for commit tests, even those that test the persistence of data in a database.

The simplest approach is to ensure that, at the conclusion of the test, you always return the data in the database to the state it was in before the test was run. You can do this manually, but the simplest approach is to rely upon the transactional nature of most RDBMS systems.

For database-related tests, we create a transaction at the beginning of the test, perform all of the operations and interactions with the database that we require within that transaction, and at the conclusion of the test (whether it passed or not), we roll back the transaction. This uses the transaction isolation properties of the database system to ensure that no other tests or users of the database will see the changes that the test makes.

A second approach to test isolation is to perform some kind of functional partitioning of the data. This is an effective strategy for both commit and acceptance tests. For tests that need to modify the state of the system as an outcome, make the principal entities that you create in your tests follow some test-specific naming convention, so that each test will only look for and see data that was created specifically for it. We describe this approach in more detail in the "State in Acceptance Tests" section on page 204.

How easy it is to find a suitable level of test isolation through partitioning the data depends a lot on the problem domain. If you domain is suitable, this is an excellent and simple strategy for keeping tests independent of one another.

Setup and Tear Down

Whatever strategy is chosen, the establishment of a known-good starting position for the test before it is run, and its reestablishment at its conclusion, is vital to avoid cross-test dependencies.

For well-isolated tests, a setup stage is usually needed to populate the database with relevant test data. This may involve creating a new transaction that will be rolled back at the conclusion of the test, or simply writing a few records of test-specific information.

Adaptive tests will be evaluating the data environment in order to establish the known starting position at startup.

Coherent Test Scenarios

There is often a temptation to create a coherent "story" that tests will follow. The intent of this approach is that the data created is coherent, so setting up and tearing down of test cases is minimized. This should mean that each test is, in itself, a little simpler, since it is no longer responsible for managing its own test data. This also means that the test suite as a whole will run faster because it doesn't spend a lot of time creating and destroying test data.

There are times when this approach is tempting, but in our view, it is a temptation that should be resisted. The problem with this strategy is that in striving for a coherent story we tightly couple tests together. There are several important drawbacks to this tight coupling. Tests become more difficult to design as the size of the test suite grows. When one test fails, it can have a cascade effect on subsequent tests that depend on its outputs, making them fail too. Changes in the business scenario, or the technical implementation, can lead to painful reworking of the test suite.

More fundamentally though, this sequential ordered view doesn't really represent the reality of testing. In most cases, even where there is a clear sequence of steps that the application embodies, at each step we want to explore what happens for success, what happens for failures, what happens for boundary conditions, and so on. There is a range of different tests that we should be running with very similar startup conditions. Once we move to support this view, we will necessarily have to establish and reestablish the test data environment, so we are back in the realm of either creating adaptive tests or isolating tests from one another.

Data Management and the Deployment Pipeline

Creating and managing data to use with automated tests can be a significant overhead. Let us take a step back for a moment. What is the focus of our testing?

We test our application to assert that it possesses a variety of behavioral characteristics that we desire. We run unit tests to protect ourselves from the effects of inadvertently making a change that breaks our application. We run acceptance tests to assert that the application delivers the expected value to users. We perform capacity testing to assert that the application meets our capacity requirements. Perhaps we run a suite of integration tests to confirm that our application communicates correctly with services it depends on.

What is the test data that we need for each of these testing stages in the deployment pipeline, and how should we manage it?

Data in Commit Stage Tests

Commit testing is the first stage in the deployment pipeline. It is vital to the process that commit tests run quickly. The commit stage is the point at which developers are sitting waiting for a pass before moving on. Every 30 seconds added to this stage are costly.

In addition to the outright performance of commit stage testing, commit tests are the primary defense against inadvertent changes to the system. The more these tests are tied to the specifics of the implementation, the worse they are at performing that role. The problem is that when you need to refactor the implementation of some aspect of your system, you want the test to protect you. If the tests are too tightly linked to the specifics of the implementation, you will find that making a small change in implementation results in a bigger change in the tests that surround it. Instead of defending the behavior of the system, and so facilitating necessary change, tests that are too tightly coupled to the specifics of the implementation will inhibit change. If you are forced to make significant changes to tests for relatively small changes in implementation, the tests are not performing effectively their role of executable specifications of behavior.

This may sound somewhat abstract in a chapter on data and databases, but tight coupling in tests is often the result of overelaborate test data.

This is one of those key points where the process of continuous integration delivers some seemingly unrelated positive behaviors. Good commit tests avoid elaborate data setup. If you find yourself working hard to establish the data for a particular test, it is a sure indicator that your design needs to be better decomposed. You need to split the design into more components and test each independently, using test doubles to simulate dependencies, as described in the "Using Test Doubles" section on page 180.

The most effective tests are not really data-driven; they use the minimum of test data to assert that the unit under test exhibits the expected behavior. Those tests that do need more sophisticated data in place to demonstrate desired behavior should create it carefully and, as far as possible, reuse the test helpers or fixtures to create it, so that changes in the design of the data structures that the system supports do not represent a catastrophic blow to the system's testability.

In our projects, we will often isolate the code creating test instances of such commonly used data structures and share them between many different test cases. We may have a `CustomerHelper` or `CustomerFixture` class that will simplify the creation of `Customer` objects for our tests, so they are created in a consistent manner with a collection of standard default values for each `Customer`. Each test can then tailor the data to meet its needs, but it starts from a known, consistent state.

Fundamentally, our objective is to minimize the data specific to each test to that which directly impacts the behavior the test is attempting to establish. This should be a goal for every test that you write.

Data in Acceptance Tests

Acceptance tests, unlike commit tests, are system tests. This means that their test data is necessarily more complex and needs to be managed more carefully if you want to avoid the tests becoming unwieldy. Again, the goal is to minimize the dependence of our tests on large complex data structures as far as possible. This approach is fundamentally the same as for commit stage tests: We aim to achieve reuse in the creation of our test cases and to minimize each test's dependence on test data. We should be creating just enough data to test the expected behavior of the system.

When considering how to set up the state of the application for an acceptance test, it is helpful to distinguish between three kinds of data.

1. **Test-specific data:** This is the data that drives the behavior under test. It represents the specifics of the case under test.

2. **Test reference data:** There is often a second class of data that is relevant for a test but actually has little bearing upon the behavior under test. It needs to be there, but it is part of the supporting cast, not the main player.

3. **Application reference data:** Often, there is data that is irrelevant to the behavior under test, but that needs to be there to allow the application to start up.

Test-specific data should be unique and use test isolation strategies to ensure that the test starts in a well-defined environment that is unaffected by the side effects of other tests.

Test reference data can be managed by using prepopulated seed data that is reused in a variety of tests to establish the general environment in which the tests run, but which remains unaffected by the operation of the tests.

Application reference data can be any value at all, even null values, provided the values chosen continue to have no effect on the test outcome.

Application reference data and, if applicable, test reference data—whatever is needed for your application to start up—can be kept in the form of database dumps. Of course you will have to version these and ensure they are migrated as part of the application setup. This is a useful way to test your automated database migration strategy.

This categorization is not rigorous. Often, the boundaries between classes of data may be somewhat blurred in the context of a specific test. However, we have found it a useful tool to help us focus on the data that we need to actively manage to ensure that our test is reliable, as opposed to the data that simply needs to be there.

Fundamentally, it is a mistake to make tests too dependent on the "universe" of data that represents the entire application. It is important to be able to consider each test with some degree of isolation, or the entire test suite becomes too brittle and will fail constantly with every small change in data.

However, unlike commit tests, we do not recommend using application code or database dumps to put the application into the correct initial state for the test. Instead, in keeping with the system-level nature of the tests, we recommend using the application's API to put it into the correct state.

This has several advantages:

- Using the application code, or any other mechanism that bypasses the application's business logic, can put the system into an inconsistent state.

Using the application's API ensures that the application is never in an inconsistent state during acceptance tests.

- Refactorings of the database or the application itself will have no effect on the acceptance tests since, by definition, refactorings do not alter the behavior of the application's public API. This will make your acceptance tests significantly less brittle.

- Your acceptance tests will also serve as tests of your application's API.

Types of Test Data: An Example

Consider testing a financial trading application. If a specific test is focused on confirming that a user's position is correctly updated when a trade is made, the starting position and finishing position are of prime importance to this test.

For a suite of stateful acceptance tests that are being run in an environment with a live database, this probably implies that this test will require a new user account with a known starting position. We consider the account and its position to be test-specific data, so for the purposes of an acceptance test, we may register a new account and provide it with some funds, to allow trading, as part of the test case setup.

The financial instrument or instruments used to establish the expected position during the course of the test are important contributors to the test, but could be treated as test reference data, in that having a collection of instruments that are reused by a succession of tests would not compromise the outcome of our "position test." This data may well be prepopulated test reference data.

Finally, the details of the options needed to establish a new account are irrelevant to the position test, unless they directly affect the starting position or the calculation of a user's position in some way. So for these items of application reference data, any default values will do.

Data in Capacity Tests

Capacity tests present a problem of scale in the data required by most applications. This problem exhibits itself in two areas: the ability to deliver a sufficient volume of input data for the test and the provision of suitable reference data to support many cases under test simultaneously.

As described in Chapter 9, "Testing Nonfunctional Requirements," we see capacity testing as primarily an exercise in rerunning acceptance tests, but for many cases at the same time. If your application supports the concept of placing an order, we would expect to be placing many orders simultaneously when we are capacity-testing.

Our preference is to automate the generation of these large volumes of data, both input and reference, using mechanisms like interaction templates, described in more detail in the "Using Recorded Interaction Templates" section on page 241.

This approach, in effect, allows us to amplify the data that we create and manage to support our acceptance tests. This strategy of data reuse is one that we tend to apply as widely as we can, our rationale being that the interactions that we encode as part of our acceptance test suite, and the data associated with those interactions, are primarily executable specifications of the behavior of the system. If our acceptance tests are effective in this role, they capture the important interactions that our application supports. Something is wrong if they don't encode the important behaviors of the system that we will want to measure as part of our capacity test.

Further, if we have mechanisms and processes in place to keep these tests running in line with the application as it evolves over time, why dump all of that and start again when it comes to capacity testing, or indeed when it comes to any other postacceptance test stage?

Our strategy, then, is to rely on our acceptance tests as a record of the interactions with our system that are of interest and then use that record as a starting point for subsequent test stages.

For capacity testing, we use tools that will take the data associated with a selected acceptance test and scale it up to many different "cases" so that we can apply many interactions with the system based on that one test.

This approach to test data generation allows us to concentrate our capacity test data management efforts on the core of the data that is, of necessity, unique to each individual interaction.

Data in Other Test Stages

At least at the level of design philosophy, if not specific technical approach, we apply the same approach to all postacceptance automated test stages. Our aim is to reuse the "specifications of behavior" that are our automated acceptance tests as the starting point for any testing whose focus is other than purely functional.

 When creating web applications, we use our acceptance test suite to derive not only our capacity tests, but also our compatibility tests. For compatibility testing, we rerun our entire acceptance test suite against all of the popular web browsers. This is not an exhaustive test—it tells us nothing about usability—but it does give us an alarm if we have made a change that breaks the user interface altogether in some browser. Since we reuse both our deployment mechanisms and our acceptance test suite, and we use virtual machines to host the tests, our ability to perform compatibility testing comes virtually for free—except for the cost of some CPU time and disk space to run the tests.

For manual testing stages, such as exploratory testing or user acceptance testing environments, there are a couple of approaches to test data. One is to run in a minimal set of test and application reference data to enable the application to start up in an empty initial state. Testers can then experiment with scenarios that occur when users initially start working with the application. Another approach is to load a much larger set of data so that testers can perform scenarios that assume the application has been in use for some time. It's also useful to have a large dataset for doing integration testing.

While it's possible to take a dump of the production database for these scenarios, we do not recommend this in most cases. This is mainly because the dataset is so large as to be too unwieldy. Migrating a production dataset can sometimes take hours. Nevertheless, there are cases where it's important to test with a dump of production—for example, when testing the migration of the production database, or determining at what point production data needs to be archived so it does not unduly slow down the application.

Instead, we recommend creating a customized dataset to use for manual testing, based either on a subset of the production data, or on a dump of the database taken after a set of automated acceptance or capacity tests have been run. You can even customize your capacity testing framework to produce a database that represents a realistic state of the application after continued use by a set of users. This dataset can then be stored and reused as part of the deployment to manual testing environments. Of course it will need to be migrated as part of this deployment process. Sometimes testers keep several database dumps around to use as starting points for various kinds of tests.

These datasets, including the minimal dataset required to start the application, should also be used by developers in their environments. On no account should developers use production datasets in their environments.

Summary

Due to its lifecycle, the management of data presents a collection of problems different from those we have discussed in the context of the deployment pipeline. However, the fundamental principles that govern data management are the same. The key is to ensure that there is a fully automated process for creating and migrating databases. This process is used as part of the deployment process, ensuring it is repeatable and reliable. The same process should be used whether deploying the application to a development or acceptance testing environment with a minimal dataset, or whether migrating the production dataset as part of a deployment to production.

Even with an automated database migration process, it is still important to manage data used for testing purposes carefully. While a dump of the production database can be a tempting starting point, it is usually too large to be useful. Instead, have your tests create the state they need, and ensure they do this in such a way that each of your tests is independent of the others. Even for manual testing, there are few circumstances in which a dump of the production database is the best starting point. Testers should create and manage smaller datasets for their own purposes.

Here are some of the more important principles and practices from this chapter:

- Version your database and use a tool like DbDeploy to manage migrations automatically.

- Strive to retain both forward and backward compatibility with schema changes so that you can separate data deployment and migration issues from application deployment issues.

- Make sure tests create the data they rely on as part of the setup process, and that data is partitioned to ensure it does not affect other tests that might be running at the same time.

- Reserve the sharing of setup between tests only for data required to have the application start, and perhaps some very general reference data.

- Try to use the application's public API to set up the correct state for tests wherever possible.

- In most cases, don't use dumps of the production dataset for testing purposes. Create custom datasets by carefully selecting a smaller subset of production data, or from acceptance or capacity test runs.

Of course, these principles will need to be adapted to your situation. However, if they are used as the default approach, they will help any software project to minimize the effects of the most common problems and issues associated with data management in automated testing and production environments.

Chapter 13

Managing Components and Dependencies

Introduction

Continuous delivery provides the ability to release new, working versions of your software several times a day. That means you have to keep your application releasable at all times. But what if you are engaged in a major refactoring or adding complex new functionality? Branching in version control might seem to be the solution to this problem. However, we feel strongly that this is the wrong answer.[1] This chapter describes how to keep your application releasable at all times, despite being under constant change. One of the key techniques for this is componentization of larger applications, so we will treat componentization, including building and managing large projects with multiple components, at length.

What is a component? This is a horribly overloaded term in software, so we will try to make it as clear as possible what we mean by it. When we talk about components, we mean a reasonably large-scale code structure within an application, with a well-defined API, that could potentially be swapped out for another implementation. A component-based software system is distinguished by the fact that the codebase is divided into discrete pieces that provide behavior through well-defined, limited interactions with other components.

The antithesis of a component-based system is a monolithic system with no clear boundaries or separation of concerns between elements responsible for different tasks. Monolithic systems typically have poor encapsulation, and tight coupling between logically independent structures breaks the Law of Demeter. The language and technology are unimportant—it has nothing to do with GUI widgets in Visual Basic or Java. Some people call components "modules." In Windows, a component is normally packaged as a DLL. In UNIX, it may be packaged as an SO file. In the Java world, it is probably a JAR file.

---

1. We discuss branching strategies in the next chapter, "Advanced Version Control."

Employing a component-based design is often described as encouraging reuse and good architectural properties such as loose coupling. This is true, but it also has another important benefit: It is one of the most efficient ways for large teams of developers to collaborate. In this chapter, we also describe how to create and manage build systems for component-based applications.

If you work on a small project, you may be thinking of skipping this chapter after reading the next section (which you should read regardless of the project size). Many projects are fine with a single version control repository and a simple deployment pipeline. However, many projects have evolved into an unmaintainable morass of code because nobody made the decision to create discrete components when it was cheap to do so. The point at which small projects change into larger ones is fluid and will sneak up on you. Once a project passes a certain threshold, it is very expensive to change the code in this way. Few project leaders will have the audacity to ask their team to stop development for long enough to rearchitect a large application into components. Working out how to create and manage components is a topic we will explore in this chapter.

The material in this chapter depends on a good understanding of the deployment pipeline. If you need a refresher, refer to Chapter 5, "Anatomy of the Deployment Pipeline." In this chapter we will also describe how components interact with branches. By the end of this chapter, we will have covered all three degrees of freedom in a build system: the deployment pipeline, branches, and components.

It is not unusual, when working on large systems, to have all three of these dimensions in play at once. In such systems, components form a series of dependencies, which in turn depend on external libraries. Each component may have several release branches. Finding good versions of each of these components that can be assembled into a system which even compiles is an extremely difficult process that can resemble a game of whack-a-mole—we have heard of projects where it takes months. Only once you have done this can you start moving the system through the deployment pipeline.

This, in essence, is the fundamental problem that continuous integration aims to solve. As usual, the solutions that we propose depend on the best practices that we hope by now are familiar to you.

Keeping Your Application Releasable

Continuous integration is designed to give you a high level of confidence that your application is working at the functional level. The deployment pipeline, an extension of continuous integration, is designed to ensure that your software is always releasable. But both of these practices depend on teams doing development on mainline.[2]

---

2. There are caveats here on the use of distributed version control systems, which we'll discuss in the next chapter.

In the course of development, teams are continually adding features, and sometimes need to make major architectural changes. During these activities the application is not releasable, although it will still pass the commit stage of continuous integration. Usually, before release, teams will stop developing new functionality and enter a stabilization phase during which only bugfixing takes place. When the application is released, a release branch is created in version control, and new development begins again on trunk. However, this process generally results in weeks or months between releases. The aim of continuous delivery is for the application to always be in a releasable state. How can we achieve this?

One approach is to create branches in version control that are merged when work is complete, so that mainline is always releasable. We examine this approach at length in the next chapter, "Advanced Version Control." However, we believe that this approach is suboptimal, since the application is not being continuously integrated if work happens on branches. Instead, we advocate that everybody checks in on mainline. How is it possible to have everybody working on mainline, and still keep your application in a releasable state at all times?

There are four strategies to employ in order to keep your application releasable in the face of change:

- Hide new functionality until it is finished.

- Make all changes incrementally as a series of small changes, each of which is releasable.

- Use branch by abstraction to make large-scale changes to the codebase.

- Use components to decouple parts of your application that change at different rates.

We'll discuss the first three strategies here. These three strategies should suffice on small projects. On larger projects, you will need to think about using components, which we cover in the rest of the chapter.

Hide New Functionality Until It Is Finished

One common problem with continuous deployment of applications is that a feature, or a set of features, can take a long time to develop. If it doesn't make sense to release a set of features incrementally, it is often tempting to start new development on a branch in version control, and integrate when the functionality is ready, so as not to interrupt the work being done on the rest of a system, which might prevent it being released.

One solution is to put in the new features, but make them inaccessible to users. For example, consider a website that provides travel services. The company running the site wants to offer a new service: hotel bookings. In order to do so, work starts on this new offering as a separate component, reached through a separate URI root /hotel. This component can still be deployed along with the rest of the system if desired—so long as access is not permitted to its entry point (this could be accomplished by a configuration setting in your web server software).

Replacing an Entire UI Incrementally

On one of Jez's projects, developers started working on a new UI using this method. While under development, the new UI was placed under the URI /new/ and no links were made to it. As we started to use parts of the new UI, we linked to them from the existing navigation. This allowed us to replace the entire UI in an incremental fashion while keeping the application working at all times. Both UIs shared stylesheets, so that they looked the same, even though they were implemented using completely different technologies; the user had no idea which technology was being used on which pages unless he or she looked at the URI.

An alternative way to ensure that semicompleted components can be shipped while not being accessible to users is to turn access to them on and off by means of configuration settings. For example, in a rich client application, you might have two menus—one with the new feature, and one without. You would use a configuration setting to switch between the two menus. This can be done either through the use of command-line options, or through other deploy-time or runtime configuration (see Chapter 2, "Configuration Management" for more on configuring software). The ability to switch features on and off (or swap them out for alternative implementations) through runtime configuration is also very useful when running automated tests.

Even huge organizations develop software this way. One world-leading search engine our colleagues worked at had to patch the Linux kernel so it could accept the large number of command-line arguments required to turn on and off the various bits of functionality in their software. This is an extreme example, and we don't recommend keeping too many options around—they should be carefully pruned away once they have served their purpose. It is possible to mark up configuration options in the codebase and use static analysis as part of the commit stage to provide a list of available configuration options for this purpose.

Shipping semicompleted functionality along with the rest of your application is a good practice because it means you're always integrating and testing the entire system as it exists at any time. This makes planning and delivering the entire application much easier, since it means dependencies and integration phases do not need to be introduced into the project plan. It ensures that the new components being developed are deployable along with the rest of the software from the beginning. It also means that you're testing your entire application, including any new or modified services required by your new components, for regressions at all times.

Writing software in this way requires a certain amount of planning, careful architecture, and disciplined development. However, the benefit in terms of being able to release new versions of your software even while adding major feature sets is usually well worth the extra effort. This alternative is also superior to using branching in version control for new feature development.

Make All Changes Incrementally

The story above—of moving an application to a completely new UI incrementally—is just a particular example of a general strategy: Make all changes incrementally. It is often tempting, when making large changes, to branch the source code and make the change on the branch. The theory is that developers can move faster if they can make large, high-level changes which break the application and then wire everything back in afterwards. However, in practice, the wiring everything up ends up being the hard part. If other teams are working in the meantime, the merge at the end can be hard—and the bigger the change, the harder it will be. The bigger the apparent reason to branch, the more you shouldn't branch.

Even if turning large changes into a series of small, incremental changes is hard work while you're doing it, it means you're solving the problem of keeping the application working as you go along, preventing pain at the end. It also means you can stop at any time if you need to, avoiding the sunk cost involved in getting halfway through a big change and then having to abandon it.

Analysis plays an important part in being able to make large changes as a series of small changes. In many ways, the thought process that goes into it is the same thought process used to break a requirement down into smaller tasks. What you then do is turn the tasks into a set of even smaller incremental changes. This additional analysis can often lead to fewer mistakes and more targeted changes—and, of course, if you make changes incrementally, you can take stock as you go along and decide how (and indeed whether) to proceed.

However, sometimes there are changes that are too hard to make in an incremental fashion. At this point, you should consider branching by abstraction.

Branch by Abstraction

This pattern is an alternative to branching when you need to make a large-scale change to an application. Instead of branching, an abstraction layer is created over the piece to be changed. A new implementation is then created in parallel with the existing implementation, and then when it is complete, the original implementation and (optionally) the abstraction layer are removed.

Creating Abstraction Layers

Creating an abstraction layer can often be hard. For example, in desktop VB applications in Windows it is quite common for all of the logic of an application to be contained in event handlers. Creating an abstraction layer for such an application involves building an object-oriented design for the logic and implementing it by refactoring the existing code out of the event handlers into a set of VB (or perhaps C#) classes. The new UI (perhaps a web UI) would then reuse the new logic. Note that there is no need to create interfaces for the logic implementation—you would only need to do that if you wanted to perform a branch by abstraction on your logic.

One example where you would not remove the abstraction layer at the end is where you want users of the system to be able to choose their implementation. In this case, you are essentially designing a plugin API. Tools such as OSGi, used in Eclipse, can simplify this process for teams using Java. In our experience, it is better not to create a plugin API up front at the start of a project. Instead, create your first implementation, then a second one, and factor out the API from these implementations. As you add more implementations and more functionality that is used in these implementations, you will find your API changing quite rapidly. If you plan to expose it publicly to allow others to develop plugins, you will want to wait for it to stabilize.

Although this pattern was named "branch by abstraction" by our colleague, Paul Hammant [aE2eP9], it is in fact an alternative to using branching to make a large-scale change to an application. When some part of the application needs a change that cannot be implemented as a series of small, incremental steps, do this:

1. Create an abstraction over the part of the system that you need to change.

2. Refactor the rest of the system to use the abstraction layer.

3. Create a new implementation, which is not part of the production code path until complete.

4. Update your abstraction layer to delegate to your new implementation.

5. Remove the old implementation.

6. Remove the abstraction layer if it is no longer appropriate.

Branch by abstraction is an alternative to using branches or implementing complex changes in one step. It allows teams to continue developing an application in continuous integration while also replacing large chunks of it, all on the mainline. If some part of the codebase needs to be changed, you first find the entry point to this part—a seam—and put in an abstraction layer which delegates to the current implementation. You then develop the new implementation alongside the new one. Which implementation gets used is decided by a configuration option that can be modified at deploy time or even run time.

You can do branch by abstraction at a very high level, such as swapping out an entire persistence layer. You can also do it at a very low level—swapping out a class for another one using the strategy pattern, for example. Dependency injection is another mechanism that enables branch by abstraction. The trick is finding or creating the seams that allow you to insert an abstraction layer.

This is also an excellent pattern to use as part of a strategy for turning a monolithic codebase that uses the ball of mud "pattern" into a more modular, better structured form. Take part of the codebase that you want to separate out as a component or rewrite. Provided you can manage the entry points to this part of the codebase, perhaps using the façade pattern, you can localize the mess and use branch by abstraction to keep the application running with the old code while you create a new, modularized version of the same functionality. This strategy is sometimes known as "sweeping it under the rug" or "Potemkin village" [ayTS3J].

The two most difficult parts of branching by abstraction are isolating the entry points to the part of the codebase in question and managing any changes that need to be made to the functionality that is under development, perhaps as part of bug-fixing. However, these problems are considerably easier to manage than they are with branching. Nevertheless, sometimes it is just too hard to find a good seam in your codebase, and branching is the only solution. Use the branch to get your codebase to a state where you can then perform branch by abstraction.

Making large-scale changes to your application, whether through branching by abstraction or any other technique, benefits enormously from a comprehensive automated acceptance test suite. Unit and component tests are simply not coarse-grained enough to protect your business functionality when big chunks of your application are being changed.

Dependencies

A dependency occurs whenever one piece of software depends upon another in order to build or run. In any but the most trivial of applications, there will be some dependencies. Most software applications have, at a minimum, a dependency on their host operating environment. Java applications depend on the JVM which provides an implementation of the Java SE API, .NET applications on the CLR, Rails applications on Ruby and the Rails framework, C applications on the C standard library, and so forth.

There are two distinctions that will be especially useful in this chapter: the distinction between components and libraries, and that between build-time and runtime dependencies.

We distinguish between components and libraries in this way: Libraries refer to software packages that your team does not control, other than choosing which to use. Libraries are usually updated rarely. In contrast, components are pieces of software that your application depends upon, but which are also developed by your team, or other teams in your organization. Components are usually updated frequently. This distinction is important because when designing a build process, there are more things to consider when dealing with components than libraries. For example, do you compile your entire application in a single step, or compile each component independently when it changes? How do you manage dependencies between components, avoiding circular dependencies?

The distinction between build-time and runtime dependencies is as follows: Build-time dependencies must be present when your application is compiled and linked (if necessary); runtime dependencies must be present when the application runs, performing its usual function. This distinction is important for several reasons. First, in your deployment pipeline you will be using many different pieces of software that are irrelevant to the deployed copy of the application, such as unit test frameworks, acceptance test frameworks, build scripting frameworks, and so forth. Second, the versions of libraries that the application uses at run time can differ from those that it uses at build time. In C and C++, of course, your build-time dependencies are simply header files, while at run time you require a binary to be present in the form of a dynamic-link library (DLL) or shared library (SO). But you can do similar things in other compiled languages too, such as building against a JAR containing just the interfaces for a system, and running against a JAR containing a full implementation (for example, when using a J2EE application server). These considerations need to be taken into account in your build system too.

Managing dependencies can be difficult. We'll start with an overview of the most common dependency problems that occur with libraries at run time.

Dependency Hell

Perhaps the most famous problem of dependency management is known as "dependency hell," sometimes colloquially called "DLL hell." Dependency hell occurs when an application depends upon one particular version of something, but is deployed with a different version, or with nothing at all.

DLL hell was a very common problem in earlier versions of Microsoft Windows. All shared libraries, in the form of DLLs, were stored in a system directory (windows\system32) without any versioning—new versions would simply overwrite old ones. Apart from this, in versions of Windows prior to XP the COM class table was a singleton, so applications that required a particular COM object would be given whichever version had been loaded first.[3] All this meant that it was impossible for different applications to depend on different versions of a DLL, or even to know which version you would be given at run time.

The introduction of the .NET framework resolves the DLL hell problem by introducing the concept of assemblies. Assemblies that are cryptographically signed can be given version numbers that allow different versions of the same library to be distinguished, and Windows stores them in a global assembly cache (known as "the GAC") which can distinguish between different versions of a library even if they have the same filename. Now you can have several different versions of a library available to your applications. The advantage of using the GAC is that, if a critical bug or security fix needs to be pushed out, you can update at a stroke all applications that use the affected DLL. Nevertheless, .NET also supports "xcopy deployment" of DLLs, whereby they are kept in the same directory as the application rather than in the GAC.

Linux avoids dependency hell by using a simple naming convention: It appends an integer to every .so file in the global library directory (/usr/lib), and uses a soft link to determine the canonical system-wide version. It's then easy for administrators to change which version is to be used by applications. If an application depends on a specific version, it asks for the file with the corresponding version number. Of course having a canonical system-wide version of a library means ensuring that every application installed works with that version. There are two answers to this problem: compiling every application from source (the approach taken by Gentoo), or doing sophisticated regression testing of every application's binaries (preferred by most creators of Linux distributions). This does mean that you can't install new binary distributions of an application that depend on a new version of a system library at will without a sophisticated dependency management tool. Fortunately, such a tool exists in the form of the Debian package management system—possibly the finest dependency management tool in existence and the primary reason why Debian is such a solid platform and why Ubuntu can produce stable releases twice a year.

A simple answer to the problem of OS-wide dependencies is the judicious application of static compilation. This means that the dependencies that are most critical to your application are aggregated into a single assembly at compile time, so that there are few runtime dependencies. However, while this makes for simpler deployments, it has some drawbacks. As well as creating large binaries, it also tightly couples the binaries thus created to a particular version of the operating system, and makes it impossible to fix bugs or security holes through operating system updates. Thus static compilation is not usually to be recommended.

---

3.   In Windows XP, the introduction of registration-free COM allowed applications to store DLLs they require in their own directory.

For dynamic languages, the equivalent approach is to ship any frameworks or libraries that the application depends upon along with it. Rails takes this approach, allowing the whole Rails framework to be shipped along with applications that use it. This means that you can have multiple Rails applications running simultaneously, each using different versions of the framework.

Java faces a particularly severe problem with runtime dependencies due to the design of its classloader. The original design prevented more than one version of a class being available in the same JVM. This restriction has been overcome in the form of the OSGi framework, which provides multiversion class loading as well as hot deployment and autoupdating. Without the use of OSGi the restriction remains, meaning that dependencies have to be managed carefully at build time. A common but unpleasant scenario is an application depending on two libraries (JARs in this case), each of which depends on the same underlying library (for example, a logging library) but a different version. The application will probably compile, but it will almost certainly fail at run time, with either a `ClassNotFound` exception (if the required method or class is not present) or with subtle bugs. This problem is known as the diamond dependency problem.

We will discuss the solution to the diamond dependency problem and another pathological case—circular dependencies—later in this chapter.

Managing Libraries

There are two reasonable ways of managing libraries in software projects. One is to check them into version control. Another is to declare them and use a tool like Maven or Ivy to download libraries from Internet repositories or (preferably) your organization's own artifact repository. The key constraint you need to enforce is that builds are repeatable—that is, if I check out the project from version control and run the automated build, I can guarantee I will get exactly the same binaries that everybody else on the project does, and that I can create exactly the same binaries three months from now when I have to debug a problem reported by a user running an old version of my software.

Checking libraries into version control is the simplest solution, and will work fine for small projects. Traditionally, a lib directory is created in your project's root to put libraries into. We suggest adding three further subdirectories: build, test, and run—for build-time, test-time, and runtime dependencies. We also suggest using a naming convention for libraries that includes their version number. So don't just check nunit.dll into your lib directory—check in nunit-2.5.5.dll. That way, you know exactly which versions you're using, and it's easy to determine whether or not you're up-to-date with the latest and greatest of everything. The benefit of this approach is that everything you need to build your application is in version control—once you have a local check-out of the project repository, you know you can repeatably build the same packages that everybody else has.

It's a good idea to check in your entire toolchain, since this represents a build-time dependency of your project. However, you should check it into a different repository from the rest of your project, because your toolchain repository can easily become very large. You should prevent your project repository from becoming so big that it takes more than a few seconds to perform common repository operations, such as seeing local changes and committing small changes to the central repository. Another alternative is to keep your toolchain on shared, network-attached storage.

There are a couple of problems with checking in libraries. First, over time, your checked-in library repository may become large and crufty, and it may become hard to know which of these libraries are still being used by your application. Another problem crops up if your project must run with other projects on the same platform. Some platforms can handle projects using multiple versions of the same library, while others (for example the JVM without OSGi, or Ruby Gems) do not allow multiple versions of the same library to be used. In this case, you need to be careful to use the same versions of libraries that other projects use. Manually managing transitive dependencies across projects rapidly becomes painful.

An automated approach to dependency management is provided by Maven and Ivy, which allow you to declare exactly which versions of your libraries you need as part of your project's configuration. The tools then download the appropriate versions of the libraries you require, transitively resolving dependencies on other projects (if applicable) and ensuring that there are no inconsistencies in the project dependency graph, such as two components requiring mutually incompatible versions of some common library. These tools will cache the libraries your project needs on your local machine, so although the project can take a long time to build when you first run it on a new machine, further builds are no slower than if you had the libraries checked into version control. The problem with Maven is that in order to enjoy repeatable builds, you must configure it to use specific versions of its plugins, and ensure that you specify the exact versions of each of your project's dependencies. There is more on dependency management with Maven later on in this chapter.

Another important practice when using dependency management tools is to manage your own artifact repository. Open source artifact repositories include Artifactory and Nexus. This helps ensure that builds are repeatable and prevents dependency hell by controlling which versions of each library are available to projects within your organization. This practice also makes it much easier to audit your libraries and prevent violations of legal constraints, such as using GPL-licensed libraries in BSD-licensed software.

If Maven and Ivy are unsuitable, it is also possible to roll your own declarative dependency management system by having a simple properties file which specifies the libraries your projects depend on and the versions of these libraries. You can then write a script which downloads the correct versions of these libraries from your organization's artifact repository—which can be as simple as a backed-up filesystem fronted with a simple web service. Of course you will need a more powerful solution if you need to handle more complex problems such as resolving transitive dependencies.

Components

Almost all modern software systems consist of a collection of components. These components may be DLLs, JAR files, OSGi bundles, Perl modules, or something else. Components have a relatively long history in the software industry. However, working out how to assemble them into deployable artifacts, and how to implement a deployment pipeline that takes account of the interactions between components, is a nontrivial task. The results of this complexity are often demonstrated by builds that take many hours to assemble a deployable, testable application.

Most applications start off as a single component. Some start off as two or three (for example, a client-server application). So why should a codebase be split into components, and how should the relationships between them be managed? Unless these relationships are managed effectively, it can compromise the ability to use them as part of a continuous integration system.

How to Divide a Codebase into Components

The idea of a "component" in software is one that most people will recognize when they see it, but that has many different, often woolly, definitions. We have already loosely defined what we mean by a component for the purposes of this chapter in the introduction, but there a few other properties of components that most people would agree upon. A fairly uncontroversial statement might look like this: "A component is reusable, replaceable with something else that implements the same API, independently deployable, and encapsulates some coherent set of behaviors and responsibilities of the system."

Clearly a single class could, in principle, have these characteristics—but generally this is not the case. The requirement for components to be independently deployable means that classes don't usually qualify. There is nothing to prevent us packaging a single class so it can be deployed, but in most cases the overhead associated with packaging doesn't make sense at this level of detail. In addition, classes usually work in clusters, with small groups of classes working closely together to deliver useful behavior and being, relatively speaking, more tightly coupled to their close collaborators.

From this we can assume that there is some lower bound for what constitutes a component. A component should have a certain level of complexity before it can be considered an independent piece of your application. So what of an upper bound? Our aim in dividing a system into components is to increase our efficiency as a team. There are several reasons why components make the software development process more efficient:

1. They divide the problem into smaller and more expressive chunks.

2. Components often represent differences in the rates of change of different parts of the system, and have different lifecycles.

3. They encourage us to design and maintain software with clear delineation of responsibilities, which in turn limits the impact of change, and makes understanding and changing the codebase easier.

4. They can provide us with additional degrees of freedom in optimizing our build and deployment process.

A significant feature of most components is that they expose an API of some form. The technical basis of this API could be provided differently: dynamic linking, static linking, a web service, file exchange, message exchange, and so forth. The nature of the API may differ, but it is important in that it represents an exchange of information with external collaborators—and so, vitally, the degree to which that component is coupled to these collaborators. Even when the interface to the component is a file format or a message schema, it still represents an informational coupling which will, in turn, require consideration of dependencies between components.

It is the degree of coupling between components, both in terms of interface and behavior, that adds complexity when they are separated and treated as independent units in a build and deployment process.

Here are some good reasons to separate out a component from your codebase:

1. Part of your codebase needs to be deployed independently (for example, a server or a rich client).

2. You want to turn a monolithic codebase into a core and a set of plugins, perhaps to replace some part of your system with an alternative implementation, or to provide user extensibility.

3. The component provides an interface to another system (for example a framework or a service which provides an API).

4. It takes too long to compile and link the code.

5. It takes too long to open the project in the development environment.

6. Your codebase is too large to be worked on by a single team.

Although the last three entries in this list may sound rather subjective, they are perfectly valid reasons to tease out components. The final point is especially critical. Teams work best when they comprise around ten people who understand a particular part of the codebase inside out, whether it's a functional component or some other boundary. If you need more than ten people to develop at the speed you need to, one very effective way to do this is to divide your system into loosely coupled components, and divide the teams too.

We do *not* recommend making teams responsible for individual components. This is because in most cases, requirements don't divide along component boundaries. In our experience, cross-functional teams in which people develop features end-to-end are much more effective. Although one team per component may seem more efficient, this is not in fact the case.

First, it is often hard to write and test requirements for a single component in isolation, since usually implementing a piece of functionality will touch more than one component. If you group teams by component, you thus require two or more teams to collaborate to complete a feature, automatically adding a large and unnecessary communication cost. Furthermore, people in component-centered teams tend to form silos and optimize locally, losing their ability to judge what is in the best interest of the project as a whole.

It is better to split teams up so that each team takes on one stream of stories (perhaps all with a common theme), and touches whatever components they need to in order to get their work done. Teams with a mandate to implement a business-level feature, and the freedom to change any component that they need to, are much more efficient. Organize teams by functional area rather than by component, ensure that everybody has the right to change any part of the codebase, rotate people between teams regularly, and ensure that there is good communication between teams.

This approach also has the benefit that making all the components work together is everybody's responsibility, not just that of the integration team. One of the more serious dangers of having a team per component is that the application as a whole won't work until the end of the project because nobody has the incentive to integrate the components.

Reasons four and five in the list above are often symptoms of a poor design which is insufficiently modular. A well-designed codebase which follows the "Don't repeat yourself" (DRY) principle, and which is composed of well-encapsulated objects that obey the Law of Demeter, is usually more efficient, easier to work on, and easier to split into components when the need arises. However, a slow build process can also be caused by overaggressive componentization. This seems to be particularly prevalent in the .NET world, where some people like to create a large number of projects within their solution, for no good reason. Doing so invariably causes compilation to slow to a crawl.

There are no hard and fast rules about how to organize your application as a collection of components, apart from the considerations of good design discussed above. There are, however, two common failings: "components everywhere" and "the one component to rule them all." Experience shows that neither extreme is appropriate, but gauging where the boundaries are remains a judgment call for developers and architects of whatever level of experience. This is one of the many factors that makes software design an art, craft, and social science as much as it is an engineering discipline.

Using Components Doesn't Imply Using an N-Tier Architecture

Sun popularized the idea of the n-tier architecture when they introduced the J2EE framework. Microsoft continues to present it as a best practice with the .NET framework. Ruby on Rails is arguably encouraging a similar architectural approach, while of course making it much simpler to get started and imposing more constraints on your system. N-Tier architectures often represent a good approach to some problems, but not necessarily all.

In our opinion, n-tier architecture is often used as a form of defensive design. It can help to prevent a large and inexperienced team from creating a tightly coupled ball of mud [aHiFnc]. It also has well-understood capacity and scalability characteristics. However, it is often not the optimal solution to many problems (this is, of course, true of all technologies and patterns). It is worth noting, in particular, that having several layers that run on physically separate environments will introduce high latencies in responding to any particular request. This, in turn, often leads to the introduction of complex caching strategies that are hard to maintain and debug. In high-performance environments, event-driven or distributed actor model architectures can offer superior performance.

The architect on one large project we encountered had mandated exactly seven layers in the architecture. Much of the time one or more of the layers was redundant. However, the requisite classes still had to be introduced, and every call to every method had to be logged. Needless to say, the application was difficult to debug because of the large number of pointless log entries. It was hard to understand because of the swathes of redundant code, and hard to modify because of the dependencies between layers.

Using components doesn't mandate the use of an n-tier architecture. It means separating logic into encapsulated modules by finding sensible abstractions that facilitate this separation. Layering can be useful—even n-tiered layering—but it is not a synonym for component-based development.

At the other end of the spectrum, if components don't automatically imply layering, layering should not automatically define components. If you use layered architectures, don't create a component per layer. You should almost always have several components within a layer, and indeed there may be components that are used by multiple layers. Component-based design is orthogonal to layering.

Finally, it's worth noting Conway's Law, which states that "organizations which design systems . . . are constrained to produce designs which are copies of the communication structures of these organizations."[4] So, for example, open source projects where developers communicate only by email tend to be very modular with few interfaces. A product developed by a small, colocated team

---

4. Melvin E. Conway, *How Do Committees Invent*, Datamation 14:5:28–31.

will tend to be tightly coupled and not modular.[5] Be careful of how you set up your development team—it will affect the architecture of your application.

If your codebase is already large and monolithic, one way to start decomposing it into components is to use branching by abstraction, as described earlier in this chapter.

Pipelining Components

Even when your application is comprised of several components, it doesn't mean that you need to have a separate build for each one. Indeed the simplest approach, and one that scales up to a surprising degree, is to have a single pipeline for your entire application. Every time a change is committed, everything is built and tested. In most cases, we would recommend building your system as a single entity until the process of getting feedback becomes too slow. As we have said, if you follow our advice in this book, you will likely find that you can build surprisingly large and complex systems this way. This approach has the advantage that it is very easy to trace which line of code broke the build.

However, realistically there are many circumstances that benefit from splitting your system into several different pipelines. Here are a few examples of circumstances where it makes sense to have separate pipelines:

- Parts of your application that have a different lifecycle (perhaps you build your own version of an OS kernel as part of your application, but you only need to do this once every few weeks).

- Functionally separate areas of your application that are worked on by different (perhaps distributed) teams may have components specific to those teams.

- Components that use different technologies or build processes.

- Shared components that are used by several other projects.

- Components that are relatively stable and do not change frequently.

- It takes too long to build your application, and creating builds for each component will be faster (but beware, the point at which this becomes true is much later than most people think).

The important thing from the perspective of the build and deployment process is that there is always some additional overhead to the management of a component-based build. In order to turn a single build into several, you need to

---

5. MacCormack, Rusnak, Baldwin, *Exploring the Duality between Product and Organizational Architectures: A Test of the Mirroring Hypothesis*, Harvard Business School [8XYofQ].

create a build system for each. This means a new directory structure and build file for each separate deployment pipeline, each of which should follow the same pattern as that for an entire system. That means the directory structure for each build should include unit tests, acceptance tests, the libraries it depends on, build scripts, configuration information, and anything else you would normally put into version control for a project. The build for each component or set of components should have its own pipeline to prove that it is fit for release. This pipeline will perform the following steps:

- Compile the code, if necessary.

- Assemble one or more binaries that are capable of deployment to any environment.

- Run unit tests.

- Run acceptance tests.

- Support manual testing, where appropriate.

The process, as for a whole system, ensures that you get feedback as early as possible, asserting the viability of each change.

Once the binaries have passed through their own mini release process, they are ready for promotion to an integration build (more on this in the next section). You will need to publish the binaries to an artifact repository, along with some metadata to identify the version of the source that was used to create the binary. A modern CI server should be able to do this for you, although if you want to do it yourself it can be as simple as storing the binaries in a directory with the name of the pipeline label that produced it. Another alternative is to use Artifactory, Nexus, or some other artifact repository software.

Please note that we are emphatically not saying that you should create a pipeline for every DLL or JAR. That's why we've been careful to say "component or set of components" repeatedly above. A component may consist of several binaries. In general, the guiding principle should be to minimize the number of builds that you operate. One is better than two, two better than three, and so on. Keep optimizing the build and making it more efficient for as long as possible before moving to a parallel pipeline approach.

The Integration Pipeline

The integration pipeline takes as its starting point the binary output from each of the components that comprise your system. The first stage of the integration pipeline should create a package (or packages) suitable for deployment by composing the appropriate collections of binaries. The second stage should deploy the resulting application to a production-like environment and run smoke tests against it to give early indication of any basic integration problems. If this stage is successful, then the pipeline should move on to a conventional acceptance test stage, running whole application acceptance tests in the usual way. Then follows the normal sequence of stages appropriate to the application, as shown in Figure 13.1.

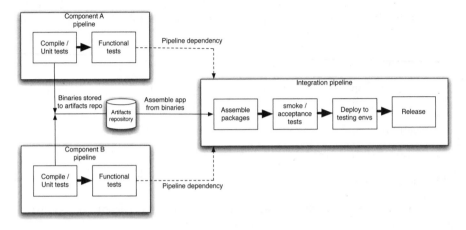

Figure 13.1 *Integration pipeline*

There are two general principles of deployment pipelines to bear in mind when creating an integration pipeline: the need for fast feedback and the need to provide visibility into the status of the build for all interested parties. Feedback can be compromised by long pipelines, or chains of pipelines. If you find yourself in this situation and you have sufficient hardware, one solution is to trigger downstream pipelines as soon as binaries are created and the unit tests pass.

In terms of visibility, if any stage of the integration pipeline fails, it should be possible to see exactly why it broke. This means that the ability to trace back from an integration build to the versions of each component that contributed to it is key. The maintenance of these relationships is essential if you are to be able to discover the changes in source code responsible for the breakage. Modern CI tools should be able to do this for you, so if yours doesn't, find one that does. It shouldn't take more than a few seconds to track down the cause of an integration pipeline failure.

It also follows that not every "green" build of an individual component will actually be good when combined with the other components that make up the application as a whole. Therefore, the team working on the components should have visibility into which versions of their component actually ended up in a green integration pipeline (and can thus be considered good for integration). *Only these versions of the components are in fact really "green."* The integration pipeline forms an extension of each individual component's pipeline. So visibility is important in both directions.

If several components change between one run of the integration pipeline and the next, it is probable that it will spend much of its time broken. This is problematic because it makes it more difficult to find which change broke your application, as there will be so many changes since the last good version of the application.

There are several different techniques to solve this problem, which we'll explore in the rest of this chapter. The simplest approach is to build every single possible combination of the good versions of your components. If your components don't change that often, or you have sufficient computing power on your build grid, you can do this. This is the best approach because it doesn't involve any human intervention or clever algorithms, and computing power is ultimately cheap compared to humans performing forensics. So if you can, do this.

The next best approach is to build as many versions of your application as you can. You can do this with a relatively simple scheduling algorithm that takes the latest version of every component and assembles your application as frequently as it can. If this operation is sufficiently fast, you can run a short smoke test suite against each version of your app. If your smoke tests take a while to run, they might only end up running against every third version of your application.

You could then have some manual way to select a given set of versions of your components and say, "Assemble these and create an instance of my integration pipeline with them," as provided by some CI tools.

Managing Dependency Graphs

It is vital to version dependencies, including libraries and components. If you fail to version dependencies, you won't be able to reproduce builds. That means, among other things, that when your application breaks due to a change in a dependency, you won't be able to trace back and find the change that broke it, or find the last "good" version of the library.

In the previous section, we discussed a set of components, each with their own pipeline, feeding into an integration pipeline which assembles the application and runs automated and manual tests on the final application. However, things are often not quite this simple: Components can have dependencies on other components, including third-party libraries. If you draw a diagram of the dependencies between components, it should be a directed acyclic graph (DAG). If this is not the case (and in particular, if your graph has cycles) you have a pathological dependency problem, which we'll address shortly.

Building Dependency Graphs

First of all, it is important to consider how we can build a graph of dependencies. Consider the set of components shown in Figure 13.2.

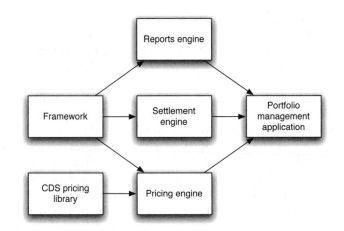

Figure 13.2   *A dependency graph*

The portfolio management application depends on a pricing engine, a settlement engine, and a reports engine. These in turn all depend on a framework. The pricing engine depends on a credit default swap (CDS) library that is provided by a (now struggling) third party. In general, we refer to a component further to the left of the diagram as an "upstream" dependency, and a component further to the right as a "downstream" dependency. Thus the pricing engine has two upstream dependencies, the CDS pricing library and the framework, and one downstream dependency, the portfolio management application.

Each component should have its own pipeline, triggered by changes in that component's source code or by changes to any upstream dependency. Downstream dependencies will be triggered by this component passing all of its automated tests. There are several possible scenarios to consider in terms of building this graph of components.

1. *A change is made to the portfolio management application.* In this scenario, only the portfolio management application needs to be rebuilt.

2. *A change is made to the reports engine.* In this scenario, the reports engine must be rebuilt and pass all its automated tests. Then the portfolio management application needs to be rebuilt, using the new version of the reports engine and the current version of the pricing and settlement engines.

3. *A change is made to the CDS pricing library.* The CDS pricing library is a third-party, binary dependency. So if the version of the CDS in use is updated, the pricing engine needs to be rebuilt against the new version and the current version of the framework. This in turn should trigger a rebuild of the portfolio management application.

4. *A change is made to the framework.* If a successful change is made to the framework, meaning that the framework pipeline passes its tests, its immediate downstream dependencies should be rebuilt: the reports engine, the pricing engine, and the settlement engine. If all three of these dependencies pass, then the portfolio management application should be rebuilt using the new versions of all three of its upstream dependencies. If any of the three intermediate component builds fail, the portfolio management application should not be rebuilt and the framework components should be treated as broken. The framework should be fixed so that all three of its downstream dependencies pass their tests, which in turn should lead to the portfolio management application passing.

There is an important observation to be drawn from this example. When considering scenario 4, it may seem that some kind of "and" relationship is required between the upstream dependencies of the portfolio management application. However, this is not the case—if a change is made to the source of the reports engine, it should trigger a rebuild of the portfolio management application whether or not the pricing engine or settlement engine are rebuilt. Furthermore, consider the following scenario.

5. *A change is made to the framework and the pricing engine.* In this case, the whole graph needs to be rebuilt. But there are several possible outcomes, each with its own considerations. The happy path is that all three intermediate components pass with the new versions of the framework and the CDS pricing library. But what if the settlement engine fails? Clearly the portfolio management application should not build against the new (but broken) version of the framework. However, you might well want the portfolio management application to build with the new version of the pricing engine, which (crucially) should be built against the new version of the CDS pricing library and the old (known good) version of the framework. Of course now you're in trouble, because no such version of the pricing library exists.

The most important constraint on these scenarios is that the portfolio management application should only build against one version of the framework. We particularly don't want to end up with a version of (say) the pricing engine built against one version of the framework, and the settlement engine built against another version. This is the classic "diamond dependency" problem—which is the build-time analogue of the runtime "dependency hell" problem we discussed earlier in this chapter.

Pipelining Dependency Graphs

So how do we construct a deployment pipeline based on the project structure we describe above? The key elements of the pipeline are that the team must get feedback as rapidly as possible on any breakages, and that we should obey the rules for building dependencies described above. Our approach is shown in Figure 13.3.

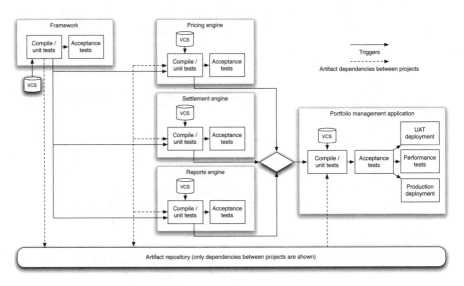

Figure 13.3   *Component pipeline*

There are a couple of important features to call out. First of all, to increase the speed of feedback, dependent projects are triggered once the commit stage of each project's pipeline is complete. You don't need to wait for the acceptance tests to pass—only for the binaries to be created which the downstream projects depend on. These are then stored in your artifact repository. Of course the acceptance tests and the various deployment stages will reuse these binaries (this is not shown on the diagram to prevent clutter).

All of the triggers are automatic, with the exception of deployments to the manual testing and production environments, which are generally manually authorized. These automatic triggers ensure that any time a change is made to (for example) the framework, it triggers a build of the pricing engine, settlement engine, and reports engine. If all three of these build successfully with the new version of the framework, the portfolio management application will get rebuilt with the new versions of all the upstream components.

It is essential that teams can trace the origins of the components that went into a particular build of the application. A good CI tool will not only do this, but will also show you which versions of your components integrated together successfully. For example in Figure 13.4, you can see that version 2.0.63 of the portfolio management application was built with version 1.0.217 of the pricing engine, version 2.0.11 of the settlement engine, version 1.5.5 of the reports engine, and version 1.3.2396 of the framework.

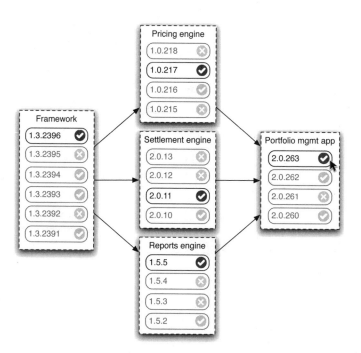

Figure 13.4 *Visualizing upstream dependencies*

Figure 13.5 shows all of the downstream components built using the selected version of the framework (1.3.2394).

Your CI tool should also ensure that consistent versions of components are used throughout the pipeline. It should prevent dependency hell, and ensure that a change in version control which affects multiple components only propagates through the pipeline once.

All the advice we gave at the beginning of this chapter on incremental development also applies to components. Make changes in an incremental way which doesn't break your dependencies. When you add new functionality, provide a new API entry point for it in the components that change. If you want to deprecate old functionality, use static analysis as part of your pipeline to detect who is consuming the old APIs. The pipeline should tell you quickly if any of your changes has broken any of your dependencies by mistake.

If you do need to make a far-reaching change to a component, you can create a new release of it. In Figure 13.6, we assume that the team working on the reports engine needs to create a new version that breaks some APIs. In order to do this, they create a branch for the 1.0 release, and start the development of 1.1 on mainline.

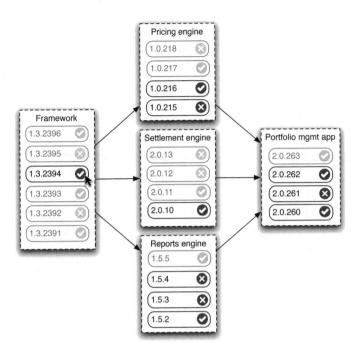

Figure 13.5   *Visualizing downstream dependencies*

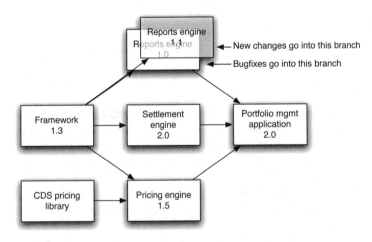

Figure 13.6   *Branching components*

The reporting engine team will continue to add new features on mainline. Meanwhile, downstream users of the reporting engine can continue to use the binaries created from the 1.0 branch. If they need a bugfix, it can be checked into the 1.0 branch and merged into trunk. Once the downstream users are ready to use the new version, they can switch. To be clear, the "branch by release" pattern, as described here, still suffers from the same downside of deferring integration, so it is second best in terms of continuous integration. However, the fact that components are (or at least should be) loosely coupled means that the risks of painful integration later are more controllable. So this is a very useful strategy for managing more complex changes to a component.

When Should We Trigger Builds?

All of the examples discussed above assume that we trigger a new build whenever there is any change to upstream dependencies. This is the right thing to do, but it is not the norm in many teams—rather, they tend to only update their dependencies once their codebase is stable, perhaps at integration time, or when development has reached some other milestone. This behavior emphasizes stability, but at the cost of potential risk of spending a great deal of time integrating.

It can be seen that there is a tension in the development process where dependencies are involved. On one hand, it is best to keep up with the newest versions of upstream dependencies to make sure that you have the most up-to-date features and bugfixes. On the other hand, there can be a cost to integrating the latest version of every dependency, because you can spend all your time fixing breakages caused by these new versions. Most teams compromise and do a refresh of all their dependencies after every release, when the risks of updating are low.

A key consideration when deciding how often to update dependencies is how much you trust new versions of these dependencies. If you have a few components depending upon a component also developed by your team, you can usually fix breakages caused by API changes very quickly and simply, so integrating often is best. If the components are sufficiently small, it is preferable to have a single build for the whole application—giving the fastest feedback of all.

If the upstream dependencies are developed by another team within your own organization, it is probably best if these components are built independently in their own pipeline. You can then decide whether or not to take the latest version of these upstream components each time that they are changed, or stick with a particular version. This decision is based on how frequently they change, and how fast the teams working on them respond to problems.

The less control, visibility, and influence you have over changes to a component, the less you trust it, the more conservative you should be about accepting new versions. Don't blindly take updates to third-party libraries, for example, if there is no obvious need to do so. If the changes don't fix problems that you have, leave the update alone, unless the version you are using is no longer supported.

In most cases, it works best for teams to be at the more continuous end in terms of integrating new versions of dependencies. Of course, continually updating all dependencies costs more in terms of resources spent integrating (both hardware and builds) and in terms of fixing bugs and the problems of integrating "unfinished" versions of components.

You need to strike a balance between getting fast feedback on whether your application is going to integrate and having hyperactive builds that continually spam you with breakages that you don't care about. One potential solution is "cautious optimism," as described in a paper by Alex Chaffee [d6tguh].

Cautious Optimism

Chaffee's proposal is to introduce a new piece of state into the dependency graph—whether a particular upstream dependency is "static," "guarded," or "fluid." Changes in a static upstream dependency do not trigger a new build. Changes in a fluid upstream dependency always trigger a new build. If a change in a "fluid" upstream dependency triggers a build and the build fails, the upstream dependency is marked "guarded," and the component is pinned to the known-good version of the upstream dependency. A "guarded" upstream dependency behaves like a static one—it doesn't take new changes—but it serves to remind the development team that there is a problem that needs to be resolved with the upstream dependency.

Effectively, we are making explicit our preferences in terms of which dependencies we do not want to take updates from continuously. We also ensure that the application is always "green"—our build system will automatically back out any breakage due to a bad new version of an upstream dependency.

Let's take part of our dependency graph, as shown in Figure 13.7. We'll assign a fluid trigger to the dependency between the CDS pricing library and the pricing engine, and a static trigger to the dependency between the framework and the pricing engine.

Consider the case where both the CDS pricing library and the framework are updated. The new version of the framework is ignored, because the trigger between the pricing engine and the framework is static. However, the new version of the CDS pricing library will trigger a new build of the pricing engine because its trigger is set to fluid. If this new build of the pricing engine fails, the trigger will get set to guarded, and further changes to the CDS pricing library will not trigger a new build of it. If the build passes, the trigger stays fluid.

However, cautious optimism can lead to complex behavior. Let's set the trigger between the framework and the pricing engine to fluid, just like the CDS pricing library is. In the case where both the CDS pricing library and the framework get updated, there will be one new build of the pricing engine. If the pricing engine breaks, you don't know what broke the build—the new version of the CDS pricing library or the new version of the framework. You'll have to try and find which it was—and in the meantime, both of your triggers will become guarded.

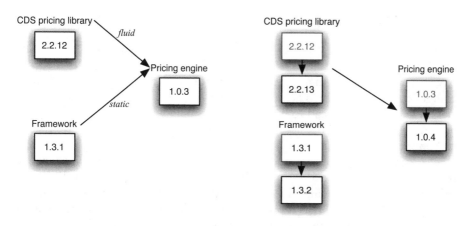

Figure 13.7 *Cautious optimism triggering*

Chaffee mentions a strategy called "informed pessimism" as a starting point for any implementation of a dependency tracking algorithm. In this strategy, every trigger is set to "static," but developers working on downstream dependencies are notified when a new version of their upstream dependency becomes available.

Apache Gump for Managing Dependencies

Apache Gump was arguably the first dependency management tool in the Java world. It was created in the early days of the Apache Java projects when all the different tools (Xerces, Xalan, Ant, Avalon, Cocoon, and so forth) depended on specific versions of each other. Developers working on these tools needed a way to select which versions of these dependencies to use, so that they could get a good version of their application working, and did so using classpath manipulation. Gump was created to automate the generation scripts to control the classpath used at build time, so that developers could experiment with different versions of dependencies to find a good build. It made a significant contribution to the stability of the builds of these projects, despite the fact that it required you to spend a good deal of time parameterizing your build. You can read more of the history of Gump at [9CpgMi]—it's a short and interesting read.

Gump became obsolete around the same time when many of the components used in Java projects became part of the standard Java API, and others such as Ant and the Commons components became backwards compatible, so you didn't need multiple versions installed in most cases. This in itself teaches a valuable lesson: Keep dependency graphs shallow, and do your best to ensure backwards compatibility—something that aggressive regression testing of your component graph at build time, as we describe in this section, will help you achieve.

Circular Dependencies

Probably the nastiest dependency problem is the circular dependency. This occurs when the dependency graph contains cycles. The simplest example is that you have a component, A, that depends on another component, B. Unfortunately component B in turn depends on component A.

This may appear to lead to a fatal bootstrapping problem. To build component A, I need to build component B, but to build component B, I need component A, and so on.

Surprisingly, we have seen successful projects with circular dependencies in their build systems. You may argue with our definition of "successful" in this case, but there was working code in production, which is enough for us. The key point is that you never begin a project with circular dependencies—they tend to creep in later. It is possible, but not recommended if you can avoid it, to survive this problem so long as there is a version of component A that you can use to build component B. You can then use the new version of B to build the new version of A. This results in a kind of "build ladder," as shown in Figure 13.8.

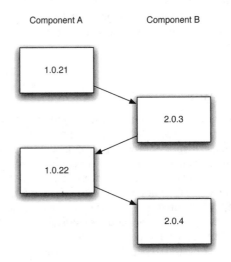

Figure 13.8 *Circular dependency build ladder*

At run time, there is no problem so long as both components, A and B, are available together.

As we have said, we don't recommend using circular dependencies. But if you ever run into one that is unfeasibly hard to avoid, then the strategy outlined above can work. No build system supports such a configuration out of the box, so you have to hack your toolchain to support it. You will also have to be cautious in how the parts of your build interact: If each component triggers a build of its dependencies automatically, the two components will be building forever because of the circularity. Always try to get rid of circular dependencies; but if you find yourself working in a codebase that has them, don't despair—you can use the build ladder as a temporary workaround until you can eliminate the problem.

Managing Binaries

We have spent a fair amount of time discussing how to organize builds in software split into components. We have described how to create a pipeline for each component, strategies for triggering downstream component pipelines when a component changes, and how to branch components. However, we have not yet discussed how to manage binaries in a component-based build. This is important because in most cases, components should have binary rather than source-level dependencies on one other. The next few pages will deal with this topic.

First, we'll discuss the general principles behind the workings of an artifact repository. We will then move on to describe how to manage binaries using only the filesystem. In the next section, we will describe the use of Maven to manage dependencies.

You don't have to roll your own artifact repository. There are several products on the market, including the open source projects Artifactory and Nexus. Several tools, such as AntHill Pro and Go, include their own artifact repository.

How an Artifact Repository Should Work

The most important property of an artifact repository is that it should not contain anything that cannot be reproduced. You should be able to delete your artifact repository without worrying that you won't be able to regain anything valuable. For this to be true, your version control system needs to contain everything required to re-create any given binary, including the automated build scripts.

The reason for the need to delete the artifacts is that they are big (and if they aren't yet, they will be). Ultimately you'll need to delete them in order to free up space. For this reason, we don't recommend checking artifacts into version control. If you can re-create them, you don't need to anyway. It is of course worth keeping around artifacts that have passed all tests and are thereby candidates for release. Anything that has been released is also worth keeping around in the event that you need to roll back to that earlier version, or to support someone using an older version of your software.

However long you keep artifacts themselves, you should always keep a hash of each one so you can verify the source of any given binary. This is important for auditing purposes—for example, if you're not sure exactly which application is deployed in a particular environment. It should be possible to get the MD5 of any given binary and use this to find out exactly which revision in source control was used to create it. You can either use your build system to store this data (some CI servers will do this for you), or your version control system. Either way, managing hashes is an important part of your configuration management strategy.

The simplest artifact repository is a directory structure on disk. Generally, this directory structure will be on a RAID or a SAN, because while artifacts should be disposable, you should be the one deciding that they can be deleted, not some badly behaved piece of hardware.

The most important constraint on this directory structure is that it should enable you to to associate a binary with the version from source control that was used to create it. Normally, your build system will generate a label, usually a sequence number, for each build that it runs. The label should be short so it can be easily communicated to others. It can include the identifier of the revision in version control used to create it (assuming you're not using a tool like Git or Mercurial which use hashes for identifiers). This label can then be included in the manifest of the binary (in the case of JARs or .NET assemblies, for example).

Create a directory for each pipeline, and within that, a directory for each build number. All the artifacts from the build can then be stored in that directory.

The next small step in sophistication is to add a simple index file that allows you to associate a status with each build, so that you can record the status of each change as it progresses through the deployment pipeline.

If you don't want to use a shared drive for your artifact repository, you can add a web service to store and retrieve artifacts. However, if you have reached this point, you should consider using one of the many free or commercial products on the market.

How Your Deployment Pipeline Should Interact with the Artifact Repository

Your deployment pipeline implementation needs to do two things: Store artifacts generated by the build process into the artifact repository, and then retrieve them for later use.

Consider a pipeline with the following stages: compile, unit test, acceptance test, manual acceptance test, and production.

- The compile stage will create binaries that need to be put into the artifact repository.

- The unit test and acceptance test stages will retrieve these binaries, run unit tests against them, and store reports generated by the unit tests in the artifact repository so that developers can see the results.

- The user acceptance test stage will take the binaries and deploy them to the UAT environment for manual testing.

- The release stage will take the binaries and release them to users or deploy them to production.

As the release candidate progresses through this pipeline, the success or failure of each stage is recorded in the index. Subsequent pipeline stages can depend on the status in this file, so only binaries that have passed the acceptance tests are made available to manual testing and further stages.

There are a couple of options for getting artifacts in and out of the artifact repository. You can store them in a shared filesystem that is accessible from every environment that you need to build on or deploy to. Your deployment scripts can then reference the path to this filesystem. Alternatively, you could use a solution like Nexus or Artifactory.

Managing Dependencies with Maven

Maven is an extensible build management tool for Java projects. In particular, it provides a sophisticated mechanism for managing dependencies. Even if you don't like the rest of Maven, you can use its powerful dependency management functionality in a standalone way. Alternatively, you could use Ivy, which tackles only the dependency management problem without the rest of Maven's build management toolchain. If you're not using Java, you can probably skip this section, unless you're interested in how Maven solves the dependency management problem.

As discussed, projects have two kinds of dependencies: dependencies on external libraries, which we discussed in the "Managing Libraries" section on page 354, and dependencies between the components of your application. Maven provides an abstraction that lets you treat them both in more or less the same way. All Maven domain objects, such as projects, dependencies, and plugins, are identified by a set of coordinates: `groupId`, `artifactId`, and `version`, which together must uniquely identify an object (these axes are sometimes referred to as GAV), as well as `packaging`. These are often written in the following format, which is also how you declare them in Buildr: `groupId:artifactId:packaging:version`. So, for example, if your project depends on Commons Collections 3.2, you would describe that dependency as follows: `commons-collections:commons-collections:jar:3.2`.

The Maven community maintains a mirrored repository that contains a large number of common open source libraries with their associated metadata (including transitive dependencies). These repositories contain almost every open source library you might need in almost any project. You can browse this repository in a web browser at http://repo1.maven.org/maven2. Declaring a dependency on a library in Maven's repository will result in Maven downloading it for you when you build your project.

You declare a project in Maven using a file called pom.xml as follows:

```
<project>
  <modelVersion>4.0.0</modelVersion>
  <groupId>com.continuousdelivery</groupId>
  <artifactId>parent</artifactId>
  <packaging>jar</packaging>
  <version>1.0.0</version>
  <name>demo</name>
  <url>http://maven.apache.org</url>
  <dependencies>
    <dependency>
      <groupId>junit</groupId>
      <artifactId>junit</artifactId>
      <version>3.8.1</version>
      <scope>test</scope>
    </dependency>
    <dependency>
      <groupId>commons-collections</groupId>
      <artifactId>commons-collections</artifactId>
      <version>3.2</version>
    </dependency>
  </dependencies>
</project>
```

This will fetch version 3.8.1 of JUnit and version 3.2 of Commons Collections to your local Maven artifact repository at ~/.m2/repository/<groupId>/ <artifactId>/<version>/ when the project is built. The local Maven artifact repository serves two purposes: It is a cache for dependencies of your projects, and it is also where Maven stores the artifacts created by your projects (more on that shortly). Notice that you can also specify the scope of the dependency: test means the dependency will only be available during test compilation and assembly. Other valid scopes include runtime for dependencies that are not required for compilation, provided for libraries that are required at compile time but will be provided at run time, and compile (the default) for dependencies that are required at compile time and run time.

You can also specify version ranges, such as [1.0,2.0) which will give you any version in the 1.x series. Brackets indicate exclusive quantifiers, and square brackets indicate inclusive quantifiers. You can leave out either the left side or the right side—so [2.0,) means any version higher than 2.0. However, even if you want to give Maven some latitude when choosing versions, it's a good idea to specify an upper bound to avoid your project picking up new major revisions which may break your application.

This project will also create an artifact of its own: a JAR file which will be stored in your local repository at the coordinates specified in your pom. In the example above, running mvn install will result in the the following directory being created in your local Maven artifact repository: ~/.m2/repository/com/ continuousdelivery/parent/1.0.0/. Since we have selected packaging type JAR,

Maven will package your code into a JAR called parent-1.0.0.jar and install it into this directory. Any other project that we run locally can now access this JAR by specifying its coordinates as a dependency. Maven will also install a modified version of your project's pom into the same directory, which includes information on its dependencies so that Maven is able to process transitive dependencies correctly.

Often you won't want to overwrite your artifacts every time you run `mvn install`. In order to do this, Maven provides the concept of snapshot builds. Simply append `-SNAPSHOT` to the version (so in the example above, it would be `1.0.0-SNAPSHOT`. Then, when you run `mvn install`, in place of the directory with the version number, Maven will create a directory in the format `version-yyyymmdd-hhmmss-n`. Projects that consume your snapshots can then specify only `1.0.0-SNAPSHOT`, not the full timestamp, and will be given the latest version that the local repository has.[6]

However, you should use snapshots with care because it can make reproducing builds harder. A better idea is to have your CI server produce canonical versions of each dependency, using the build label as part of the artifact's version number, and store these in your organization's central artifact repoistory. You can then use Maven's version quantifiers in your pom file to specify a range of acceptable versions to use. If you really need to do some exploratory work on your local machine, you can always edit your pom definition to temporarily enable snapshots.

We have only scratched the surface of Maven in this section. In particular, we haven't discussed managing your own Maven repositories, which is important if you want to manage dependencies across your organization, or multimodule projects which are Maven's way of creating a componentized build. While these are important topics, they go beyond what we can reasonably cover in this chapter. If you're interested in more advanced Maven-fu, we recommend you consult the excellent *Maven: The Definitive Guide* written by Sonatype and published by O'Reilly. Meanwhile, we do want to cover some of the basic dependency refactorings you can do in Maven.

Maven Dependency Refactorings

Say you have a set of dependencies that are used by mutiple projects. If you only want to define the versions of the artifacts to use once, you can do so by defining a parent project which includes the versions of each artifact to use. Just take the POM definition provided above, and wrap `<dependencyManagement>` around the `<dependencies>` block. Then you can define a child project like this:

---

6. Local repositories will periodically update from remote repositories—although it is possible to store snapshots in remote repositories, it is not a good idea.

```
<project>
  <modelVersion>4.0.0</modelVersion>
  <parent>
    <groupId>com.continuousdelivery</groupId>
    <artifactId>parent</artifactId>
    <version>1.0.0</version>
  </parent>
  <artifactId>simple</artifactId>
  <packaging>jar</packaging>
  <version>1.0-SNAPSHOT</version>
  <name>demo</name>
  <url>http://maven.apache.org</url>
  <dependencies>
    <dependency>
      <groupId>junit</groupId>
      <artifactId>junit</artifactId>
      <scope>test</scope>
    </dependency>
    <dependency>
      <groupId>commons-collections</groupId>
      <artifactId>commons-collections</artifactId>
    </dependency>
  </dependencies>
</project>
```

This will use the versions of these dependencies defined in the parent project—notice that the junit and commons-collections references have no version number specified.

You can also refactor your Maven build to remove duplication of common dependencies. Instead of creating a JAR as its end product, you can have a Maven project create a pom which is then referenced by other projects. In the first code listing (with artifactId parent), you would change the value of <packaging> to pom instead of jar. You can then declare a dependency on this pom in any projects that you want to use the same dependencies:

```
<project>
  ...
  <dependencies>
    ...
    <dependency>
      <groupId>com.thoughtworks.golive</groupId>
      <artifactId>parent</artifactId>
      <version>1.0</version>
      <type>pom</type>
    </dependency>
  </dependencies>
</project>
```

One really useful feature of Maven is that it can analyze your project's dependencies and tell you about both undeclared dependencies and unused declared dependencies. Simply use mvn dependency:analyze to run this report. There's more on managing dependencies with Maven here: [cxy9dm].

Summary

In this chapter, we have discussed techniques to ensure that your team can develop as efficiently as possible, while keeping your application always in a releasable state. As usual, the principle is to ensure that teams get fast feedback on the effect of their changes on the production-readiness of the application. One strategy for meeting this goal is to ensure every change is broken down into small, incremental steps which are checked into mainline. Another is to break your application down into components.

Dividing an application into a collection of loosely coupled, well-encapsulated, collaborating components is not only good design. It allows for more efficient collaboration and faster feedback when working on large systems. Until your application gets sufficiently large, there is no need to build your components individually—the simplest thing is to have a single pipeline that builds your whole application at once as the first stage. If you concentrate on efficient commit builds and fast unit testing, and implement build grids for acceptance testing, your project can grow to a much larger degree that you might think possible. A team of up to 20 people working full-time for a couple of years should not need to create multiple build pipelines, although of course they should still separate their application into components.

Once you exceed these limits, though, the use of components, dependency-based build pipelines, and effective artifact management are the key to efficient delivery and fast feedback. The beauty of the approach described in this chapter is that it builds on the already beneficial practice of component-based design. This approach avoids the use of complex branching strategies, which usually leads to serious problems in integrating your application. However, it does depend on having a well-designed application that is amenable to a componentized build. Unfortunately, we have seen too many large applications that cannot be easily componentized in this way. It is very hard to coax such an application into a state where it can be easily modified and integrated. So, make sure that you are using your technology's toolchain effectively to write code that can be built as a set of independent components once it gets large enough.

Chapter 14

Advanced Version Control

Introduction

Version control systems, also known as source control and revision control systems, are designed to allow organizations to maintain a complete history of every change made to their applications, including source code, documentation, database definitions, build scripts, tests, and so forth. However, they also serve another important purpose: They enable teams to work together on separate parts of an application while maintaining a system of record—the definitive codebase of the application.

Once your team grows beyond a handful of developers, it becomes hard to have many people working full-time on the same version control repository. People break each other's functionality by mistake, and generally tread on each others' toes. The aim of this chapter is thus to examine how teams can work productively with version control.

We'll start off with a little history, and then dive straight into the most controversial topic in version control: branching and merging. We then go on to discuss some modern paradigms that avoid some of the problems of traditional tools: stream-based revision control and distributed revision control. Finally, we'll present a set of patterns for working with branches—or, in some cases, for avoiding them.

We'll be spending a lot of time discussing branching and merging in this chapter. So let's take a moment to think of how it fits into the deployment pipeline we've spent so much time discussing. The deployment pipeline is a paradigm for moving code from check-in to production in a controlled way. However, it is only one of the three degrees of freedom that you have to work with in large software systems. This and the previous chapter address the other two dimensions: branches and dependencies.

There are three good reasons to branch your code. First, a branch can be created for releasing a new version of your application. This allows developers to continue working on new features without affecting the stable public release. When bugs are found, they are first fixed in the relevant public release branch, and then the changes are applied to the mainline. Release branches are never merged back to mainline. Second, when you need to spike out a new feature or a refactoring; the spike branch gets thrown away and is never merged. Finally, it is acceptable to create a short-lived branch when you need to make a large change to the application that is not possible with any of the methods described in the last chapter—an extremely rare scenario if your codebase is well structured. The sole aim of this branch is to get the codebase to a state where further change can be made either incrementally or through branch by abstraction.

A Brief History of Revision Control

The grand-daddy of all version control systems was SCCS, written in 1972 by Marc J. Rochkind at Bell Labs. From it evolved most of the venerable open source version control systems, all still in use: RCS, CVS, and Subversion.[1] Of course there are many commercial tools on the market, each with its own approach to helping software developers manage collaboration. The most popular of these are Perforce, StarTeam, ClearCase, AccuRev, and Microsoft Team Foundation System.

The evolution of revision control systems has not slowed, and currently there is an interesting movement toward distributed version control systems. DVCSs were created to support the working patterns of large open source teams, such as the Linux kernel development team. We'll look at distributed version control systems in a later section.[2]

Since SCCS and RCS are so rarely used today, we won't discuss them here; dedicated VCS junkies can find plenty of information online.

CVS

CVS stands for Concurrent Versions System. "Concurrent" in this context means that multiple developers can work at the same time on the same repository. CVS is an open source wrapper implemented on top of RCS,[3] which provides extra features such as a client-server architecture and more powerful branching and tagging facilities. Originally written in 1984–1985 by Dick Grune and made publicly available in 1986 as a set of shell scripts, it was ported to C in 1988 by Brian Berliner. For many years, CVS was the best known and most popular version control system in the world, mainly because it was the only free VCS.

CVS brought a number of innovations both to versioning and to the software development process. Probably the most important of these is that the default

---

1. While the distinction between open source and commercial systems is important for your freedoms as a consumer, it is worth noting that Subversion is maintained by a commercial organization, Collabnet, which provides paid support.
2. For a humorous look at the major open source version control systems, see [bnb6MF].
3. RCS, like SCCS, only works on local filesystems.

behavior of CVS is not to lock files (hence "concurrent")—in fact, this was the principal motivation for CVS' development.

Despite its innovations, CVS has many problems, some of which are due to its inheriting a per-file change tracking system from RCS.

- Branching in CVS involves copying every file into a new copy of the repository. This can take a long time and use a lot of disk space if you have a big repository.

- Since branches are copies, merging from one branch into another can give you lots of phantom conflicts, and does not automatically merge newly added files from one branch into another. There are workarounds, but they are time-consuming, error-prone, and altogether thoroughly unpleasant.

- Tagging in CVS involves touching every file in the repository—another time-consuming process in large repositories.

- Check-ins to CVS are not atomic. This means that if your check-in process gets interrupted, your repository will be left in an intermediate state. Similarly, if two people try to check in at the same time, the changes from both sources may be interleaved. This makes it hard to see who changed what, or to roll back one set of changes.

- Renaming a file is not a first-class operation: You have to delete the old file and add a new one, losing the revision history in the process.

- Setting up and maintaining a repository is hard work.

- Binary files are just blobs in CVS. It makes no attempt to manage changes to binary files, so disk usage is inefficient.

Subversion

Subversion (SVN) was designed to be "a better CVS." It fixes many of CVS' problems, and in general can be used as a superior replacement to CVS in any situation. It was designed to be familiar to users of CVS, and retains essentially the same command structure. This familiarity has helped Subversion rapidly replace CVS in application software development.

Many of the good qualities of SVN derive from abandoning the format common to SCCS, RCS, and their derivatives. In SCCS and RCS, files are the unit of versioning: There is a file in the repository for every file checked in. In SVN, the unit of versioning is the *revision*, which comprises a set of changes to the files in a set of directories.[4] You can think of each revision as containing a snapshot of all the files in the repository at that time. In addition to describing changes to files,

---

4. We prefer the more general term "change set" to "revision," but Subversion exclusively uses "revision."

deltas can include instructions for copying and deleting files. In SVN, every commit applies all changes atomically and creates a new revision.

> Subversion provides a facility known as "externals" which allows you to mount a remote repository to a specified directory in your repository. This facility is useful if your code depends on some other codebase. Git offers a similar facility called "submodules." This provides a simple and cheap way to manage dependencies between components in your system, while still maintaining one repository per component. You can also use this method to separate your source code and any large binaries (compilers, other parts of your toolchain, external dependencies) into separate repositories, while still enabling users to see the links between them.

One of the most important characteristics of Subversion's repository model is that revision numbers apply globally to the repository rather than to individual files. You can no longer talk about an individual file moving from revision 1 to revision 2. Instead, you would want to know what happened to a particular file when the repository changed from revision 1 to revision 2. Subversion treats directories, file attributes, and metadata the same way it treats files, which means that changes to these objects can be versioned in the same way as changes to files.

Branching and tagging in Subversion are also much improved. Instead of updating each individual file, Subversion leverages the speed and simplicity of its copy-on-write repository. By convention, there are three subdirectories in every Subversion repository: trunk, tags, and branches. To create a branch, you simply create a directory with the branch name under the branches directory, and copy the contents of trunk at the revision you want to branch from to the new branch directory you just created.

The branch you just created is thus simply a pointer to the same set of objects that the trunk points to—until the branch and trunk begin to diverge. As a result, branching in Subversion is an almost constant-time operation. Tags are handled in exactly the same way, except they are stored under a directory called tags. Subversion does not distinguish between tags and branches, so the difference is simply a convention. If you want, you can treat a tagged revision as a branch in Subversion.

Subversion also improves on CVS by keeping a local copy of the version of every file as it existed when you last checked it out from the central repository. This means that many operations (for example, checking what you have changed in your working copy) can be performed locally, making them much faster than in CVS. They can even be done when the central repository is not available, which makes it possible to continue working while disconnected from the network.

However, the client-server model still makes some things difficult:

- You can only commit changes while online. This might sound obvious, but one of the main advantages of distributed version control systems lies in the fact that checking in is an operation separate from sending your changes to another repository.

- The data that SVN uses to track changes on local clients is stored in .svn directories in each folder in the repository. It is possible to update different directories on your local system to different revisions, and even to different tags or branches. While this may be desirable, in some cases it can lead to confusion and even errors.

- While server operations are atomic, client-side operations are not. If a client-side update is interrupted, the working copy can end up in an inconsistent state. Generally, this is fairly easy to fix, but in some cases it is necessary to delete whole subtrees and check them out again.

- Revision numbers are unique in a given repository, but not globally unique across different repositories. This means, for example, that if a repository is broken into smaller repositories for some reason, the revision numbers in the new repositories will not bear any relationship to the old ones. While this may sound like a small thing, it means that SVN repositories cannot support some features of distributed version control systems.

Subversion certainly represents a great advance over CVS. More recent versions of Subversion have features such as merge tracking which make it approach commercial tools like Perforce in feature-richness, if not in performance and scalability. However, when compared to the new crop of distributed version control systems such as Git and Mercurial, it begins to show the limitations imposed by its original inspiration to be "a better CVS." As Linus Torvalds notably said, "There is no way to do CVS right" [9yLX5I].

Nevertheless, if you are comfortable with the limitations of a centralized version control system, Subversion may be good enough for you.

Commercial Version Control Systems

The world of software tools moves fast, so this section is likely to go out of date. Check http://continuousdelivery.com for the most up-to-date information. At the time of writing, the only commercial VCSs that we are able to wholeheartedly recommend are:

- *Perforce.* Superior performance, scalability, and excellent tool support. Perforce is used in some truly huge software development organizations.

- *AccuRev.* Offers ClearCase-like ability to do stream-based development without the crippling administrative overhead and poor performance associated with ClearCase.

- *BitKeeper.* The first truly distributed version control system, and still the only commercial one.

Microsoft's Team Foundation Server (TFS) may be your default choice if you use Visual Studio—its tight integration is perhaps its only distinction. Otherwise, there is no good reason to use its source control offering, since it is essentially an inferior knock-off of Perforce. Subversion wins over TFS hands down. We strongly suggest that you avoid ClearCase, StarTeam, and PVCS wherever possible. Anybody still using Visual SourceSafe should immediately migrate to a tool which doesn't corrupt its database (a big no-no in a version control system) in quite so many situations[5] [c5uyOn]. For an easy migration path, we'd suggest SourceGear's excellent product Vault (TFS also offers an easy migration path, but we cannot recommend it).

Switch Off Pessimistic Locking

If your version control system supports optimistic locking, in which editing a file in your local working copy doesn't prevent others from editing it in theirs, you should use it. Pessimistic locking, in which you must obtain an exclusive lock on a file in order to edit it, may seem like a good way to prevent merge conflicts. However, in practice it reduces the efficiency of the development process, especially in larger teams.

Version control systems that take the pessimistic lock approach deal in terms of ownership. The pessimistic locking strategy ensures that only one person can work on any given object at any time. If Tom attempts to acquire a lock on component A while Amrita has it checked out of revision control, he will be sent packing. If he attempts to commit a change without first acquiring the lock, the operation will fail.

Optimistic lock systems work in a completely different manner. Instead of controlling access, they work on the assumption that most of the time, people won't be working on the same thing, and so allow free access for all users of the system to all objects under their control. These systems track changes to the objects under their control, and when the time comes to commit changes, they use algorithms to merge the changes. Usually the merging is completely automatic, but if the revision control system detects a change that it cannot merge automatically, it will highlight the change and ask for help from the person committing the change.

The way optimistic lock systems work usually varies depending on the nature of the content they are managing. For binary files, they tend to ignore deltas, and just take the last change submitted. However, their power lies in the way they deal with source code. For such objects, optimistic lock systems often assume

---

5. Indeed VSS recommends that you run a database integrity checker at least once a week when running VSS [c2M8mf].

that a single line within a file is a sensible unit of change. So if Ben works on component A and changes line 5 while, simultaneously, Tom is working on component A and changes line 6, after both commit the revision control system will keep Ben's line 5 and Tom's line 6. If both decide to change line 7, and Tom checks in first, Ben will be prompted by the version control system to resolve the resulting merge conflict when he makes his check-in. He will be asked to either keep Tom's change, keep his own, or manually edit them together to keep the important bits of both.

For people accustomed to the pessimistic lock revision control systems, optimistic lock systems sometimes look, well, hopelessly optimistic. "How can they possibly work?" Actually, they work surprisingly well, in many respects significantly better than pessimistic locking.

We have heard users of pessimistic locking systems express fears that users of optimistic locking systems will spend all of their time resolving merge conflicts, or that the automated merging will result in code that doesn't execute or even compile. These fears are simply not realized in practice. Merge conflicts do happen—on large teams they happen fairly frequently—but usually nearly all of them are fixed in a matter of seconds rather than minutes. They only take longer than that if you ignore our earlier recommendation and don't commit changes frequently enough.

The only time when pessimistic locking makes sense is for binary files, such as images and documents. In this case, it's impossible to merge the results meaningfully, so pessimistic locking is a reasonable approach. Subversion allows you to lock files on demand, and also to apply a property, `svn:needs-lock`, to such files to enforce pessimistic locking.

Pessimistic systems often force development teams to allocate behavior by component to avoid lengthy delays caused by waiting for access to the same code. The flow of creativity—a natural and essential part of the development process—is frequently interrupted by the need to check out a file that the developer hadn't realized would be needed. They also make it almost impossible to make changes that affect a large number of files without inconveniencing many other users. On large teams working off mainline, it is virtually impossible for teams to refactor with pessimistic locking switched on.

Optimistic locking imposes fewer constraints on the development process. The version control system doesn't impose any strategy on you. Overall, it feels significantly less intrusive and lighter-weight in use, without losing any flexibility or reliability and with a great increase in scalability, particularly for large, distributed teams. If your revision control system has the option, pick optimistic locking. If it doesn't, consider migrating to a revision control system that does.

Branching and Merging

The ability to create branches, or streams, in a codebase is a first-class feature of every version control system. This operation creates a replica of the chosen baseline within the version control system. This replica can then be manipulated in the same way as (but independently from) the original, allowing the two to diverge. The main purpose of branches is to facilitate parallel development: the ability to work on two or more work streams at the same time without one affecting the other. For example, it is common to branch on release, allowing for ongoing development on mainline and bugfixing in the release branch. There are several other reasons why teams may choose to branch their code.[6]

- **Physical:** branching of the system's physical configuration—branches are created for files, components, and subsystems.

- **Functional:** branching of the system's functional configuration—branches are created for features, logical changes, both bugfixes and enhancements, and other significant units of deliverable functionality (e.g., patches, releases, and products).

- **Environmental:** branching of the system's operating environment—branches are created for various aspects of the build and runtime platforms (compilers, windowing systems, libraries, hardware, operating systems, etc.) and/or for the entire platform.

- **Organizational:** branching of the team's work efforts—branches are created for activities/tasks, subprojects, roles, and groups.

- **Procedural:** branching of the team's work behaviors—branches are created to support various policies, processes, and states.

These categories aren't mutually exclusive, but they provide an insight into the reasons why people branch. Of course, you could create branches across several dimensions at the same time; this is fine if the branches never have to interact with each other. However, this is normally not the case—usually we have to take a set of changes from one branch and copy it to another branch in a process known as merging.

Before we get on to merging, it is worth thinking about the problems that branching creates. In most cases where you branch, your entire codebase is going to evolve separately in each branch—including test cases, configuration, database scripts, and so forth. First of all, it highlights the imperative of keeping absolutely everything in version control. Before you start branching your codebase, make sure that you're ready—ensure you have absolutely everything you need to build your software in version control.

---

6.   Taken from Appleton et al., 1998 [dAI5I4].

> **Version Control Horror Stories: #1**
>
> By far the most common reason to branch is functional. However, creating branches for a release is just the beginning. One large network infrastructure provider we worked with had branches for every major customer of their product. They also had subbranches for each bugfix and new feature. Version numbers for their software went *w.x.y.z* where *w* was a major version, *x* was a release, *y* was a customer identifier, and *z* was a build. We were called in because it took them 12–24 months to make a major release. One of the first problems we spotted was that their tests were in a separate version control repository from their code. As a result, they had a really hard time working out which tests applied to which build. This, in turn, prevented them from adding more tests to their codebase.

Branching and streaming may seem like a great way to solve many problems affecting the process of software development on large teams. However, the requirement to merge branches means it's important to think carefully before branching and to make sure you have a sensible process to support it. In particular, you need to define a policy for each branch describing its role in the delivery process and prescribing who is allowed to check into it and under what circumstances. For example, a small team might have a mainline which all developers can check into and a release branch that only the testing team is able to approve changes to. The testing team would then be responsible for merging bugfixes into the release branch.

In a larger and more heavily regulated organization, each component or product might have a mainline that developers check into, and integration branches, release branches, and maintenance branches that only operations personnel are authorized to make changes to. Getting changes into these branches might require creating change requests and having the code pass a set of tests (manual or automated). There will be a promotion process defined, so that, for example, changes must go from mainline to the integration branch before they can be promoted to the release branch. Code line policies are discussed in more detail in Berczuk (2003), pp. 117–127.

Merging

Branches are like the infinitude of universes postulated by the many-worlds interpretation of quantum mechanics. Each one is completely independent and exists in blissful ignorance of the others. However, in real life, unless you are branching for releases or for spikes, you will reach a point where you need to take the changes you have made in one branch and apply them to another. Doing this can be very time-consuming, although pretty much every VCS on the market has some functionality to make it easier, and distributed VCSs make merging branches with no conflicts relatively straightforward.

The real problem arises when two different and conflicting changes have been made in the two branches that you want to merge. Where changes literally overlap each other, your revision control system will detect them and warn you. However, your conflicts may just be differences in intent which are missed by the revision control system and "merged" automatically. When a long time passes between merges, merge conflicts are often symptoms of conflicting implementations of functionality, leading to rewrites of large chunks of the code in order to harmonize the changes that have occurred in the two branches. It is impossible to merge such changes without knowing what the authors of the code intended—so conversations have to happen, perhaps weeks after the code being merged was originally written.

Semantic conflicts that are not caught by your version control system can be some of the most pernicious. For example, if Kate perform a refactoring that renames a class in one of her changes, and Dave introduces a new reference to the class in one of his changes, their merge will work just fine. In a statically typed language, this problem will be found when somebody tries to compile the code. In a dynamic language, it won't be found until run time. Much more subtle semantic conflicts can be introduced through merges, and without a comprehensive body of automated tests, you may not even catch them until a defect occurs.

The longer you leave things before merging the branches, and the more people you have working on them, the more unpleasant your merge is going to be. There are ways of minimizing this pain:

- You could create more branches to reduce the number of changes made to a given branch. For example, you could create a branch every time you start working on a feature; this is an example of "early branching." However, this means more work to keep track of all the branches, and you're just delaying the pain of having to do more merges.

- You could be parsimonious about creating branches, perhaps creating a branch per release. This is an example of "deferred branching." To minimize the pain of merging, you could merge often, which means the merges will be less unpleasant. However, you have to remember to do it at regular intervals—every day, for example.

In fact, there are many possible branching patterns, each with their own policies, advantages, and disadvantages. We'll explore some possible branching styles later on in this chapter.

Branches, Streams, and Continuous Integration

Keen readers will notice that there is a tension between using branches and continuous integration. If different members of the team are working on separate branches or streams, then by definition they're not continuously integrating. Perhaps the most important practice that makes continuous integration possible is that everybody checks in to mainline at least once a day. So if you merge your branch to (not just from) mainline once a day, you're OK. If you're not doing that, you're not doing continuous integration. Indeed, there is a school of thought that any work on a branch is, in the lean sense, waste—inventory that is not being pulled into the finished product.

It's not uncommon to see continuous integration basically ignored and people branching promiscuously, leading to a release process that involves many branches. Our colleague Paul Hammant provided the example in Figure 14.1 from a project he worked on.

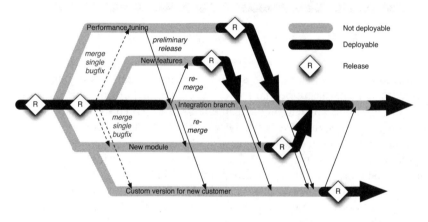

Figure 14.1   *A typical example of poorly controlled branching*

In this example, branches are created for various projects that occur as part of the program of work to develop the application. Merges happen back to trunk (or the "integration branch," as it's referred to here) fairly irregularly, and when they do happen, they tend to break it. As a result, trunk stays broken for long periods of time until the "integration phase" of the project prior to release.

The problem with this, unfortunately fairly typical, strategy is that the branches tend to stay in an undeployable state for large amounts of time. Furthermore, it is usually the case that branches have soft dependencies on one other. In the example given, every branch needs to take bugfixes from the integration branch, and every branch takes performance fixes from the performance tuning branch. The branch for the custom version of the application is a work in progress that doesn't become deployable for an extended period of time.

Keeping track of branches, working out what to merge and when, and then actually performing these merges consumes significant resources, even with the merge point tracking facilities provided by tools like Perforce or Subversion. Even after this is done, the team still has to get the codebase into a deployable state—the exact problem that continuous integration is supposed to solve.

A more manageable branching strategy—our strong recommendation, and arguably the industry standard—is to create long-lived branches only on release, as shown in Figure 14.2.

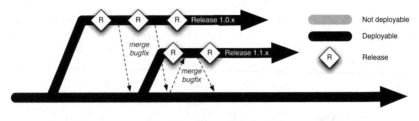

Figure 14.2   *Release branching strategy*

In this model, new work is always committed to the trunk. Merging is only performed when a fix has to be made to the release branch, from which it is then merged into mainline. Critical bugfixes might also be merged from mainline into release branches. This model is better because the code is always ready to be released, and the releases are therefore easier. There are fewer branches, so much less work has to be done merging and keeping track of the branches.

You may be concerned that not branching will hinder your ability to create new features without affecting other people. How can you perform a large restructuring without creating a new branch to isolate the work? We addressed this at length in the previous chapter, in the "Keeping Your Application Releasable" section on page 346.

The incremental approach certainly requires more discipline and care—and indeed more creativity—than creating a branch and diving gung-ho into re-architecting and developing new functionality. But it significantly reduces the risk of your changes breaking the application, and will save you and your team a great deal of time merging, fixing breakages, and getting your application into a deployable state. Such activity tends to be very hard to plan, manage, and track, making it ultimately much more costly than the more disciplined practice of developing on mainline.

If you work in medium or large teams, you may be shaking your head skeptically at this point. How is it possible to work on a large project without having people branch? If 200 people are checking in every day, that's 200 merges and 200 builds. Nobody is going to get any work done—they will spend all of their time merging instead!

In practice, even if everybody is working in one huge codebase, things can work with large teams. Two hundred merges are fine, provided everyone is working in a different area of the code and each change is small. On a project that large, if several developers routinely touch the same bits of code, that indicates that the codebase is poorly structured, with insufficient encapsulation and high coupling.

Things are much, much worse if merges are left until the end of the release. By that point, it is practically guaranteed that every branch will have merge conflicts with every other. We have seen projects where the integration phase *began* with weeks of trying to resolve merge conflicts and get the application into a state where it could even be run. Only then could the *testing* phase of the project even get off the ground.

The correct solution for medium and large teams is to split up your application into components and ensure there is loose coupling between components. These are the properties of well-designed systems. A consequence of taking this incremental approach to merging, in which the application is always kept working on mainline, is the gentle, subtle pressure it applies to make the design of your software better. Integrating the components into a working application is then a complex and interesting problem in its own right, which we explored in the previous chapter. However, it is an infinitely superior way to solve the problem of developing large applications.

It's worth saying again: You should never use long-lived, infrequently merged branches as the preferred means of managing the complexity of a large project. Doing so stores up trouble for when you come to try and deploy or release your application. Your integration process will be an extremely high-risk exercise that will be unpredictable, costing you considerable time and money. Any version control system vendor telling you that all you have to do is use their merge tools to solve your problem is simply being economical with the truth.

Distributed Version Control Systems

In the last few years, distributed version control systems (DVCSs) have become increasingly popular. Several powerful open source DVCSs exist, such as Git [9Xc3HA] and Mercurial. In this section, we'll examine what is special about DVCSs and how to use them.

What Is a Distributed Version Control System?

The fundamental design principle behind a DVCS is that each user keeps a self-contained, first-class repository on their computer. There is no need for a privileged "master" repository, although most teams designate one by convention (otherwise it is impossible to do continuous integration). From this design principle, many interesting characteristics follow.

- You can start using a DVCS in a few seconds—just install it, and commit your changes into a local repository.

- You can pull updates individually from other users without them having to check their changes into a central repository.

- You can push updates to a selected group of users without everyone being forced to take them.

- Patches can effectively propagate through networks of users, making it much easier to approve or reject individual patches (a practice known as *cherry-picking*.

- You can check your changes into source control while you are working offline.

- You can commit incomplete functionality regularly to your local repository to check point without affecting other users.

- You can easily modify, reorder, or batch up your commits locally before you send changes to anybody else (this is known as *rebasing*).

- It's easy to try out ideas in a local repository without the need to create a branch in a central repository.

- Due to the ability to batch check-ins locally, the central repository doesn't get hit so often, making DCVSs more scalable.

- Local proxy repositories are easily established and synchronized, making it easy to provide high availability.

- Since there are many copies of the full repository, DCVSs are more fault-tolerant, although master repositories should still be backed up.

If you think that using a DVCS sounds rather like everyone having their own SCCS or RCS, you are right. Where distributed version control systems differ from the approaches in the previous section is in the way they handle multiple users, or concurrency. Instead of using a central server with a version control system on it to ensure that several people can work on the same branch of the codebase at the same time, it takes the opposite approach: Every local repository is effectively a branch in its own right, and there is no "mainline" (Figure 14.3).

Much of the work that goes into the design of a DVCS is spent on making it easy for users to share their changes with each other. As Mark Shuttleworth, founder of Ubuntu's parent company Canonical, notes, "The beauty of distributed version control comes in the form of spontaneous team formation, as people with a common interest in a bug or feature start to work on it, bouncing that work between them by publishing branches and merging from one another. These teams form more easily when the cost of branching and merging is lowered, and taking this to the extreme suggests that it's very worthwhile investing in the merge experience for developers."

This phenomenon is especially visible with the advent of GitHub, BitBucket, and Google Code. Using these sites, it's easy for developers to make a copy of an existing project's repository, make a change, and then make their changes easily available to other users who might be interested in them. The maintainers

Implemented the stage history page.	H	2008-04-23 12:
Added the pipeline history page.	H	2008-04-23 12:
change localhost to copy data from server/t	ricky	2008-04-23 16:
fix build by reverting back to Prototype.js versi	ricky	2008-04-23 15:
Fixed the failed build.	Tian Yue <ytian@thoughtwo	2008-04-22 19:
Merge and upgrade database template	LYH & GL	2008-04-22 18:
rename pipeline- to stage- for the pipeline_plan_li	ricky	2008-04-22 18:
Automated merge with http://cruise@bjcruise.tho	tin & ricky	2008-04-22 17:
Automated merge with http://cruise@bjcruise.1	HK	2008-04-22 17:
Refactored the Selenium test and add the P	HK	2008-04-22 17:
minor fix to vm template	tin & ricky	2008-04-22 17:
merge	ricky & tin	2008-04-22 17:
refactor and rename pipeline.js; added white	ricky & tin	2008-04-22 17:
Added pauseCause and pauseBy to pipelin	LYH & GL	2008-04-22 18:
Automated merge with http://cruise@bjcruie	GL	2008-04-22 16:
Automated merge with http://cruise@bjcruie	GL	2008-04-22 16:
Display nothing rather than ... when build dc	GL	2008-04-22 16:
merge	ricky & tin	2008-04-22 16:
Automated merge with http://cruise@bjcruie	H & C	2008-04-22 15:
Return 404 when specified tab dosen't exist	LYH & GL	2008-04-22 15:
Automated merge with http://cruise@bjcruie	C & H	2008-04-22 15:
Automated merge with http://cruise@bjcruise.1	GL & LYH	2008-04-22 15:
Fixed the UI issue when ErrorBuildCause h	GL & LYH	2008-04-22 15:

Figure 14.3   *Lines of development in a DCVS repository*

of the original project can see the changes and pull them back into their project's master repository if they like.

This represents a paradigm shift in collaboration. Instead of having to submit their patches to the project owner for committing back to the project's repository, people can now publish their own version for others to experiment with. This leads to much faster evolution of projects, much more experimentation, and faster delivery of features and bugfixes. If somebody does something clever, other people can and will use it. That means that commit access is no longer a bottleneck to people creating new functionality or fixing bugs.

A Brief History of Distributed Version Control Systems

For a number of years, the Linux kernel was developed without the use of source control. Linus Torvalds developed on his own machine and made the source available as tarballs which were rapidly copied to a vast number of systems worldwide. All changes were sent to him as patches, which he could easily apply and back out. As a result, he didn't need source control—neither for backing up his source code nor to allow multiple users to work on the repository at the same time.

However, in December 1999, the Linux PowerPC project began using BitKeeper, a proprietary distributed version control system which became available in 1998. Linus began to consider adopting BitKeeper for maintaining the kernel. Over the course of the following years, some of the maintainers of sections of the kernel began to use it. Eventually, in February 2002, Linus adopted BitKeeper, describing it as "the best tool for the job," despite not being an open source product.

BitKeeper was the first widely used distributed version control system, and it was built on top of SCCS. In fact, a BitKeeper repository consists simply of a set of SCCS files. In keeping with the philosophy of distributed version control systems, each user's SCCS repository is a first-class repository in its own right. BitKeeper is a layer on top of SCCS which allows users to treat deltas, or changes against a particular revision, as first-class domain objects.

Following BitKeeper, a number of open source DVCS projects started. The first of these was Arch, begun by Tom Lord in 2001. Arch is no longer maintained, and has been superseded by Bazaar. Today there are many competing open source DVCSs. The most popular and feature-rich of these are Git (created by Linus Torvalds to maintain the Linux kernel and used by many other projects), Mercurial (used by the Mozilla Foundation, OpenSolaris, and OpenJDK), and Bazaar (used by Ubuntu). Other open source DVCSs under active development include Darcs and Monotone.

Distributed Version Control Systems in Corporate Environments

At the time of writing, commercial organizations had been slow to adopt DVCSs. Apart from general conservatism, there are three obvious objections to the use of DVCSs in companies.

- Unlike centralized version control systems, which only store a single version of the repository on the user's computer, anyone who makes a copy of the local repository of a DVCS has its entire history.

- Auditing and workflow are more slippery concepts in the realm of DVCS. Centralized version control systems *require* users to check all their changes into a central repository. DVCSs allow users to send changes to each other, and even to change history in their local repository, without these changes being tracked in the central system.

- Git actually does allow you to change history. This may well be a red line in corporate environments subject to regulatory regimes, who will have to back up their repository regularly in order to keep a record of everything that has happened.

In practice, these considerations should not provide a barrier to corporate adoption in many cases. While users could, in theory, avoid checking in to the designated central repository, it makes little sense to do so because, given a continuous integration system, it is impossible to get builds based on your code without pushing changes. Pushing changes to your colleagues without checking in centrally is often more trouble than it's worth—except of course in the case where you need to, at which point having a DVCS is incredibly useful. As soon as you designate a central repository, all of the properties of a centralized version control system are available.

The thing to bear in mind is that with a DVCS, many workflows are possible with very little effort on the part of developers and administrators. Conversely, centralized VCSs can only support noncentralized models (such as distributed teams, the ability to share workspaces, and approval workflows) through adding complex features that subvert the underlying (centralized) model.

Using Distributed Version Control Systems

The main difference between distributed and centralized version control systems is that when you commit, you are committing to your local copy of the repository—effectively, to your own branch. In order to share your changes with others, there is an *additional* set of steps you need to perform. To do this, DVCSs have two new operations: pulling changes from a remote repository and pushing changes to it.

For example, here is a typical workflow on Subversion:

1. `svn up`—Get the most recent revision.

2. Write some code.

3. `svn up`—Merge my changes with any new updates to the central repository and fix any conflicts.

4. Run the commit build locally.

5. `svn ci`—Check my changes, including my merge, into version control.

In a distributed version control system, the workflow looks like this:

1. `hg pull`—Get the latest updates from the remote repository into your local repository.

2. `hg co`—Update your local working copy from your local repository.

3. Write some code.

4. `hg ci`—Save your changes to your local repository.

5. `hg pull`—Get any new updates from the remote repository.

6. `hg merge`—This will update your local working copy with the results of the merge, but will *not* check in the merge.

7. Run the commit build locally.

8. `hg ci`—This checks in the merge to your local repository.

9. `hg push`—Push your updates to the remote repository.

We are using Mercurial as our example here because the command syntax is similar to that of Subversion, but the principles are precisely the same with other DCVSs.

It looks a bit like Figure 14.4 (each box represents one revision with the arrows indicating a revision's parent).

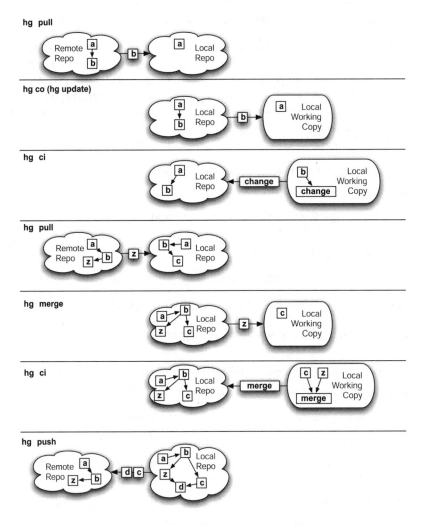

Figure 14.4 *DVCS workflow (diagram by Chris Turner)*

The merge process is a little safer than the Subversion equivalent because of step 4. This extra check-in step ensures that even if the merge is bad, you can step back to where you were before merging and try again. It also means that you have recorded a change representing just the merge, so that you can see precisely what the merge did and (assuming you haven't yet pushed your changes) undo it if you decide later that it was a poor one.

You can repeat steps 1–8 as many times as you like before executing step 9 to send your changes to the continuous integration build. You can even use a great feature available in Mercurial and Git known as rebasing. This lets you change the history of your local repository, so you can (for example) roll up all your changes into one single commit. This way you can continue to check in to save your changes, merge changes others have made, and of course run your commit suite locally without affecting other users. When the functionality that you are working on is complete, you can rebase and send all of your changes to the master repository as a single commit.

As for continuous integration, it works exactly the same with a DVCS as it would with a centralized version control system. You can still have a central repository, and it will still have your deployment pipeline implementation triggering off it. However, a DVCS gives you the option to try out several other possible workflows if you prefer. We discuss these in detail in the "Distributed Version Control Systems" section on page 79.

Until you commit changes from your local repository to the central repository that feeds your deployment pipeline, your changes aren't integrated. Committing changes frequently is a fundamental practice of continuous integration. For integration to take place, you must push changes to the central repository at least once a day, and ideally much more frequently than that. So, some of the benefits of DVCS can compromise the effectiveness of CI if misused.

Stream-Based Version Control Systems

IBM's ClearCase is not only one of the most popular version control systems in large organizations; it also introduced a new paradigm into version control systems: streams. In this section, we'll discuss how streams work and how to do continuous integration with stream-based systems.

What Is a Stream-Based Version Control System?

Stream-based version control systems such as ClearCase and AccuRev are designed to ameliorate the merge problem by making it possible to apply sets of changes to multiple branches at once. In the stream paradigm, branches are replaced by the more powerful concept of streams, which have the crucial distinction that they can inherit from each other. Thus, if you apply a change to a given stream, all of its descendent streams will inherit those changes.

Consider how this paradigm helps with two common situations: applying a bugfix to several versions of your application and adding a new version of a third-party library to your codebase.

The first situation is common when you have long-lived branches for your releases. Say you need to make a bugfix to one of your release branches. How do you apply that bugfix to all other branches of your code at the same time? Without stream-based tools, the answer is to manually merge it. This is a boring and error-prone process, especially when you have several different branches to apply the change to. With stream-based version control, you simply promote the change in your branch to the common ancestor of all the branches that need the change. Consumers of these branches can then update to get these changes, and create a new build which includes the fix.

The same consideration applies when managing third-party libraries or shared code. Say you want to update an image processing library to a new version. Every component will need to update to depend on the same version. With a stream-based VCS, you can check in the new version to an ancestor of every stream that needs to take the update, and all the streams inheriting from it will pick it up.

You can think of a stream-based version control system as being rather like a union filesystem, but with filesystems forming a tree structure (a connected directed acyclic graph). So, every repository has a root stream, from which all other streams inherit. You can create new streams based on any existing stream.

In the example in Figure 14.5, the root stream contains a single file, foo, at revision 1.2, and an empty directory. Both the release 1 and release 2 streams inherit from it. In the release 1 stream, the files present in the root stream can be found, as well as two new files: a and b. In the release 2 stream, two different files are present: c and d. foo has been modified and is now at version 1.3.

Two developers are working on the release 2 stream in their workspaces. Developer 1 is modifying file c, and developer 2 is modifying file d. When developer 1 checks in her changes, everybody working on the release 2 stream will see them. If file c is a bugfix that is required for release 1, developer 1 could promote file c to the root stream, in which case it would be visible from all streams.

So, making changes to one stream won't affect any other stream, unless those changes are promoted. Once promoted, they will be visible to every other stream that inherits from the original stream. It is important to bear in mind that promoting changes in this way doesn't change history. Rather, it's like adding an overlay with the new changes in it on top of the existing contents of the stream.

Development Models with Streams

In stream-based systems, developers are encouraged to develop in their own workspaces. This way, developers can perform refactorings, experiment with

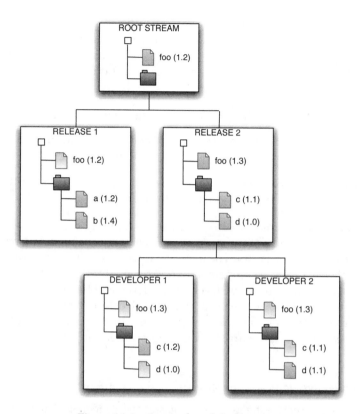

Figure 14.5 *Stream-based development*

solutions, and develop functionality without affecting other users. When they are ready, they can promote their changes to make them available to others.

For example, you might be working on a stream you've created for a particular feature. When the feature is complete, you can promote all the changes in that stream to the team's stream, which can be continuously integrated. When your testers want to test completed functionality, they could have their own stream, to which all functionality ready for manual testing can be promoted. Functionality that has passed testing can then be promoted to a release stream.

Thus, medium and large teams can work on multiple pieces of functionality at the same time without affecting each other, and testers and project managers can cherry-pick the functionality that they want. This is a real improvement when compared to the conundrum most teams face when they come to release. Typically, creating a release involves branching the entire codebase and then stabilizing the branch—but of course when you branch, there is no simple way to cherry-pick the bits you want (see the "Branch for Release" section on page 409 for more details on this problem and ways out of it).

Of course, in real life things are never quite so simple. Features are never really independent of one another and, especially if your team refactors as vigorously as it should, merge problems occur frequently as you promote large chunks of code between streams. So it is no surprise that integration issues are common as a result of:

- Complex merges, as different teams change shared code in different ways.

- Dependency management problems, when new features depend on code introduced in other features that haven't been promoted.

- Integration issues, as integration and regression tests break on the release stream because the code is in a new configuration.

These problems are made worse when you have more teams or more layers. This effect is often multiplicative, because a common reaction to having more teams is to create more layers. The intention is to isolate the impact of the teams on each other. One large company reported having five levels of streams: team level, domain level, architecture level, system level, and finally production level. Each change had to move through every level before getting to production. Needless to say, they faced significant problems getting releases out of the door as these issues regularly occurred upon every promotion.

> ### ClearCase and the Rebuilding-from-Source Antipattern
>
> One of the problems with the stream model of development is that promotion is done at the source level, not the binary level. As a result, every time you promote a change to a higher stream, you have to check out source and rebuild the binary. In many ClearCase shops, it is normal for the operations team to insist on deploying only binaries that have been rebuilt from scratch based on the source that is checked out from their release branch. Apart from anything else, this leads to a great deal of waste.
>
> Furthermore, it violates one of our key principles—that the binaries you release should be the same binaries that have been through the rest of your deployment pipeline, so you can be sure that what you release is what you tested. Apart from the fact that nobody has tested the binaries that came from the release stream, there is also a chance that differences could be introduced in the build process, perhaps by the operations team using a different minor revision of the compiler or a different version of some dependency. Such differences can lead to bugs in production that take days to track down.

It's important to remember that not committing to a shared mainline several times a day is inimical to the practice of continuous integration. There are ways to manage this, but they require a great deal of discipline—and still won't fully resolve the dilemma that medium and large teams find themselves in. The rule of thumb is to promote as often as possible, and run as many of the automated tests as frequently as you can on streams that are shared between developers. In this respect, this pattern is similar to branch by team, described later on in this chapter.

It's not all bad news though. The Linux kernel development team uses a process very similar to that described above, but each branch has an owner whose job it is to keep that stream stable, and of course the "release stream" is maintained by Linus Torvalds who is very choosy about what he pulls in to his stream. The way the Linux kernel team works, there is a hierarchy of streams with Linus' at the top, and changes are pulled by the stream owners, rather than pushed up to them. This is quite the opposite of the structure that exists in most organizations, where the operations or build teams have the unfortunate duty of trying to merge everything.

Finally, a note about this style of development: You don't need a tool with explicit stream support to do this. Indeed, the Linux kernel development team uses Git to manage their code, and the new breed of distributed version control systems such as Git and Mercurial are versatile enough to handle this kind of process—albeit without some of the fancy graphical tools that products like AccuRev bring to the table.

Static and Dynamic Views

ClearCase has a feature known as "dynamic views." This updates every developer's view the moment a file is merged into a stream from which their stream inherits. This means that developers automatically pick up any changes to their stream immediately. In the more traditional static view, changes won't be seen until the developer decides to update.

Dynamic views are a great way to get changes the moment they are committed, which helps to remove merge conflicts and eases integration—assuming developers check in frequently and regularly. However, there are problems both at a technical level and at a practical change management level. At the technical level, this feature is desperately slow: In our experience, it dramatically slows down access to the developer's filesystem. As most developers are frequently performing filesystem-intensive tasks like compilation, the cost is unacceptable. More practically, if you are in the middle of a piece of work and a merge is forced on you, it can break your train of thought and confuse your picture of the problem.

Continuous Integration with Stream-Based Version Control Systems

One of the purported benefits of stream-based development is to make it easier for developers to work on their own private streams, with the promise that merging will be easier later. From our perspective, this approach has a fundamental flaw: Everything is fine when changes are promoted regularly (i.e., more than once a day), but promoting that frequently tends to limit the benefits of the approach in the first place. If you are promoting frequently, simpler solutions work as well or better. If you don't promote frequently, your team is much more likely to run into problems when it is time to release. They will spend an indeterminate amount of time getting everything into shape, patching together functionality that everybody thought was working, and fixing bugs that were introduced by the complex merges. This is the problem that continuous integration is supposed to solve.

Tools like ClearCase certainly have powerful merging capabilities. However, ClearCase also has an entirely server-based model where everything from merging to tagging to deleting files requires a great deal of server activity. Indeed, promoting changes to a parent stream in ClearCase requires the committer to resolve any bad merges that take place on sibling streams.

Our ClearCase experience, and that of our colleagues, has been that with a repository of any size, operations that you would expect to be straightforward—such as checking in, deleting a file, and (especially) tagging—take an inordinate length of time. This alone adds a very significant cost to developing with these tools if you want to check in at all regularly. Indeed unlike Accurev, which has atomic commits, ClearCase requires tagging in order to be able to roll back to a known version of the repository. If you've got an experienced, talented team of ClearCase administrators helping out, your development process may be manageable. We are afraid that our experience has been universally bad. As a result, we have often taken the approach of using a tool such as Subversion within the development team, and doing a one-way automated merge to ClearCase periodically as a way of keeping everybody happy.

The most important feature of stream-based version control systems—the ability to promote change sets—also causes a bit of a problem when it comes to continuous integration. Consider an application which has several streams for various point releases. If a bugfix is promoted to the ancestor of all these streams, it will trigger a new build of every single descendant stream. This could use up all the capacity of your build system very quickly. On a team which has a number of streams active at any given time, and which promotes regularly, builds will be running continuously on every stream.

There are two options to deal with this problem: spend an awful lot of money on build hardware or virtual resources, or change the way builds are triggered. One useful strategy is to trigger builds only when a change is made to the stream that your deployment pipeline is associated with, not when changes are promoted to its ancestors. Of course, release candidates thus created should still pick up the latest version of the stream, including any changes promoted to its ancestors. Builds that are triggered manually would then also cause such changes to be included in the release candidate, and the infrastructure team will need to make sure that they trigger manual builds where appropriate to ensure that the relevant release candidates get created when necessary.

Develop on Mainline

In this and the following sections, we'll look at various patterns for branching and merging, their various advantages and disadvantages, and the circumstances under which they are appropriate. We'll begin with developing on mainline, because this method of development is often overlooked. In fact, it is an extremely effective way of developing, and the only one which enables you to perform continuous integration.

In this pattern, developers almost always check in to mainline. Branches are used only rarely. The benefits of developing on mainline include

- Ensuring that all code is continuously integrated

- Ensuring developers pick up each others' changes immediately

- Avoiding "merge hell" and "integration hell" at the end of the project

In this pattern, in normal development, developers work on mainline, committing code at least once a day. When faced with the need to make a complex change, be it developing new functionality, refactoring part of the system, making far-reaching capacity improvements, or rearchitecting layers of the system, branches are not used by default. Instead, changes are planned and implemented as a set of small, incremental steps that keep tests passing and so do not break existing functionality. This is described at length in the "Keeping Your Application Releasable" section on page 346.

Mainline development does not preclude branching. Rather, it means "that all ongoing development activities end up on a single codeline at some time" (Berczuk, 2003, p. 54). However, branches should only be created when they won't have to be merged back to mainline, such as when performing a release or spiking out a change. Berczuk (idem) quotes Wingerd and Seiward on the advantages of mainline development: "90% of SCM 'process' is enforcing codeline promotion to compensate for lack of a mainline" (Wingerd, 1998).

One of the consequences of mainline development is that not every check-in to mainline will be releasable. This may appear to be a knock-down refutation of the mainline development practice if you are used to branching for feature development or using stream-based development to promote changes up through several levels to a release stream. How do you manage large teams of developers working on multiple releases if you check every change in to mainline? The answer to this is good componentization of your software, incremental development, and feature hiding. This requires more care in architecture and development, but the benefits of not having an unpredictably long integration phase, where work from multiple streams has to be merged to create a viable release branch, far outweighs this effort.

One of the objectives of the deployment pipeline is to allow frequent check-ins to mainline on large teams which may result in temporary instabilities, while still allowing you to get rock-solid releases out of the door. In this sense, the deployment pipeline is antithetical to the source promotion model. The main advantage of the deployment pipeline lies in the rapid feedback you get on the effect of every change on the fully integrated application—something that is impossible in the source promotion model. The value of this feedback is that you know for sure exactly what the state of your application is at any time—you don't have to wait until the integration phase to discover that your application needs weeks or months of extra work to be releasable.

Making Complex Changes without Branching

In a situation where you want to make a complex change to the codebase, creating a branch on which to make changes so that you don't interrupt other developers' work may seem the simplest course of action. However, in practice, this approach leads to multiple long-lived branches which diverge substantially from mainline. Merging branches, towards release time, is almost always a complex process that takes an unpredictable amount of time. Each new merge breaks different pieces of existing functionality and is followed by a process to stabilize the mainline before the next merge occurs.

As a result, releases take much longer than planned, have less scope, and are of lower quality than desired. Refactoring is harder in this model, unless your codebase is loosely coupled and obeys the Law of Demeter, which means the technical debt also gets paid off very slowly. This rapidly leads to unmaintainable codebases that make it even harder to add new functionality, fix bugs, and refactor.

In short, you face all the problems that continuous integration is supposed to address. Creating long-lived branches is fundamentally opposed to a successful continuous integration strategy.

Our proposal is not a technical solution but a practice: Always commit to trunk, and do it at least once a day. If this seems incompatible with making far-reaching changes to your code, then we humbly submit that perhaps you haven't tried hard enough. In our experience, although it may sometimes take longer to implement a feature as a series of small, incremental steps that keep the code in a working state, the benefits are immense. Having code that is always working is fundamental—we can't emphasize enough how important this practice is in enabling continuous delivery of valuable, working software.

There are times when this approach won't work, but they really are very rare, and even then there are strategies that will mitigate the effects (see the "Keeping Your Application Releasable" section on page 346). However, even then it is better to avoid the need for doing this in the first place. Moving from A to B via incremental changes which are regularly checked in to mainline is almost always the right thing to do, so always put it on top of your list of options.

Version Control Horror Stories: #2

In one very large development project, we were forced to maintain a series of parallel branches. At one stage we had one release in production, which had some bugs (release 1). As these bugs were in production, it was imperative that they were fixed, so we had a small team dedicated to that task. We had a second branch in active development, with more than a hundred people working on it (release 2). This branch was intended for an imminent release, but had a series of fairly serious structural problems that we knew we had to address for the future health of the project. In order to prepare the ground for a more stable future release, we had another small team working on a fairly fundamental restructuring of the code (release 3).

Releases 1 and 2 fundamentally shared their overall structure to a significant degree. Release 3 rapidly diverged once its development began: It had to because of the technical debt that had accrued in the other two releases. Release 3's function was to repay the most costly parts of that technical debt.

It quickly became clear that we would have to be extremely disciplined in our approach to merging changes. The changes made in release 1 were less wide-ranging than the changes made in the others, but were vital production bugfixes. The volume of change being made by the release 2 development team would be overwhelming if not carefully managed, and the changes in release 3 were vital to the success of the project in the long term.

We established several things that helped us:

1. A clearly described merge strategy

2. A separate continuous integration server for each of these relatively long-lived branches

3. A small, dedicated merge team to manage the process, and in most cases perform the merge operations

Figure 14.6 shows a diagram of the strategy that we employed on this project. This is not the right strategy for every project but it was correct for us. Release 1 was in production, with only critical changes made to this branch of the code because there was another release imminent. Any change to release 1 was important; it was made there as quickly as possible and, if necessary, went through a release process to get the "fix" into production. All release 1 changes were then made to release 2 in the order that they were made in release 1.

Release 2 was under very active development. All changes, whether initiated from release 1 or made directly in release 2, were subsequently made to release 3. Again, these changes were made in order.

The merge team worked full-time to move changes between the three release branches, using the revision control system to maintain the order of change. They used the best code merge tools that we could find, but because of the widespread functional changes between releases 1 and 2, and the widespread structural changes between releases 2 and 3, often merging wasn't enough. In many cases, fixes to bugs in an earlier release disappeared in the new release 3 because we were improving things. In other cases, they had to be rewritten from scratch because while the problem remained in some form, the implementation was now wholly different.

This was difficult, frustrating work that the team became very good at. We rotated people through the team, but a core of developers decided to see it through because they understood how important the job was. At its peak, the merge team was four individuals working full-time for several months.

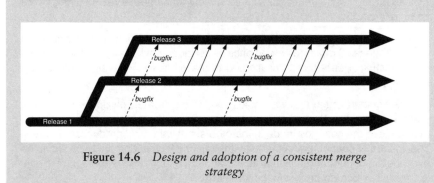

Figure 14.6   *Design and adoption of a consistent merge strategy*

Branching is not always so costly, but it always comes with some cost. If we had our time again, we would have chosen a different strategy, such as branching by abstraction to allow refactoring to occur while work continued on mainline.

Branch for Release

The one situation when it's always acceptable to create a branch is shortly before a release. Once the branch is created, testing and validation of the release is done from code on the branch, while new development is performed on mainline.

Creating a branch for release replaces the evil practice of the code freeze, in which checking in to version control is entirely switched off for days and sometimes weeks. By creating a release branch, developers can keep checking in to mainline, while changes to the release branch are made for critical bugfixes only. Branching by release is shown in Figure 14.2.

In this pattern:

- Features are always developed on mainline.

- A branch is created when your code is feature-complete for a particular release and you want to start working on new features.

- Only fixes for critical defects are committed on branches, and they are merged into mainline immediately.

- When you perform an actual release, this branch is optionally tagged (this step is mandatory if your version control system only manages changes on a per-file basis, like CVS, StarTeam, or ClearCase).

The scenario which motivates branching for release is as follows. The development team needs to start working on new features while the current release is being tested and prepared for deployment, and the testing team wants to be able to fix defects for the current release without affecting ongoing new feature development. In this scenario, it makes sense to logically separate work on new features from bugfixing on the branch. It is important to remember that bugfixes must ultimately be merged back into trunk; in general, it is wise to do this immediately after a bugfix is committed to a branch.

In product development, maintenance releases are needed to address issues that must be fixed before the next version is ready. For example, security problems need to be fixed in point releases. Sometimes the line between features and bugfixes can be hard to see, leading to quite complex development on a branch. Paying customers still using earlier releases of the software may not be willing (or able) to upgrade to the newest version, and will need some features to be implemented on the older branch. Teams should always aim to minimize this as much as possible.

This style of branching doesn't work very well on really large projects because it's hard for large teams or multiple teams to finish work on a release simultaneously. In this case, the ideal approach is to have a componentized architecture with a release branch for each component, so that teams can branch and move ahead on new work for their component while other teams are finishing their components. If this isn't possible, take a look at the branch by team pattern later on in this chapter and see if it makes more sense to apply that pattern. If you need to be able to cherry-pick features, take a look at the next pattern, branch by feature.

It is important, when branching for release, not to create further branches off the release branch. Branches for later releases should always be made off mainline, not off existing release branches. Creating branches off existing branches creates a "staircase" structure (Berczuk, 2003, p. 150) which makes it hard to find out what code is common between releases.

Once you achieve a certain frequency of releases, around once a week or so, it no longer makes sense to branch for release. In this scenario, it's cheaper and easier to simply put out a new version of the software instead of patching on the release branch. Instead, your deployment pipeline keeps a record of which releases were performed, when, and what revision in version control they came from.

Branch by Feature

This pattern is designed to make it easier for large teams to work simultaneously on features while keeping mainline in a releasable state. Every story or feature is developed on a separate branch. Only after a story is accepted by testers, it is merged to mainline so as to ensure that mainline is always releasable.

This pattern is generally motivated by the desire to keep the trunk always releasable, and therefore do all of the development on a branch so you don't interfere with other developers or teams. Many developers don't like to have their work exposed and publicly available until they are completely done. In addition, it makes version control history more semantically rich if each commit represent a complete feature or a complete bugfix.

There are some prerequisites for this pattern to work at all, let alone well.

- Any changes from mainline must be merged onto every branch on a daily basis.

- Branches must be short-lived, ideally less than a few days, never more than an iteration.

- The number of active branches that exist at any time must be limited to the number of stories in play. Nobody should start a new branch unless the branch representing their previous story is merged back to mainline.

- Consider having testers accept stories *before* they are merged. Only allow developers to merge to trunk once a story has been accepted.

- Refactorings must be merged immediately to minimize merge conflicts. This constraint is important but can be painful, and further limits the utility of this pattern.

- Part of the technical lead's role is to be responsible for keeping the trunk releasable. The tech lead should review all merges, perhaps in patch form. The tech lead has the right to reject patches that may potentially break the trunk.

Having many long-lived branches is bad because of the combinatorial problem of merging. If you have four branches, each of them will only be merging from mainline, not with each other. All four branches are diverging. It only takes two branches performing a refactoring in a tightly coupled codebase to bring the entire team to a halt when one of them merges. It bears repeating that branching is fundamentally antithetical to continuous integration. Even if you perform continuous integration on every branch, it doesn't actually address the problem of *integration*, since you're not in fact integrating your branch. The nearest you can get to true continuous integration is to have your CI system merge every branch into a hypothetical "trunk" that represents what the trunk would look like if everybody were to merge, and run all automated tests against that. This is a practice we describe in the context of distributed version control systems on page 79. Of course, such a merge would likely fail most of the time, which nicely demonstrates the problem.

Feature Crews, Kanban, and Branch by Feature

Branch by feature is often mentioned in the literature on the "feature crews" pattern [cfyl02] and by some advocates of the kanban development process. However, you can do both kanban development and feature crews without creating branches for each feature, and it works great (better, even, than using branch by feature). These patterns are completely orthogonal.

Our criticisms of branch by feature should not be interpreted as an attack on feature crews or the kanban development process—we have seen both of these development processes working extremely effectively.

Distributed version control systems (DVCSs) are designed with exactly this kind of pattern in mind, and make it absurdly easy to merge to and from trunk and create patches against head. Open source projects that use GitHub (for example) can achieve large gains in development speed by making it easy for users to branch a repository to add a feature and then make the branch available to a committer to pull from. However, there are some key attributes of open source projects that make them especially suitable for this pattern.

- Although many people can contribute to them, they are managed by a relatively small team of experienced developers who have the ultimate power to accept or reject patches.

- Release dates are relatively flexible, allowing the committers of open source projects a wide degree of latitude in rejecting suboptimal patches. While this can also be true of commercial products, it is not the norm.

Therefore, in the open source world this pattern can be very effective. It can also work for commercial projects where the core development team is small and experienced. It can work in larger projects, but only where the following conditions apply: The codebase is modular and well factored; the delivery team is split into several small teams, each with experienced leaders; the whole team is committed to checking in and integrating with mainline frequently; and the delivery team is not subject to undue pressure to release which might lead to suboptimal decision making.

We are cautious about recommending this pattern because it is so closely related to one of the most common antipatterns of commercial software development. In this evil, but extremely common, mirror universe, developers branch to create features. This branch stays isolated for a long time. Meanwhile, other developers are creating other branches. When it comes close to release time, all the branches get merged into trunk.

At this point, with a couple of weeks to go, the entire testing team that has been basically twiddling their thumbs finding the odd bug on trunk suddenly has a whole release worth of integration and system-level bugs to discover, as well as all the feature-level bugs which have not yet been found because nobody bothered to have the testers check the branches properly before they got integrated. The testers may as well not bother anyway, because the development team doesn't have the time to fix many of the bugs before the release date. Management, testers, and the development team will spend a week or four in a fury of reprioritizing and fighting to get critical bugs fixed before the whole sorry mess is dumped on the operations team to somehow get it into production or otherwise make it available to users—who are not thrilled to be on the receiving end of the resulting dog's dinner.

This force is very strong, and it will take an extremely disciplined team to avoid this problem. It is all too easy to use this pattern to defer the pain of making sure your application is in a releasable state. We have seen even small, experienced, ninja-level agile teams mess this pattern up, so there is little hope for the rest of us. You should always start with the "develop on mainline" pattern and then, if you want to try branching by feature, proceed rigidly according to the rules above. Martin Fowler wrote an article that demonstrates vividly the risks of branching by feature [bBjxbS], in particular its uneasy relationship with continuous integration. There is more on using DVCS with continuous integration in the "Distributed Version Control Systems" section on page 79.

Overall, you need to be pretty certain that the benefits of this pattern outweigh the considerable overhead, and that it will not lead to meltdown when release time arrives. You should also consider other patterns, such as branch by abstraction using components instead of branches to manage scaling, or just apply the solid engineering discipline to make every change small and incremental and check in to mainline regularly. All of these practices are described at length in the previous chapter.

It is worth emphasizing that branching by feature is really the antithesis of continuous integration, and all of our advice on how to make it work is only about ensuring that the pain isn't too horrible come merge time. It is much simpler to avoid the pain in the first place. Of course, like all "rules" in software development, there are exceptions where this may make sense, such as open source projects or small teams of experienced developers working with distributed version control systems. However, be aware that you are "running with scissors" when you adopt this pattern.

Branch by Team

This pattern is an attempt to address the problem of having a large team of developers working on multiple work streams while still maintaining a mainline that can always be released. As with branch by feature, the main intent of this pattern is to ensure that the trunk is always releasable. A branch is created for every team, and merged into trunk only when the branch is stable. Every merge to any given branch should immediately be pulled into every other branch.

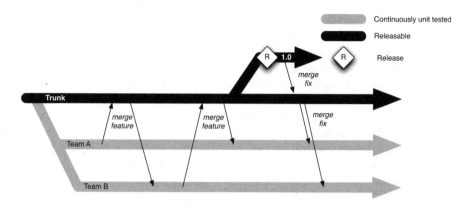

Figure 14.7   *Branch by team*

Here is the workflow for branching by team.[7]

1.   Create small teams, each working on its own branch.

2.   Once a feature/story is completed, the branch is stabilized and merged to trunk.

3.   Any changes on trunk get merged to every branch daily.

4.   Unit and acceptance tests are run on every check-in on the branch.

5.   All tests, including integration tests, are run on trunk every time a branch is merged into it.

When you have developers checking directly into trunk, it is hard to ensure that you can always release your work at regular intervals, as required by iterative development methods. If you have several teams working on stories, the trunk will almost always contain half-completed work that prevents the application from being released as is, unless you are disciplined about following the rules in the "Keeping Your Application Releasable" section on page 346. In this pattern, developers only check in to their team's branch. This branch is only merged to trunk when all the features being worked on are complete.

---

7.   As described in *Version Control for Multiple Agile Teams* by Henrik Kniberg [ctlRvc].

This pattern works when you have several small, relatively independent teams working on functionally independent areas of the system. Crucially, every branch needs to have an owner responsible for defining and maintaining its policy, including governing who checks in to the branch. If you want to check in to a branch, you must find one whose policy your check-in will not violate. Otherwise, you must create a new branch.

This pattern aims to maintain the trunk in a releasable state. However, each branch in this pattern faces exactly the same problem—it can only be merged into trunk when it is "stable." The actual policy considers a branch stable if it can be merged into trunk without breaking any of the automated tests, including acceptance and regression tests. Thus each branch effectively needs its own deployment pipeline, so that the team can determine which builds are good and thus which versions of the source code can be merged to mainline without violating the policy. Any such version should have had the latest version of mainline merged into it before the build is kicked off, so as to ensure that merging the branch to mainline will not cause the mainline build to fail.

From a CI perspective, this strategy has some drawbacks. One fundamental problem is that the unit of work under this strategy is scoped to a whole branch, not just a particular change. In other words, you can't merge a single change to mainline—you have to merge the whole branch, otherwise there is no way of knowing whether you have violated the mainline policy. If the team discovers a bug after it has merged to trunk, and there are other changes in the branch, they can't just merge the fix. In this situation, the team would either have to get the branch stable again, or create yet another branch just for the fixes.

Some of these problems can be mitigated through the use of a distributed version control system (DVCS). The Linux kernel development team uses a version of this pattern, keeping logical branches for different parts of the operating system—the scheduler and the networking stack, for example—in independent repositories. DVCSs have the ability to send selected changesets from one repository to another, a process known as cherry-picking. This means that rather than always merging the whole branch, you can merge just the features you want. Modern DVCSs also have sophisticated rebasing facilities so that you can retroactively apply patches to previous changesets and bundle them up. So if you discover a bug in your patch, you can add the bugfix to the patch, run this version through your pipeline to verify it won't break the mainline, and merge the additional patch. The use of a DVCS turns this pattern from one we would not recommend to one that we might recommend under certain circumstances, provided the teams merge to mainline on a regular basis.

If merges aren't sufficiently frequent, this pattern suffers from the same drawback as every pattern where the whole team does not check in directly to trunk: True continuous integration is compromised. This means there is always the risk of frequent, serious merge conflicts. For this reason, Kniberg recommends that every team merges to trunk whenever a story is completed, and merges from trunk every day. However, even with these provisos, there will always be a consistent overhead—possibly a substantial one—due to the need to keep every branch synchronized with mainline. If the branches diverge substantially from each other, by performing a refactoring on a tightly coupled codebase for example, teams will need to synchronize these changes as soon as possible to avoid merge conflicts. This, in turn, means performing refactorings against a stable version of the branch, so they can be merged to mainline immediately.

In practice, this pattern is not dissimilar to branch by feature. Its advantage is that there are fewer branches, so integration happens more frequently—at the team level at least. Its disadvantage is that branches diverge much more rapidly, because a whole team is checking in to each branch. Thus merges can become significantly more complex than they would be if branching by feature. The main risk is that teams are not sufficiently disciplined about merging changes to and from the mainline. Team branches will diverge rapidly from the mainline and from each other, and merge conflicts can quickly become extremely painful. Where we have seen this pattern in real life, this was, almost inevitably, the outcome.

As we have already described at length in the "Keeping Your Application Releasable" section on page 346, we recommend an incremental approach to development along with feature hiding as the best way to keep your application releasable even when you're in the middle of developing new features. In general, while it requires more discipline, it is considerably less risky than managing several branches, having to constantly merge, and not having the rapid feedback on the effects of your changes on the whole application that true continuous integration provides.

However, it if you are working on a large, monolithic codebase, this pattern (along with branch by abstraction) can form a useful part of a strategy of moving to loosely coupled components.

Version Control Horror Stories: #3

We worked on a large project where a subset of the team worked in India. At that time, the network infrastructure between the development sites was both slow and unreliable. The cost of each commit was high. We created a separate local repository for the team in India to which they committed changes frequently, using a normal continuous integration cycle. They ran a local copy of CruiseControl and so had a wholly independent, local CI cycle. At the end of each day, one lucky member of the Indian team merged the team's changes to mainline which was based in England, and ensured that the local repository was brought up-to-date with mainline so that development could resume afresh the following day.

Summary

Effective control of the assets that you create and depend upon in the course of software development is essential for the success of a project of any size. The evolution of version control systems and the configuration management practices that surround them is an important part of the history of the software industry. The sophistication of modern version control systems and their easy availability is a statement of their central importance to modern team-based software development.

The reason we spend so much time on this arguably tangential topic is twofold: Firstly, version control patterns are central to the way you design your deployment pipeline. Secondly, it has been our experience that poor version control practices are one of the most common barriers to fast, low-risk releases. Some of the powerful features of these version control systems can be applied in ways that endanger the chances of safe, reliable, low-risk software releases. Understanding the available features, picking the correct tools, and using them appropriately is an important attribute of a successful software project.

We have spent some time comparing different version control system paradigms: the standard centralized model, the distributed model, and the stream-based model. We believe that distributed version control systems in particular will continue to have a massive positive impact on the way software is delivered. However, it is still possible to create an efficient process using the standard model. For most teams, a more important consideration is which strategy to use for branching.

There is a fundamental tension between the desire for continuous integration and the desire to branch. Every time you make a decision to branch in a CI-based development system, you compromise to some degree. The question of which pattern to use is a choice that should be based on identifying the optimal process for your team and your software project. On one hand, an absolute view of CI says that every change should be committed as soon as possible to trunk. The trunk is always the most complete and up-to-date statement of the state of your system, because you will deploy from it. The longer the changes are kept separate from trunk—no matter what the technology is, or how sophisticated the merge tools are—the greater the risk that, when the eventual merge takes place, there will be a problem. On the other hand, there are factors, such as bad networks, slow builds, or convenience, that make it more efficient to branch.

This chapter has presented a series of options to cope with such situations in which it is more efficient for a development team to compromise CI to some extent. However, it is important that every time you branch, you recognize that there is a cost associated with it. That cost comes in increased risk, and the only way to minimize that risk is to be diligent in ensuring that any active branch, created for whatever reason, should be merged back to mainline daily or more frequently. Without this, the process can no longer be considered to be based on continuous integration.

As we have said, the only reasons to branch we can recommend without any caveats are for releases, for spiking, and *in extremis* when there is no other reasonable way to get your application to a point where it will be possible to make further changes by other methods.

Chapter 15

Managing Continuous Delivery

Introduction

This book is mainly aimed at practitioners. However, implementing continuous delivery involves more than just buying some tools and doing some automation work. It depends on effective collaboration between everyone involved in delivery, support from executive sponsors, and willingness of people on the ground to make changes. This chapter is written to provide guidance on how to make continuous delivery work within your organization. First, we present a maturity model for configuration and release management. Next, we will explore how to plan your project's lifecycle, including release. Then we describe an approach to risk management of build and release in software projects. Finally, we take a look at the common organizational risks and antipatterns involved in deployment, along with best practices and patterns to help you to avoid them.

Before we get started, we wanted to present the overall value proposition of continuous delivery. Continuous delivery is more than just a new delivery methodology. It is a whole new paradigm for running a business that depends on software. To understand why this is so, we need to examine a fundamental tension at the heart of corporate governance.

CIMA defines enterprise governance as "the set of responsibilities and practices exercised by the board and executive management with the goal of providing strategic direction, ensuring that objectives are achieved, ascertaining that risks are managed appropriately, and verifying that the organization's resources are used responsibly." It goes on to differentiate corporate governance, which is concerned with *conformance*—in other words, compliance, assurance, oversight, and responsible, transparent management—from business governance, concerned with the *performance* of the business and value creation.

On the one hand, the business wants to get valuable new software out of the door as fast as possible in order to keep increasing revenue. On the other hand,

417

people responsible for corporate governance want to ensure that the organization understands any risks that could lead to the business losing money or being shut down, such as violation of applicable regulations, and that processes are in place to manage these risks.

While everybody in the business ultimately has a shared goal, performance and conformance are forces that can often come into conflict. This can be seen in the relationship between development teams, who are under pressure to ship as quickly as possible, and operations teams who treat any change as a risk.

We contend that these two parts of the organization are not participating in a zero sum game. It is possible to achieve both conformance and performance. This principle is right at the heart of continuous delivery. The deployment pipeline is designed to achieve performance by ensuring the delivery teams get constant feedback on the production-readiness of their application.

It is also designed to help teams achieve conformance by making the delivery process transparent. Both IT and the business can try out the application at any time, perhaps to test some new feature, by self-servicing a deployment of the application to a UAT environment. For audit purposes, the pipeline provides a system of record as to exactly which versions of each application have been through which parts of the delivery process, and the ability to trace back from what's in every environment to the revision it came from in version control. Many of the tools in this space provide the facility to lock down who can do what, so that deployments can only be performed by authorized people.

The practices in this book, in particular incremental delivery and automation of the build, testing, and deployment process, are all designed to help manage the risk of releasing new versions of the software. Comprehensive test automation provides a high level of confidence in the quality of the application. Deployment automation provides the ability to release new changes and back out at the press of a button. Practices such as using the same process to deploy into every environment and automated environment, data, and infrastructure management are designed to ensure that the release process is thoroughly tested, the possibility for human error is minimized, and any problems—whether functional, nonfunctional, or configuration-related—are discovered well before release.

Using these practices, even large organizations with complex applications can deliver new versions of their software rapidly and reliably. That means not only that businesses can get a faster return on their investment, but that they can do so with reduced risks and without incurring the opportunity cost of long development cycles—or worse, delivering software that is not fit for purpose. To use an analogy with lean manufacturing, software that is not being delivered frequently is like inventory stored up in a warehouse. It has cost you money to manufacture, but is not making you any money—indeed, it is costing you money to store it.

A Maturity Model for Configuration and Release Management

In discussing the topic of governance, it is extremely useful to have a clear view of the objectives of organizational change. Over many years of working in consultancy—an occupation that gives an opportunity to see many different organizations and understand the detail of their working practices—we and our colleagues have distilled a model for evaluating the organizations that we work in. This model helps to identify where an organization stands in terms of the maturity of its processes and practices and defines a progression that an organization can work through to improve.

In particular, we have been careful to address all the roles involved in the delivery of software across an organization, and how they work together. Figure 15.1 shows the model.

Practice	Build management and continuous integration	Environments and deployment	Release management and compliance	Testing	Data management	Configuration management
Level 3 - Optimizing: Focus on process improvement	Teams regularly meet to discuss integration problems and resolve them with automation, faster feedback, and better visibility.	All environments managed effectively. Provisioning fully automated. Virtualization used if applicable.	Operations and delivery teams regularly collaborate to manage risks and reduce cycle time.	Production rollbacks rare. Defects found and fixed immediately.	Release to release feedback loop of database performance and deployment process.	Regular validation that CM policy supports effective collaboration, rapid development, and auditable change management processes.
Level 2 - Quantitatively managed: Process measured and controlled	Build metrics gathered, made visible, and acted on. Builds are not left broken.	Orchestrated deployments managed. Release and rollback processes tested.	Environment and application health monitored and proactively managed. Cycle time monitored.	Quality metrics and trends tracked. Non functional requirements defined and measured.	Database upgrades and rollbacks tested with every deployment. Database performance monitored and optimized.	Developers check in to mainline at least once a day. Branching only used for releases.
Level 1 - Consistent: Automated processes applied across whole application lifecycle	Automated build and test cycle every time a change is committed. Dependencies managed. Re-use of scripts and tools.	Fully automated, self-service push-button process for deploying software. Same process to deploy to every environment.	Change management and approvals processes defined and enforced. Regulatory and compliance conditions met.	Automated unit and acceptance tests, the latter written with testers. Testing part of development process.	Database changes performed automatically as part of deployment process.	Libraries and dependencies managed. Version control usage policies determined by change management process.
Level 0 – Repeatable: Process documented and partly automated	Regular automated build and testing. Any build can be re-created from source control using automated process.	Automated deployment to some environments. Creation of new environments is cheap. All configuration externalized / versioned.	Painful and infrequent, but reliable, releases. Limited traceability from requirements to release.	Automated tests written as part of story development.	Changes to databases done with automated scripts versioned with application.	Version control in use for everything required to recreate software: source code, configuration, build and deploy scripts, data migrations.
Level -1 – Regressive: processes unrepeatable, poorly controlled, and reactive	Manual processes for building software. No management of artifacts and reports.	Manual process for deploying software. Environment-specific binaries. Environments provisioned manually.	Infrequent and unreliable releases.	Manual testing after development.	Data migrations unversioned and performed manually.	Version control either not used, or check-ins happen infrequently.

Figure 15.1 *Maturity model*

How to Use the Maturity Model

The ultimate aim is for your organization to improve. The outcomes you want are:

- Reduced cycle time, so that you can deliver value to your organization faster and increase profitability.

- Reduced defects, so that you can improve your efficiency and spend less on support.

- Increased predictability of your software delivery lifecycle to make planning more effective.

- The ability to adopt and maintain an attitude of compliance to any regulatory regime that you are subject to.

- The ability to determine and manage the risks associated with software delivery effectively.

- Reduced costs due to better risk management and fewer issues delivering software.

We believe that this maturity model can act as a guide to help you achieve all of these outcomes. We recommend, as ever, that you apply the Deming cycle—plan, do, check, act.

1. Use the model to classify your organization's configuration and release management maturity. You may find that different parts of your organization achieve different levels in each of the different categories.

2. Choose an area to focus on where your immaturity is especially painful. Value stream mapping will help you identify areas that need improvement. This book will help you understand what each improvement brings to the table and how to implement it. You should decide which improvements make sense for your organization, estimate their costs and benefits, and prioritize. You should define acceptance criteria to specify the results that you expect and how they will be measured, so that you can decide if the changes were successful.

3. Implement the changes. First, create an implementation plan. It will probably make sense to begin with a proof of concept. If so, choose a part of your organization that is really suffering—these people will have the best motivation to implement change, and it is here that you will see the most dramatic change.

4. Once the changes have been made, use the acceptance criteria you created to measure if the changes had the desired effect. Hold a retrospective meeting of all stakeholders and participants to find out how well the changes were executed and where the potential areas for improvement are.

5. Repeat these steps, building upon your knowledge. Roll out improvements incrementally, and roll them out across your whole organization.

Organizational change is hard, and a detailed guide is beyond the scope of this book. The most important advice that we can offer is to implement change incrementally, and measure the impact as you go. If you try and go from level one to level five across your whole organization in one step, you will fail. Changing large organizations can take several years. Finding the changes that will deliver the most value and working out how to execute them should be treated scientifically: come up with a hypothesis, then test. Repeat, and learn in the process. No matter how good you are, it is always possible to improve. If something doesn't work, don't abandon the process; try something else.

Project Lifecycle

Every software development project is different, but it is not too hard to abstract common elements. In particular, we can usefully generalize the lifecycle of software delivery. Every application, like every team, has a narrative arc. It has become common to talk about teams passing through five phases: forming, storming, norming, performing, and mourning/reforming. In the same way, every piece of software goes through several phases. An initial high-level picture might include the following phases: identification, inception, initiation, development and deployment, and operation. We'll briefly go through these phases before moving on to a more detailed examination of how build and deployment engineering fits into the picture.

ITIL and Continuous Delivery

The Information Technology Infrastructure Library provides a framework for software service delivery that believe is broadly compatible with the approach to delivery we describe in this book. We share an overriding focus on delivering increased value to customers by making IT a strategic asset for the business. In the same way as ITIL focuses on services having *utility*, or fitness for purpose, and *warranty*, or fitness for use, we discuss systems meeting clearly defined functional and nonfunctional requirements.

However, ITIL has a much wider scope than this book. It aims to provide good practices for all stages of a service's lifecycle, from practices and funtions for managing IT strategy and the service portfolio right through to how to manage a service desk. In contrast, this book assumes that you already have a strategy in place, along with processes for managing it, and that you have some high-level idea of the services you want to provide. We focus primarily on the ITIL phase known as service transition, with some discussion of service operation (particularly in Chapter 11, "Managing Infrastructure and Environments").

In the context of ITIL, the majority of this book can be thought of as providing good practices for the release and deployment management and service testing and validation processes, including their relationship to the service asset and configuration management and change management processes. However, since we take a holistic view of delivery, what we discuss in the book also has implications for service design and service operation.

> The main difference between our approach and that of ITIL is our focus on iterative and incremental delivery and cross-functional collaboration. ITIL considers these things important from the point of view of service design and service operation, but it is somewhat neglected when service transition—particularly development, testing, and deployment—is discussed. We consider iterative and incremental delivery of valuable, high-quality software to be absolutely critical to the ability of businesses to create and maintain a competitive advantage.

Identification

Medium-sized and large organizations will have a governance strategy. Businesses will determine their strategic objectives, leading to programs of work being identified which will enable the business to achieve its strategic objectives. These programs are in turn broken down into projects.

Nevertheless, in our experience it is startlingly common to begin an IT program without a business case. That will likely lead to failure, because it is impossible to know what success looks like without a business case. You might as well be the Underpants Gnomes in South Park, whose strategy is

1. Collect underpants.

2. ?

3. Profit.

It is very hard to do requirements gathering, and impossible to objectively prioritize the requirements thus gathered, without a business case (this also applies to services that are provided internally). Even with it, you can be certain that the application or service you end up with will differ significantly from the solution you had in your head during the initial requirements gathering.

The other essential thing to have in place before you start gathering requirements is a list of stakeholders, the most important of whom is the business sponsor (known in PRINCE2 as the senior responsible owner). There should only be one business sponsor for each project or, inevitably, any reasonably sized project will collapse from political infighting long before it is finished. This business owner is known in Scrum as the product owner, and in other agile disciplines as the customer. However, in addition to the business owner, every project needs a steering committee of interested parties—in a corporation, this will include other executives and representatives of the users of the service; for a product, it may include high-profile or otherwise representative customers of the product. Other internal stakeholders of an IT project include the operations, sales, marketing, and support personnel, and of course the development and testing teams. All these stakeholders should be represented during the next phase of the project: inception.

Inception

This is most simply described as the phase before any production code is written. Typically, requirements are gathered and analyzed during this time, and the project is loosely scoped and planned. It can be tempting to dismiss this phase as being of low value, but even your hardcore agilista authors have learned from bitter experience that this phase needs to be carefully planned and executed for a software project to be successful.

There are many deliverables from an inception, some of which will vary depending on methodology and the type of project. However, most inceptions should include the following:

- A business case, including the estimated value of the project.

- A list of high-level functional and nonfunctional requirements (addressing in particular capacity, availability, service continuity, and security) with just enough detail to be able to estimate the work involved and plan the project.

- A release plan which includes a schedule of work and the cost associated with the project. In order to get this information, it is usual to estimate the relative size of the requirements, coding effort required, risk associated with each requirement, and a staffing plan.

- A testing strategy.

- A release strategy (more on this later).

- An architectural evaluation, leading to a decision on the platform and frameworks to use.

- A risk and issue log.

- A description of the development lifecycle.

- A description of the plan to execute this list.

These deliverables should contain enough detail that work can begin on the project, with the aim of having something delivered in a few months at most, and much less if possible. A reasonable maximum project horizon, in our experience, is about three to six months—with a preference for the lower limit. A go/no-go decision should be made following the inception process as to whether the project should go ahead, based on the estimated value of the project, estimated costs, and the predicted risks.

The most important part of an inception—the bit that ensures that the project has a chance of success—is getting all the stakeholders together face-to-face. That means developers, customers, operations people, and management. The conversations between these people, leading to a shared understanding of the problem to be solved and the way to solve it, are the real deliverables. The list above is designed to structure the conversations so that the important issues are discussed, risks are identified, and strategies to deal with them are put in place.

These deliverables should be written down, but since they are living documents, we expect that each will change throughout the project. To keep track of these changes in a reliable way—so that everyone can easily see what the current picture is—you should commit these documents into a version control system.

One word of warning: Every decision you make at this stage of a project is based on speculation, and will change. What you produce is a best guess, based on the small amount of information you have. Expending too much effort at this stage of the project—the stage when you know the least that you will ever know about it—is a mistake. These are essential planning discussions and direction setting, but expect to refine and redefine many of them as you go. Successful projects cope with change successfully. Those that attempt to avoid it often fail. Detailed planning, estimation, or design at this stage of a project are wasted time and money. Broad-based decisions are the only kind of decisions durable at this stage.

Initiation

Following inception, you should establish initial project infrastructure. This is the initiation phase that will typically last one or two weeks. The following list describes typical initiation stage activities.

- Making sure that the team (analysts and managers, as well as developers) has the hardware and software that they need to begin work

- Making sure that basic infrastructure is in place—such as an Internet connection, a whiteboard, paper and pens, a printer, food, and drinks

- Creating email accounts and assigning people permissions to access resources

- Setting up version control

- Setting up a basic continuous integration environment

- Agreeing upon roles, responsibilities, working hours, and meeting times (for example, stand-ups, planning meetings, and showcases)

- Preparing the work for the first week and agreeing on targets (not deadlines)

- Creating a simple test environment and test data

- A slightly more detailed look at the intended system design: exploring the possibilities is really the aim at this stage

- Identify and mitigate any analysis, development, and testing risks by doing spikes (throwaway implementations of a particular requirement designed as a proof of concept)

- Developing the story or requirement backlog

- Setting up the project structure and using the simplest possible story, the architectural equivalent of a "hello world," including a build script and some tests to get continuous integration under way

It is vitally important to assign enough time to comfortably complete these tasks. It is unproductive and demoralizing to attempt to start work if nobody has acceptance criteria for the initial requirements being developed, and if team members are using poorly provisioned computers with bad tools and flaky Internet access.

While this stage in the project is really targeted at getting the basic project infrastructure in place, and should not be treated as a true development iteration, it is extremely useful to use a real-world problem to get things working. Building a test environment when there is nothing to test, or setting up a version control system when there is nothing to store, is a sterile and inefficient way to start. Pick the simplest possible requirement that you can find that is, nevertheless, solving a real problem and establishing some initial directions in terms of design. Use this story to make sure that you can version-control the results properly, that you can run your tests in your CI environment, and that you can deploy the results to a manual test environment. The target is to get this story complete and demonstrable, and establish all of the supporting infrastructure, by the end of the initiation phase.

Once you're done, you can get started on actual development.

Develop and Release

Naturally, we would recommend an iterative and incremental process for developing and releasing software. The only time this might not be applicable is when you are working on a large defense project involving many parties—but even the space shuttle software was implemented using an iterative process.[1] Although many people agree on the benefits of an iterative process, we have often seen teams that claim to be doing iterative development but actually aren't. So it's worth reiterating what we consider to be the essential, basic conditions for an iterative process.

- Your software is always working, as demonstrated by an automated test suite including unit, component, and end-to-end acceptance tests that run every time you check in.

---

1.   ACM, 1984, vol. 27 issue 9.

- You deploy working software, at every iteration, into a production-like environment to showcase it to users (this is what makes the process incremental in addition to being iterative).

- Iterations are no longer than two weeks.

There are several reasons for using an iterative process:

- If you prioritize features with high business value, you may find that your software starts being useful long before the end of your project. There are often good reasons not to launch new software the moment that it has useful functionality—but there is no better way to turn worrying over the project's eventual success into excitement over the new features than a working system that people can use.

- You get regular feedback from your customer or sponsor on what works and what requirements need clarifying or changing, which in turn means that what you are doing is considerably more likely to be useful. Nobody knows what they really want at the beginning of a project.

- Things are only really done when the customer signs them off. Having regular showcases where this happens is the only remotely reliable way to track progress.

- Having your software working at all times (because you have to showcase it) instills discipline in your team that prevents problems such as long integration phases, refactoring exercises that break everything, and experiments that lose focus and go nowhere.

- Perhaps most importantly, iterative methods place an emphasis on having *production-ready* code at the end of each iteration. This is the only really useful measure of progress in software projects, and one that only iterative methods provide.

An often-cited reason *not* to do iterative development is when the project as a whole won't deliver any value until some huge quantity of features is complete. While this threshold may be real for many projects, the last point in our list above is especially applicable in this situation. When managing large projects that aren't developed iteratively, all measures of progress are subjective, and there is no way to quantify the project's actual progress. The nice charts you see in noniterative methods are based on estimations of time remaining and guesses at the risks and costs of later integration, deployment, and testing. Iterative development provides objective measures of the rate of progress based on the rate at which development teams produce working software that users agree is fit for purpose. Only working code that is production-ready, code that you can interact with, even if only in a UAT environment, provides any guarantee that any given feature is really finished.

Crucially, production-readiness also means that the software has had its nonfunctional requirements tested on a production-like environment with a production-sized data set. Any nonfunctional characteristics you care about, such as capacity, availability, security, and so forth, should be tested using a realistic load and usage pattern. These tests should be automated and run against every build of the software that passes the acceptance tests so that you know your software is always fit for use. We cover this in more detail in Chapter 9, "Testing Nonfunctional Requirements."

The keys to an iterative development process are prioritization and parallelization. Work is prioritized so that analysts can begin analyzing the most valuable features, feed work to developers, and thence to testers and on to a showcase to real users or their proxies. Using techniques from lean manufacturing, this work can be parallelized and the number of people working on each task altered to remove bottlenecks. This leads to a very efficient development process.

There are many approaches to iterative and incremental development. One of the most popular is Scrum, an agile development process. We have seen Scrum succeed on many projects, but we have also seen it fail. Here are the three most common reasons for failure:

- *Lack of commitment.* The transition to Scrum can be a scary process, especially for project leadership. Make sure that everybody meets regularly to discuss what is going on, and establish regular retrospective meetings to analyze performance and seek improvements. Agile processes rely on transparency, collaboration, discipline, and continuous improvement. The sudden wealth of useful information that appears when agile processes are implemented can thrust inconvenient truths, previously hidden, into the spotlight. The key is to realize that these issues were there all along. Now that you know about them, you can fix them.

- *Ignoring good engineering.* Martin Fowler, amongst others, has described what happens if people following Scrum think that you can ignore technical practices like test-driven development, refactoring, and continuous integration [99QFUz]. A codebase mangled by junior developers won't be automatically fixed by any development process alone.

- *Adapting until the process is no longer an agile one.* It is common for people to "adapt" agile processes into something they think will work better in their particular organization. Agile processes are designed to be tailored to meet the needs of individual projects, after all. However, the elements of agile processes often interact in subtle ways, and it is very easy to misunderstand where the value lies, particularly for people with no background in these iterative processes. We can't emphasize enough how important it is to start by assuming that what is written is correct, and first follow the process as written. Only then, once you have seen how it works, should you start adapting it to your organization.

This last point was so troubling to Nokia that they created a test to evaluate whether their teams were really doing Scrum. It is divided into two parts.

Are you doing iterative development?

- Iterations must be time-boxed to less than four weeks.[2]

- Software features must be tested and working at the end of each iteration.

- The iteration must start before the specification is complete.

Are you doing Scrum?

- Do you know who the product owner is?

- Is the product backlog prioritized by business value?

- Does the product backlog have estimates created by the team?

- Are there project managers (or others) disrupting the work of the team?

To clarify the last point, we believe project managers can play a useful role by managing risks, removing roadblocks such as a lack of resources, and facilitating efficient delivery. But there are some project managers who do none of these things.

Operation

Typically, the first release is not the last. What happens next very much depends on the project. The development and release phase may continue at full tilt, or the team might be reduced in size. If the project is a pilot, the opposite may happen and the team may grow.

An interesting aspect of a genuinely iterative and agile process is that in many ways, the operational phase of a project is not necessarily any different from the regular development phase. Most projects, as we said, don't stop at the point of first release, and will continue to develop new functionality. Some projects will have a series of maintenance releases, perhaps fixing unforeseen problems, perhaps tailoring the project to meet newly discovered user needs, perhaps as part of a rolling program of development. In all these cases, new features will be identified, prioritized, analyzed, developed, tested, and released. This is no different from the regular development phase of the project. In this respect, making these phases collapse together is one of the best ways to eliminate risk, and is at the core of continuous delivery as described in the rest of this book.

As we mentioned earlier in this section, it is very useful to pull the time of release to the earliest possible point that makes sense for any given system. The

---

2.   As we say above, we believe iterations should be time-boxed to two weeks, not four.

best feedback you will get is that from real users; the key here is to release your software for real use as soon as you can. Then you can react to any problems or feedback about the usability and utility of your software as quickly as possible. Despite this, there are some differences to consider between the phases of the project before and after the system has been released for general use. Change management, particularly that concerned with data generated by the application and its public interfaces, becomes a significant issue once the first public release has occurred (see Chapter 12, "Managing Data").

A Risk Management Process

Risk management is the process of making sure that:

- The main project risks have been identified.

- Appropriate mitigating strategies have been put in place to manage them.

- Risks continue to be identified and managed throughout the course of the project.

There are several key characteristics that a risk management process should have:

- A standard structure for project teams to report status

- Regular updates, following the standard, from the project team on their progress

- A dashboard where program managers can track current status and trends across all projects

- Regular audits by someone outside the project to ensure that risks are being managed effectively

Risk Management 101

It is important to note that not all risks need to have a mitigating strategy put in place. Some events are so catastrophic that, should they occur, nothing could be done to mitigate them. A huge asteroid destroying all life on the planet is an extreme example, but you take our point. There are often real-life project-specific risks that would lead to the project being cancelled, such as legislative or economic changes, changes to the management structure of an organization, or the removal of a key project sponsor. There is little point planning a mitigation strategy that would be too costly or time-consuming to be worth putting in place—for example, a multisite multinode backup system for a small company's time and expenses application.

A common model of risk management (See *Dancing with Bears* by Tom DeMarco and Timothy Lister) categorizes all risks in terms of their *impact*—how much damage they would cause if they materialize—and their *likelihood*—how likely they are to occur. These are combined to assess each risk's severity. It is easiest to consider the impact in financial terms: how much money would be lost if the risk materializes? Then the likelihood can be modeled as a probability between 0 (impossible) and 1 (certain). Severity is then the impact multiplied by the probability, which gives you an estimate of the severity of the risk in terms of an amount of money. This allows you to make a very simple calculation when deciding what strategies to put in place to mitigate the risk: does the mitigation strategy cost more than the severity of the risk? If so, it's probably not worth implementing.

Risk Management Timeline

In terms of the project lifecycle model that we presented earlier in this chapter, the risk management process should begin at the end of the inception phase, be revisited at the end of the initiation phase, and then regularly revisited throughout the development and deployment phase.

End of Inception

There are two important deliverables that should be ready at this stage. The first is the release strategy that has been created as part of inception. You should verify that all the considerations we discuss in the section on creating a release strategy have been taken into account. If they haven't, how is the team planning to manage the relevant risks?

The second deliverable is a plan for the initiation phase. Sometimes there is a gap between the inception and initiation phases, in which case this plan can be delayed until a few days before the start of initiation. Otherwise, it needs to happen as part of the end of initiation.

End of Initiation

The key here is to make sure that the team is ready to start developing software. They should already have a continuous integration server running which compiles the code (if applicable) and runs an automated test suite. They should have a production-like environment that they are deploying to. A testing strategy should be in place that lays out how the functional and nonfunctional (in particular capacity) requirements of the application will be tested through an automated test suite run as part of the deployment pipeline.

Develop and Release Risk Mitigation

Even with the best preparation, there are many ways in which a development and deployment phase can go horribly wrong, sometimes more quickly than you thought possible. We have all experienced or heard horror stories about projects that deliver no code until past the deployment date, or systems that deployed but failed instantly because of capacity problems. Throughout this phase, the question that you need to ask yourself is, "What can possibly go wrong?" because if you don't ask yourself the question, you won't have any answers ready when things do go wrong.

In many ways the real value of risk management is that it establishes a context for development, and so engenders a thoughtful, risk-aware approach to development activities. The act of considering, as a team, what may go wrong can be a source of concrete requirements that may otherwise have been missed, but it also allows us to pay enough attention to a risk to avert it before it becomes an issue. If you think that a third-party supplier may slip their deadline, you will monitor their progress ahead of time, and thus have time to plan for and accommodate the slip before the deadline arrives.

In this phase you are aiming to identify, track, and manage any manageable risks that you can think of. There are several ways of identifying risks:

- Look at the deployment plan.

- Have regular project miniretrospectives after every showcase and get the team to brainstorm risks during this meeting.

- Make risk identification part of your daily stand up meeting.

There are several common build-related and deployment-related risks to look out for—we'll cover these in the next section.

How to Do a Risk-Management Exercise

It's important not to disturb a team that is regularly delivering working software on schedule with few defects. However, it is important to discover quickly if there is a project that appears to be doing fine from the outside but is actually going to fail. Fortunately, one of the great benefits of iterative methods is that it is relatively simple to discover if this is the case. If you are doing iterative development, you should be showcasing working software at the end of every iteration from a production-like environment. This is possibly the best demonstration of tangible progress. The rate at which your team produces real working code, good enough for real users to use, and deploys it into a production-like host environment—velocity—doesn't lie, even if estimates do.

Compare this to noniterative methods—or, for that matter, iterative methods where the iterations are too long. In such projects it is necessary to go into the details of the working of the team, dive into the various project documents and tracking systems to find out how much work is left to be done and how much work has been done. Once this analysis has been done, it becomes necessary to validate your results against reality, which is an extremely hard and unreliable process, as anybody who has tried to do it can verify.

A good starting point to analyze any project is to pose these questions (this list has worked well for us on several projects):

- How are you tracking progress?

- How are you preventing defects?

- How are you discovering defects?

- How are you tracking defects?

- How do you know a story is finished?

- How are you managing your environments?

- How are you managing configuration, such as test cases, deployment scripts, environment and application configuration, database scripts, and external libraries?

- How often do you showcase working features?

- How often do you do retrospectives?

- How often do you run your automated tests?

- How are you deploying your software?

- How are you building your software?

- How are you ensuring that your release plan is workable and acceptable to the operations team?

- How are you ensuring that your risk-and-issue log is up-to-date?

These questions are not prescriptive, which is important because every team needs to have a certain amount of flexibility to choose the most suitable process for their specific needs. Instead, they are open-ended, ensuring that you can get as much information as possible on the project's context and approach. However, they focus on the outcome, so you can validate that the team will actually be able to deliver, and you will be able to spot any warning signs.

Common Delivery Problems—Their Symptoms and Causes

In this section we describe a few common problems that arise during the process of building, deploying, testing, and releasing software. Although almost anything *could* go wrong with your project, some things are more likely to go wrong than others. It is usually quite hard to work out what is *actually* going wrong with your project—all you have is symptoms. When things do go wrong, work out how that could have been spotted early, and ensure that these symptoms are monitored.

Once you have observed the symptoms, you need to discover the root cause. Any given symptom can be a manifestation of a number of possible underlying causes. To do this, we use a technique called "root cause analysis." This is a fancy name for a very simple procedure. When confronted with a set of symptoms, simply behave like a small child and repeatedly ask the team, "Why?" It is recommended that you ask "Why?" at least five times. Although this process sounds almost absurd, we have found it to be incredibly useful and totally foolproof.

Once you know the root cause, you have to actually fix it. However this is beyond the remit of assurance. So, without further ado, here's a list of common symptoms, grouped by their root cause.

Infrequent or Buggy Deployments

Problem
It takes a long time to deploy the build, and the deployment process is brittle.

Symptoms

- It takes a long time for bugs to be closed by testers. Note that this symptom may not be exclusively caused by infrequent deployments, but it is one possible root cause.

- It takes a long time for stories to be tested or signed off by the customer.

- Testers are finding bugs that developers fixed a long time ago.

- Nobody trusts the UAT, performance, or CI environments, and people are skeptical as to when a release will be available.

- Showcases rarely happen.

- The application can rarely be demonstrated to be working.

- The team's velocity (rate of progress) is slower than expected.

Possible causes
There are many possible reasons. Here are a few of the commonest causes:

- The deployment process is not automated.

- There is not enough hardware available.

- The hardware and operating system's configuration are not managed correctly.

- The deployment process depends on systems outside the team's control.

- Not enough people understand the build and deployment process.

- Testers, developers, analysts, and operations personnel are not collaborating sufficiently during development.

- Developers are not being disciplined about keeping the application working by making small, incremental changes, and so frequently break existing functionality.

Poor Application Quality

Problem

Delivery teams are failing to implement an effective testing strategy.

Symptoms

- Regression bugs keep popping up.

- The number of defects keeps increasing even when your team spends most of its time fixing them (of course this symptom will only be manifested if you have an effective testing process).

- Customers complain of a poor-quality product.

- Developers groan and look horrified whenever a new feature request arrives.

- Developers complain about the maintainability of the code, but nothing ever gets better.

- It takes an ever-increasing amount of time to implement new functionality, and the team starts falling behind.

Possible causes

There are essentially two sources of this problem: ineffective collaboration between testers and the rest of the delivery team, and poorly implemented or inadequate automated tests.

- Testers do not collaborate with developers during development of features.

- Stories or features are marked as "done" without comprehensive automated tests written, without being signed off by testers, or without being showcased to users from a production-like environment.

- Defects are routinely entered into a backlog without being fixed on the spot with an automated test to detect regression problems.

- The developers or testers don't have sufficient experience developing automated test suites.

- The team does not understand the most effective types of tests to write for the technology or platform that they are working on.

- The developers are working without sufficient test coverage, perhaps because their project management doesn't allow them time to implement automated testing.

- The system is a prototype that will be discarded (though we have come across a few important production systems that were originally developed as prototypes but were never discarded).

Please note that it is, of course, possible to go over the top with automated tests—we know of one project where the entire team spent several weeks writing nothing but tests. When the customer discovered that there was no working software, the team was fired. However, this cautionary tale should be taken in context: The most common failure mode, by far, is that there is too little automated testing, not too much.

Poorly Managed Continuous Integration Process

Problem

The build process is not properly managed.

Symptoms

- Developers don't check in often enough (at least once a day).

- The commit stage is permanently broken.

- There is a high number of defects.

- There is a long integration phase before each release.

Possible causes

- The automated tests take too long to run.

- The commit stage takes too long to run (less than five minutes is ideal, more than ten minutes is unacceptable).

- The automated tests fail intermittently, giving false positives.

- Nobody is empowered to revert check-ins.

- Not enough people understand, and can make changes to, the CI process.

Poor Configuration Management

Problem

Environments can't be commissioned, and applications installed reliably, using an automated process.

Symptoms

- Mysterious failures in production environments.

- New deployments are tense, scary events.

- Large teams are dedicated to environment configuration and management.

- Deployments to production often have to be rolled back or patched.

- Unacceptable downtime of production environment.

Possible causes

- UAT and production environments are different.

- A poor or badly enforced change management process for making changes to production and staging environments.

- Insufficient collaboration between operations, data management teams, and delivery teams.

- Ineffective monitoring of production and staging environments to detect incidents.

- Insufficient instrumentation and logging built into applications.

- Insufficient testing of the nonfunctional requirements of applications.

Compliance and Auditing

Many large companies are required to comply with legally binding regulations that govern their industry. For example, all US registered public companies are required to comply with the Sarbanes-Oxley Act of 2002 (often abbreviated to Sarbox or SOX). US health care companies have to comply with the provisions of HIPAA. Systems that deal with credit card information must conform to the PCI DSS standard. Pretty much every field is regulated in one way or another, and IT systems frequently have to be designed with some regulations in mind.

We have neither the space nor the willpower to examine the regulations covering every industry in every country, which in any case change frequently. However, we would like to spend some time discussing regulation in general, specifically in environments that define close controls on the software release process. Many such regulatory regimes require audit trails that make it possible to identify, for every change in a production environment, what were the lines of code that it came from, who touched them, and who approved the steps in the process. Such regulations are common in many industries from finance to health care.

Here are some common strategies we have seen employed for enforcing these kinds of regulations:

- Locking down who is able to access "privileged" environments.

- Creating and maintaining an effective and efficient change management process for making changes to privileged environments.

- Requiring approvals from management before deployments can be performed.

- Requiring every process, from building to release, to be documented.

- Creating authorization barriers to ensure that the people who create the software are not able to deploy it into production environments, as a protection against potential malicious interventions.

- Requiring every deployment to be audited to see exactly what changes are being made.

Strategies like these are essential in organizations subject to regulation, and can lead to drastic reductions in downtime and defect counts. Nonetheless they have a bad reputation because it is all too easy to implement them in ways that make change more difficult. However, the deployment pipeline makes it possible to enforce these strategies fairly easily while enabling an efficient delivery process. In this section, we present some principles and practices to ensure compliance with such regulatory regimes while maintaining short cycle times.

Automation over Documentation

Many companies insist that documentation is central to auditing. We beg to differ. A piece of paper that says you did something in a certain way is no guarantee that you actually did that thing. The world of consultancy abounds in tales of people passing (for example) ISO 9001 audits by supplying a bunch of documents which "proved" they had implemented them and coaching their staff on how to give the correct answers when questioned by inspectors.

Documentation also has a nasty habit of going out of date. The more detailed a document is, the more quickly it is likely to go out of date. When it does so, people don't usually bother to update it. Everybody has heard the following conversation at least once:

Operator: "I followed the deployment process you emailed me last month, but it doesn't work."

Developer: "Oh, we changed the way deployment works. You need to copy this new set of files over and set permission x." Or worse, "That's strange, let me take a look . . . " followed by hours of working out what has changed and how to get it deployed.

Automation solves all of these problems. Automated scripts are the documentation of your processes that *must* work. By enforcing their use, you ensure both that they are up-to-date and that the process has been performed precisely as you intend.

Enforcing Traceability

It is often necessary to be able to trace the history of changes, from what is in production to the source control versions that produced it. There are two practices that help with this process that we want to emphasize.

- Only create binaries once, and deploy the same binaries into production that you created in the first stage of your build process. You can ensure that the binaries are the same by taking a hash of them (using MD5 or SHA1, for example), and storing them in a secure database. Many tools will do this for you automatically.

- Use a fully automated process to take your binaries through the deployment, test, and release process which records who did what when. Again, there are several tools on the market that can help with this.

Even with these precautions, there is a window when unauthorized changes can be introduced: when the binaries are first created from source code. All it takes is somebody gaining access to the box where this is done and inserting files into the filesystem during the compile or assembly process for this to happen. One way to solve this problem is to create binaries in a single step, using an automated process which executes on a box which is access-controlled. In this case it is essential to be able to provision and manage this environment automatically so that it is possible to debug any problems with the creation process.

Access Control and Enforcing Traceability

One of our colleagues, Rolf Russell, worked in a financial services company which was particularly strict about traceability to protect their intellectual property. In order to ensure that the code that was deployed into production really was the same as the code checked into the revision control system, they decompiled the binaries to be deployed. The results of the decompilation were compared against a decompiled version of what was in production to see what changes were being made.

At the same company, only the CTO was authorized to deploy certain business-critical applications to their production environment. Every week, the CTO set aside a couple of hours for releases, during which people would come to her office so that she could run the script to perform the deployment. At the time of writing, the company was moving to a system where users were allowed to deploy some applications themselves, from a single terminal in a room which required ID card access. This room contained a CCTV camera which recorded all activity 24 hours a day.

Working in Silos

It is often the case that large organizations have separate departments for different functions. Many organizations have independent teams for development, testing, operations, configuration management, data management, and architecture. In much of this book we have promoted open and free communication and collaboration between and within teams, so there are some dangers to creating barriers between the parts of your organization responsible for different aspects of software creation and release. However, there are some responsibilities that should clearly belong in one group and not another. In regulated environments, many important activities are subject to review by auditors and security teams, whose job it is to ensure that the organization is not exposed to legal risks or security breaches of any kind.

Such separation of responsibilities, at the right point and managed in the right way, need not be a bad thing. In theory, everybody who works for an organization will keep the best interests of that organization at heart, which means that they will cooperate effectively with other departments. However, this is often not the case. Almost without exception, such a lack of collaboration results from poor communication between groups. We believe very strongly that the most effective teams develop software in cross-functional groups that are composed of people from all of the different disciplines required to define, develop, test, and release software. These groups should sit together—when they don't, they don't benefit from each other's knowledge.

Some regulatory regimes make such cross-functional teams difficult to establish. If you are in a more siloed organization, the processes and techniques described throughout this book—in particular, implementing a deployment pipeline—help to prevent these silos from making the delivery process inefficient. However, the most important solution is communication between silos from the beginning of a project. This should take several forms:

- Everybody involved in the delivery of a project, including somebody from each of the silos, should meet at the beginning of every project. We'll call this group of people the release working group, because their job is to keep the release process working. Their task should be to put together a release strategy for the project, as detailed in Chapter 10, "Deploying and Releasing Applications."

- The release working group should meet regularly throughout the project. They should run a retrospective on the project since the last time they met, plan how to improve things, and execute the plan. Use the Deming cycle: plan, do, check, act.

- Even if it has no users yet, the software should be released as often as possible—this means at least every iteration—to a production-like environment. Some teams practice continuous deployment, which means releasing every change that passes all the stages in your pipeline. This is an application of the principle: "If it hurts, do it more frequently." We can't stress enough how important this practice is.

- Project status, including the dashboard we mentioned in the "A Risk Management Process" section on page 431, should be available to everyone involved in the build, deploy, test, and release process, preferably on big monitors that everybody can see.

Change Management

In regulated environments, it is often essential for parts of the build, deploy, test, and release process to require approval. In particular, manual testing environments, staging, and production should always be under strict access control so that changes to them can only be made through the organization's change management process. This may seem unnecessarily bureaucratic, but in fact research has demonstrated that organizations which do this have lower mean time between failures (MTBF) and mean time to repair (MTTR) (see *The Visible Ops Handbook*, p. 13).

If your organization has a problem meeting its service levels due to uncontrolled changes to testing and production environments, we suggest the following process for managing approvals:

- Create a Change Advisory Board with representatives from your development team, operations team, security team, change management team, and the business.

- Decide which environments fall under the purview of the change management process. Ensure that these environments are access-controlled so that changes can only be made through this process.

- Establish an automated change request management system that can be used to raise a change request and manage approvals. Anyone should be able to see the status of each change request and who has approved it.

- Any time anybody wants to make a change to an environment, whether deploying a new version of an application, creating a new virtual environment, or making a configuration change, it must be done through a change request.

- Require a remediation strategy, such as the ability to back out, for every change.

- Have acceptance criteria for the success of a change. Ideally, create an automated test that now fails but will pass once the change is successful. Put an indicator on your operations management dashboard with the status of the test (see the "Behavior-Driven Monitoring" section on page 323).

- Have an automated process for applying changes, so that whenever the change is approved, it can be performed by pressing a button (or clicking a link, or whatever).

The last part sounds difficult, but we hope that by now it also sounds familiar, since it has been the primary focus of this book. The mechanism for deploying a change that is audited and authorized to a production environment is the same as deploying the same change to any other environment, with the addition of the authorization: Adding access control to a deployment pipeline is a trivial exercise. It is so simple that it often makes sense to extend the auditing and authorization further: All changes are approved by whoever owns the environment. This means that you can use the same automation you created for your testing environments to make changes to environments that fall under the change management process. It also means you have already tested the automated processes you created.

How does the CAB decide whether a change should be executed? This is simply a matter of risk management. What is the risk of making the change? What is the benefit? If the risks outweigh the benefits, the change should not be made, or another less risky change should be made. The CAB should also be able to make comments on tickets, request more information, or suggest modifications. All these processes should be able to be managed through the automated ticketing system.

Finally, there are three more principles that should be followed when implementing and managing a change approval process:

- Keep metrics on the system and make them visible. How long does it take for a change to be approved? How many changes are waiting for approval? What proportion of changes are denied?

- Keep metrics that validate the success of the system and make them visible. What's the MTBF and MTTR? What is the cycle time for a change? There is a more complete list of metrics defined in the ITIL literature.

- Hold regular retrospectives on the system, inviting representatives from each of your organization's units, and work to improve the system based on feedback from these retrospectives.

Summary

Management is vital to the success of every project. Good management creates processes enabling efficient delivery of software, while ensuring that risks are managed appropriately and regulatory regimes are complied with. Nevertheless, too many organizations—with the best of intentions—create poor management structures that meet none of these goals. This chapter is intended to describe an approach to management that deals with both conformance and performance.

Our build and release maturity model is targeted at improving organizational performance. It allows you to identify how effective your delivery practices are, and suggests ways to improve them. The risk management process described here, along with our list of common antipatterns, is designed to help you create a strategy to identify problems as soon as they occur, so you can rectify them early when they are easy to fix. We have spent a good proportion of this chapter (and this book) discussing iterative, incremental processes; this is because iterative, incremental delivery is the key to effective risk management. Without an iterative, incremental process, you have no objective way to gauge your project's progress or your application's fitness for purpose.

Finally, we hope that we have demonstrated that iterative delivery, combined with an automated process for building, deploying, testing, and releasing software embodied in the deployment pipeline, is not only compatible with the goals of conformance and performance, but is the most effective way of achieving these goals. This process enables greater collaboration between those involved in delivering software, provides fast feedback so that bugs and unnecessary or poorly implemented features can be discovered quickly, and paves the route to reducing that vital metric, cycle time. This, in turn, means faster delivery of valuable, high-quality software, which leads to higher profitability with lower risk. Thus the goals of good governance are achieved.

Bibliography

1. Adzic, Gojko, *Bridging the Communication Gap: Specification by Example and Agile Acceptance Testing*, Neuri, 2009.

2. Allspaw, John, *The Art of Capacity Planning: Scaling Web Resources*, O'Reilly, 2008.

3. Allspaw, John, *Web Operations: Keeping the Web on Time*, O'Reilly, 2010.

4. Ambler, Scott, and Pramodkumar Sadalage, *Refactoring Databases: Evolutionary Database Design*, Addison-Wesley, 2006.

5. Beck, Kent, and Cynthia Andres, *Extreme Programming Explained: Embrace Change (2nd edition)*, Addison-Wesley, 2004.

6. Behr, Kevin, Gene Kim, and George Spafford, *The Visible Ops Handbook: Implementing ITIL in 4 Practical and Auditable Steps*, IT Process Institute, 2004.

7. Blank, Steven, *The Four Steps to the Epiphany: Successful Strategies for Products That Win*, CafePress, 2006.

8. Bowman, Ronald, *Business Continuity Planning for Data Centers and Systems: A Strategic Implementation Guide*, Wiley, 2008.

9. Chelimsky, Mark, *The RSpec Book: Behaviour Driven Development with RSpec, Cucumber, and Friends*, The Pragmatic Programmers, 2010.

10. Clark, Mike, *Pragmatic Project Automation: How to Build, Deploy, and Monitor Java Applications*, The Pragmatic Programmers, 2004.

11. Cohn, Mike, *Succeeding with Agile: Software Development Using Scrum*, Addison-Wesley, 2009.

12. Crispin, Lisa, and Janet Gregory, *Agile Testing: A Practical Guide for Testers and Agile Teams*, Addison-Wesley, 2009.

13. DeMarco, Tom, and Timothy Lister, *Waltzing with Bears: Managing Risk on Software Projects*, Dorset House, 2003.

14. Duvall, Paul, Steve Matyas, and Andrew Glover, *Continuous Integration: Improving Software Quality and Reducing Risk*, Addison-Wesley, 2007.

15. Evans, Eric, *Domain-Driven Design*, Addison-Wesley, 2003.

16. Feathers, Michael, *Working Effectively with Legacy Code*, Prentice Hall, 2004.

17. Fowler, Martin, *Patterns of Enterprise Application Architecture*, Addison-Wesley, 2002.

18. Freeman, Steve, and Nat Pryce, *Growing Object-Oriented Software, Guided by Tests*, Addison-Wesley, 2009.

19. Gregory, Peter, *IT Disaster Recovery Planning for Dummies*, For Dummies, 2007.

20. Kazman, Rick, and Mark Klein, *Attribute-Based Architectural Styles*, Carnegie Mellon Software Engineering Institute, 1999.

21. Kazman, Rick, Mark Klein, and Paul Clements, *ATAM: Method for Architecture Evaluation*, Carnegie Mellon Software Engineering Institute, 2000.

22. Meszaros, Gerard, *xUnit Test Patterns: Refactoring Test Code*, Addison-Wesley, 2007.

23. Nygard, Michael, *Release It!: Design and Deploy Production-Ready Software*, The Pragmatic Programmers, 2007.

24. Poppendieck, Mary, and Tom Poppendieck, *Implementing Lean Software Development: From Concept to Cash*, Addison-Wesley, 2006.

25. Poppendieck, Mary, and Tom Poppendieck, *Lean Software Development: An Agile Toolkit*, Addison-Wesley, 2003.

26. Sadalage, Pramod, *Recipes for Continuous Database Integration*, Pearson Education, 2007.

27. Sonatype Company, *Maven: The Definitive Guide*, O'Reilly, 2008.

28. ThoughtWorks, Inc., *The ThoughtWorks Anthology: Essays on Software Technology and Innovation*, The Pragmatic Programmers, 2008.

29. Wingerd, Laura, and Christopher Seiwald, "High-Level Best Practices in Software Configuration Management," paper read at *Eighth International Workshop on Software Configuration Management*, Brussels, Belgium, July 1999.

Index

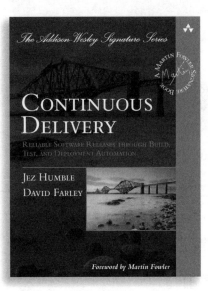

FREE Online Edition

Your purchase of **Continuous Delivery: Reliable Software Releases through Build, Test, and Deployment Automation** includes access to a free online edition for 45 days through the Safari Books Online subscription service. Nearly every Addison-Wesley Professional book is available online through Safari Books Online, along with more than 5,000 other technical books and videos from publishers such as Cisco Press, Exam Cram, IBM Press, O'Reilly, Prentice Hall, Que, and Sams.

SAFARI BOOKS ONLINE allows you to search for a specific answer, cut and paste code, download chapters, and stay current with emerging technologies.

Activate your FREE Online Edition at www.informit.com/safarifree

> **STEP 1:** Enter the coupon code: NYGIQVH.

> **STEP 2:** New Safari users, complete the brief registration form.
> Safari subscribers, just log in.

If you have difficulty registering on Safari or accessing the online edition, please e-mail customer-service@safaribooksonline.com